gilbert
LAW SUMMARIES

CONSTITUTIONAL LAW

Twenty-Seventh Edition

Jesse H. Choper
Professor of Law
University of California, Berkeley

Supplement in Back of Book

HARCOURT BRACE LEGAL AND PROFESSIONAL PUBLICATIONS, INC.
EDITORIAL OFFICES: 176 W. Adams, Suite 2100, Chicago, IL 60603

REGIONAL OFFICES: New York, Chicago, Los Angeles, Washington, D.C.
Distributed by: **Harcourt Brace & Company** 6277 Sea Harbor Drive, Orlando, FL 32887 (800)787-8717

PROJECT EDITOR
Steven J. Levin, B.A., J.D.

SERIES EDITOR
Elizabeth L. Snyder, B.A., J.D.

QUALITY CONTROL EDITOR
Megan Knowles, B.A.

SUMMARY OF CONTENTS

Page

CONSTITUTIONAL LAW CAPSULE SUMMARY I

TEXT CORRELATION CHART i

APPROACH TO EXAMS . . . . . (i)

I. POWERS OF THE FEDERAL GOVERNMENT 1
- Chapter Approach 1
- A. Judicial Power 2
  - 1. Source and Scope of Power 2
  - 2. Jurisdiction of the Supreme Court 4
  - 3. Limitations on Jurisdiction of Federal Courts 6
  - 4. Effect of Declaration of Unconstitutionality 21
- B. Legislative Power 22
  - 1. Power of Congress—In General 22
  - 2. Commerce Power 24
  - 3. Taxing and Spending Powers 24
  - 4. War Power 27
  - 5. Power Over External Affairs 28
  - 6. Power Over Naturalization and Citizenship 28
  - 7. Property Power 29
  - 8. Investigatory Power 29
  - 9. Congressional Immunity 30
- C. Executive Power 31
- D. Power Over Foreign Affairs 35

II. THE FEDERAL SYSTEM—INTERGOVERNMENTAL RELATIONS 39
- Chapter Approach 39
- A. Nature and Scope of Federal and State Powers 39
- B. Intergovernmental Privileges and Immunities 41
- C. Intergovernmental Immunity 43

III. REGULATION AND TAXATION OF COMMERCE 47
- Chapter Approach 47
- A. Regulation of Foreign Commerce—Exclusive Federal Power 48
- B. Regulation of Interstate Commerce 48
- C. Power of States to Tax Interstate Commerce 62
- D. Power of States to Tax Foreign Commerce 70

IV. INDIVIDUAL RIGHTS—LIMITATIONS ON THE EXERCISE OF GOVERNMENTAL POWER 72
- Chapter Approach 72
- A. Introduction 74
- B. Due Process 76
- C. Equal Protection 91
- D. The "State Action" Requirement 124
- E. Congressional Power to Enforce Constitutional Rights 128

F. Freedom of Speech, Press, and Association 133
G. Freedom of Religion 187
H. Other Limitations on Governmental Power 203
I. Safeguards in the Administration of Criminal Justice 211

REVIEW QUESTIONS AND ANSWERS 229

SAMPLE EXAM QUESTIONS AND ANSWERS 247

TABLE OF CASES 265

INDEX 279

gilbert
capsule summary
constitutional law

Text Section

I. POWERS OF THE FEDERAL GOVERNMENT

A. JUDICIAL POWER

1. **Source and Scope of Power**
   a. **Source:** The Constitution provides for one Supreme Court and such inferior courts as Congress may establish . . . . [1]
   b. **Scope:** Jurisdiction of federal courts is generally limited to ***cases:*** . . . [3]
      (1) Involving the ***Constitution, acts of Congress,*** or ***federal treaties;***
      (2) In which the ***United States is a party;***
      (3) Between a ***state and citizens of another state;***
      (4) Between ***citizens of different states.***
   c. **Limitations on scope of federal judicial power**
      (1) **Sovereign immunity doctrine:** Under this doctrine, the United States may not be sued without its consent. Suits against federal officers acting in their official capacity may also be subject to sovereign immunity . . . . [4]
      (2) **Eleventh Amendment:** The Eleventh Amendment bars a citizen of one state from suing another state (without its consent) in federal court. It also has been interpreted as prohibiting federal suits by citizens of the state being sued. It does ***not*** bar suits by the federal government, Supreme Court review, suits against state subdivisions, or suits against state officials who allegedly have violated plaintiff's constitutional rights . . . . [6]
2. **Jurisdiction of the Supreme Court**
   a. **Original jurisdiction:** The Supreme Court's original (trial) jurisdiction is derived from Article III, Section 2 and is limited mainly to ***controversies between two or more states*** . . . . [16]
   b. **Appellate jurisdiction:** Article III, Section 2 also gives the Supreme Court appellate jurisdiction over the cases listed above (*supra,* §3) . . . . [20]
      (1) **Power of judicial review:** Judicial review has ***evolved from Supreme Court decisions*** and allows the Court to hold acts of other branches of government unconstitutional, to hold state statutes unconstitutional, and to review state court judgments . . . . [21]
      (2) **Methods for invoking appellate jurisdiction:** Supreme Court review may be had either by ***appeal*** (mandatory) or ***certiorari*** (discretionary). However, mandatory appeal jurisdiction is very limited and so the Court's appellate jurisdiction is almost entirely by ***certiorari*** . . . . [22]
      (3) **Limitations on statutory regulation:** *Ex parte McCardle* has been interpreted as allowing Congress full power, subject to the language of Article III, to limit the Supreme Court's appellate jurisdiction . . . . [26]
3. **Limitations on Jurisdiction of Federal Courts**
   a. **"Case or controversy":** Article III, Section 2 limits federal court jurisdiction to "cases and controversies." There must be a ***real dispute affecting rights of parties with adverse interests.*** The action must also be ***ripe*** and pose a ***real and immediate danger*** to complainants' interests. Thus, the Court will ***not*** render any ***advisory opinions*** (or review state court advisory options), nor opinions in ***moot cases*** (issue resolved) or ***collusive suits*** . . . . [27]

b. **Standing:** To have standing to raise a constitutional issue, a claimant must show the following: .... [43]

(i) **Direct and immediate injury:** The claimant must show a direct and immediate ***personal*** injury due to the challenged action. The injury may be aesthetic, conservational, or recreational, as well as economic .... [44]

(ii) **Causation:** The injury must be traced to the challenged action and one that will be redressed by the remedy sought .... [46]

(iii) **Congressional conferral of standing:** Standing may be conferred by federal statutes that create new interests if an injury to those interests can be shown .... [47]

(1) **Citizens' standing:** Persons have ***no standing*** as citizens to claim that federal statutes are unconstitutional because the injury is too indirect, and Congress cannot change this by statute .... [48]

(2) **Taxpayers' standing:** Although generally federal taxpayers have no standing to attack federal expenditures, a taxpayer can challenge spending or appropriation measures if there is a ***nexus*** between claimant's status and the issue in question (*i.e.*, taxpayer may challenge the validity of a tax assessed against her). Standing may also exist where taxpayer alleges that a ***specific constitutional limitation*** on the taxing and spending power (so far only Establishment Clause) has been ***exceeded***. State taxpayer standing is governed by these same rules .... [49]

(3) **Assertion of third party rights:** Absent a federal statute conferring standing, an injured party can assert ***only his own*** constitutional rights .... [54]

(a) **Exceptions:** In certain special circumstances, a claimant may assert the rights of third parties: (i) where it is ***difficult for a third party to assert rights*** or (ii) where a ***special relationship*** exists between the claimant and third party .... [55]

(b) **Standing of an association:** An association ***may*** have standing to represent its members if (i) the ***members have standing;*** (ii) the interest asserted is ***germane to the association's purpose;*** and (iii) the members are ***not required to participate*** in the suit .... [58]

(4) **Standing of a state:** A state may attack the validity of federal action affecting the state's own ***property*** interest. However, absent authorization by Congress, the state ***cannot*** attack federal statutes on the ground that Congress exceeded its delegated powers, nor can a state assert as parens patriae the claims of its citizens against the federal government, although it ***can*** assert such claims against another state .... [59]

c. **Additional conditions for review of state court decisions:** These include the requirements that claimant must have ***exhausted all available state remedies*** and that the ***state judgment must be final.*** The case also must involve a state decision that ***turned on a substantial federal question.*** There must be no ***adequate and independent state ground*** for the Court to review the case .... [63]

d. **Other policies of "strict necessity":** In adhering to its policy of ***judicial self-restraint,*** the Court decides only those constitutional issues ***raised in a case.*** Furthermore, the Court attempts to interpret federal statutes so as to ***avoid*** constitutional questions and may ***decline*** to decide a case if the record is sketchy concerning the constitutional issue .... [77]

e. **Challenges to state action in federal courts:** In appropriate circumstances, a person may bring an action in federal court against a state officer seeking damages, an injunction, or a declaratory judgment to vindicate her rights .... [80]

(1) **Restrictions on injunctions:** Usually, federal statutes ***bar*** the issuance of federal injunctions against enforcement of state tax laws, pending state criminal proceedings, state criminal statutes or prosecutions, pending state civil proceedings, and the ongoing supervision of state executive activities .... [81]
(2) **Exhaustion of state remedies:** This is ***not*** required when seeking a federal injunction against state administrative actions .... [94]
(3) **Abstention:** A federal court may ***abstain*** from granting an injunction or declaratory judgment and remand the parties to the state court for interpretation of the statute. However, where a statute is ambiguous, an ***overbroad or vague regulation of speech or association,*** or where the court finds ***further delay unjustifiable,*** it may grant the relief .... [95]

f. **Political questions:** The Court will ***not*** decide a case that presents a political question rather than a justiciable controversy .... [100]

4. **Effect of Declaration of Unconstitutionality:** Theoretically, a decision declaring an act unconstitutional is binding only on the parties to the suit. Practically, the decision establishes a principle of law applicable to all persons .... [111]
   a. **Retroactive effect:** A declaration of unconstitutionality has full retroactive effect in all cases still open on appeal and as to all events, regardless of when they occur .... [112]
   b. **Partial invalidity:** Where part of a statute is invalid, the Court looks to legislative intent (*i.e.*, ***severability***) in deciding whether the entire statute should be ruled invalid .... [114]

B. LEGISLATIVE POWER

1. **Power of Congress—In General:** Legislative power is basically the power of Congress to make laws, but also includes the power to do other things necessary and proper to enactment of legislation .... [118]
   a. **Scope of federal powers:** Undelegated powers that are not prohibited are ***reserved to the states*** by the Tenth Amendment. ***Enumerated powers*** are those expressly delegated by the Constitution. Additionally, *McCulloch v. Maryland* held that certain broad federal powers may be ***implied*** from the Necessary and Proper Clause .... [119]
      (1) **Appropriate means:** Congress may use ***any*** appropriate means to achieve the ends expressed in the enumerated powers. Moreover, the Necessary and Proper Clause applies to ***all*** powers delegated to ***any*** federal branch .... [122]
      (2) **Doctrine of inherent sovereign powers:** The theory that the government has inherent powers, independent of the Constitution, has been given some effect, but ***only over external or foreign affairs*** . [125]
   b. **Delegation of legislative power:** To delegate, Congress must ***possess*** the particular power, that power must be ***delegable,*** and ***intelligible standards*** must be established to govern the exercise of the delegated power .... [126]
      (1) **Judicial branch:** Note that nonadjudicatory functions (*e.g.*, rule making) may be delegated to the judicial branch as long as the task does not encroach upon another branch's power and is an appropriate judicial duty .... [129]
2. **Commerce Power:** This extensive congressional power is discussed *infra* .. [130]
3. **Taxing and Spending Powers**
   a. **Constitutional provision:** Congress has the power to tax, pay debts, and provide for the common defense and general welfare (Article I, Section 8) . [131]
   b. **Independent powers:** The powers to tax and to spend for the general welfare are independent powers, *i.e.*, power to tax and spend in manner not specified under any of Congress's enumerated regulatory powers .. [132]

c. **Taxation with purpose or effect of regulation:** Where Congress has the power to regulate, a tax is valid as a necessary and proper exercise of its regulatory power. Where there is ***no*** regulatory power, the tax will be upheld if its ***dominant intent*** is to raise revenue (*i.e.*, fiscal rather than penal) .... [133]
   (1) **No power to regulate:** The objective approach will uphold a tax with an apparent regulatory purpose if it does ***in fact*** raise revenue. Under a subjective standard the Court looks to the statute's language and operative effect to determine its dominant intent. Both approaches have been used to examine tax statutes .... [137]

d. **Spending with purpose or effect of regulation:** Many federal spending programs are expressly conditioned on regulating the recipient's activities. If Congress may ***directly regulate*** the target activity, the spending program is valid as a necessary and proper exercise of the regulatory powers .... [139]
   (1) **No power to regulate:** Congress rarely lacks the power to regulate activities related to federal spending programs. Federal funds have been used to "entice" states to conform to federal standards under the theory that Congress can act for the general welfare, *e.g.*, conditioning receipt of certain highway funds on a recipient state's adoption of a minimum drinking age .... [141]
   (2) **Limitations:** Congress's power to spend ***must be exercised for the general welfare*** and it may ***not violate an independent constitutional right*** .... [142]

4. **War Power:** Congress has the power to declare war, raise and support armed forces, and promulgate rules for regulation of the military (Article I, Section 8). Congressional power during war is quite broad and may continue ***after*** war ends so as to remedy resultant problems (*e.g.,* rent controls) ..... [144]
5. **Power Over External Affairs:** This is discussed *infra* .... [148]
6. **Power Over Naturalization and Citizenship:** Congress has ***plenary*** power over aliens (Article I, Section 8, Clause 4) and can prescribe the conditions upon which they may come to or remain in the country .... [149]
   a. **Plenary power over aliens**
      (1) **Exclusion of aliens seeking entry:** An alien seeking entry must follow whatever procedure is required by Congress, and Congress may exclude aliens altogether ***without*** a hearing .... [151]
      (2) **Deportation of resident aliens:** Once an alien is physically present legally or illegally—in the United States, he is entitled to certain ***due process*** rights before deportation (*i.e.*, notice and a hearing) .... [152]
   b. **Naturalization:** Congress has the exclusive power over naturalization, but may not discriminate between naturalized and native-born citizens . [154]
   c. **Loss of citizenship:** Congress cannot revoke citizenship of a native-born or naturalized citizen without his consent, but it can provide for revocation of naturalization obtained wrongfully or by fraud .... [157]
7. **Property Power:** Congress has ***unlimited*** power to dispose of U.S. property as long as the method used is in the public interest (Article IV, Section 3) .. [158]
8. **Investigatory Power:** Investigatory power is implied from the power to legislate .... [160]
   a. **Scope of investigatory power:** The power to investigate is ***limited*** to inquiries of which that particular House has jurisdiction .... [161]
   b. **Enforcement of investigatory power:** Enforcement is usually accomplished by ***contempt*** proceedings in which either House acts as a court to try, convict, and fine and/or imprison the contemnor. Congressional investigatory power is limited by certain constitutional rights of the witnesses (*e.g.*, self-incrimination privilege) .... [162]

9. **Congressional Immunity:** The Speech and Debate Clause forbids civil or criminal prosecution against members of Congress (or aides) for acts that occur in the ***regular course of the legislative process*** (Article I, Section 6, Clause 1) .... [164]
   a. **Scope:** Immunity does ***not*** extend to state legislators who violate federal law. Neither promises by a federal legislator to perform a future act nor political acts are protected .... [167]

C. EXECUTIVE POWER

1. **Source of Presidential Powers:** Article I, Section 1 confers upon the President the ***whole executive power;*** he may delegate and appoint members of the executive branch, but all executive power remains with the office of the presidency .... [170]
2. **Scope of Powers**
   a. **Appointment power:** The President has the power to appoint, with the advice and consent of the Senate, "officers of the United States" (*e.g.*, ambassadors). Appointment of "inferior" officers may be vested in other departments (*e.g.*, special prosecutors appointed by courts) .... [171]
   b. **Removal power:** Although the Constitution is silent on the President's power to remove most of his appointees (*exception:* he cannot remove federal judges), the Court has held that he can remove some purely executive appointees even though the appointment required congressional approval (*e.g.*, postmaster) .... [174]
   c. **Pardon power:** The President can grant reprieves and pardons for "offenses against the United States," except for impeachment (Article II, Section 2). *But note:* Civil contempt is ***not*** subject to presidential pardon, although criminal contempt is .... [179]
   d. **"Legislative" power of President:** In certain areas, the President has limited legislative powers. Congress may ***delegate*** legislative power subject to the separation of powers doctrine .... [182]
      (1) **Veto power:** The President's veto power applies to ***all*** legislative action unless expressly excepted by the Constitution. If vetoed, Congress can repass legislation by a two-thirds vote of each House. Decisions of the executive branch and its agencies may ***not*** be vetoed by Congress .... [185]
      (2) **Military powers:** The President has ***no power*** to declare war, but as Commander-in-Chief, he has extensive legislative power in "theaters of war." As such, he can deploy military forces against insurrection or invasion (foreign or domestic) without congressional action .... [187]
      (3) **Inherent "emergency" power:** It is ***probable*** that the President has inherent power to act, without congressional authorization, in cases of great national emergency. The inherent power is limited by congressional denial of a specific power (*e.g.*, no power to seize steel mills) .... [189]
   e. **Impoundment:** The President has ***no power*** to refuse to spend appropriated funds ***expressly mandated*** by Congress to be spent .... [191]
   f. **Executing laws:** Presidential action may also be upheld as an exercise of the President's power to execute the laws .... [192]
3. **Executive Privilege:** This privilege is for protection against disclosure of presidential communications made in the exercise of executive power. It derives from both the separation of powers doctrine and the need for confidentiality .... [193]
   a. **Scope:** The claim of privilege for military, diplomatic, or national security secrets is given great ***deference*** by the courts. However, other presidential communications are only ***presumptively*** privileged .... [194]

b. **Civil damages:** Damages are ***not allowed*** for private suits based on any presidential acts within the outer perimeters of presidential constitutional authority. This blanket immunity does ***not*** extend to presidential aides .... [198]

D. POWER OVER FOREIGN AFFAIRS

1. **Constitutional Provisions:** Article I, Section 8 grants ***Congress*** the power to regulate commerce with foreign nations, to declare war, to raise and support armies, and to provide and maintain a navy. Article II, Sections 2 and 3 provide that the President is Commander-in-Chief of the armed forces, has certain treaty-making powers, shall receive foreign ambassadors, and shall nominate and appoint U.S. ambassadors and ministers, subject to Senate confirmation .... [200]
2. **Comparison with Domestic Powers:** Federal power as to domestic affairs is shared with the powers of the states. In ***foreign affairs,*** the federal power is ***exclusive.*** Congress may delegate greater powers concerning foreign affairs to the President than is permissible in domestic affairs .... [201]
3. **Treaty Power:** The President can make treaties with the advice and consent of ***two-thirds of the Senate*** .... [206]
   a. **Status of treaties:** A treaty is "the supreme law of the land" and supersedes state law. The Supremacy Clause places self-executing treaties on ***an equal footing*** with the Constitution. Where there is a conflict between a treaty and an act of Congress, the ***last expression*** of the sovereign will stand .... [207]
   b. **Types of treaties:** A treaty may be ***self-executing*** (no further congressional action necessary) or it may expressly or impliedly require that Congress must pass ***effectuating legislation*** .... [210]
   c. **Independent source of power:** The treaty power is an independent source of federal power, thus permitting federal action over subjects outside the other constitutionally enumerated federal powers .... [211]
      (1) **Limitations:** The major limitations on federal treaty power and legislation thereunder are the formal requirements of presidential proposal and Senate ratification. But, a treaty must not contravene individual rights protected by the Constitution, and the Court has ***suggested*** that a treaty must concern a ***proper subject of negotiation*** .... [212]
4. **Executive Agreements:** The President may enter into agreements with other countries; this power is independent of the treaty power and does not need Senate consent. Executive agreements have a status similar to treaties and prevail over any inconsistent state law. It is unclear whether they also prevail over inconsistent congressional acts .... [215]

II. THE FEDERAL SYSTEM—INTERGOVERNMENTAL RELATIONS

A. NATURE AND SCOPE OF FEDERAL AND STATE POWERS

1. **In General:** Powers of government may be ***exclusive*** to the state or the federal government, or they may be ***exercised concurrently*** .... [220]
2. **Exclusive vs. Concurrent Powers**
   a. **Exclusive state powers:** The Tenth Amendment reserves to the states all powers not constitutionally delegated to the federal government. However, federal powers are now broadly interpreted .... [221]
   b. **Exclusive federal power:** Whether the power is exclusive depends on ***constitutional limitations*** on state power, the ***nature*** of the power, and the ***words granting the power*** .... [222]

c. **Concurrent federal and state power:** Under the Supremacy Clause, state laws that are "inconsistent" with federal power are invalid even where the power is concurrent. The mere existence of certain federal power (*e.g.*, the commerce power) inhibits state power to a certain degree even where Congress has not yet acted .... [226]

B. INTERGOVERNMENTAL PRIVILEGES AND IMMUNITIES

1. **National Citizenship:** The Fourteenth Amendment guarantees the privileges and immunities stemming from the national government to all citizens (*e.g.*, right to travel interstate, right to vote for national officers) .... [229]

   a. **Bill of Rights not included:** The *Slaughterhouse Cases* held that the rights protected against federal action by the first eight Amendments were ***not*** privileges and immunities of national citizenship so as to be protected from state action under the Fourteenth Amendment. However, the Amendment contains an ***Enabling Clause*** (Section 5) that grants Congress power to enforce the protection of citizens' privileges and immunities .... [231]

2. **State Citizenship:** The Interstate Privileges and Immunities Clause (Article IV, Section 2) prohibits state discrimination against noncitizens of the state in respect to essential activities or basic rights—unless the discrimination is ***closely*** or ***substantially related*** to a ***substantial state purpose*** .... [233]

C. INTERGOVERNMENTAL IMMUNITY

1. **In General:** The Supremacy Clause impliedly limits state power to regulate and tax the property and activities of the federal government; the Tenth Amendment places similar limitations on federal power regarding state governments .... [241]

2. **Federal Regulation of State Governments:** The Tenth Amendment limits the federal government's power to interfere with state and local functions. However, the Court's view is that state interests are more properly protected by inherent restraints built into the structure of the federal system (*e.g.*, state representation in Congress) than by judicial review. Thus, unless such safeguards are extraordinarily defective, the ***Court*** will ***not*** find that an otherwise permissible exercise of congressional power violates the Tenth Amendment because it regulates the states as well as private persons .... [243]

   a. **Exception:** The Tenth Amendment limits Congress's power to regulate the states alone by directing the states to act in a particular way ..... [244]

3. **Federal Taxation of State Governments:** The same rule seemingly applies to federal taxation of state property and activities .... [245]

4. **State Taxation of Federal Government**

   a. **When Congress has spoken:** Congress has complete power to regulate state taxation of federal property and activities, and the Court in *McCulloch v. Maryland* held that property or activities of the federal government itself (or of federal agencies) may not be taxed by the states [246]

   b. **When Congress has not spoken:** The Supremacy Clause impliedly prohibits (i) state taxes that ***discriminate*** against federal property and activities; and (ii) nondiscriminatory state taxes that place a ***substantial burden*** on the federal government .... [247]

5. **State Regulation of Federal Government:** Congress has complete power to forbid or permit state regulation of federal property or activities. Absent congressional consent, the Supremacy Clause impliedly immunizes agents of the federal government from state regulations that interfere with the performance of federal functions. The state regulation is also invalid if inconsistent with the policy of a federal statute .... [258]

III. REGULATION AND TAXATION OF COMMERCE

	Text Section
A. REGULATION OF FOREIGN COMMERCE—EXCLUSIVE FEDERAL POWER Because the federal government must speak with one voice when regulating relations with foreign governments, regulation of foreign commerce is exclusively a federal power	[260]
B. REGULATION OF INTERSTATE COMMERCE	
1. **Concurrent Power:** The federal power to regulate interstate commerce is concurrent with state power over transactions occurring within the state	[261]
2. **Scope of Federal Power:** There are two principal theories upon which congressional exercise of the Commerce Clause power "to regulate commerce . . . among—the several states" may be upheld: (i) Congress's power over the ***channels or facilities*** of interstate commerce and (ii) Congress's power over activities that have a ***"national economic effect"***	[262]
a. **"Channels" or "facilities" of interstate commerce:** Congress has ***plenary*** power to regulate the "channels" and "facilities" of interstate commerce. This includes the authority to ***exclude*** from shipment or travel in the channels of interstate commerce any goods, persons, or activities found by Congress to be harmful to the public health, safety, welfare, or morals. This includes the power to regulate even ***after*** interstate commerce has ended	[263]
b. **National economic effect:** Congress has the power to regulate all "commerce" or "activity" that ***affects more than one state.*** This includes the power to ***prohibit*** as well as to ***encourage*** both ***commercial and noncommercial*** activities and even if they occur wholly intrastate	[271]
(1) **Congressional findings:** If Congress has made findings that the activity in question affects more than one state, the Court will give great deference to the finding	[273]
(2) **Volume of commerce affected:** Congress may regulate any business or individual, no matter how small the impact on interstate commerce, as long as there is an ***aggregate*** effect on other states by the ***class of activities*** regulated	[274]
(3) **Limitless power?** Under the "national economic effect" theory, Congress may not regulate activities that (i) are completely internal to a single state or (ii) so remotely affect other states that to uphold congressional regulation would obliterate our concept of federalism.	[275]
3. **State Regulation of Interstate Commerce:** The federal power over interstate commerce is potentially all pervasive, but it is not exclusive. Whether a state may regulate interstate commerce turns significantly on whether there is relevant federal legislation	[278]
a. **Power of Congress to permit or prohibit state regulation:** The Commerce Clause gives Congress complete power to permit or prohibit state regulation of what is concededly interstate commerce	[279]
(1) **Where Congress expressly authorizes or prohibits state regulation:** An authorizing or prohibiting enactment by Congress can change a prior decision of the Supreme Court regarding state regulation of interstate commerce. However, while state regulations are immune from attack under the Commerce Clause if authorized by Congress, they may be attacked by use of the ***Equal Protection Clause*** since Congress cannot authorize states to violate this Clause	[280]
(2) **Where no express congressional authorization or prohibition of state law:** When there is relevant federal legislation, but no express authorization or prohibition of state law, the Court determines whether the ***general intent*** of the relevant statute authorizes or forbids the state regulation in question. If the state regulation is found to be ***superseded*** or ***preempted*** by federal law, it will be held invalid under the Supremacy Clause. In determining congressional	

intent, the Court will look to: (i) whether there is an interest in uniform, national regulation, (ii) historical or traditional classifications of the subject matter as federal or local, (iii) completeness of the federal regulatory scheme, and (iv) the coincidence between federal and state statutes . . . . [283]

b. **Power of states to regulate where Congress has not acted:** Where Congress has not enacted legislation regarding the subject matter, states may regulate local transactions even though they affect interstate commerce—subject to certain limitations . . . . [290]

(1) **Discrimination:** State regulations that discriminate against interstate commerce are ***almost always invalid*** (*e.g.*, statutes excluding incoming or restricting outgoing trade in order to protect economic interests of local industry) as an invasion of the federal commerce power. However, even discriminatory regulations may be upheld to protect health and safety interests if no reasonable and adequate nondiscriminatory alternatives are available (*e.g.*, state may prohibit importation of live baitfish from other states where they pose a health threat to state's fragile fisheries) . . . . [291]

(2) **Nondiscriminatory regulation:** State regulations that do not discriminate against interstate commerce are given greater deference by the Court . . . . [305]

(a) **"Subject matter" test (older approach):** If the subject matter involved does not require a uniform, national rule, but is of local concern and permits diverse regulation, the state regulation has usually been upheld if it has some rational basis . . . . [306]

(b) **"Balancing" test (modern approach):** Under this current approach, the ***burden on interstate commerce*** imposed by the regulation is weighed against the ***strength of the state interest*** in the regulation, with the Court deciding whether the regulation imposes an ***unreasonable burden*** on interstate commerce. The Court gives greater weight to statutes that further local health, safety, or social welfare interests than to statutes that seek to protect local economic interests . . . . [309]

1) **Judicial role:** The Court makes its own determination as to the purposes of the state regulation and is not bound by recitals of purpose by the enacting legislature. However, the Court generally will defer to state legislative determinations of disputed factual questions on whether the state's purpose is served by the regulation or on the cost of compliance . . . . [311]

2) **Economic regulations:** The fact that a nondiscriminatory state regulation is designed to protect local economic interests does not automatically invalidate it under the Commerce Clause . . . . [317]

3) **Reciprocity agreements:** Reciprocity agreements between states respecting sale of products do not automatically violate the Commerce Clause; but a ***mandatory*** reciprocity requirement forbidding sale of products from another state unless that state reciprocates is invalid absent a substantial state interest that cannot be obtained by alternative means . . . . [319]

(3) **Permits or licenses for interstate business:** The traditional rule is that a state cannot require a permit or license for the privilege of engaging in interstate transportation, or of engaging in business that is ***exclusively*** interstate commerce, but the state may require a permit to promote safety rather than to prevent competition . . . . . . [320]

(4) **Broader state power over liquor regulation:** The Twenty-First Amendment has been held to give the states broader regulatory power over regulation of liquor than over any other type of interstate commerce. A state is unconfined by traditional Commerce Clause limitations when deciding whether to ***permit importation or sale*** of liquor ***destined for local use or consumption*** .... [322]

(a) **Limitation—noncentral state interests:** Even state liquor regulations concerning local sale and use may be subject to Congress's commerce power when the federal policies are particularly strong and the state's central interests in regulating the time, place, and manner of liquor importation and sale are not directly implicated .... [323]

C. POWER OF STATES TO TAX INTERSTATE COMMERCE

1. **General Considerations:** Congress has complete power to authorize or forbid state taxation of interstate commerce. Where Congress has not acted, state taxes that ***discriminate*** against interstate commerce violate the Commerce Clause (and possibly the Interstate Privileges and Immunities Clause or Equal Protection Clause). ***Nondiscriminatory*** taxes may be valid ...... [328]
2. **Ad Valorem Property Taxes:** These are taxes based on the value of property .... [337]
   a. **Tax on property used to transport goods interstate:** The validity of such taxes depends on (i) whether the property has a ***nexus*** with the taxing state (*i.e.*, receives benefits or protection from that state), and (ii) whether its value has been ***properly apportioned*** according to its contacts with each taxing state. An unfair apportionment may violate both the Due Process and Commerce Clauses .... [338]
   b. **Tax on cargo in transit:** States ***cannot*** levy an ad valorem tax on property being shipped interstate that happens to be in the taxing state on tax day. However, a break in transit intended to end or suspend a shipment renders the property subject to state taxation .... [347]
3. **"Doing Business" Taxes:** These are imposed for engaging in business within the state. States may impose such taxes if they meet a four-part test: .... [350]
   a. The activity taxed must have a ***substantial nexus*** to the taxing state;
   b. The tax must be ***fairly apportioned;***
   c. The tax must ***not discriminate*** against interstate commerce; and
   d. It must ***fairly relate to services provided*** by the taxing state.
4. **Severance Taxes:** A nondiscriminatory state tax on extraction of minerals from the state is valid, based on the four-part test (above) .... [358]
5. **Taxes on Solicitors:** Flat license fees may not be levied on solicitors of local orders to be filled from goods shipped interstate .... [359]
6. **Highway Use Taxes:** License and similar taxes on interstate carriers will be upheld if they are nondiscriminatory and are imposed to compensate states for costs of maintaining roads .... [361]
7. **Airport Use Fees:** Similarly, a state or municipal tax imposed on emplaning commercial airline passengers is valid if the tax is not excessive when compared to governmental benefits and it does not discriminate against interstate commerce .... [364]
8. **Sales and Use Taxes:** A sales tax is a tax on sales consummated ***within the state;*** a use tax is imposed on the user of goods purchased ***outside the state*** .... [365]
   a. **Use tax by "consumer" state:** Such tax is valid as long as the rate is not higher than the sales tax rate (determined by each locality where the state sales tax rate varies among localities) .... [366]
   b. **Sales tax by "seller" state:** Such tax is valid when imposed on sales consummated ***within*** the state .... [370]

c. **Sales tax by "consumer" state:** Such tax is valid if the interstate seller has ***substantial contacts*** in the consumer state. Solicitation of orders subject to acceptance at seller's out-of-state office ("drummers") is ***not*** sufficient contact . . . . [373]

d. **Collection of use tax:** A requirement by the "consumer" state that the interstate seller collect the tax ***is*** permissible if the seller has the "minimum contacts" necessary to satisfy the Due Process Clause ***and*** the substantial nexus required by the Commerce Clause. "Drummers" ***are*** sufficient bases, as is maintenance of an office in the state. However, solicitation of sales by mail is insufficient . . . . [376]

9. **Taxes on Foreign Corporations:** A state is not required to admit foreign corporations to do business locally. However, under the Equal Protection Clause, a state cannot impose more burdensome taxes on foreign corporations than on domestic ones unless such discrimination is ***rationally related*** to a ***legitimate*** state purpose . . . . [381]

D. **POWER OF STATES TO TAX FOREIGN COMMERCE**

1. **Import-Export Clause**

a. **Imports:** No state may impose a tax on imports or related activity as such without congressional consent (Article 1, Section 10, Clause 2). However, a nondiscriminatory property tax on all goods in the state is valid . . . . [383]

b. **Exports:** State taxation of exports is prohibited only ***after*** the goods enter the "export stream" . . . . [387]

2. **Commerce Clause:** The Commerce Clause gives Congress plenary power to regulate foreign commerce, and thus inherently limits a state's power to tax such commerce . . . . [388]

IV. **INDIVIDUAL RIGHTS—LIMITATIONS ON THE EXERCISE OF GOVERNMENTAL POWER**

A. **INTRODUCTION**

1. **Bill of Rights—Limitation on Federal Power:** The Bill of Rights as originally applied limits the actions of the ***federal*** government . . . . [390]

2. **Fourteenth Amendment—Limitation on State Power:** This Amendment incorporates many of the rights protected by the first 10 Amendments as restrictions on ***state*** action . . . . [391]

a. **Privileges and Immunities Clause:** This is ***not*** applicable to the states . [392]

b. **Fourteenth Amendment Due Process Clause:** Most provisions of the Bill of Rights have been held to be so fundamental as to be applicable to the states by incorporation through this clause ("selective incorporation") . . . [393]

(1) **Extent of incorporation:** If a right is incorporated by the Fourteenth Amendment, then ***all aspects and elements*** of the right are incorporated and are applicable ***both*** to federal and state action, according to a majority of the Court. *But note:* Some Justices hold that some aspects of a right are not so fundamental that they should receive as much protection from state action as from federal action (*e.g.*, unanimous verdict required in federal jury trial not required in state jury trial) . . . . [397]

(2) **Other rights:** Due process also protects fundamental rights beyond those enumerated in the Bill of Rights (*e.g.*, "beyond a reasonable doubt" standard in criminal actions) . . . . [400]

c. **Equal Protection Clause:** This clause limits ***only state action***. However, federal discrimination may violate the Fifth Amendment Due Process Clause . . . . [401]

Text Section

B. DUE PROCESS

1. **Introduction:** Both the Fifth and Fourteenth Amendments protect against the deprivation of ***"life, liberty or property without due process of law"*** ..... [402]
2. **Procedural Due Process:** Certain procedural safeguards (notice and hearing) limit government actions that affect a citizen's ***"liberty"*** and ***"property"*** interests .... [403]
   a. **Definitions:** ***"Liberty"*** includes more than freedom from physical restraints (*e.g.*, right to contract, to engage in gainful employment, to be free of defamation by government, and the right to develop certain parental interests). ***"Property"*** includes ownership and entitlements granted by state or federal law (*i.e.*, a legitimate claim to certain benefits such as public education, continued welfare benefits, and, under certain circumstances, public employment). ***Deprivation*** of life, liberty, or property without due process requires more than negligent conduct .... [404]
   b. **Timing and scope of required hearing:** Whether a ***prior*** evidentiary hearing is required, and the ***extent*** of procedural requirements, is determined by (i) the importance of the interest; (ii) the value of specific procedural safeguards to that interest; and (iii) the government interest in fiscal and administrative efficiency .... [414]
      (1) **Civil forfeiture of real property used in a crime:** There must be a notice and adversary proceeding ***prior*** to seizure of ***real property*** .. [415]
      (2) **Termination of welfare benefits:** There must be ***prior*** notice and a ***prior hearing*** before an ***impartial*** decisionmaker before benefits can be terminated .... [416]
      (3) **Termination of disability benefits:** ***Prior notice*** and a ***subsequent hearing*** are sufficient because disability benefits are ***not*** based on financial need .... [417]
      (4) **Termination of public employment:** An employee subject to removal only "for cause" must be given a ***pretermination notice and opportunity to respond*** followed by a ***subsequent*** full ***evidentiary*** hearing .... [419]
      (5) **Public education—disciplinary suspension:** Although ***no*** prior hearing is required for ***temporary*** suspensions (10 days or less), ***some notice*** of charges and ***some opportunity to explain*** is usually required .... [421]
      (6) **Public education—academic dismissal:** Due process is satisfied if the student is ***adequately informed*** of the deficiency and given an ***opportunity to respond*** .... [423]
      (7) **License suspension:** Under certain circumstances, the state's interest may ***sometimes*** be important enough to suspend a license ***without a prior hearing,*** provided there is a ***prompt*** post-suspension hearing .... [424]
      (8) **Creditor remedies:** ***Prior notice and hearing*** are required for a prejudgment ***garnishment*** of wages. Exceptions are allowed for certain prejudgment seizure procedures and in ***extraordinary circumstances*** (*e.g.*, debtor preparing to flee with assets) ...... [426]
      (9) **Attachment of real property:** Prejudgment attachment is not permitted without prior notice and hearing unless facts show plaintiff is likely to recover .... [427]
      (10) **Commitment to a mental institution:** The standard of proof used at an ***adult's*** precommitment adversarial hearing must be at least that of ***"clear and convincing"*** evidence. Parents or a governmental agency can institutionalize a child without a prior hearing if a ***prior neutral inquiry*** and ***subsequent periodic reviews*** are made .... [428]
      (11) **Antipsychotic drugs for prisoners:** A trial-type hearing and right

to counsel are ***not*** required to administer drugs against a prisoner's will, as long as decisionmakers are not biased . . . . [430]

(12) **Termination of parental status:** Parental unfitness must be shown by at least ***"clear and convincing"*** evidence. Counsel must be appointed for indigent parents in termination hearings ***only*** where fundamental fairness demands it . . . . [431]

3. **Substantive Due Process**

a. **Economic and social regulations:** Until the mid-1930s, the Court reviewed the ***substance*** of legislation and used the Due Process Clause to invalidate economic and social regulations if the ***means*** used were not ***reasonably related*** to a ***legitimate*** end. Today, the Court defers to legislative judgments in this area unless the regulations are demonstrably ***arbitrary or irrational.*** The effect has been the upholding of nearly all social and economic regulations . . . . [434]

b. **Fundamental personal rights:** Due process is used to protect certain fundamental rights not enumerated in the Constitution. Infringement of such rights is subject to ***strict scrutiny*** . . . . [441]

(1) **Right of privacy:** Although not mentioned in the Constitution, this is one of those ***basic human rights*** that are of fundamental importance. It cannot be impaired except where the law is narrowly drawn and serves a ***compelling state interest*** . . . . [442]

(a) **Scope:** The right to privacy includes familial rights such as marriage, procreation, contraception, abortion, and a right to educate children as one chooses . . . . [443]

(2) **Right to interstate travel:** The right to travel from state to state is ***virtually unqualified.*** However, the right to travel abroad ***may*** be regulated within the traditional limitations of due process . . . . [464]

(3) **Right to vote:** This is a fundamental right and is constitutionally protected . . . . [473]

(4) **Rights of mentally ill:** Involuntary commitment to a mental hospital is subject to due process protection. A person must be found to be (i) ***mentally ill*** and (ii) ***dangerous*** (to himself or others) or ***incapable of surviving*** safely outside an institution. The rights of involuntarily committed persons ***also*** include adequate food, shelter, clothing, and medical care . . . . [474]

(5) **Right to reject medical treatment:** A competent person has the right to refuse unwanted medical treatment . . . . [479]

C. EQUAL PROTECTION

1. **Constitutional Provisions:** Equal protection is applied to the states through the Fourteenth Amendment Equal Protection Clause and to the federal government through the Due Process Clause of the Fifth Amendment . . . . [481]

2. **In General:** Discriminatory treatment is not necessarily prohibited, as long as the statutory classification meets the relevant test: (i) the ***traditional*** (or rational basis) test, (ii) the ***strict scrutiny*** (or compelling interest) test, or (iii) the ***intermediate level of scrutiny*** (or quasi-suspect class) test . . . . [483]

3. **Traditional Test—Economic and Social Regulations:** Because most economic and social regulations are not based on suspect or quasi-suspect criteria, nearly all such regulations are reviewed by the Court under the ***traditional*** equal protection test . . . . [484]

a. **Extreme judicial deference:** Under this test, the classification is valid if it is ***rationally related to a proper state interest.*** The classification will be presumed valid unless it is applied in an ***arbitrary or capricious*** manner . . . . [485]

b. **Less deferential formulation:** Sometimes the Court states the traditional test in a slightly less deferential way: The classification must have a ***fair***

and substantial relation to the object of the legislation. However, even using this formulation, the Court almost always ***sustains*** the classification . [488]

4. **Suspect Classification—"Strict Scrutiny":** Government action that ***intentionally*** discriminates against racial or ethnic minorities is suspect and subject to strict scrutiny . . . . [489]
   a. **Test:** Equal protection is violated unless the suspect classification is ***necessary to promote a compelling state interest*** . . . . [490]
      (1) **"Necessary" to promote compelling state interest:** This may be found when there is ***no less burdensome, alternative means*** to accomplish the state interest . . . . [491]
      (2) **Requirement of intentional discrimination:** Intentional or "de jure" discrimination may be found in three ways: . . . . [493]
         (i) ***On its face;***
         (ii) ***By unequal administration*** of the law; or
         (iii) ***By impermissible motive*** in enacting the law.
      (3) **Compare—"de facto" discrimination:** A law, neutral on its face, may have a racially disproportionate ***impact*** and thus may violate equal protection. Such statutes are judged by the ***"traditional"*** test . [506]
   b. **What is "suspect" classification?**
      (1) **Racial (or ethnic) classifications:** Some classifications based on race or national origin do not impose burdens on the basis of race but merely draw lines on the basis of a racial criterion . . . . [510]
         (a) **In general—strict scrutiny:** Racial classifications are ***prohibited*** unless ***necessary*** to a ***compelling*** state interest . . . . . . [511]
         (b) **Racial segregation:** Deliberate segregation in public schools and public facilities violates equal protection. To establish a constitutional violation, the court must find ***segregative intent,*** which may be inferred from actions having a foreseeable, disparate impact . . . . [512]
            1) **Remedying segregation:** School boards have an affirmative duty to eliminate intentional racial segregation. The remedy in each case is determined by the nature and scope of the violation . . . . [520]
         (c) **"Benign" discrimination:** Government action that ***favors*** racial or ethnic minorities is subject to strict scrutiny review just as is government action that discriminates ***against*** minorities . . . [533]
            1) **Remedying past discrimination:** Under some circumstances, the government may give preference to persons who are members of a minority group discriminated against in the past if the discrimination is identified by an authorized government body. However, such plans ***cannot*** be used to remedy ***general*** past societal discrimination . . . . [534]
            2) **Student diversity in higher education:** Apart from the government's interest in remedying past discrimination, the Court has also held that a state university ***may*** consider race or ethnicity in order to achieve diversity in its admissions . . . . [539]
            3) **Congressional power:** Congress may use benign, race-conscious measures if substantially related to important government objectives, even if the measures are not designed to remedy past governmental or societal discrimination . . . . [541]
            4) **Legislative apportionment:** Racial or ethnic criteria may be used to create or preserve minority strength as long as no racial group has its overall voting strength minimized or the shape of districts is not so bizarre as to be explainable only on grounds of race . . . . [543]

(d) **Repeal of remedies for discrimination or segregation:** A state may repeal or modify an antidiscrimination law if the remedy was not constitutionally required. However, a state ***does*** violate equal protection if it reallocates decisionmaking authority regarding racial issues so as to make it more difficult for minorities to get favorable laws passed . . . . [544]

(2) **Discrimination against aliens:** Discrimination in the admission or exclusion of aliens is permissible under Congress's plenary power over aliens. However, ***most*** state discriminations against lawfully admitted aliens are ***"suspect"*** (*e.g.*, those involving welfare, civil service, land ownership) . . . . [545]

(a) **Exception—participation in government process:** The courts use the ***traditional equal protection test*** for state laws that exclude aliens from ***participation*** in its democratic institutions (voting, public offices, etc.). Such laws are usually upheld [551]

(b) **Illegal aliens:** Although state discrimination against illegal aliens is ***not*** suspect, denial of free public education to children of illegal aliens usually violates equal protection . . . . [552]

5. **Quasi-Suspect Classifications—Intermediate Level of Scrutiny:** Classifications based on gender or legitimacy are ***not*** "suspect." They are ***"quasi-suspect"*** and violate equal protection unless they are ***substantially related*** to ***important*** government objectives. (This test is more strict than the traditional test) . . . . [554]

a. **"De facto" discrimination:** The ***traditional*** test is used for laws that do not intentionally discriminate but have a disproportionate impact . . . . . . [556]

b. **Gender discrimination:** All recent decisions have held that laws discriminating ***against*** women violate equal protection, but several discriminatory laws against ***men*** have been upheld . . . . [557]

(1) **Laws compensating women for past discrimination:** These have been upheld as being substantially related to an important government objective . . . . [561]

c. **Discrimination against illegitimate children:** Although most state laws that discriminate against illegitimate children have been invalidated, some discrimination has been upheld (*e.g.*, in areas of social security, probate, and immigration) . . . . [562]

6. **Classifications that Are Not Suspect or Quasi-Suspect**

a. **Discrimination against the poor:** Poverty standing alone is ***not*** a suspect classification and the traditional test is used . . . . [565]

(1) **De facto discrimination:** The major developments in discrimination against the poor have involved state laws or other official practices that have a disproportionate impact on poor people (in the areas of criminal appeals, fines or imprisonment, divorce, and paternity actions) . . . . [567]

(2) **Compare:** In cases involving bankruptcy, welfare appeals, and abortion, the Court has upheld laws that place a burden on the poor . . [574]

b. **Discrimination against the elderly:** This is judged by the traditional test . . . . [578]

c. **Discrimination against nonresidents:** Legitimate residency requirements are not suspect and are judged by the rational basis test . . . . . . [579]

d. **Discrimination against mentally retarded:** Laws that discriminate against mentally retarded persons are judged by the rational basis test . . [580]

7. **"Fundamental Rights"—Strict Scrutiny:** A fundamental right is one ***explicitly or implicitly*** guaranteed by the Constitution. Government action impinging on a fundamental right is subject to ***strict scrutiny*** . . . . [582]

a. **Freedom of association:** ***Burdensome requirements*** for new political parties to get candidates on the election ballot were held invalid because they impaired freedom of association, and no ***compelling state interest*** was shown to justify the discrimination. However, state requirements that candidates or new political parties demonstrate public support to get on the ballot have been upheld . . . . [583]

b. **Right to travel interstate:** This right has been held impaired by state ***durational residence requirements*** for welfare and medical benefits, and for certain voting registrations. However, residence requirements for reduced tuition and divorce have been upheld because they are neither ***necessities of life*** nor serve ***momentous government purposes*** . . . . [590]

c. **Right of privacy:** This right has been recognized as implicit in the "liberty" protected by the Due Process Clause, and ***burdensome*** classifications are subject to ***strict scrutiny.*** The rights to ***marry, procreate,*** and have an ***abortion*** are classified as fundamental rights . . . . [601]

d. **Freedom of speech:** Any governmental restrictions on this fundamental right must be ***finely tailored*** to serve ***substantial*** state interests. Strict scrutiny applies . . . . [606]

e. **Right to vote:** Several amendments prohibit specific restrictions on the right to vote. Apart from these, there is no general right to vote in the Constitution. However, the Court has held that government discrimination regarding voting is subject to ***strict scrutiny*** under the Equal Protection Clause . . . . [607]

(1) **Denial of the vote:** Denial of this right to some residents who meet the age and citizenship requirements, while granting the right to other citizens, has usually been held to violate equal protection because the classification failed to meet the ***compelling state interest*** standard (*e.g.*, poll taxes) . . . . [608]

(a) **Exceptions:** The Court has upheld laws denying certain persons the right to vote: . . . . [615]

1) ***Denying felons*** the right to vote is sanctioned by constitutional language (Fourteenth Amendment, Section 2) and is ***not*** subject to strict scrutiny;

2) ***"Special purpose" elections*** which apply to a limited group are judged by the ***traditional*** test; and

3) ***Laws denying voting rights to nonresidents*** are subject only to the ***traditional*** test.

(2) **Limiting "effectiveness" of the vote:** Laws that ***substantially*** impair the effectiveness of the right to vote are subject to ***fairly*** strict—scrutiny (*e.g.*, primary election registration, absentee ballot restrictions, ballot qualification restrictions) . . . . [620]

(3) **"Dilution" of the vote—apportionment:** In the past, the Court considered apportionment a political question, but now will hear such cases to assure to each voter equal protection . . . . [625]

(a) **Congressional districts:** Under the Constitution, ***"precise mathematical equality"*** (one person-one vote) is the goal in determining congressional districts ***within a state***. The preservation of ***political boundaries*** (*i.e.*, city or county lines) does ***not*** justify deviations from the ***equal population*** requirement. Congress's apportionment of districts ***among the states*** is not subject to the same mathematical standard . . . . [626]

(b) **State legislative districts:** In ***state*** legislative districts, mathematical exactness is not required, and so a ***10% deviation*** between any two districts is permissible. However, larger deviations ***cannot*** be upheld unless explained by some acceptable state policy. Existing political boundaries ***may*** be given consideration . . . . [631]

1) **Multi-member districts:** These do ***not*** violate the "one person-one vote" rule, but are violative of equal protection

if they effectively minimize the voting power of a particular racial or political group . . . . [637]

2) **Gerrymandering:** State districting plans that disadvantage an identifiable racial or political group on a statewide basis may violate equal protection . . . . [639]

3) **Relevant population:** Districting need not be based on ***total*** population (*e.g.*, aliens, transients, and convicts may be excluded) . . . . [640]

4) **Relevant officials:** The "one person-one vote" rule applies to the ***election*** of ***all*** officials who perform normal governmental functions. The rule also applies to the ***nomination*** of officials, but not to appointed officials . . . [641]

(c) **Supermajority requirements:** Provisions requiring approval (by the legislature or referendum) by more than a majority are ***valid*** as long as they do not discriminate against any identifiable class . . . . [646]

(d) **Remedies for malapportionment:** The federal courts usually defer to state remedies (by courts or the legislature). If the state fails to act, the federal court will draw up a plan. Federal courts have less flexibility than the states and thus their plans are subject to stricter review . . . . [647]

f. **Right to be a candidate:** This has ***not*** been recognized as a fundamental right, but laws that impose burdensome requirements on candidates are subject to ***fairly strict*** review . . . . [649]

8. **"Nonfundamental" Rights:** Rights that are not implicitly or explicitly guaranteed by the Constitution are reviewable under the traditional ***"rational basis"*** test. Rights to welfare, disability benefits, housing, or a particular quality of education have been held to be ***important,*** but not fundamental, rights . . . . [652]

9. **"Irrebuttable Presumptions" and the Right to a Hearing:** In several "important interests" cases, the Court invalidated ***over-inclusive*** state classifications because they created improper irrebuttable presumptions. In such cases ***procedural due process*** requires some opportunity for persons to show that they should be treated differently. *Examples:* . . . . [663]

a. **Parental custody:** An unwed father must be given a hearing to determine his fitness as a parent . . . . [664]

b. **Residency status:** A state law may require higher fees for nonresident students but applicants are entitled to a hearing to present evidence of their bona fide residency . . . . [665]

c. **Pregnancy and employee fitness:** Due process requires a case-by-case determination of when a pregnant teacher is physically incapable of continuing her duties . . . . [666]

d. **Food stamps:** Similarly, a household must have an opportunity to present evidence as to whether it is needy for food stamp purposes . . . [667]

e. **Disability benefits for illegitimate children:** Social Security benefits may not be denied some illegitimate children born after the parent's disability without giving them the opportunity to establish their dependency . . . . . . [668]

f. **Decline of doctrine:** The last of these "important interests" cases (in 1975) recognized that limiting Social Security benefits to wives and step-children who were such for more than nine months prior to the wage earner's death may be over- or under-inclusive in some cases. However, it was ***upheld*** on the basis of government efficiency . . . . [669]

D. THE "STATE ACTION" REQUIREMENT

1. **Introduction:** The Fourteenth and Fifteenth Amendments restrict only ***governmental*** action, not the acts of private individuals. But "state action" includes more than acts by the legislative, executive, judicial, and administrative branches of government . . . . [670]

2. **Acts of Government "Agents":** State action includes conduct of government officials acting in their official capacity (*i.e.*, under color of law) even if they act illegally [671]
3. **"Public" or "Government" Functions:** Occasionally, activities undertaken by private individuals or organizations are ones that are "traditionally the ***exclusive*** prerogative of the State," and are then treated as state action. These actions include ***elections*** (and primaries and preprimaries) and the operation of ***company towns*** [672]
   a. **Limits of doctrine:** In most cases, the Court has ***not*** found privately conducted activity to be a government function. *Examples:* [677]
      (1) **Shopping centers:** A shopping center is ***not*** the functional equivalent of a municipality (as is a company town), because it does not possess ***all*** the attributes of a town [678]
      (2) **Monopoly businesses:** A heavily regulated utility granted a monopoly by the state did ***not*** engage in state action when it terminated a user's service without notice or hearing because utility service is not traditionally the exclusive province of the state [679]
      (3) **Regulated businesses:** The same is true of businesses such as nursing homes or specialized private schools [680]
      (4) **Creditor's remedies:** A warehouseman authorized by state statute to sell stored goods for unpaid charges is ***not*** engaged in state action [681]
4. **Significant State "Involvement":** More frequently, state action by private individuals (usually racial discrimination violating equal protection) is found because the government has ***required*** or ***significantly encouraged*** the acts of discrimination. Allowing the conduct to occur is not sufficient for "state action"; the state must ***compel*** or ***significantly participate*** in the private conduct. State action has been found in: [682]
   a. ***Government compulsion*** of private discrimination (ordinance requiring segregation in restaurants);
   b. ***Government administration*** of private discrimination (state as trustee of segregated park);
   c. ***Joint action*** by government officials and private persons concerning creditors' remedies (*e.g.*, attachment laws);
   d. ***Judicial enforcement*** of private discrimination ***through restrictive covenants;***
   e. ***Government approval*** of private conduct, but mere licensing by the state is ***not*** equivalent to state action; and
   f. ***"Symbiotic" relationships*** between government and individual.

E. CONGRESSIONAL POWER TO ENFORCE CONSTITUTIONAL RIGHTS

1. **In General:** The Necessary and Proper Clause and the Enabling Clauses of the Thirteenth, Fourteenth, and Fifteenth Amendments empower Congress to enforce and fashion remedies for violations of constitutional rights. Sometimes, Congress even has the power to legislate against practices that the Court would not find unconstitutional [692]
   a. **Government action:** Congress may impose ***criminal or civil*** remedies for a violation of constitutional rights by government action [693]
   b. **Private action:** If the constitutional right operates against private individuals as well as government action, Congress may legislate remedies against ***anyone*** who interferes [694]
2. **Necessary and Proper Clause:** Several rights "arise from the relationship of the individual and the federal government" and are protected from interference by both private and government actions under the Necessary and Proper Clause (*e.g.*, the right to travel interstate, the right to vote in federal elections and primaries, and the right to petition Congress for redress of wrongs) [695]

3. **Thirteenth Amendment:** Under the amendment's Enabling Clause, Congress may prohibit ***virtually all*** racial discrimination against ***blacks,*** and ***some*** discrimination against whites .... [702]
4. **Fourteenth Amendment:** Under the Enabling Clause, Congress has the power to ***define*** the ***substantive*** terms of the Fourteenth Amendment, and the Court will uphold such legislation as long as it perceives a ***basis*** for the congressional determination (*e.g.*, congressional ban on English literacy tests for voting upheld even though the Court would not have held such tests unconstitutional) .... [704]
   a. **Remedial power:** Congress may also prohibit conduct that is not itself unconstitutional, if it has a ***rational basis*** for so doing (*e.g.*, a racially disproportionate impact). Remedies may be legislated for ***prior violations*** or to ***prevent future violations*** .... [705]
   b. **Limitations:** Although the extent is still unclear, certain limitations on congressional power regarding the Fourteenth Amendment exist: (i) Congress may not define nor remedy discrimination by enactments that ***conflict with other constitutional provisions;*** and (ii) although Congress has the power to enforce guarantees of the amendment, it has ***no power to restrict, abrogate, or dilute*** these guarantees .... [708]
   c. **Government vs. private action:** Although state action is required for violation of the Fourteenth Amendment, certain ***private actions*** (*e.g.*, by state or local officials, private citizens collaborating with officials, and perhaps private individuals alone) ***may*** be remedied by Congress's broad powers under the Enabling Clause .... [712]
5. **Fifteenth Amendment:** Where Congress has a ***rational basis*** for finding government racial discrimination in voting, it has broad remedial powers under the Enabling Clause .... [716]
6. **Other Sources of Power:** Provisions of the Civil Rights Act of 1964 prohibiting racial discrimination have been upheld under the ***Commerce Clause.*** Similarly, the federal government may indirectly, through its ***taxing and spending powers,*** compel recognition of the constitutional rights of others . [718]

F. FREEDOM OF SPEECH, PRESS, AND ASSOCIATION

1. **In General:** The right is based on the First Amendment and is applied to the states through the Fourteenth Amendment. It encompasses the right to hold beliefs, the rights to speak and to remain silent, the right to associate and refrain from associating, and the rights to communicate and to receive information. The right protects individuals and, in some cases, corporations, and affords some protection to symbolic conduct .... [721]
   a. **Rights not absolute:** There is ***no*** absolute right to speak or publish what ever one chooses. Restrictions regarding defamation, obscenity, or incitement to violence may be valid. The right also does not include the right to be heard by public bodies .... [736]
   b. **Validity of restrictions:** The Court must ***balance*** First Amendment rights against the interest served by the imposed restraint. There usually exists a presumption against the validity of restraints upon this right. Content-based speech regulations are unconstitutional absent a showing that a regulation is ***necessary*** to serve a ***compelling*** interest and is ***narrowly drawn*** to achieve that end .... [737]
   c. **"Overbreadth" and "vagueness":** The Court may permit regulations to be challenged ***on their face*** if they are overbroad or vague because such regulations may ***chill*** the exercise of free speech. If a law is ***vague on its face,*** it is totally ***invalid.*** Thus persons are immune from regulation under the law, even if their conduct is not constitutionally protected .... [739]
      (1) **Overbreadth:** An overbroad law is one that regulates constitutionally protected expression or association along with unprotected conduct .... [741]

Text Section

(2) **Overbreadth due to vagueness:** Where vagueness in a regulation may be ***interpreted*** as proscribing protected as well as unprotected conduct, it may be overbroad .... [745]

(3) **Vagueness alone:** A law may be impermissibly vague even though not overbroad, *e.g.*, a law making unlawful "speech not protected by the Constitution" .... [746]

2. **Advocacy of Unlawful Action**

a. **Speech that is abusive of government or officials:** Unpatriotic or disrespectful speech is protected as long as it does not incite unlawful action or breach of the peace .... [750]

b. **Criminal penalties for advocacy of illegal action**

(1) **Earlier view:** In the past, speech that advocated forceful overthrow of the government could be penalized .... [751]

(2) **Holmes-Brandeis test:** However, Holmes and Brandeis dissented in these early cases by contending that government may punish speech only if it ***produces (or is intended to produce) a clear and imminent danger of a serious substantive evil*** .... [752]

(3) ***Dennis-Yates*** **test:** There must be a ***substantial governmental interest*** (determined by the courts) and a ***call to illegal action*** (rather than a mere belief in such action) before speech may be punished .... [753]

(4) ***Brandenburg*** **test:** More recently, the Court has held that speech advocating illegal actions may be penalized only when directed to inciting or producing ***imminent*** lawless action and the speech is likely to result in such action. Note that ***imminence*** and ***evil intent*** appear to be independent requirements for this test .... [754]

3. **Defamation:** This is generally ***not*** protected and may be punished by criminal or civil libel laws; however, mere opinion on public issues is not actionable .... [755]

a. **Matters of public interest:** A constitutional privilege exists for ***certain*** public interest matters. Statements concerning the official conduct of public officials or candidates is privileged unless made with ***actual malice*** (*i.e.*, statement was ***known*** to be false or was published with ***reckless disregard*** as to its truth or falsity—*New York Times* rule) .... [756]

b. **Public figures:** The *New York Times* rule also applies to those who, for ***"all purposes and in all contexts,"*** have achieved general fame or notoriety, or to those who voluntarily involve themselves in a ***particular*** public controversy .... [768]

c. **Private individuals:** The *New York Times* rule does ***not*** apply to defamation of private individuals. States may define standards for private person suits as long as (i) they do not impose ***liability without fault,*** (ii) the factual misstatement ***warns a reasonably prudent*** publisher of its defamatory potential, and (iii) only ***actual damages*** are permitted .... [772]

d. **"Fact" vs. "opinion":** Any statement that may be reasonably interpreted as stating ***facts*** about an individual may be actionable—as long as it is proven false when a public figure or matter of public concern is involved .... [778]

e. **Intentional infliction of emotional distress:** The *New York Times* rule applies to damage actions by public figures for this tort .... [779]

f. **Invasion of privacy suits:** After the *Gertz* case in 1974, there is serious doubt as to whether the *New York Times* rule applies to damage actions by private individuals for invasion of privacy—even where the matter reported was of ***substantial public interest*** .... [780]

4. **Obscenity:** Obscene expression is ***not*** protected by the First Amendment ... [781]

a. **Definition:** Obscene material is a description or depiction of sexual conduct which, taken ***as a whole,*** by the ***average person,*** applying current ***community standards:*** .... [782]

(1) ***Appeals to the prurient interest in sex;***
(2) ***Portrays sex in a patently offensive way;*** and
(3) ***Has no serious social value*** (applying a reasonable person standard rather than the community standard).

b. **Community standards:** These may be determined on a ***statewide*** (or even more local) basis; a nationwide standard is ***not*** required . . . . [789]

c. **Special considerations affecting obscenity:** Greater proof (*i.e.*, a showing of ***knowledge*** of the contents of the materials) is required for prosecution of ***book dealers.*** A state may restrict ***minors'*** access to obscene materials more so than that of adults. And a state may prohibit distribution of child pornography even though not "obscene." Except for child pornography, a state may ***not*** prohibit obscene materials in a person's own home but the sale or distribution of such materials may be punishable . . . . [795]

5. **"Fighting Words" and "Hostile Audiences":** Certain expressions may be prohibited under "breach of the peace" or "disorderly conduct" statutes ***if*** the regulations are ***narrowly drawn*** . . . . [805]

   a. **"Fighting words":** Words that by their utterance inflict injury or tend to incite an ***immediate*** breach of the peace are ***not*** protected by the First Amendment . . . . [806]

   b. **"Hostile audience":** If the speaker's actions produced ***imminent danger*** of ***uncontrolled violence*** by the audience, the exercise of First Amendment rights is outweighed by the public interest in order . . . . [808]

6. **Commercial Speech:** Commercial speech is speech in which the ***dominant*** theme is simply to ***propose a commercial transaction*** . . . . [810]

   a. **Regulation of content permissible:** Commercial speech is subject to ***greater regulation*** than other forms of protected speech. Thus, a state may prohibit ***illegal*** or ***misleading*** ads, or prohibit ***billboards*** (except those advertising the business of the property's occupant) in the interest of traffic safety and aesthetics . . . . [814]

   b. **Scope of protection:** Truthful ads may ***not*** be prohibited unless the ban ***directly advances a substantial government interest*** and is ***only extensive*** enough to serve that interest (*e.g.*, lawyer advertising) . . . . [819]

7. **Censorship and Prior Restraint:** There is a strong presumption ***against*** the constitutional validity of censoring or enjoining in advance unprotected speech. This presumption ***also*** applies to informal government action that has the effect of preventing speech in advance . . . . [832]

   a. **Exceptional cases in which prior restraints allowed:** This occurs generally where the utterance is deemed so inimical to the public good that subsequent remedies would be inadequate (*e.g.*, preserving a fair trial) . . . . [835]

   b. **Procedural safeguards:** Even in exceptional cases, procedural requirements (***notice and hearing,*** etc.) must be observed. Cases where prior restraints have been allowed include certain obscene publications, CIA employee's writings about his employment, and movie censorship . . [842]

   c. **Censorship of the mails:** Censorship of obscene mail or imports is permissible if the proper procedural safeguards are followed. *Note:* An individual has a right to request the government to prohibit a mailer from sending materials to him . . . . [856]

8. **Symbolic Conduct:** Conduct used to communicate an idea may be regulated if there is an important state interest ***independent*** of the speech aspects of the conduct, ***especially*** if the state has no less restrictive means of regulation . . . . [861]

   a. **But note:** A symbolic ***conduct*** conviction must be ***reversed*** if the protected ***speech*** is made part of the offense or may have been relied upon to convict . . . . [866]

Text Section

9. **First Amendment Rights in Public Places**
   a. **Public forum:** Some places are so historically associated with the exercise of First Amendment rights that they cannot be totally closed to protected expression (*e.g.*, streets, sidewalks, parks, public schools). Other public property, although not a traditional public forum, may become one for such time as the state opens it for public use as a place for expressive activity . . . . [869]
   b. **Time, place, and manner regulations:** These are permissible on both types of public forums if (i) they are not based on the ***content*** of the speech: (ii) they are ***narrowly tailored*** to serve (iii) a significant ***government interest;*** and (iv) if banned, an ***alternative forum*** is available for the protected expression . . . . [871]
   c. **Total ban:** A total ban is permissible if it meets the above criteria. Thus, the justification of a state interest in ***protecting privacy*** allows bans on door-to-door solicitations, unwanted mail, etc.; however, it is an open question whether billboards may be totally banned . . . . [889]
   d. **Not a public forum:** Certain public property that is traditionally or by government designation ***not open to the general public*** may be closed to the exercise of First Amendment rights if the prohibition is nondiscriminatory and reasonable (*e.g.*, jailhouse grounds, military bases). Generally, ***private property*** owners may prohibit protected activities, although where the property is held to be equivalent to a public place, no prohibition of the ***reasonable*** exercise of rights is allowed (*e.g.*, "company town") . . . . [893]
   e. **Licensing:** This is a valid means of regulating speech in public areas when the requirements contain ***clearly defined standards*** as to time, place, manner, and duration. Furthermore, denial of a license may ***not*** be based on speech ***content*** (except perhaps under special circumstances) and the issuance of licenses must ***not*** be discretionary with local officials. But a ***reasonable fee*** for the license may be charged . . . [897]
   f. **Injunction:** Injunctions that impose "time, place, and manner" restrictions on exercise of First Amendment rights in ***public*** forums must burden no more speech than ***necessary*** to serve a ***significant*** government interest . . . . [905]

10. **First Amendment Freedoms and Special Government Interests**
   a. **Administration of justice:** Restrictions on First Amendment rights during the judicial process will be sustained to the extent necessary to assure the orderly administration of justice . . . . [906]
      (1) **In court:** Disruptive or disrespectful statements directed to the judge during court proceedings are punishable by contempt . . . . . [907]
      (2) **Out of court:** Utterances out of court are not punishable unless they pose a ***clear and present danger of serious interference*** with the administration of justice. Note that freedom of the press in these circumstances is broadly allowed. The permissible amount of freedom of speech or press depends substantially upon the ***type*** of judicial proceeding involved . . . . [908]
   b. **Electoral process:** The degree of scrutiny the Court applies to election regulation depends on how great a restriction the regulation imposes on the right to vote (*e.g.*, ballot qualifications, restrictions on political parties) may be subject to the ***compelling state interest*** test. Campaign financing laws are generally permitted, but are subject to limitations. Note that the amount that political action committees spend on campaigns may ***not*** be limited . . . . [918]
   c. **Subsidies:** The government need not subsidize speech, and so it can deny tax benefits to lobbying groups. And the government may fund certain programs and not others (*e.g.,* government need not fund abortion counseling) . . . . [937]

d. **Public schools:** Student speech on school grounds may not be prohibited unless it interferes with the educational process; *e.g.*, vulgar and offensive speech in classroom may be prohibited . . . . [940]

e. **Academic freedom:** The First Amendment protects against government attempts to influence academic speech. However, in appropriate proceedings, the government may force disclosure of academic peer review materials . . . . [944]

f. **Prison administration:** Prison regulations that impinge on prisoners' constitutional rights are ***valid*** if reasonably related to a penological interest. Courts generally must give ***broad deference to reasonable*** judgments of prison administrators . . . . [945]

g. **Military personnel:** The First Amendment does protect military personnel, but speech that undermines the military's effectiveness may be restricted, even though such speech would be permissible in a civilian setting . . . . [951]

h. **Practice of law:** Restrictions on the professional conduct of attorneys cannot interfere with a group's freedom of expression and association. To overcome this right, the state must show a ***substantial interest*** in order to regulate attorneys' conduct . . . . [952]

i. **Labor picketing:** This is a protected activity, but may be limited in advancement of an overriding state law or policy (*e.g.*, labor laws) or where a ***clear, immediate danger*** of violence exists . . . . [954]

j. **Boycotts:** Boycotts that are nonviolent and seek to secure ***constitutional rights*** are protected, absent a narrowly tailored law prohibiting certain anti-competitive conduct . . . . [959]

k. **Trademarks:** Congress may grant a limited property right in a word that has acquired special value through the efforts of an entity, thus allowing the entity to prevent others from using the word . . . . [961]

l. **Copyright:** Congress may grant authors exclusive control of their writing for a limited period . . . . [962]

11. **Freedom of Association—Special Rules**

a. **Association with groups engaging in unprotected advocacy or activities:** An individual may be punished for membership in certain types of groups, but only if (i) the group itself engages in activities not constitutionally protected (*see* above), ***and*** (ii) the individual has ***knowledge*** of the group's illegal advocacy and the ***specific intent*** that the illegal aims be accomplished . . . . [963]

b. **Compulsory disclosure of membership:** Compulsory disclosure is permissible only where it ***directly*** serves a ***substantial*** government interest that ***outweighs*** the individual's need for privacy or anonymity . . . [966]

(1) **Privilege against self-incrimination:** Even though the government interest in disclosure prevails, if the membership admission is used to prosecute the registrant under criminal statutes, registration of membership may violate the individual's Fifth Amendment privilege against self-incrimination . . . . [968]

c. **Disclosures required in legislative investigations:** The legislative power to compel disclosure of one's political beliefs or associations is limited by the privilege against self-incrimination, due process ("pertinency" requirement), and the First Amendment. The last requires an ***overriding*** legislative interest, a ***nexus*** between the disclosure and the investigation, and current ***relevancy*** . . . . [969]

d. **Civil penalties for unprotected association (or advocacy):** Government may impose penalties such as denial of government benefits (*e.g.*, tax exemptions) on those who engage in illegal association (or speech) . . . . . . [975]

(1) **Burden of proof:** If the civil disability is imposed to ***penalize*** the actions rather than to serve an important government interest, the

government has the burden of showing the person engaged in unprotected association (or advocacy) . . . . [976]

(2) **Liability of organization:** Organizations may be liable for damages only if the acts of their representatives were performed within the scope of actual or apparent authority, or if specifically ratified . . . . [978]

e. **Restrictions on public employment, licensed professions, and other public benefits**

(1) **Standards of conduct and loyalty oaths:** The government ***may*** require employees to take an oath to support the Constitution and may summarily discharge those who refuse to comply. Compulsory disclosure of memberships, as an employment prerequisite, is ***limited*** to associations in which the government has a ***legitimate interest,*** and even then, an individual may be excluded from employment only if the ***knowledge and intent test*** (*supra*) has been met. Neither standards of conduct concerning past or future conduct nor loyalty oaths may be ***vague;*** precision is required be cause of the potential "chilling effect." Similar principles are applied to cases involving licensed professions and use of public facilities, etc. . . . . [980]

(a) **Patronage:** A public employee may ***not*** be hired, promoted, transferred, fired, or recalled because of political party affiliation unless that affiliation is necessary for the effective performance of the work . . . . [988]

(b) **Expression of views:** Public employment cannot be denied for speech on matters of public concern. However, in situations where the need for confidentiality is great or the speech impairs job performance, the Court will ***balance*** the public employee's First Amendment rights against the government's interest in efficient performance of public service . . . . [989]

(c) **Political activities:** Some limits are permissible on a public employee's right to engage in political activities (*e.g.*, the Hatch act). Such conditions of employment are allowed because of the overriding government interest in efficient, nonpartisan employees and to protect employees from being forced to work for the election of their superiors . . . . [991]

(2) **Disclosure:** Requirements of disclosure of ***certain*** past or present organizational affiliations that are relevant to loyalty, fitness, and suitability are permissible for public employees, lawyers, and recipients of other public benefits. The requirements must not be ***overbroad*** so as to have a "chilling effect" . . . . [995]

(a) **Privilege against self-incrimination:** An individual may not be denied public employment, bar membership, or other public benefits simply because she refuses to answer on a claim of the privilege . . . . [1001]

12. **Freedom of Press—Special Problems:** Generally, the press is afforded no greater First Amendment rights than a private citizen. There is ***no*** privilege to refuse to answer good faith grand jury questions and no guaranteed access to prisons, prisoners, or government information. However, the public ***and*** the press have a right to attend criminal (and probably civil) trials and elaborate preliminary hearings unless the judge finds that right outweighed by a compelling and narrowly tailored interest . . . . [1002]

a. **Broadcasting:** Radio and television broadcasting may be more closely regulated than the press because the number of broadcasting licenses is limited. Thus, the paramount right is the right of the ***viewers and listeners*** to receive information of public concern rather than a broadcaster's right to broadcast what she pleases . . . . [1011]

(1) **Note:** The FCC can order a right to reply, forbid common ownership, or censor indecent speech. However, broadcasters need ***not*** accept

political advertisements. Also, Congress may ***not*** ban editorials by noncommercial broadcasters or by broadcasters who receive government subsidies . . . . [1012]

b. **Taxation:** The press is subject to general taxes and regulations, but a tax that applies only to the press is invalid unless necessary to a compelling interest . . . . [1018]

c. **Cable television:** The relaxed standard of First Amendment scrutiny applicable to regulation of general broadcasting is not applicable to cable television because there is no practical limit on the number of cable channels, but neither does the strict scrutiny applicable to newspaper regulation apply because of the physical connection to viewer's televisions . . . . [1019]

G. FREEDOM OF RELIGION

1. **Constitutional Provisions:** "Congress shall make no law respecting an ***establishment*** of religion, or prohibiting the ***free exercise*** thereof" . . . . [1021]
2. **Application to States:** The First Amendment's protection of religion is applied to the states under the Fourteenth Amendment . . . . [1022]
3. **Scope of Establishment Clause:** The Establishment Clause insures government ***neutrality*** in religious matters. It bars government ***sponsorship*** of religion, government ***financial support*** of religion, active government ***involvement*** in religious activities, and ***official preference*** of one religious denomination over another . . . . [1023]

a. **Three-pronged test:** To be valid under the Establishment Clause, a statute (or other government action) must: . . . . [1026]

(1) Have a ***secular purpose;***

(2) Have a ***principal or primary effect*** that ***neither advances nor inhibits*** religion; and

(3) Not foster ***excessive government entanglement*** with religion.

b. **Aid to parochial school students:** Some government aid that provides assistance to ***all*** students (public and parochial) satisfies the test (*e.g.*, transportation, textbooks, health services, guidance counseling outside the parochial school). But tuition grants and tax credits have been held to violate the Establishment Clause . . . . [1027]

(1) **But note:** The Court has upheld a state income tax deduction to ***all*** taxpayers for school expenses since the purpose and primary effect is secular . . . . [1038]

c. **Direct aid to church-related institutions:** Aid has usually been held valid in cases involving hospitals, colleges, and counseling agencies where the aid was used only for ***secular*** purposes. However, most direct aid to elementary and secondary schools has been held invalid, usually on the basis of ***excessive government entanglement*** with religion . . . [1040]

d. **Tax exemption for religious property:** An exemption from property tax is valid on the basis that not to do so would ***increase*** church-state entanglement. However, a tax limited to ***only*** religious organizations is invalid . . . . [1051]

e. **Use of public facilities:** Using public facilities for religious worship and discussion is ***valid*** because there is a ***secular purpose*** in providing a public forum for the exchange of ideas, the benefit to religion would be ***incidental*** with no ***primary*** effect of advancing religion, and exclusion would create greater church-state ***entanglement*** . . . . [1053]

f. **Religion and public schools:** Prayers (including a time set aside for silent prayers), Bible reading, and anti-evolution laws have been held ***invalid*** in public schools. But the academic study of religion or the Bible and the recitation of religious references in historic documents are permissible since their purpose and effect are secular. Similarly, secondary schools that allow student groups to meet on school premises during noninstructional time may allow religious groups to do so, even for religious purposes .... [1054]

g. **Policies of public schools to "accommodate" religion:** Such policies (*e.g.,* released time off premises) are valid if they do not involve religious programs in the public schools and they ***further,*** rather than threaten, the free exercise of religion .... [1066]

h. **General government regulation benefiting religion:** Such regulations are valid if they have a secular purpose and effect (*e.g.,* religious oath for public office—invalid, Sunday closing laws—valid) .... [1070]

i. **Public acknowledgments of religion:** Traditionally, government has recognized our religious heritage and has permitted official expressions of religious beliefs. This does ***not*** violate the Establishment Clause unless, in reality, it establishes (or tends to establish) a religion (*e.g.*, prayers at opening sessions of public bodies, a Nativity scene in a city's annual Christmas display, national motto of "In God We Trust" are allowed, but prayers at public school graduations are not allowed) ...... [1075]

4. **Scope of Free Exercise Clause**

a. **Purpose:** If the purpose of a statute (or government action) is to treat adversely or discriminate against a specific religion, it violates the Free Exercise Clause unless it is narrowly tailored to advance a compelling interest .... [1080]

b. **"Beliefs" vs. "action" or "conduct":** The freedom to hold religious beliefs is absolute, but religious ***conduct*** is not absolutely protected. Under prior law, the Court would balance the severity of the burden on the conduct against the importance of the state interest and consider the availability of alternative means. Recently, the Court has held that there is ***no right*** to a religious exemption from a ***neutral*** law that happens to impose a substantial burden on religious practice .... [1083]

(1) **Application:** Thus, the Court has upheld laws prohibiting polygamy, requiring the closing of businesses on Sundays, limiting conscientious objectors to the draft, requiring military service or training for certain benefits, and taxing activities even though such laws burdened the exercise of religious practices .... [1089]

(2) **Decisions upholding "free exercise" claims:** In a few cases, the Court has required religious exemptions from neutral laws, including exemptions from: compelled secondary school attendance (for Amish); and accepting any suitable work under workers' compensation statutes (for Sabbatarians who refuse to accept jobs requiring work on the Sabbath) .... [1099]

c. **"Accommodations" that benefit only some religions:** Government action effecting de facto discrimination is ***not*** violative of either religion clause if there is a neutral, secular basis for the government delineations ...... [1106]

5. **What Are Protectible "Religious Beliefs"?** Courts may not delve into the ***truth*** of religious beliefs, but they may judge the ***sincerity*** of a believer. Religious beliefs need not be theistic for constitutional protection .... [1107]

6. **Judicial Resolution of Disputes Involving Church Doctrine:** Courts are prohibited (on entanglement grounds) from determining ***ecclesiastical*** questions. However, civil courts may use neutral principles of property law to resolve church property disputes .... [1111]

7. **Standing:** A person claiming a violation of the ***Free Exercise Clause*** must show ***direct personal injury*** and ***interference*** with her own religious beliefs. For an ***Establishment Clause*** claim, the only standing requirement is that the person be ***directly affected*** .... [1113]

H. OTHER LIMITATIONS ON GOVERNMENTAL POWER

Text Section

1. **Restrictions on Power of Eminent Domain:** The Fifth and Fourteenth Amendments permit no ***taking*** of private property (for public use) without just compensation . . . . [1115]
   a. **Substantive requirements**
      (1) **Public use:** If the "taking" is not for public use, the government may not appropriate the property—even if "just compensation" is paid . . . . [1119]
      (2) **"Taking" vs. "regulation":** A ***taking*** requires just compensation, while a ***regulation*** under the police power does not. In determining whether a taking occurs, the court asks whether ***justice and fairness require government compensation.*** A taking will almost always be found if there is an ***actual appropriation*** or a ***permanent physical invasion*** of private property . . . . [1121]
      (3) **"Just" compensation:** Usually this means the ***fair market value*** of the property taken . . . . [1130]
   b. **Procedural requirements:** Requirements of reasonable notice and opportunity to be heard must be met. However, due process does ***not*** require that the condemnation occur in advance of occupying the property . . . . [1132]
2. **Prohibition Against Involuntary Servitude:** The Thirteenth Amendment prohibits involuntary servitude anywhere in the United States. However, exceptional cases may justify enforcement of a personal obligation (*e.g.*, military conscription) . . . . [1133]
3. **Impairment of Contractual Obligations:** ***State*** legislatures (but not courts) are prohibited from impairing public or private contracts by the Contract Clause (Article I, Section 10); not all impairments are considered unconstitutional . . . . [1136]
   a. **Private contracts:** These can be ***modified*** if the legislation is a reasonable, narrowly tailored means of promoting an important public interest . [1141]
   b. **Public contracts:** Modifications of public contracts must satisfy the same requirements necessary for modification of private contracts. The courts give ***less deference*** to the legislative judgment of public contracts. Additionally, the state cannot bargain away any essential attributes of sovereignty (*e.g.*, police powers) . . . . [1146]
   c. **Federal government:** The Contract Clause does ***not apply*** to the federal government. Congress can adjust economic interests retroactively if there is a rational purpose . . . . [1150]
4. **Prohibition Against Ex Post Facto Laws:** This prohibition is based on Article I, Sections 9 and 10, and applies to both federal and state governments. A law is unconstitutional if it involves a ***retroactive alteration*** of the law in a ***substantially prejudicial*** manner which deprives a person of a right previously enjoyed, for the purpose of ***punishing*** that person for ***some past activity*** . . . . [1151]

I. SAFEGUARDS IN THE ADMINISTRATION OF CRIMINAL JUSTICE

1. **Right to Counsel:** This is guaranteed by the Sixth and Fourteenth Amendments in ***criminal prosecutions that result in imprisonment.*** Indigents have a right to appointed counsel . . . . [1154]
2. **Use of Involuntary Confessions:** The Fifth and Fourteenth Amendments prohibit the use of ***involuntary*** confessions. ***Voluntary*** confessions may also be inadmissible if an accused's *Miranda* rights were violated . . . . [1160]
3. **Privilege Against Self-Incrimination:** This right is guaranteed by the Fifth and Fourteenth Amendments. An accused cannot be compelled to give ***testimony*** that might subject him to a criminal prosecution . . . . [1165]
   a. **No comment on failure to testify:** Defendant's failure to take the witness stand in his own defense is assumed to be a claim of the privilege and ***no adverse inference*** of guilt may be drawn from such an action . [1168]

4. **Exclusion of Evidence Obtained by Illegal Searches and Seizures:** The exclusionary rule is based on the Fourth and Fourteenth Amendments. Illegally obtained evidence is ***inadmissible*** and encompasses all evidence (*e.g.*, physical evidence, wiretapping, evidence obtained through a privacy invasion, etc.). However, evidence obtained by an invalid search warrant is admissible if issued by a neutral magistrate and the officer had a reasonable, ***good faith*** belief that it was valid . . . . [1169]
5. **Cruel and Unusual Punishment:** This is prohibited by the Eighth and Fourteenth Amendments and imposes substantive limits on ***what can be made "criminal"*** (*e.g.*, drug addiction), limits the ***kinds of punishment*** (*i.e.*, barbaric), and proscribes punishments that are ***excessive or grossly disproportionate*** to the crime . . . . [1176]
   a. **Capital punishment:** The death penalty is ***not*** cruel and unusual punishment under all circumstances. If the sentencing body is allowed to consider ***aggravating and mitigating factors*** and if there is a ***review procedure,*** the death penalty is permissible . . . . [1187]
6. **Right to Trial by Jury**
   a. **Petit jury**
      (1) **Constitutional provision:** Under the Sixth Amendment (and by incorporation, the Due Process Clause of the Fourteenth Amendment), a defendant charged with any ***serious*** offense is entitled to a jury trial in both federal and state courts . . . . [1197]
      (2) **What constitutes "trial by jury":** Federal statute requires 12 jurors in federal criminal trials. The Constitution requires a ***sufficient number*** to provide adequate deliberation and a representative cross section of the community. Thus, some states have a minimum of six jurors. Unanimous verdicts are required in federal court, but generally not in state courts (unless it is a six-member jury) . . . . . . [1199]
      (3) **"Serious" vs. "petty" offenses:** Any offense that carries a potential sentence of ***more than six months*** is a serious offense, and a jury trial ***must*** be given on demand . . . . [1203]
   b. **Selection of jurors:** The Sixth Amendment guarantees the right to trial before an impartial jury drawn from a fair cross section of the community. Thus, systematic exclusions of an identifiable segment of the community violates this right. *But note:* Proportionate representation on the petit jury is not required . . . . [1205]
      (1) **Impartial jury:** Factors used to consider whether a jury was impartial include pretrial publicity, possible influence of prejudicial associations with jury during trial, and in death penalty cases, the composition of the jury. A defendant has standing to challenge a verdict based on unfair jury selection . . . . [1215]
7. **Right to Public Trial:** This right is guaranteed by the Sixth and Fourteenth Amendments. The press (or public) has no ***Sixth Amendment*** ground to complain of exclusion from pretrial hearings . . . . [1219]
8. **Right to a Fair Trial:** Certain types of conduct may be so unfair as to violate due process, and actual prejudice need ***not*** be shown. Inflammatory publicity may be unfair, although media coverage (including television) of the trial, when properly controlled, does not necessarily violate due process. A conviction must be reversed when it is found that a jury was not impartial . . . . [1223]
9. **Burden of Proof:** Due process requires proof ***beyond a reasonable doubt*** of every element of the crime with which the defendant is charged . . . . [1227]
10. **Requirement of Certainty in Criminal Statutes:** Vagueness in criminal statutes renders them invalid. This requirement ***prevents arbitrary and discriminatory enforcement*** . . . . [1231]
11. **Rights on Appeal:** A state is ***not required*** to provide appellate review, but if it does so, it cannot discriminate on the basis of poverty. An indigent has the ***right to counsel*** and the right to a ***free transcript*** to prepare his appeal . . . [1234]

Text Section

12. **Post-Conviction Procedures:** Federal procedures are mostly statutory. State convictions may be reviewed in state courts, and after exhaustion of state remedies, a petitioner with a claim of a constitutional or federal statute violation may appeal to the federal courts on a writ of habeas corpus ...... [1238]
13. **Retroactive Application of Determinations Regarding Constitutional Rights of Accused:** Whether a Court decision is to be applied retroactively depends on the ***purpose*** of the new standards, the ***extent of reliance*** on the old standards, and the ***effect*** of retroactivity on administration of justice .... [1241]
    a. **Rules applied retroactively:** The Court has given such effect only where the decision affects the ***very integrity of the fact-finding process*** (*e.g.*, right to counsel) .... [1243]
    b. **Cases on appeal:** Even if the new rule is not applied retroactively, it will still be applied to cases ***pending*** on direct appeal at the time of the decision (unless the rule is an unanticipated new principle of law) .... [1245]

TEXT CORRELATION CHART

Gilbert Law Summary **Constitutional Law**	Brest, Levinson **Processes of Constitutional Decisionmaking** 1992 (3rd ed.) 1993 Supp.	Cohen, Varat **Constitutional Law: Cases and Materials** 1993 (9th ed.)	Gunther **Cases and Materials on Constitutional Law** 1991 (12th ed.)	Lockhart, Kamisar, Choper, Shiffrin **Constitutional Law: Cases—Comments—Questions** 1991 (7th ed.)	Rotunda **Modern Constitutional Law** 1993 (4th ed.)	Stone, Seidman, Sunstein, Tushnet **Constitutional Law** 1991 (2nd ed.)
I. POWERS OF THE FEDERAL GOVERNMENT						
A. Judicial Power						
1. Source and Scope of Power	71-95	24-38	1-39, 51-66	1-26	1-25	21-78
2. Jurisdiction of the Supreme Court	1538-1550	38-50	39-51	50-56, 59-66	25-32	78-84, 125-127
3. Limitations on Jurisdiction of Federal Courts						
a. "Case or controversy"	1466-1468	90-94	1593-1598	1575-1630	1079-1088	84-86
b. Standing	1466-1468	94-134	1598-1639	1581-1616	1088-1126	87-106
c. Additional conditions for review of state court decisions	1474-1475	50-58	1639-1651	1630-1633	1115-1126	48-50
d. Other policies of "strict necessity"	1470-1472	58-77	1639-1651	56-59	32-39	87
e. Challenges to state action in federal courts	1472-1474	77-90	1639-1651	1633-1643	21-25	50-54
f. Political questions	1469-1470	134-153	1593-1598	26-50	39-56	106-123
4. Effect of Declaration of Unconstitutionality	1468-1469	36-38	28-29		1-8	21-29
B. Legislative Power						
1. Power of Congress—In General		212	66-93	66-76	138-339	127-140
2. The Commerce Power	379-386, 399-400	212-227	106-157	76-128	138-169	140-225
3. Taxing and Spending Powers	386-389, 397-399	227-233	176-201	128-143	169-184	230-248
4. War Power		233-244	202-204	203-206		225-226
5. Power Over External Affairs		233-244	204-210	143-148	216-253	227-230, 461-471
6. Power Over Naturalization and Citizenship	1355-1392	248	685-686		253-266	413-420
7. Property Power		244-246				
8. Investigatory Power			373-374			415-420, 1412-1417
9. Congressional Immunity		460-468	374-375	215-218	266-275	
C. Executive Power	216-229, 480-504, 513-516; Supp. 98-99		312-351	169-182, 210-215, 218-222	216-253, 275-294	367-413
D. Power Over Foreign Affairs		419-433	351-371	143-148	216-253	461-471

TEXT CORRELATION CHART—continued

Gilbert Law Summary Constitutional Law	Brest, Levinson **Processes of Constitutional Decisionmaking** 1992 (3rd ed.) 1993 Supp.	Cohen, Varat **Constitutional Law: Cases and Materials** 1993 (9th ed.)	Gunther **Cases and Materials on Constitutional Law** 1991 (12th ed.)	Lockhart, Kamisar, Choper, Shiffrin **Constitutional Law: Cases—Comments—Questions** 1991 (7th ed.)	Rotunda **Modern Constitutional Law** 1993 (4th ed.)	Stone, Seidman, Sunstein, Tushnet **Constitutional Law** 1991 (2nd ed.)
II. THE FEDERAL SYSTEM—INTERGOVERNMENTAL RELATIONS						
A. Nature and Scope of Federal and State Powers	400-406	251-383	66-93, 291-305	76-128, 222-294	193-216	265-276
B. Intergovernmental Privileges and Immunities	173-177, 422-424; Supp. 92-95	349-362	281-291, 307-308	280-287	114-122	301-310
C. Intergovernmental Immunity	406-422; Supp. 58-92	383-418	305-311	148-167	63-66	224-225, 310-315
III. REGULATION AND TAXATION OF COMMERCE						
A. Regulation of Foreign Commerce					136	
B. Regulation of Interstate Commerce						
1. Concurrent Power	424-433; Supp. 92-98	178-186	93-94	222-233		348-359
2. Scope of Federal Power	389-400	187-227	94-176	115-128	138-216	140-224
3. State Regulation of Interstate Commerce	433-474	251, 255-349	210-291	233-294	67-129	276-359
C. Power of States to Tax Interstate Commerce		252	306-307	307-316	129-137	312-315
D. Power of States to Tax Foreign Commerce			306-307	328-336	136	
IV. INDIVIDUAL RIGHTS: LIMITATIONS ON THE EXERCISE OF GOVERNMENTAL POWER						
A. Introduction	554-576		411-429	391		471, 759-768
B. Due Process						
1. Introduction	943-946, 1122	514	432-439	391-410	339	777-786
2. Fundamental Personal Rights	946-1053; Supp. 161-226	577-679	491-583	410-571	591-701	814-985
3. Substantive Due Process—Economic and Social Regulations	280-302	514-552	439-453, 476-491	336-361	339-359	786-814

TEXT CORRELATION CHART—continued

Gilbert Law Summary Constitutional Law	Brest, Levinson **Processes of Constitutional Decisionmaking** 1992 (3rd ed.) 1993 Supp.	Cohen, Varat **Constitutional Law: Cases and Materials** 1993 (9th ed.)	Gunther **Cases and Materials on Constitutional Law** 1991 (12th ed.)	Lockhart, Kamisar, Choper, Shiffrin **Constitutional Law: Cases—Comments—Questions** 1991 (7th ed.)	Rotunda **Modern Constitutional Law** 1993 (4th ed.)	Stone, Seidman, Sunstein, Tushnet **Constitutional Law** 1991 (2nd ed.)
4. Procedural Due Process	970-982, 1122-1188; Supp. 258-259	1070-1104	583-601	611-645	359-385	985-1011
C. Equal Protection						
1. Constitutional Provisions	546-550	679	601-608	1202		471
2. In General	546-550	679-686	601-608	1202-1220		471
3. Traditional Test—Economic and Social Regulations	554-581; Supp. 101-123	686-710	615-636	1202-1220	475-481	532-565
4. Suspect Classification—Strict Scrutiny						
a. Test	642-687; Supp. 152-159	710-711	608-615	1220-1226	481	565-566
b. What is "suspect" classification?						
(1) Racial (or ethnic) "classifications"	581-709; Supp. 125-159	711-722	636-646	1226-1258	481-544	565-566
(a) In general—strict scrutiny	474-480		636-646	1220-1226		565-617
(b) Racial segregation	581-604	722-770	646-656, 704-751	1226-1279	481-512	482-532
(c) "Benign" discrimination	709-805	829-906	757-819	1279-1329	512-544	617-676
(d) Repeal of remedies for discrimination or segregation	700-709		757-819	1323-1329		
(2) Discrimination against aliens		906-915	680-688	1329-1339	544-557	718-732
5. Quasi-Suspect Classifications—Intermediate Level of Scrutiny						
a. Test	574-581, 805-813; Supp. 101-123		658-659	1340-1341		676-692
b. Gender discrimination	813-877	770-801	656-680	1339-1362	563-582	692-718
c. Discrimination against illegitimate children		915-926	688-693	1421-1432	557-563	732-741
6. Classifications that Are Not Suspect or Quasi-Suspect						
a. Discrimination against the poor	813-877	938-939	702-704	1432-1439	582-591	741-752
b. Discrimination against the elderly	877, 1210-1301; Supp. 330-342	926, 1022-1049	701-702		582-591	753-759

TEXT CORRELATION CHART—continued

Gilbert Law Summary Constitutional Law	Brest, Levinson **Processes of Constitutional Decisionmaking** 1992 (3rd ed.) 1993 Supp.	Cohen, Varat **Constitutional Law: Cases and Materials** 1993 (9th ed.)	Gunther **Cases and Materials on Constitutional Law** 1991 (12th ed.)	Lockhart, Kamisar, Choper, Shiffrin **Constitutional Law: Cases—Comments—Questions** 1991 (7th ed.)	Rotunda **Modern Constitutional Law** 1993 (4th ed.)	Stone, Seidman, Sunstein, Tushnet **Constitutional Law** 1991 (2nd ed.)
c. Discrimination against non-residents		988-1022	861-871	1421-1432	616-626	752, 870-877
d. Discrimination against the mentally retarded	878-887	926-939	693-701	1367-1376	590	752-753
7. Fundamental Rights—Strict Scrutiny	946-958	939-1022	819-871	1376-1439	591-701	814-818
8. "Nonfundamental" Rights	1018-1033; Supp. 161-226	1022-1070	871-878	1439-1464	684-692	883-906, 968-974
9. "Irrebuttable Presumptions" and the Right to Hearing	1129	1093-1103	875-878	1464-1473		1007-1009
D. The "State Action" Requirement						
1. Introduction	1301-1304	1104	883-889	1473-1477	414-420	1593-1601
2. Acts of Government "Agents"	1326-1355; Supp. 343-351		912-926			1637-1645
3. "Public" or "Government" Functions	1304-1326	1110-1119	891-899	1477-1489	420-432	1645-1658
4. Significant State "Involvement"	1304-1326	1129-1150	899-912	1489-1514	432-468	1626-1637
E. Congressional Power to Enforce Constitutional Rights						
1. In General		1104	926-928, 952-954	1536-1539	701	248-265
2. Necessary and Proper Clause						54-68
3. Thirteenth Amendment		1155-1162	946-952	1567-1575	706-717	485-486, 1593-1596
4. Fourteenth Amendment		1162-1167	928-941, 952-994	1548-1554	701-706	54-68
5. Fifteenth Amendment		1167		1539-1541, 1558-1568	717-725	54-68
6. Other Sources of Power		1167-1190		120-126	184-193	54-68
F. Freedom of Speech, Press, and Association						
1. In General	889-896	1194-1202	994-1008	645	725	1011-1025
2. Advocacy of Unlawful Action		1202-1238	1026-1040, 1061-1069	645-692	725-737	1025-1077
3. Defamation		1256-1282	1075-1095	692-727	874-905	1145-1181
4. Obscenity		1282-1298	1095-1131, 1137-1167	727-756, 825-838	966-1005	1203-1232
5. "Fighting Words" and "Hostile Audiences"		1298-1231	1070-1075, 1261-1279	756-767	800-819	1082-1102
6. Commercial Speech		1331-1352	1167-1190	838-863	855-874	1182-1203
7. Censorship and Prior Restraint	920-935	1238-1256	1008-1217	869-895	737-751	1257-1265

TEXT CORRELATION CHART—continued

Gilbert Law Summary Constitutional Law	Brest, Levinson **Processes of Constitutional Decisionmaking** 1992 (3rd ed.) 1993 Supp.	Cohen, Varat **Constitutional Law: Cases and Materials** 1993 (9th ed.)	Gunther **Cases and Materials on Constitutional Law** 1991 (12th ed.)	Lockhart, Kamisar, Choper, Shiffrin **Constitutional Law: Cases—Comments—Questions** 1991 (7th ed.)	Rotunda **Modern Constitutional Law** 1993 (4th ed.)	Stone, Seidman, Sunstein, Tushnet **Constitutional Law** 1991 (2nd ed.)
8. Symbolic Conduct	896-920	1429-1448	1217-1249		931-949	1289-1308
9. First Amendment Rights in Public Places		1352-1429	1190-1357	911-935	751-800	1265-1289
10. First Amendment Freedoms and Special Governmental Interests	1177-1186	1478-1537	1410-1455	1029-1048		1337-1397
11. Freedom of Association—Special Rules	1159-1167	1448-1478	1399-1410	998-1029	905-922	1403-1418
12. Freedom of Press—Special Problems		1537-1590	1455-1501	962-998	922-931	1418-1455
G. Freedom of Religion	1417-1426; Supp. 353-358	1590-1693	1501-1590	1091-1202	819-855	1455-1547
H. Other Limitations on Governmental Power		552-679	465-491	361-391	1005-1079	1547-1593
I. Safeguards in the Administration of Criminal Justice		490-514		571-611	391-414	

approach to exams

Constitutional law problems almost always involve action by an arm of federal or state government (*e.g.*, a statute, an executive order, an administrative or judicial decision, a legislative or administrative investigation, conduct of government officers) that affects an individual or group of persons (including artificial persons such as corporations). But the range of constitutional issues that may arise concerning action by the federal government is greater than those that may arise from action by state (or local) governments.

As an initial matter, any exercise of power by any branch of the federal government must find its source in the Constitution. In addition, action by the federal government sometimes may abridge constitutional limitations that protect individual rights.

State governments, on the other hand, possess inherent, sovereign powers which have their source outside the Constitution. Furthermore, although state constitutions and statutes may designate the powers of the different branches and levels of state government, the Constitution does not ordinarily require any particular separation of powers within the states. [Sweezy v. New Hampshire, 354 U.S. 234 (1957)] Thus, the only federal constitutional issues that arise from the actions of state (or local) governments are whether those actions conflict with constitutional limitations on state power.

A. ACTION BY THE FEDERAL GOVERNMENT

For exam questions concerning action by the federal government, first determine what type of action is involved (*e.g.*, statute, executive order, etc.), and then use the specific analytical approach below.

1. **Congressional Statutes:** If a federal statute is under consideration, two general issues may arise:

   (i) ***Whether Congress has the delegated power*** to enact such a statute (*e.g.*, under the commerce, taxing, or spending power), since Congress generally may legislate only by virtue of its powers enumerated in the Constitution; and

   (ii) ***Whether the statute***, either on its ***face or as applied*** in the particular case, ***violates a limitation of the Constitution*** that protects individual rights (*e.g.*, a provision in the Bill of Rights).

   Furthermore, your question may require you to determine whether a federal statute ***preempts*** certain state action (by virtue of the Supremacy Clause). Finally, remember that the federal statute may be ***interpreted so as to avoid a constitutional question***—thus requiring discussion of constitutional problems to demonstrate how they may be avoided.

2. **Executive Orders:** Executive orders usually present the same general problems as congressional statutes:

   (i) ***Whether the executive*** (usually the President) has been ***specifically delegated*** such power by the Constitution or whether the executive has ***"inherent" constitutional power*** to undertake such action; and

   (ii) ***Whether the order violated a constitutional limitation*** that protects individual rights.

Similar issues of ***preemption*** or ***interpretation*** may also arise. Also, watch for the presence of a federal statute that is relevant to an executive order. This may present an issue of whether (or to what extent) Congress may or has ***delegated or limited*** executive authority in this area.

3. **Administrative Actions:** Two general issues may arise concerning administrative actions:

   (i) ***Whether Congress has granted the general power*** exercised by the administrative agency (not itself a constitutional matter, but possibly requiring a discussion of constitutional problems in the context of avoiding constitutional questions); and

   (ii) ***Whether the action—on its face***, or more frequently, ***as applied*** in the particular instance—***violates a constitutional limitation*** that protects individual rights.

   Besides these main issues, you may need to consider the ***scope of congressional delegation*** to the administrative agency (a constitutional issue), and ***preemption*** of state action by the administrative action or interpretation thereof, depending on your question.

4. **Legislative and Administrative Investigations:** The usual issues that arise concerning legislative or administrative investigations are:

   (i) ***What specific authority***, both substantive and procedural, has been ***granted by Congress*** to the investigative body (again, not itself a constitutional matter, but possibly requiring a discussion of constitutional problems in the context of interpreting the authorization to avoid a constitutional question); and

   (ii) ***Whether the specific action*** taken against the person investigated ***violates any constitutional limitation*** that protects individual rights (*e.g.*, privilege against self-incrimination, freedom of expression or association).

   Other possible issues may concern problems of ***delegation***, and there may be a question of whether the investigation authorized is in pursuit of a ***valid legislative purpose***—*i.e.*, whether Congress's authorization is within the scope of its constitutionally delegated powers.

5. **Conduct of Government Officers:** Exam questions concerning conduct of government officers involve action taken by law enforcement officers (*e.g.*, searches and seizures), prosecutors (*e.g.*, obtaining confessions), judges (*e.g.*, appointment of counsel), and executive officials (*e.g.*, condemnation of property). The usual issue is whether the action taken against a person ***violates any constitutional limitation*** that protects individual rights.

B. ACTION BY STATE (OR LOCAL) GOVERNMENT

For exam questions raising issues of state action, use the following approaches:

1. **Statutes (or Ordinances):** As indicated above, the only federal constitutional issues that arise regarding a state statute or municipal ordinance are whether the statute or ordinance, on its face or as applied in the particular case:

(i) ***Violates a constitutional limitation*** that protects individual rights against state action (*e.g.,* bill of attainder, due process, equal protection, right of privacy);

(ii) ***Is contrary to an implied constitutional limitation*** on state power (*e.g.,* the grant of the "commerce power" to the federal government operates as an implied limitation on state regulation of interstate commerce); or

(iii) ***Has been preempted*** by federal treaty, statute, or an administrative rule.

Note: The interpretation of state statutes and municipal ordinances is a matter of state law for state courts and generally presents no federal constitutional issues.

2. **State Executive, Judicial, or Administrative Orders or Rules:** The issues here are generally the same as for state statutes (above).

3. **Conduct of Government Officers:** The issues here are generally the same as for conduct of federal officers (*supra*).

C. JURISDICTION OF FEDERAL COURTS AND REQUIREMENTS FOR SUPREME COURT REVIEW

For questions that ask for a federal court decision or for review by the Supreme Court, consider:

1. **The Constitution and Acts of Congress:** Remember that the Constitution and federal statutes (i) designate the ***jurisdiction*** of the federal courts (*e.g.,* federal courts may only decide "cases or controversies"); and (ii) specify ***procedural requirements*** that must be met to obtain Supreme Court review (*e.g.,* a decision from a state court is reviewable only by certiorari).

2. **Judicial Self-Restraint:** And even though a case may clearly fall within the constitutional and statutory jurisdiction of the federal courts, the Supreme Court has adopted certain "prudential" principles of "judicial self-restraint" to ***limit the occasions on which it will decide constitutional questions*** (*e.g.,* the Court will ordinarily not decide a constitutional issue before the time that it is necessary to do so, or when the record presents some other ground upon which the case may be decided).

I. POWERS OF THE FEDERAL GOVERNMENT

chapter approach

This chapter examines the sources and scope of federal judicial, legislative, and executive power. Under our system of federalism, the general power to govern is reserved to the individual states, and the federal government is granted only certain enumerated powers. Thus, whenever an exam question deals with any act by the federal government, you must first determine whether the federal government has been granted the power to so act. To make this determination, look first to the Constitution. However, keep in mind that certain indisputably federal powers are not explicitly granted therein. Moreover, judicial interpretation has often expanded federal power well beyond what is obvious from the explicit language of the Constitution.

1. **Judicial Power:** The federal courts generally have power to hear most cases where federal law is in issue, where the United States is a party, or where the suit is between a state and a citizen of another state or between citizens of different states. But there are a number of limitations that you must remember for exam purposes: (i) The doctrine of ***sovereign immunity*** prevents suits against the United States and its officers without its consent. (ii) The ***Eleventh Amendment*** provides some limitation on suits against states in federal courts, although states can be sued on causes of action passed by Congress pursuant to delegated powers, and state officials can be sued for violating complainants' constitutional rights. (iii) The federal courts can hear only ***cases or controversies***, meaning that there must be a genuine, present dispute. (iv) The harm complained of must be ***real*** (although not necessarily economic) and the litigants must have a ***personal stake*** in the outcome. (v) The injury must be ***remediable*** by the judicial relief sought. (vi) The Supreme Court will not review a state court decision unless ***all state procedures have been exhausted***, judgment is ***final***, and a ***federal issue is conclusive***. (vii) The Court will also refrain from deciding ***political questions***.

2. **Legislative Power:** The Constitution grants Congress the power to legislate in many specific areas. Recall that Congress also has power to enact any law that is ***necessary and proper*** to effectuate any specifically enumerated power of any branch of the federal government. ("Necessary" includes any ***appropriate*** means.) In addition to its enumerated powers, Congress has the ***inherent power*** to regulate external or foreign affairs.

   Regarding Congress's specifically enumerated powers, the most important for exam purposes is the commerce power, discussed in Chapter III. Some important things to know about other enumerated powers are: Congress's specifically enumerated power to tax allows it to regulate through taxation where it otherwise lacks power to regulate, provided that the tax has a revenue raising purpose. Similar results are possible under Congress's spending power. The war power gives Congress broad authority to declare war and to enact necessary legislation in times of war. Congress also has plenary power over naturalization and citizenship.

3. **Executive Power:** The executive power is vested in the President. Some key things to remember concerning executive power are: The President has ***broad appointment powers*** for federal judges, ambassadors, and federal officers, with the advice and consent of the Senate. However, Congress may vest the power to appoint inferior officers in the heads of departments or the courts instead of the President. The President's ***veto power***

allows him to veto acts of the legislature, which then must be repassed by a two-thirds vote of each House to be effective. Although the President ***cannot declare war***, he does have power to commit armed forces in the event of insurrection or invasion without waiting for Congress to declare war. The President also has an extensive ***privilege against disclosure*** of presidential communications.

4. **Power Over Foreign Affairs:** Unlike the power over domestic affairs, the power over foreign affairs is ***exclusively vested in the federal government***. Congress has the power to regulate foreign commerce. The President has the power to make treaties with foreign nations with the consent of two-thirds of the Senate, and such treaties are the supreme law of the land—of equal weight with acts of Congress. The President also has power to enter into agreements or compacts with other countries without the consent of the Senate, but the scope of this power is uncertain.

A. JUDICIAL POWER

1. Source and Scope of Power

a. **Source of federal judicial power:** [§1] Article III, Section 1 of the United States Constitution provides that the federal judicial power "shall be vested in one Supreme Court, and in such inferior Courts as the Congress may from time to time ordain and establish."

(1) **Lower courts:** [§2] Congress need not establish ***any*** lower federal courts (*e.g.*, district courts, circuit courts of appeal), nor grant them full jurisdiction to decide all matters within the federal judicial power. [Sheldon v. Sill, 49 U.S. 441 (1850)]

(a) **Limitation:** However, congressional power over lower federal courts may be limited by other constitutional provisions (*e.g.*, a federal statute withholding jurisdiction of lower federal courts to decide cases in which one party is a Methodist would probably violate the First Amendment).

b. **Scope of federal judicial power:** [§3] Article III, Section 2 limits the jurisdiction of federal courts to ***cases*** (among others):

(1) ***Whose disposition depends upon construction of the Constitution, an act of Congress, or a federal treaty*** (*i.e.*, cases "arising under" one of these);

(2) ***In which the United States is a party***;

(3) ***Between a state and citizens of another state***; and

(4) ***Between citizens of different states ("diversity" cases)***.

c. **Limitations on scope of federal judicial power**

(1) **Sovereign immunity doctrine:** [§4] Although the Constitution gives federal courts the power to hear suits in which the United States is a party,

the United States may not be sued without its consent—which is generally afforded by a federal statute. [United States v. McLemore, 45 U.S. 286 (1846)]

(a) **Suits against federal officers acting in their official capacity:** [§5] Suits against federal officers acting in their official capacity are deemed actions against the United States itself if the relief sought would expend the public treasury, interfere with public administration, or restrain the government from acting or compel it to act, and thus may be subject to sovereign immunity. [Larson v. Domestic & Foreign Commerce Corp., 337 U.S. 682 (1949)]

1) **Exception:** Suits against federal officers are ***not*** subject to sovereign immunity if the officer's action was plainly beyond the officer's delegated statutory powers, ***or*** if the powers themselves (or the manner in which they are exercised) are constitutionally void. [Malone v. Bowdoin, 369 U.S. 643 (1962)]

(2) **Eleventh Amendment:** [§6] The Eleventh Amendment provides that a citizen of one state may not sue another state in federal court without the state's consent. It has also been interpreted to prevent federal court suits by citizens of the state being sued. [Hans v. Louisiana, 134 U.S. 1 (1890)]

(a) **Suits against state officials:** [§7] If the Eleventh Amendment would bar the suit if brought against the state, it also usually bars private suits against state officials that require a federal court to award money damages for ***past conduct*** which must be paid from the state treasury. [Edelman v. Jordan, 415 U.S. 651 (1974)—suit against state official for retroactive payment of wrongfully withheld welfare benefits]

(b) **Limitations on scope of Eleventh Amendment**

1) **Suits by federal government:** [§8] The Eleventh Amendment does ***not*** bar federal court suits by the federal government against the states. [United States v. Texas, 143 U.S. 621 (1892)]

2) **Supreme Court review:** [§9] The Eleventh Amendment also does not block appellate review in the Supreme Court of a civil or criminal action from a state court that would (because a state is a party) have been barred if it had been brought originally in a federal court. [McKesson Corp. v. Florida Division of Alcoholic Beverages & Tobacco, 496 U.S. 18 (1990)]

3) **State subdivisions:** [§10] The Eleventh Amendment also does not prevent suits against state subdivisions (*e.g.*, counties, municipalities) or state governmental corporations. [Lincoln County v. Luning, 133 U.S. 529 (1890)]

4) **Suits against state officials:** [§11] Subject to the situation described *supra*, §7, the Eleventh Amendment does not bar

suits against state officials acting pursuant to state law but allegedly in violation of the complainant's ***constitutional rights***.

a) **Rationale:** A suit against a state official for ***injunctive relief*** or damages to be paid ***by the official*** is not one against the state. The official is allegedly enforcing an unconstitutional enactment (which is void) and is therefore held to be "stripped of his official or representative character." [*Ex parte* Young, 209 U.S. 123 (1908); Scheuer v. Rhodes, 416 U.S. 232 (1974)]

1/ **Compare—violations of state law:** The Eleventh Amendment does, however, bar federal court suits against state officials for alleged violations of ***state*** law. Unlike claimed violations of plaintiff's constitutional rights, the federal court suit in this instance is not needed to "vindicate the supreme authority of federal law." [Pennhurst State School & Hospital v. Halderman, 465 U.S. 89 (1984)]

b) **Retroactive vs. prospective relief from state funds:** [§12] Nor does the Eleventh Amendment forbid suits against state officials that have a financial impact on the state treasury by requiring ***prospective*** payment of state funds. Unlike retroactive payments from the state treasury, such prospective relief will not affect already defined allocations of state funds. [Edelman v. Jordan, *supra*, §7]

c) **Attorneys' fees:** [§13] Nor does the Eleventh Amendment forbid an award of attorneys' fees against a state official, to be paid from state funds, as a penalty for bad faith violation of a prospective injunction. [Hutto v. Finney, 437 U.S. 678 (1978)]

5) **Congressionally created causes of action:** [§14] The broadest exception to state immunity from private suits in federal court concerns statutory causes of action passed by Congress pursuant to its power under either the Commerce Clause [Pennsylvania v. Union Gas Co., 491 U.S. 1 (1989)] or Section 5 of the Fourteenth Amendment (authorizing Congress to enforce the amendment) [Fitzpatrick v. Bitzer, 427 U.S. 445 (1976)]. *Rationale:* In approving them, the states consented to suits based on these powers.

6) **Courts of other states:** [§15] Neither the Eleventh Amendment nor any other provision of the Constitution affords a state immunity from being sued in the courts of another state. [Nevada v. Hall, 440 U.S. 410 (1979)]

2. **Jurisdiction of the Supreme Court**

a. **Original (trial) jurisdiction:** [§16] Under Article III, Section 2, the Supreme Court has original jurisdiction "in all Cases affecting Ambassadors, other public Ministers and Consuls and those in which a State shall be a Party."

(1) **Provision is self-executing:** [§17] Congress may neither restrict nor enlarge the Supreme Court's original jurisdiction. [Marbury v. Madison, 5 U.S. 137 (1803)]

(2) **Concurrent jurisdiction:** [§18] But Congress may give concurrent jurisdiction to lower federal courts.

(3) **"Controversies between two or more States":** [§19] At present, the Supreme Court's original jurisdiction is mainly occupied by "controversies between two or more States." [28 U.S.C. §1251]

b. **Appellate jurisdiction:** [§20] Article III, Section 2 further provides that "in all other Cases before mentioned [*see supra*, §3], the Supreme Court shall have appellate Jurisdiction, both as to Law and Fact, with such Exceptions, and under such Regulations as the Congress shall make."

(1) **Power of judicial review:** [§21] Although the Constitution does not expressly so provide, the Court early held that it has the power to hold acts of other ***branches of the federal government*** (Congress and Executive) unconstitutional [Marbury v. Madison, *supra*]; to hold ***state statutes*** unconstitutional [Fletcher v. Peck, 10 U.S. 87 (1810)]; and to review the ***judgments of state courts*** in cases that fall within the federal "judicial power" (*see supra,* §9) [Martin v. Hunter's Lessee, 14 U.S. 304 (1816)].

(2) **Statutory regulation of appellate jurisdiction:** [§22] Congress has provided two methods for invoking Supreme Court appellate jurisdiction: (i) ***appeal*** (where jurisdiction is mandatory) and (ii) ***certiorari*** (where it is within the Court's discretion). However, mandatory appeal is very limited, and so the Court's appellate jurisdiction is almost entirely by certiorari.

(a) **Review of state court judgments:** [§23] A party may file a ***petition for certiorari*** for review of final judgments or decrees rendered by the highest court of a state in which a decision could be had where:

(i) The ***constitutionality of a United States statute or treaty*** is in question: or

(ii) A ***state statute*** is drawn into question on the ground that it is ***repugnant to the Constitution, treaties, or other federal law***.

(b) **Review of federal court judgments:** [§24] A party may file a ***petition for certiorari*** from a federal court of appeals in ***any*** civil or criminal case, whether or not constitutional issues are involved. [28 U.S.C. §1254] Mandatory appellate jurisdiction (by ***appeal***) is available only as to decisions of three-judge federal district court panels that grant or deny injunctive relief. [28 U.S.C. §1253]

(3) **Denials of certiorari:** [§25] Certiorari will be granted "only when there are special and important reasons"—*e.g.*, conflict of decisions in lower courts, important federal question not yet decided by the Supreme Court. [U.S. Sup. Ct. R. 17] Denial of certiorari carries no implication of the Court's view on the merits of the case. It simply means that fewer than four members of the Court believed it desirable to review the decision in question. [Maryland v. Baltimore Radio Show, Inc., 338 U.S. 912 (1950)]

(4) **Limitations on statutory regulation:** [§26] *Ex parte McCardle*, 74 U.S. 506 (1868), has been read as giving Congress full power—under the "exceptions and regulations" language of Article III (*supra,* §20)—to limit the Supreme Court's appellate jurisdiction. ***Possible*** limitations on such congressional power have been suggested:

(a) ***Congress may eliminate certain avenues*** for Supreme Court review, ***but not all*** avenues—since this would destroy the Court's essential role in the constitutional plan.

(b) ***Although Congress may eliminate Supreme Court review of certain cases*** within the federal judicial power, it must permit jurisdiction to remain in ***some lower federal court***.

(c) ***If Congress were to deny all Supreme Court review of an alleged violation*** of constitutional rights—or go even further and deny a hearing before any federal judge on such a claim—this would ***violate due process*** of law.

3. **Limitations on Jurisdiction of Federal Courts**

a. **"Case or controversy":** [§27] Article III, Section 2 limits the jurisdiction of federal courts to "cases" and "controversies." The terms are interchangeable and refer to a matter "appropriate for judicial determination," as distinguished from disputes that are hypothetical, academic, or moot. The matter must be "***definite and concrete***, touching the legal relations of parties having ***adverse legal interests***. It must be a ***real and substantial controversy*** admitting of specific relief through a decree of a conclusive character." [Aetna Life Insurance Co. v. Haworth, 300 U.S. 227 (1937)]

(1) **Advisory opinions:** [§28] Thus, the Court will not render an advisory opinion to Congress or the President on the constitutionality of some contemplated action or legislation.

(a) **Review of advisory opinions also foreclosed:** [§29] Some state courts may be allowed to give advisory opinions. The Supreme Court will refuse to review such opinions, even if they decide constitutional issues, because they do not constitute cases or controversies.

(b) **Compare—declaratory judgments:** [§30] A federal court may issue a final judgment declaring the rights and liabilities of parties even though no affirmative relief is sought.

1) **Genuine controversy required:** [§31] However, there must be an actual controversy. There is a "case or controversy" when there is an ***actual dispute***—a definite threat of interference with defined rights—between parties having ***adverse legal interests***. [United Public Workers v. Mitchell, 330 U.S. 75 (1947)]

2) **"Ripeness":** [§32] Both under the "case or controversy" requirement and pursuant to "prudential principles of ***judicial self-restraint***," the Court will ordinarily not decide constitutional questions before it is necessary to do so. [Rescue Army v. Municipal Court, 331 U.S. 549 (1947)]

3) **Real threat of harm required:** [§33] Complainants must demonstrate that they have engaged (or wish to engage) in specific (not hypothetical) conduct ***and*** that the challenged action poses a ***real and immediate danger*** to their interests. [Boyle v. Landry, 401 U.S. 77 (1971)]

   a) **Example—no enforcement by state:** [§34] The Court will not determine the constitutionality of a statute when it has never been enforced and there is no real fear that it ever will be—even though the state prosecutor says that it will be enforced. [Poe v. Ullman, 367 U.S. 497 (1961)—anticontraceptive law not enforced for 80 years despite "ubiquitous, open, public sales"]

   b) **Example—no specific conduct by complainants:** [§35] Nor will the Court afford equitable relief in respect to the constitutionality of bail and sentencing practices when complainants fail to show that they are in imminent danger of being prosecuted (or even that they expect to violate any laws) and thus will become subject to the allegedly invalid practices. [O'Shea v. Littleton, 414 U.S. 488 (1974)]

      1/ **Compare—suit for damages:** This is true even if complainants have suffered injury from such practices in the past, and thus, have standing to sue for damages. [City of Los Angeles v. Lyons, 461 U.S. 95 (1983)]

   c) **Example—no claim of harm:** [§36] The Court found no "justiciable controversy" in an action alleging that the complainants' First Amendment rights were being "chilled" by the mere existence of military data-gathering activities—at least where there was no claim of a specific present harm or threat of specific future harm, but only the fear that the military "might" take some additional action "detrimental" to complainants. [Laird v. Tatum, 408 U.S. 1 (1972)]

(2) **Moot cases:** [§37] The Court will not review moot cases. Since the matter has been resolved, there is no "case or controversy." [Liner v. Jafco, Inc., 375 U.S. 301 (1964)]

(a) **Collateral legal consequences:** [§38] Even if a jail sentence has been fully served, a criminal conviction is not moot for purposes of Supreme Court review (or postconviction attack such as habeas corpus) unless there is no possibility that any collateral legal consequences (*e.g.*, loss of civil rights, impeachment as a witness) will be imposed because of the challenged conviction. [Sibron v. New York, 392 U.S. 40 (1968)]

(b) **Recurring issue:** [§39] An attack on a periodic event (*e.g.*, alleged denial of right to vote) is not moot even though the event occurs before the case is decided (election already held). The claim is "capable of repetition, yet evading review" since it will apply equally to the next election, and the judicial machinery may again be too slow for determination before the election. [Moore v. Ogilvie, 394 U.S. 814 (1969)]

(c) **Voluntary cessation:** [§40] If defendant voluntarily stops allegedly unlawful practices when a suit is threatened or filed, the case need not be held moot because "otherwise, the defendant is free to return to his old ways." [United States v. W. T. Grant Co., 345 U.S. 629 (1953)]

(d) **Class actions:** [§41] The class representative may continue to pursue a class action even though the representative's controversy has become moot, as long as the claims of others in the class are still viable. [United States Parole Commission v. Geraghty, 445 U.S. 388 (1980)]

(3) **Collusive or friendly suits:** [§42] The Court will not hear a claim where there is no antagonistic assertion of conflicting claims. Generally, in collusive suits, one side finances and controls the whole litigation; there is no real "case or controversy," and the Court will not decide such a case—particularly on a constitutional issue. [Chicago & Grand Trunk Railway v. Wellman, 143 U.S. 339 (1892)]

(a) **Compare—"test" cases:** Collusive suits may be distinguished from "test" cases, which are true controversies but planned by the parties in order to expedite a decision on certain issues.

b. **Standing:** [§43] The doctrine of standing concerns both the "case or controversy" requirement of Article III and "prudential principles of judicial self-restraint." The second, which is a judicially self-imposed "policy limitation," is "not always clearly distinguished from the constitutional limitation." [Flast v. Cohen, 392 U.S. 83 (1968)]

(1) **Direct and immediate injury:** [§44] Article III requires that a person asserting the violation of a constitutional (or statutory) right show ***a direct and immediate personal injury*** due to the challenged action. Otherwise, he

has no standing, and the Court will not decide the issue. [Sierra Club v. Morton, 405 U.S. 727 (1972)]

(a) **Rationale:** The person must allege "such a personal stake in the outcome of the controversy as to assure that concrete adverseness which sharpens the presentation of issues." [Baker v. Carr, 369 U.S. 186 (1962)]

(b) **Example:** A statute making it a crime to be a member of the Communist Party may be attacked by a Communist Party member as denying freedom of association, since a member suffers direct and immediate personal injury due to the statute. In contrast, a non-Party member would have no standing to attack the statute on these grounds.

(c) **Nature of injury:** [§45] Neither criminal sanctions nor economic harm is necessary—the injury "may reflect aesthetic, conservational, and recreational as well as economic values." [Association of Data Processing Service Organizations, Inc. v. Camp, 397 U.S. 150 (1970)] And the fact that the injury is widely shared and relatively insubstantial to any particular litigant will not defeat a showing of "injury in fact." [United States v. SCRAP, 412 U.S. 669 (1973)]

(2) **Causation:** [§46] Besides requiring an assertion of injury, Article III requires that a person asserting the violation of a constitutional (or statutory) right show that the injury suffered (i) "can fairly be ***traced to the challenged action***" and (ii) will be ***redressed by the judicial relief*** sought. [Simon v. Eastern Kentucky Welfare Rights Organization, 426 U.S. 26 (1976)—denial of hospital services to plaintiffs not traceable to allegedly invalid I.R.S. rule that allegedly "encouraged" such denial; Allen v. Wright, 468 U.S. 737 (1984)—racially segregated public schools not traceable to alleged I.R.S. laxity in denying tax exemptions to racially discriminatory private schools]

(a) **Example:** One who seeks to challenge exclusionary zoning practices must show more than that the challenged zoning makes housing too expensive for him to buy. He must allege specific facts showing that, absent the zoning, there is a "substantial probability" that he would be able to buy—*i.e.*, that he would benefit in a tangible way from judicial intervention. [Warth v. Seldin, 422 U.S. 490 (1975)]

(3) **Congressional conferral of standing:** [§47] A federal statute may create new interests, injury to which may be sufficient for standing. But Congress may not go beyond Article III's requirement of "injury in fact." [Trafficante v. Metropolitan Life Insurance Co., 409 U.S. 205 (1972)—federal statute may give standing to tenants of an apartment complex who allege loss of important benefits from lack of interracial association by claiming rental discrimination by the owner in violation of the Civil Rights Act; *but see* Sierra Club v. Morton, *supra*—club had no standing to challenge construction of recreation area in a national forest as violating a federal statute since club failed to allege that it or its members used the site or would be significantly affected by the proposed construction]

(4) **Citizens' standing:** [§48] Persons have ***no standing*** as citizens to claim that federal statutes violate the Constitution. Any interest in constitutional governance is only a "generalized interest of all citizens," resulting in an "abstract injury," which is no substitute for the actual injury needed to focus litigation efforts and judicial decision-making. The fact that ***no one*** may have sufficient injury to establish standing is not a reason to find standing when no injury exists. [Schlesinger v. Reservists Committee, 418 U.S. 208 (1974)—citizens have no standing to contend that a senator's or representative's membership in Armed Forces Reserve violates art. I, §6, cl. 2 forbidding the same from "holding any office under the United States"]

(a) **Application—federal statutes:** The limitation prevents Congress from creating an individual right in "any citizen" (even though such person has not suffered any distinctive concrete injury) to bring suit to enforce government observance of the Constitution or federal laws. [Lujan v. Defenders of Wildlife, 112 S. Ct. 2130 (1992)—no "citizen" standing to challenge regulation under the Endangered Species Act, despite statutory language allowing "any person [to] commence a civil suit on his own behalf (A) to enjoin any person . . . who is alleged to be in violation of" the Act]

(5) **Taxpayers' standing**

(a) **Municipal taxpayers:** [§49] Taxpayers have standing to challenge municipal actions involving ***measurable expenditures*** (*e.g.*, expenditure for busing children to parochial schools). [Everson v. Board of Education, 330 U.S. 1 (1947)]

1) **Compare:** A taxpayer has ***no*** standing as such to challenge Bible reading in public schools since there is no measurable expenditure and hence no "good-faith pocketbook action." [Doremus v. Board of Education, 342 U.S. 429 (1952)]

(b) **Federal taxpayers:** [§50] Taxpayers generally have ***no standing*** to attack allegedly unconstitutional federal expenditures; the theory is that their interest in such expenditures is too remote, indeterminate, and minute, and that any injury is suffered in common with people generally. [Frothingham v. Mellon, 262 U.S. 447 (1923)] However, this is merely self-imposed judicial restraint, to which there are ***exceptions***.

1) **Personal liability exception:** [§51] A taxpayer may attack the validity of a federal tax ***assessed against her***. If the taxpayer prevails, she will have reduced her tax liability—and her interest is therefore substantial, definite, and personal. [United States v. Butler, 297 U.S. 1 (1936)]

2) **Unconstitutional spending program exception:** [§52] Likewise, a taxpayer may challenge a federal expenditure if (i) she alleges that it "***exceeds a specific constitutional limitation*** on the taxing and spending power," and (ii) it is part of a ***federal***

spending program (as opposed to an incidental expenditure under a regulatory statute).

a) **Example—Establishment Clause:** The Establishment Clause of the First Amendment—designed to bar taxation and spending for support of religion—is such a "specific constitutional limitation." Thus, a federal taxpayer has standing to challenge federal ***expenditures*** to aid parochial schools on the ground that they violate the Establishment Clause. [Flast v. Cohen, *supra*, §43]

1/ **Inapplicable to Property Clause:** In *Valley Forge Christian College v. Americans United*, 454 U.S. 464 (1982), a federal taxpayer was ***denied*** standing to challenge a gift of federal surplus property to a church college as violating the Establishment Clause. *Rationale:* The challenge was not to a federal expenditure under Congress's taxing and spending power, but to an exercise of Congress's power under Article IV, Section 3, Clause 2, to "dispose of . . . property belonging to the United States."

b) **Note:** The taxpayer must allege that the expenditure exceeds a specific constitutional provision. In *Frothingham, supra,* the taxpayer did not argue that the federal expenditure (for maternity care programs) exceeded "specific constitutional limitations," but only that it was "generally beyond the powers delegated to Congress" and was reserved to the states by the Tenth Amendment.

c) **And note:** In *United States v. Richardson*, 418 U.S. 166 (1974), a federal taxpayer was denied standing to contend that a federal statute permitting summary C.I.A. reports on expenditure of its funds violated Article I, Section 9, Clause 7 (which requires a "regular statement and account" of how all public money is expended). *Rationale:* The challenge was not addressed to "a specific constitutional limitation upon the taxing and spending power" but only to statutes regulating the C.I.A.

(c) **State taxpayers:** [§53] The standing rules for state taxpayers to attack allegedly unconstitutional state expenditures in a federal court are the ***same*** as for federal taxpayers challenging federal expenditures. [Asarco, Inc. v. Kadish, 490 U.S. 605 (1989)]

(6) **Assertion of third party rights:** [§54] Absent a federal statute conferring standing, the Court—pursuant to principles of judicial self-restraint—will permit only the injured person to claim a violation of his own constitutional (or statutory) rights. [Tileston v. Ullman, 318 U.S. 44 (1943)—doctor bringing a declaratory judgment action had no standing to contend that anticontraceptive law violated his patients' constitutional rights]

(a) **Exceptions:** [§55] In certain special circumstances, a claimant may assert the rights of third parties (provided he himself has also suffered injury).

1) **Where difficult for third party to assert rights:** [§56] A claimant may assert the rights of a third party where the latter would find it difficult or impossible to vindicate his own rights.

a) **Example:** A state statute required the NAACP to disclose its membership lists. The Court held that the NAACP—which was ***injured*** because disclosure would result in its losing members—could assert the freedom-of-association rights of its members. If members had to assert their own rights, the rights would be nullified in the process of assertion (since they depended on anonymity). [NAACP v. Alabama, 357 U.S. 449 (1958)]

b) **Example:** Defendant, a white homeowner, sold her home to a black buyer. Another white homeowner sued for damages for breach of a racially restrictive covenant. Defendant—who would be ***injured*** by an award for damages—had standing to assert equal protection rights of blacks. If defendant could not assert such rights, they would be lost—since whites would not sell to blacks and the latter would find it very difficult to bring their grievance before any court. [Barrows v. Jackson, 346 U.S. 249 (1953)]

2) **Where special relationship exists between claimant and third party:** [§57] Several cases have permitted assertion of the rights of third parties when the injury suffered by claimant deters his relationship with the third party, thereby indirectly resulting in a violation of the third party's rights.

a) **Example:** Vendor of beer had standing to assert constitutional rights of males under 21 years of age against law prohibiting sale of beer to them. [Craig v. Boren, 429 U.S. 190 (1976)]

b) **Example:** Seller of contraceptives had standing to assert constitutional rights of potential purchasers against law regulating distribution to them. [Carey v. Population Services International, 431 U.S. 678 (1977)]

(b) **Standing of an association:** [§58] Even if an association has itself suffered no injury, it may have standing to assert the rights of its members in a representative capacity ***if*** (i) the ***members themselves have standing***, (ii) the interest asserted is ***germane to the association's purpose***, and (iii) ***neither the claim asserted nor the relief requested requires that the members participate*** in the suit. [Hunt v. Washington State Apple Advertising Commission, 432 U.S. 333 (1977)]

(7) **Standing of a state**

(a) **Property interests:** [§59] A state may attack the validity of federal action affecting the state's own property interests. [Missouri v. Holland, 252 U.S. 416 (1920)]

(b) **Tenth Amendment claims:** [§60] Absent congressional authorization of such a suit, however, a state has no standing to attack a federal statute on the ground that Congress has exceeded its delegated powers. The state has suffered no injury as such, and the matter is merely a "political question." [Massachusetts v. Mellon, 262 U.S. 447 (1923)]

(c) **Parens patriae:** [§61] Similarly, a state has no standing, as parens patriae, to assert the claims of its citizens against the federal government—at least with respect to a federal spending program. Where citizens' rights respecting their relations with the federal government are concerned, "it is the United States, and not the state, which represents them as parens patriae." [*Compare* Massachusetts v. Mellon, *supra*, *with* South Carolina v. Katzenbach, 383 U.S. 301 (1966)]

1) **Compare:** A state has standing, as parens patriae of the general welfare of its citizens, to challenge the constitutionality of another state's law that causes substantial injury to the complaining state's population. [Maryland v. Louisiana, 451 U.S. 725 (1981)—Maryland successfully challenged Louisiana use tax that discriminated against interstate commerce]

(8) **Freedoms of expression and religion:** [§62] Special applications of the "standing" doctrine related to these substantive provisions of the Constitution are discussed *infra*, §§739 *et seq., and see infra,* §§1113-1114.

c. **Additional conditions for review of state court decisions:** [§63] Apart from the matters discussed above, several other requirements must be satisfied before the Supreme Court will review a state court decision.

(1) **Exhaustion of state procedures:** [§64] The Supreme Court will not review a state court judgment unless the claimant has exhausted all available state remedies (*e.g.*, has appealed to the highest court in the state in which a decision could be had).

(2) **Final judgments:** [§65] The Court will review only final judgments of state courts; *i.e.*, no further proceedings can be pending that could alter or modify the judgment. The Supreme Court decides for itself whether a judgment is final, but in at least the following four categories of cases, a judgment may be considered "final" even when further proceedings may be had in the state courts. [Cox Broadcasting Corp. v. Cohn, 420 U.S. 469 (1975)]

(a) **Federal issue is conclusive:** [§66] For example, if a criminal defendant admits the facts charged but moves to dismiss the indictment on the ground that his action is constitutionally protected, and a denial of this motion is affirmed on appeal, the judgment may be treated as "final" even though a trial on the facts could still be had. [Mills v. Alabama, 384 U.S. 214 (1966)]

(b) **Federal issue will survive:** [§67] If a state appellate court decides a federal issue and remands for retrial on damages, the judgment may be treated as "final" because the issue will require federal review regardless of the outcome of the retrial. [Radio Station WOW, Inc. v. Johnson, 326 U.S. 120 (1945)]

(c) **Later federal review impossible:** [§68] If a state appellate court reverses a criminal conviction (on the ground that defendant was denied a constitutional right) and orders a new trial, the judgment may be treated as "final" because the prosecution could not appeal the reversal if the defendant is acquitted on retrial. [California v. Stewart, 384 U.S. 436 (1966)]

(d) **Delayed review would seriously erode federal policy:** [§69] If a state appellate court holds that a state law does not violate a newspaper's First Amendment freedom of the press and remands for trial, the judgment may be treated as "final" because the newspaper might win at trial on nonfederal grounds and the unreviewed state court decision would leave the law on the books—thus possibly chilling First Amendment rights on other newspapers. [Cox Broadcasting Corp. v. Cohn, *supra*]

(3) **"Federal question":** [§70] The Supreme Court will review state court judgments or the validity of state statutes only if they involve a "substantial federal question"—*i.e.*, a purported violation of the Constitution, a federal statute, or treaty. The Court will ***not*** review a state act challenged solely on the ground that it violates state law or the state constitution.

(a) **Review of state statute:** [§71] When reviewing a ***state*** statute or municipal ordinance, the Court is ordinarily bound by the final interpretation of the state courts.

(b) **State procedure:** [§72] The federal question must be ***properly and timely raised*** in the state proceedings, in a reasonably clear fashion and in accordance with ***reasonable*** state rules of procedure.

1) **But note:** The state procedure may not be used to ***evade*** decision of the federal question. It must afford the claimant a fair opportunity to present the question. Thus, the state court may not prescribe a novel procedure and then claim that failure to comply therewith precludes review. [NAACP v. Alabama, *supra*, §56]

(4) **"Adequate and independent state ground":** [§73] It must appear that the state court decision ***turned*** on the federal question. If the state court judgment can be ***supported entirely on a state ground*** (*e.g.*, state court refuses to decide federal issue because of claimant's failure to comply with a reasonable state rule of procedure in asserting the federal

claim), the Supreme Court will ***not*** review. To do so would be to render an "advisory opinion" on the federal question, since the state judgment would not be changed. [Herb v. Pitcairn, 324 U.S. 117 (1945)]

(a) **Independent state ground:** [§74] Even if the state court decides a federal question in the case, the Supreme Court will not review if the state court ***also*** grounded its decision on a matter of state law ***and if*** a decision on the federal question was not required in light of disposition of the state question. [Murdock v. City of Memphis, 87 U.S. (20 Wall.) 590 (1875)]

(b) **Adequacy of state ground:** [§75] The state ground must be "adequate." It may not be unreasonable or unfair, and it must serve a legitimate state interest. [Henry v. Mississippi, 379 U.S. 443 (1965)]

(c) **Unclear whether state or federal ground:** [§76] If it is unclear as to whether the state court decision turned on state or federal law, the Supreme Court may:

(i) ***Dismiss*** because its jurisdiction is ambiguous; or

(ii) ***Remand*** to the state court for clarification.

However, the Court disfavors these alternatives and has adopted a rule that requires a clear and express statement by the state court that its decision actually rests on state law. Thus, if the state court decision appears to rest primarily on federal law or is interwoven with federal law, absent a clear statement to the contrary, the Court will assume that there is ***no*** adequate state ground. [Michigan v. Long, 463 U.S. 1032 (1983)]

d. **Other policies of "strict necessity":** [§77] The Court has developed additional prudential principles of judicial self-restraint pursuant to its practice of "strict necessity in disposing of constitutional issues"—"the most important and the most delicate of the Court's functions." [Rescue Army v. Municipal Court, *supra*, §32] Ordinarily, the Court will decide only those constitutional issues that are actually raised in the case before it, and will not decide them in broader terms than are required by the precise facts to which the ruling is to be applied.

(1) **Construction of federal statutes:** [§78] Where serious doubts are raised as to the constitutionality of an act of Congress, the Court will first ascertain "whether a construction of the statute is fairly possible by which the questions may be avoided." [Ashwander v. Tennessee Valley Authority, 297 U.S. 288 (1936)]

(2) **Sketchiness of record:** [§79] Even when the Court clearly has jurisdiction of an appeal from a state or federal court, and even when there is no nonconstitutional ground for decision, the Court may decline to decide a case raising a constitutional issue if the facts in the record concerning the precise reach or meaning of the law being challenged, or its

consequences for the litigants, are not sufficiently in a "clean cut and concrete form." [Socialist Labor Party v. Gilligan, 406 U.S. 583 (1972)]

e. **Challenges to state action in federal courts:** [§80] In appropriate circumstances, a person may bring an action in federal court—for damages, an injunction, or a declaratory judgment—against a state officer (but not against the state itself) to remedy or to prevent a violation of rights under the Constitution, federal law, or treaty. *Rationale:* Such an action is not one against the state itself (and thus barred by the Eleventh Amendment, *supra*, §6) because, by attempting to enforce a state law that violates a federal right, the state officer is "stripped of his official capacity"—and hence is personally accountable for his actions. [*Ex parte* Young, *supra*, §11]

(1) **Statutory restrictions on federal injunctions:** [§81] Statutes restrict the use of federal injunctions regarding state action.

(a) **Tax laws and rate orders:** [§82] Federal statutes bar the issuance of a federal injunction against certain types of state action (*e.g.*, enforcement of state tax laws [28 U.S.C. §1341], rate orders of a state administrative agency [28 U.S.C. §1342]), as long as there are "plain, speedy and efficient" remedies available in the state courts.

(b) **Pending proceedings:** [§83] A federal statute [28 U.S.C. §2283] provides that federal courts may ***not*** enjoin state court proceedings ***already instituted*** "except as expressly authorized by Act of Congress." An express congressional exception [42 U.S.C. §1983] ***authorizes*** federal injunctions to correct the deprivation of constitutional rights. However, section 1983 injunctions against pending state court proceedings may be issued only if consistent with "announced principles of equity, comity, and federalism"—amplified and illustrated in the discussion that follows. [Mitchum v. Foster, 407 U.S. 225 (1972)]

(2) **Enjoining state criminal statutes or prosecutions:** [§84] Because of principles of "equity, comity, and federalism," a federal court will ***not*** enjoin state criminal statutes or prosecutions absent ***"irreparable injury"*** or ***"exceptional circumstances"***—*i.e.*, a showing of significant harm that could not be avoided by state adjudication and appellate review of the proceedings. [Douglas v. City of Jeannette, 319 U.S. 157 (1943); Wooley v. Maynard, 430 U.S. 705 (1977)—injunction may issue against further prosecutions which would seriously burden one already convicted of violating state law, where such prosecutions violate his constitutional rights]

(a) **Compare—declaratory judgment:** [§85] However, no special circumstances or "irreparable injury" need be shown for a federal court to issue a declaratory judgment that a state criminal statute (under which a prosecution is genuinely threatened) is unconstitutional—either on its face or as applied. [Steffel v. Thompson, 415 U.S. 452 (1974)]

1) **Rationale:** A declaratory judgment is "a less harsh and abrasive remedy than the injunction." Furthermore, denying all federal relief would place a citizen in the dilemma of either intentionally flouting state law (and risking imprisonment) or forgoing what she believes to be a constitutionally protected activity.

2) **Preliminary injunction permitted:** [§86] If a proper federal declaratory judgment proceeding has been initiated by plaintiff, the federal judge may grant a preliminary injunction against threatened prosecution by state officials pending final resolution of the federal declaratory judgment action. [Doran v. Salem Inn, Inc., 422 U.S. 922 (1975)]

(b) **Free speech:** [§87] A federal injunction may be issued if a state criminal statute or regulation is alleged to be invalid on its face as an "overbroad" or "vague" regulation of freedom of expression or association (discussed *infra*, §§739-749). [Dombrowski v. Pfister, 380 U.S. 479 (1965)]

1) **Limitation for pending prosecution:** [§88] But principles of "equity, comity, and federalism" forbid ***injunctions***—or ***declaratory judgments***—against pending state criminal proceedings even when the state statute affects freedom of expression or association, except perhaps where the statute is "flagrantly and patently" unconstitutional in every way. [Younger v. Harris, 401 U.S. 37 (1971); Samuels v. Mackell, 401 U.S. 66 (1971)]

(3) **Pending civil proceedings:** [§89] The prohibition against federal injunctions or declaratory judgments against pending state criminal proceedings also extends to pending state-initiated civil proceedings that are "akin to a criminal prosecution"—*e.g.*, civil suit by state prosecutor to close a theater exhibiting obscene films [Huffman v. Pursue, Ltd., 420 U.S. 592 (1975)], and a civil action to remove a child from parents for child abuse [Moore v. Sims, 442 U.S. 415 (1979)].

(a) **Applications:** [§90] The prohibition against federal injunctions also applies in the following situations.

1) **Contempt proceedings:** The prohibition applies to pending state contempt proceedings—even where the contempt is civil in nature (*e.g.*, to enforce a court subpoena). [Juidice v. Vail, 430 U.S. 327 (1977)—contempt power is at the core of state judicial system]

2) **Execution of judgments:** It also applies to state laws that seek to ensure compliance with court judgments. [Pennzoil Co. v. Texaco, Inc., 481 U.S. 1 (1987)—law permitting judgment creditor to execute lien on debtor's property unless debtor posts bond in amount of judgment]

3) **Proceedings to recover state funds:** It applies to a pending civil action by the state to recover state funds fraudulently obtained, since this vindicates the important state policy of safeguarding its treasury. [Trainor v. Hernandez, 431 U.S. 434 (1977)]

4) **Bar disciplinary proceedings:** It also applies to state bar disciplinary proceedings. [Middlesex County Ethics Committee v. Garden State Bar Association, 457 U.S. 423 (1982)]

5) **Administrative proceedings:** It applies to state administrative proceedings involving ***important*** state interests. [Ohio Civil Rights Commission v. Dayton Christian Schools, Inc., 477 U.S. 619 (1986)—sex discrimination charge]

(b) **Definition of "pending":** [§91] If the relevant state proceeding (criminal or civil) is begun after an action for a federal injunction (or declaratory judgment) is filed, but before any substantial proceedings on the merits in federal court, the federal action ordinarily must be dismissed. [Hicks v. Miranda, 422 U.S. 332 (1975)]

(c) **"Bad faith" exception:** [§92] A federal injunction (or declaratory judgment) may issue against a pending state criminal prosecution (or state-initiated civil action) if the claimant shows that state officials are acting in bad faith—*i.e.*, with no hope of prevailing, to harass claimants and deter them from engaging in constitutionally protected activities—and will continue to do so regardless of what the state courts do. [Dombrowski v. Pfister, *supra*; Younger v. Harris, *supra*]

(4) **Ongoing supervision of state executive activities:** [§93] Principles of "equity, comity, and federalism" also impose significant restrictions on federal court supervision of the practices of state executive or administrative agencies—*e.g.*, disciplining of police [Rizzo v. Goode, 423 U.S. 362 (1976)], and bail, sentencing, and jury fee policies [O'Shea v. Littleton, *supra*, §35].

(a) **Note:** Such federal equitable relief will not be granted unless plaintiff shows "the likelihood of substantial and immediate irreparable injury, and the inadequacy of remedies at law." [O'Shea v. Littleton, *supra*]

(5) **Exhaustion of state remedies:** [§94] Although the rule had been that a person seeking a federal injunction against state administrative action must have exhausted all adequate state administrative remedies, federal law [28 U.S.C. §1983] has been interpreted to excuse this requirement. [Damico v. California, 389 U.S. 416 (1967)] Thus, there is ***no*** requirement of exhausting state judicial remedies.

(6) **"Abstention" doctrine:** [§95] In "narrowly limited special circumstances" [Zwickler v. Koota, 389 U.S. 241 (1967)], a federal court may abstain from granting an injunction or declaratory judgment and remand

the parties to state court for an interpretation of the statute. [Railroad Commission v. Pullman Co., 312 U.S. 496 (1941)] *Rationale:* This promotes harmonious federal-state relations, since the state court may interpret the statute so as to make a decision of the constitutional question unnecessary.

(a) **Ambiguity:** [§96] The federal court may abstain if the state statute or regulation is unclear, giving state courts the opportunity to avoid the constitutional issue. [Harris County Commissioners' Court v. Moore, 420 U.S. 77 (1975)]

(b) **"Free speech" exception:** [§97] However, where the state statute is attacked on the ground that it is an "overbroad" or "vague" regulation of expression or association (*infra*, §§739-749), a federal court generally will ***not abstain***, even where the statute might be given a limiting interpretation.

1) **Rationale:** The right of free speech is fundamental in a democratic society, and the mere existence of a vague or overbroad regulation might deter people from exercising that right. If the statute is invalid on its face, the federal court should generally so hold unless the statute can be clarified in a single state proceeding. [Dombrowski v. Pfister, *supra*]

2) **Note:** If the state official wishes to avoid federal adjudication, she may promptly seek a declaratory judgment in the state courts, clarifying the scope of the statute.

(c) **"Unjustifiable delay" exception:** [§98] The federal court may decline to abstain if it finds further delays unjustifiable—especially in civil rights cases. [Griffin v. County School Board, 377 U.S. 218 (1964)—further delay in integration of school system unjustified]

(d) **Procedure to be followed:** [§99] If the parties are remanded to state court, the claimant may expressly reserve the right to litigate the federal question ultimately in federal court and still present constitutional arguments in the state court. [England v. Louisiana State Board of Medical Examiners, 375 U.S. 411 (1963)]

f. **Political questions:** [§100] When a case presents a "political question" rather than a justiciable controversy, the Court will not decide the question (on the basis of separation of powers). Final determination of such questions is left to the political branches—*i.e.*, Congress and/or the executive branch.

(1) **Criteria:** [§101] The basic criteria for determining whether a question is "political" are [Baker v. Carr, *supra*, §44]:

(i) ***A "textually demonstrable" constitutional commitment*** of the issue ***to the political branches***;

(ii) ***Lack of manageable standards*** for judicial resolution;

(iii) ***A need for finality*** in the action of the political branches; and

(iv) ***Difficulty or impossibility*** of devising effective judicial remedies.

(a) **Note—interrelationship:** The lack of judicially manageable standards may strengthen the conclusion that there is a textually demonstrable commitment to a coordinate branch. [Nixon v. United States, 113 S. Ct. 732 (1993)]

(2) **Case-by-case determination:** [§102] Beyond these criteria, the Court decides each matter on a case-by-case basis.

(3) **Application**

(a) **Foreign relations:** [§103] Certain basic issues of foreign relations (*e.g.*, what the recognized government of a foreign country is; on what date hostilities ceased against a foreign government) may be "political questions." [Martin v. Mott, 25 U.S. 19 (1827)]

1) **Rationale:** Resolution of such issues frequently turns on standards that defy judicial application, involves the exercise of discretion demonstrably committed to Congress or the President, or uniquely demands a single-voiced statement of the government's views.

2) **Example:** A plurality of the Court has stated that the issue of whether the President has unilateral power to terminate a treaty (*i.e.*, without the consent of Congress) is a "political question"; there are no judicially manageable standards. [Goldwater v. Carter, 444 U.S. 996 (1979)]

(b) **Military organization:** [§104] Detailed issues concerning the composition, training, equipping, and disciplining of U.S. military forces are "political questions" committed to Congress by Article I, Section 8, Clause 16. [Gilligan v. Morgan, 413 U.S. 1 (1973)]

(c) **Constitutional amendments:** [§105] Details respecting proposed constitutional amendments (*e.g.*, how long they remain open to ratification, or what effect a prior rejection by the state legislature may have on subsequent ratification) have been held to involve "political questions." They are committed to Congress by Article V, and there are no manageable judicial standards. [Coleman v. Miller, 307 U.S. 433 (1939)]

(d) **Impeachment:** [§106] The provision of Article I, Section 3, Clause 6 that the "Senate shall have the sole power to try all impeachments" commits to the Senate the determination of procedures for trying an impeached official, which are unreviewable by the courts. [Nixon v. United States, *supra*]

(e) **Republican form of government:** [§107] Questions under Article IV, Section 4, providing that the United States shall guarantee every state a republican form of government, have been held "political," because there are no judicially manageable standards to determine whether the form of government is "republican." [Pacific States Telegraph & Telephone Co. v. Oregon, 223 U.S. 118 (1912)]

(f) **Internal political party disputes:** [§108] The Court has indicated "grave doubts" whether the federal judiciary should intervene in certain disputes at political party conventions. [O'Brien v. Brown, 409 U.S. 1 (1972)—"the convention itself is the proper forum for determining intraparty disputes to which delegates shall be seated"]

(g) **Political rights:** [§109] Constitutional issues concerning political rights or the allocation of political power within a state (such as deprivation of the right to vote, or legislative apportionment) are ***not*** necessarily "political questions." They may involve claims under the Fifteenth Amendment or the Equal Protection Clause of the Fourteenth Amendment, which have well-developed and familiar judicial standards. [Baker v. Carr, *supra*, §101; Gomillion v. Lightfoot, 364 U.S. 339 (1960)]

(h) **Congressional membership:** [§110] The Constitution prescribes certain minimum requirements for membership in each House [Art. I, §2] and provides that "each House shall be the judge of the elections, returns and qualifications of its members" [Art. I, §5].

1) **Example:** Since Article I, Section 5 commits to the House of Congress the final decision of which candidate "received more lawful votes," the issue is a "political question." [Roudebush v. Hartke, 405 U.S. 15 (1972)]

2) **Compare:** But Article I, Section 5 does not constitute a demonstrable commitment of nonreviewable power to Congress to set and evaluate qualifications of members beyond the age, citizenship, and residence requirements of Article I, Section 2, Clause 2. Thus, such issues are ***not*** "political questions." [Powell v. McCormack, 395 U.S. 486 (1969)]

4. **Effect of Declaration of Unconstitutionality:** [§111] In legal theory, a decision declaring an act unconstitutional is binding on no one but the parties to the suit. In fact, of course, such a decision establishes a principle of law applicable to all persons. However, certain problems may arise in applying the declaration to litigation involving other parties:

a. **Retroactive effect**

(1) **General rule:** [§112] The Court's declaration of unconstitutionality is the controlling interpretation of federal law. It has full retroactive effect in all cases still open on appeal, and as to all events regardless of when they occur. [Harper v. Virginia Department of Taxation, 113 S. Ct. 2510 (1993)]

(2) **Application—criminal cases:** [§113] The issue of retroactivity has been encountered repeatedly in recent years in connection with rulings by the Court that declare unconstitutional some statute or procedure affecting

those charged with a crime. Are persons imprisoned under the invalid statute or procedure whose convictions have been affirmed on appeal entitled to be freed, or at least given a new trial? (*See infra*, §§1241-1245.)

b. **Partial invalidity:** [§114] When part of a statute has been declared invalid, whether the remaining portion shall also be declared unconstitutional, or enforced as valid, depends upon the intention of the legislature.

(1) **Statute severable:** [§115] Where the parts are so ***distinctly severable*** that each can stand alone, and it was the apparent intention of the legislature that the valid part should be enforceable even though another part should fail, then one part of the statute may be enforced even if another is declared unconstitutional. [Carter v. Carter Coal Co., 298 U.S. 238 (1936)]

(2) **Statute not severable:** [§116] On the other hand, if the different parts of a statute are so mutually ***connected and interdependent*** that the legislature must have intended them to be effective only as a whole, then all provisions dependent on or connected with the unconstitutional portion must also fall. [Pollock v. Farmers' Loan & Trust Co., 158 U.S. 601 (1895)]

(3) **"Severability clause":** [§117] A statute may provide that "if any section or provision of this act shall be held to be invalid, this shall not affect the validity of other sections or provisions hereof." A legislative declaration of this type ("severability clause") provides a ***rebuttable*** presumption as to the intent of the legislature, but it is not conclusive. [Williams v. Standard Oil, 278 U.S. 235 (1929)]

B. LEGISLATIVE POWER

1. **Power of Congress—In General:** [§118] Legislative power is basically the power to make laws, but it also includes the power to investigate, hear, and consider matters upon which legislation may be enacted, and do all other things necessary or proper to the enactment of legislation. Article I, Section 1 of the Constitution provides: "All legislative powers herein granted shall be vested in a Congress of the United States. . . ."

a. **Scope of federal powers**

(1) **Doctrine of enumerated powers:** [§119] The Tenth Amendment provides: "The powers not delegated to the United States by the Constitution, nor prohibited by it to the States, are ***reserved to the States*** respectively, or to the people." Thus, the doctrine early developed that the federal government was one of "enumerated" or "delegated" powers, and that the powers not expressly delegated were "reserved" to the states. [Kansas v. Colorado, 206 U.S. 46 (1907)]

(2) **Doctrine of implied powers:** [§120] Nevertheless, the Court (per Chief Justice Marshall) in *McCulloch v. Maryland*, 17 U.S. (4 Wheat.) 316 (1819), held that in addition to those powers specifically enumerated in the Constitution, certain broad federal powers are to be implied from the ***Necessary and Proper Clause***. [Art. I, §8, cl. 18]

(a) **Necessary and Proper Clause:** [§121] Article I, Section 8, Clause 18 provides that Congress has the power "[t]o make all laws which shall be ***necessary and proper*** for carrying into execution the foregoing powers, and all other powers vested by this Constitution in the Government of the United States, or in any Department or Officer thereof."

(b) **Congress may use any appropriate means:** [§122] Congress is not limited to only those means that are absolutely necessary. Rather, it may use ***any appropriate means*** to achieve the ends specified in the enumerated powers—*i.e.*, any means not prohibited by the Constitution. The need for a particular means is for Congress—not the Supreme Court—to determine.

1) **Example:** The enumerated powers do not include the power to incorporate a national bank, but Congress may do so as a "necessary and proper" means of carrying out its delegated powers to lay and collect taxes [Art. I, §8, cl. 1], borrow money [Art. I, §8, cl. 2], regulate commerce among the several states [Art. I, §8, cl. 3], declare and conduct war [Art. I, §8, cl. 11], and raise and support armies and navies [Art. I, §8, cls. 12, 13]. [McCulloch v. Maryland, *supra*]

(c) **Powers traceable to grants of power to other branches:** [§123] The provisions of the Necessary and Proper Clause apply to ***all*** powers delegated to ***any*** branch of the federal government.

1) **Admiralty and maritime power:** [§124] Thus, Congress has the power to legislate concerning admiralty and maritime matters even though the Constitution contains no express grant of such power to Congress. Article III, Section 2 extends the federal ***judicial*** power to "all cases of admiralty and maritime jurisdiction"; and the Court has held that the framers intended to place the entire subject—substantive as well as procedural aspects—under national control. [*Ex parte* Garnett, 141 U.S. 1 (1891)]

(3) **Inherent powers:** [§125] There is one broad exception to the doctrine that Congress's authority is limited to the enumerated powers. ***International powers*** (*i.e.*, powers over ***external or foreign affairs***) are considered inherent federal powers even though not expressly recited in the Constitution. [United States v. Curtiss-Wright Export Corp., 299 U.S. 304 (1936)]

b. **Delegation of legislative power:** [§126] Several decisions in the 1930s held that congressional delegations of lawmaking power to the executive branch or administrative agencies were impermissible because they were unduly broad. [Panama Refining Co. v. Ryan, 293 U.S. 388 (1935); Schechter Poultry Co. v. United States, 295 U.S. 495 (1935)]

(1) **Requirement of standards:** [§127] To avoid "delegation running riot," and to ensure that the fundamental purposes of the separation of

powers are observed, the Court required that delegations of legislative power contain "intelligible standards" to confine the discretion of the delegate. [Yakus v. United States, 321 U.S. 414 (1944)]

(2) **Effective demise of the nondelegation doctrine:** [§128] But no decision since 1935 has invalidated a congressional delegation of power, and the Court has been extremely liberal on the sufficiency of "standards," no matter how broadly phrased (*e.g.*, upholding "public interest, convenience, or necessity").

(a) **Note:** In recent years, some justices have invoked the nondelegation doctrine in arguing that a delegation of legislative power was invalid because Congress had not made the critical policy decisions. [*See, e.g.*, American Textile Manufacturers Institute v. Donovan, 452 U.S. 490 (1981)]

(3) **Delegation to judicial branch:** [§129] Congress may delegate rule-making authority (and other nonadjudicatory functions) to the judicial branch (as well as to the executive branch or administrative agencies) as long as the task delegated does not invade the prerogatives of some other branch and is appropriate to the duties of the judicial branch. [Mistretta v. United States, 488 U.S. 361 (1989)—upholding placement in judicial branch of commission to promulgate sentencing guidelines]

2. **Commerce Power:** [§130] Congress's all important powers under Article I, Section 8, Clause 3, "to regulate commerce with foreign nations, and among the several states . . ." are discussed in a separate section (*see infra*, §§260 *et seq.*).

3. **Taxing and Spending Powers**

a. **Constitutional provision:** [§131] Article I, Section 8, Clause 1 provides that "Congress shall have the power to lay and collect taxes . . . to pay the debts and provide for the common defense and general welfare of the United States."

b. **Independent powers:** [§132] The powers (i) to tax to raise revenue; and (ii) to spend for the general welfare are ***independent*** powers. That is, Congress may (i) tax subjects and (ii) spend money on activities that it could not regulate directly under any of its enumerated regulatory powers (such as the commerce power).

c. **Taxation with purpose or effect of regulation:** [§133] Virtually all taxes have some ancillary regulatory effect, in that they tend to encourage or discourage various types of activity.

(1) **Where Congress has power to regulate:** [§134] If Congress has the power to regulate the subject or activity taxed, the tax—even though enacted for a regulatory rather than a revenue-raising purpose—can be upheld as a "necessary and proper" exercise of one of Congress's regulatory powers.

(a) **Example:** A tax levied on banknotes issued by state banks was upheld (even though it drove the banknotes out of existence), because

Congress has the power to regulate the national currency. [Art. I, §8, cl. 5] Its validity as a revenue-raising measure was immaterial. [Veazie Bank v. Fenno, 75 U.S. (8 Wall.) 533 (1869)]

(b) **Effect:** Since Congress has almost limitless regulatory power under the Commerce Clause (discussed *infra*), virtually ***all*** federal taxes may be upheld as "necessary and proper" exercises of the commerce power, without reliance on the taxing power at all.

(2) **Where Congress has no power to regulate:** [§135] In those rare instances where Congress has no power to regulate the subject or activity taxed, the tax must be justified under the taxing power. But even here, the tax is not necessarily invalid merely because it regulates the activity taxed to some extent—since virtually every tax has this effect.

(a) **Test:** [§136] The tax will be upheld under the taxing power if its ***dominant intent*** is revenue-raising (rather than prohibition or regulation). Phrased another way, the tax will be invalid only if its dominant intent is penal (rather than fiscal).

(b) **Objective approach:** [§137] The Court has sometimes applied this test very objectively. If the tax ***in fact*** raises revenue, it will be upheld: *i.e.*, its dominant intent will be considered fiscal, despite the apparent regulatory purpose.

1) **Examples:** The following taxes that obviously had substantial regulatory effects were nonetheless upheld as revenue-raising measures:

a) ***Tax of 10¢ per pound on yellow oleomargarine***, as compared to one-fourth of a cent per pound on white oleo [McCray v. United States, 195 U.S. 27 (1904)];

b) ***Special excise tax on dealers in narcotics*** [United States v. Doremus, 249 U.S. 86 (1919)];

c) ***Tax on dealers in firearms*** [Sonzinsky v. United States, 300 U.S. 506 (1937)]; and

d) ***Tax on bookmaking activities*** [United States v. Kahriger, 345 U.S. 22 (1953)].

(c) **Subjective approach:** [§138] On other occasions, the Court has examined the statute more carefully, looking to the ***language*** and ***operative effect*** to determine its dominant intent. The following factors may be important:

(i) ***Who enforces*** the tax statute. (If the Treasury Department enforces, this evidences fiscal intent; if the Labor Department, regulatory intent.)

(ii) ***How much detailed activity*** one must engage in to be subject to, or to avoid, the tax. (The more detailed the activity, the greater the evidence of a penal or regulatory intent.)

(iii) Whether ***scienter*** is required. (A scienter requirement usually indicates a penal or regulatory intent.)

(iv) ***Amount*** of the tax. (If the amount is so great that virtually all activity is structured to avoid liability—resulting in almost no revenue—this evidences a penal or regulatory intent.)

1) **Examples of penal or regulatory taxes:** A special tax on those who employ child labor was held invalid; several of the above factors were present. [Bailey v. Drexel Furniture Co., 259 U.S. 20 (1922)] A special tax on liquor businesses conducted contrary to state law was also held invalid; the purpose was held to be imposition of a federal penalty for commission of a state crime. [United States v. Constantine, 296 U.S. 287 (1935)]

2) **Compare:** But a special tax on those engaged in gambling has been upheld, since the tax produced revenue despite its regulatory effect. Although the tax statute requires the filing of much detailed information, this ***aids in collection of the tax***. Since gambling is not illegal everywhere, this is ***not*** an added federal penalty for state law violation. [United States v. Kahriger, *supra*] (*Note:* This doctrine concerning the taxing power is still "good law," although the gambling tax statute was subsequently held to violate the Fifth Amendment privilege against self-incrimination. [Marchetti v. United States, 390 U.S. 39 (1968)])

d. **Spending with purpose or effect of regulation:** [§139] Almost all spending programs likewise produce an ancillary regulatory effect, since they tend to encourage or discourage various activities by individuals. Indeed, many federal spending programs ("grants-in-aid") are specifically conditioned on the recipient states using the funds pursuant to federally designated standards.

(1) **Where Congress has power to regulate:** [§140] As in the case of the taxing power, if Congress may ***directly regulate*** the activity or conduct in which persons must engage to receive funds under a federal spending program, the spending program is valid as a "necessary and proper" exercise of the regulatory powers.

(2) **Where Congress has no power to regulate:** [§141] As in the case of the taxing power, Congress rarely lacks the power to regulate activities related to federal spending programs.

(a) **Example:** A congressional program has been upheld solely under the spending power (the Court assuming no regulatory power available) where federal funds were granted to all states enacting unemployment compensation schemes conforming to federal requirements. [Steward Machine Co. v. Davis, 301 U.S. 548 (1937)] The Court found that the federal program did not "coerce" state adoption of unemployment plans, but merely served as a "temptation."

1) The Court also noted that the federal program satisfied a ***federal fiscal purpose***—since if the states did not provide unemployment

compensation, Congress could clearly do so for the general welfare. This theory could sustain broad exercises of the spending power that have substantial regulatory effects.

(b) **Example:** Assuming (but ***not*** deciding) that the Twenty-First Amendment (*see infra*, §§322-327) would bar Congress from enacting a national minimum drinking age, the Court has held that Congress may condition some percentage of federal highway funds on a recipient state's adopting a minimum drinking age. [South Dakota v. Dole, 483 U.S. 203 (1987)]

(c) **Limitations on the spending power**

1) **"General welfare":** [§142] Congress's power to spend must be exercised for the "general welfare"; *i.e.*, the expenditure must be "for the common benefit as distinguished from some mere local purpose." [United States v. Gerlach Live Stock Co., 339 U.S. 725 (1950)] However, the determination of what is in the nation's "general welfare" is left to Congress. [Helvering v. Davis, 301 U.S. 619 (1937)]

2) **Individual rights:** [§143] Congress may not use the spending power to violate an independent constitutional limitation, *e.g.*, by inducing states to engage in activities that would themselves be unconstitutional (such as to inflict cruel and unusual punishment).

4. **War Power**

a. **Constitutional provisions:** [§144] Article I, Section 8 grants Congress the power to declare war, to raise and support armies, to provide and maintain a navy, to make rules for the government and regulation of the land and naval forces, and to provide for organizing, arming, disciplining, and calling forth the militia.

(1) **Broad scope of powers:** [§145] These powers give Congress a wide scope of authority ***during war*** to wage war effectively. For example, Congress may take action affecting domestic matters, such as the national economy, independent of its authority to regulate such matters under any other enumerated power.

(a) **After war:** [§146] Congressional authority under the war power may also continue after cessation of hostilities to remedy evils created by the war. [Woods v. Cloyd W. Miller Co., 333 U.S. 138 (1948)—post-World War II rent controls held valid because housing shortage was attributable to the war]

1) **Limits on power:** [§147] This ***post-war*** power is probably not so unlimited as to "swallow up" the limits on congressional power; although, absent a constitutionally protected personal liberty, the Court would probably give very limited judicial review to an exercise of such power.

5. **Power Over External Affairs:** [§148] The scope of Congress's power over external affairs is discussed elsewhere (*see infra*, §§200 *et seq.*).

6. **Power Over Naturalization and Citizenship**

   a. **Constitutional provision:** [§149] Article I, Section 8, Clause 4 provides that Congress shall have power "to establish a uniform rule of naturalization. . . ."

   b. **Plenary power over aliens:** [§150] The authority of Congress over admission, exclusion, and deportation of aliens is plenary. Congress may exclude aliens altogether, or prescribe the conditions upon which they may come into or remain in the country. [Kleindienst v. Mandel, 408 U.S. 753 (1972)]

      (1) **Exclusion of aliens seeking entry:** [§151] An alien who seeks admission to the country does so only upon such terms as Congress shall prescribe. Whatever procedure Congress authorizes is "due process," as far as the alien is concerned. [United States *ex rel.* Knauff v. Shaughnessy, 338 U.S. 537 (1950)]

         (a) **Example:** Congress may authorize the Attorney General to determine (upon the basis of confidential information the disclosure of which, in the Attorney General's judgment, would endanger the public security) that the admission of an alien would be prejudicial to the interests of the United States; and ***without a hearing***, the government may constitutionally order an alien ***excluded*** from the United States. [United States *ex rel.* Knauff v. Shaughnessy, *supra*; Shaughnessy v. United States *ex rel.* Mezei, 345 U.S. 206 (1953)]

      (2) **Deportation of resident aliens:** [§152] While Congress may prescribe conditions for expulsion and deportation of resident aliens, such aliens in a deportation proceeding do have constitutional protections not available to nonresident aliens seeking entry into the country; *i.e.*, an alien physically present in the United States (legally or illegally) is a "person" within the provisions of the Fifth Amendment and is entitled to ***certain procedural due process rights***.

         (a) **Example:** Before a resident alien may be expelled and deported, he is at least entitled to notice of the nature of the charges against him and a hearing before an executive or administrative tribunal. [Kwong Hai Chew v. Colding, 344 U.S. 590 (1953)]

         (b) **Comment:** Note that the Alien Registration Act of 1940, which authorized the deportation of resident aliens because of membership in the Communist Party (even though such membership terminated before the enactment of the Act), was held ***not*** to be an ex post facto law (*see infra*, §1152) since deportation was not deemed to constitute "punishment." [Harisiades v. Shaughnessy, 342 U.S. 580 (1952)]

      (3) **State regulation of aliens:** [§153] This subject is discussed elsewhere (*see infra*, §§545 *et seq.*).

c. **Naturalization:** [§154] The constitutional basis for federal and state citizenship is found in Section 1 of the Fourteenth Amendment, which states that "all persons born or ***naturalized*** in the United States, and subject to the jurisdiction thereof, are citizens of the United States and the State wherein they reside."

(1) **Congressional power:** [§155] The power of naturalization is vested ***exclusively*** in Congress. [Holmgren v. United States, 217 U.S. 509 (1910)]

(2) **Rights of naturalized citizens:** [§156] The rights of native-born and naturalized citizens are of the ***same dignity*** and are ***coextensive*** (except that only a native-born citizen can be elected President). Hence, a statute that attempts to discriminate between the two classes of citizenship is unconstitutional. [Schneider v. Rusk, 377 U.S. 163 (1964)—statute that deprived naturalized citizens of their citizenship if they resumed foreign residence held to violate equal protection]

d. **Loss of citizenship:** [§157] Under Section 1 of the Fourteenth Amendment, Congress does ***not*** have the power to take away the citizenship of a citizen born or naturalized in the United States unless the government establishes, by a preponderance of evidence, that the citizen ***intended to relinquish citizenship***. Such intent can be expressed in words or found as a fair inference from proven conduct. [Afroyim v. Rusk, 387 U.S. 253 (1967)—holding unconstitutional statute that provided for loss of citizenship for voting in a foreign election; Vance v. Terrazas, 444 U.S. 252 (1980)—upholding a rebuttable presumption that, when a statutory expatriating act is proven, there was intent to relinquish citizenship; but the government must still prove that the act was performed with the necessary intent to relinquish citizenship]

(1) **Compare:** Congress does have power to revoke the citizenship of persons who are not "born or naturalized in the United States"—*e.g.*, by being born abroad to an American parent. [Rogers v. Bellei, 401 U.S. 815 (1971)]

(2) **And note:** Statutes that provide for revocation of naturalization obtained unlawfully or by fraud have also been upheld. [Schneiderman v. United States, 320 U.S. 118 (1945)]

7. Property Power

a. **Power over property of the United States:** [§158] Article IV, Section 3, Clause 2 provides that Congress shall have power "to dispose of and make all needful rules and regulations respecting the territory or other property belonging to the United States."

b. **Scope of power:** [§159] The power over United States property—including the power to determine what are "needful" rules "respecting" the public lands—is vested in Congress ***without limitation***. [Kleppe v. New Mexico, 426 U.S. 529 (1976)]

8. Investigatory Power

a. **Implied from power to legislate:** [§160] While there is no constitutional provision expressly conferring upon Congress the power to make investigations and exact testimony, it has long been recognized as a necessary incident of the power to legislate. [McGrain v. Daugherty, 273 U.S. 135 (1927)]

(1) **Application:** Pursuant to this implied power, either House of Congress may compel the attendance of witnesses before that House (or any duly constituted committee thereof), and order that the witnesses answer questions. [McGrain v. Daugherty, *supra*; Sinclair v. United States, 279 U.S. 263 (1929)]

b. **Scope of investigatory power:** [§161] The power to investigate is limited to inquiries of which the particular House has ***jurisdiction—i.e.***, in respect to which it rightfully may take legislative action. Neither House of Congress possesses a general power to inquire into the private affairs of citizens. [Kilbourn v. Thompson, 103 U.S. 168 (1880)]

(1) **Application:** For the purpose of determining the essential character of a congressional inquiry, recourse is usually had to the statute or resolution under which the investigation is authorized. Furthermore, it is not required that the information be pertinent to any pending legislation. The investigatory power extends to ***all matters upon which Congress could choose to act***.

c. **Enforcement of investigatory power:** [§162] The principal method for enforcing the congressional investigative power is punishment by ***contempt***. Congress has the power to punish a person, other than a member, for contempt in order to assure the integrity of its authority. [Anderson v. Dunn, 19 U.S. (6 Wheat.) 204 (1821)] Either House of Congress may convene as a court to try, convict, and direct a fine against and/or imprisonment of the contemnor, but any imprisonment is limited to the duration of the current term of Congress.

d. **Limits on investigatory power:** [§163] The principal grounds upon which witnesses may refuse to answer questions before congressional committees are discussed elsewhere; *e.g.*, privilege against self-incrimination (*infra*, §§1165-1168); interference with First Amendment rights (*infra*, §§972-974); and lack of due process safeguards in hearing procedures (*infra*, §971).

9. **Congressional Immunity:** [§164] Article I, Section 6, Clause 1 provides that "Senators and Representatives . . . shall not be questioned in any other Place . . . for any Speech or Debate in either House." The Speech or Debate Clause forbids criminal or civil proceedings against members of Congress for "legislative acts." [United States v. Johnson, 383 U.S. 169 (1966)]

a. **Rationale:** [§165] Defending criminal or civil actions of all kinds (including suits for injunctions or damages) diverts the time, energy, and attention of members of Congress from their legislative tasks. [Eastland v. United States Servicemen's Fund, 421 U.S. 491 (1975)]

b. **Persons covered:** [§166] Besides Senators and Representatives, the immunity also covers aides who engage in acts that would be immune if performed by the legislator. [Gravel v. United States, 408 U.S. 606 (1972)]

(1) **Compare:** The Speech or Debate Clause does ***not*** extend to state legislators who are prosecuted for violation of federal law. [United States v. Gillock, 445 U.S. 360 (1980)]

c. **Scope of immunity:** [§167] Neither "acts that occur in the ***regular course of the legislative process***" nor "the ***motivation*** for those acts" may be used against the legislator in a judicial proceeding.

(1) **Compare:** Note that ***promises*** by a legislator to perform a ***future*** legislative act are not immune and may be introduced into evidence. [United States v. Brewster, 408 U.S. 501 (1972)—permitting prosecution for bribery to influence legislation]

d. **"Legislative acts":** [§168] In addition to statements or acts on the floor of Congress, this includes such matters as how a legislator voted or decided to vote, and extends to conducting committee hearings, introducing material at such hearings, and preparing committee reports.

(1) **But note:** It does ***not*** extend to ***public distribution*** of committee reports, even when authorized by statute [Doe v. McMillan, 412 U.S. 306 (1973)], nor to ***republication*** (*e.g.*, in press releases or newsletters) of defamatory statements originally made in Congress [Hutchinson v. Proxmire, 443 U.S. 111 (1979)].

e. **"Political acts":** [§169] Political acts are ***not*** subject to the protection of the Speech or Debate Clause. They include communications with and services for constituents, and speeches and publications outside of Congress. [United States v. Brewster, *supra*]

C. EXECUTIVE POWER

1. **Source of Presidential Powers:** [§170] Article I, Section 1 confers the ***whole*** executive power to the President. The President is given broad authority to delegate and to appoint members of the executive branch, but all executive power ultimately rests in the hands of the President.

2. **Scope of Powers**

a. **Appointment power:** [§171] Article II, Section 2 specifies that the President shall nominate and appoint "with the advice and consent of the Senate" all "Ambassadors, other public Ministers and Consuls, Judges of the Supreme Court, and all other Officers of the United States, whose appointments are not herein otherwise provided for . . . but Congress may vest the appointment of inferior officers as they think proper in the President alone, in the Courts of Law, or in the Heads of Departments."

(1) **Congressional appointees:** [§172] Although Congress may appoint officials to exercise such investigative power as it might delegate to one of its own committees, it may ***not*** appoint members of an agency or commission with administrative powers (*e.g.*, promulgating rules or issuing advisory opinions) or law enforcement powers (*e.g.*, conducting litigation in the courts). Such persons are "officers of the United States" and

must be appointed pursuant to Article II, Section 2. [Buckley v. Valeo, 424 U.S. 1 (1976)]

(2) **"Principal" vs. "inferior" officers:** [§173] "Principal" officers may be appointed only by the President with the advice and consent of the Senate. Appointment of "inferior" officers may be vested in other departments. [Morrison v. Olson, 487 U.S. 654 (1988)]

(a) **Example:** Independent prosecutors—who are appointed with limited tenure and authority, and are subject to removal by executive officials—have been held to be "inferior" officers and thus may be appointed by the "courts of law." [Morrison v. Olson, *supra*]

(b) **Limits on power:** Congress may not vest courts with appointment power if it is "incongruous" with the functions normally performed by courts; *e.g.*, if the courts were given undue discretion over the appointees' jurisdiction. [Morrison v. Olson, *supra*]

b. **Removal power:** [§174] The Constitution is silent on the President's power to remove most presidential appointees.

(1) **Federal judges:** [§175] The President has ***no power*** to remove Supreme Court justices or lower court judges appointed by him, as the Constitution provides that they are to remain in office "during good behavior." [Art. III, §1]

(2) **Executive appointees:** [§176] However, in order that the President may accomplish his constitutional role, there are ***some*** "purely executive" officials that must be removable by the President at will, even though the appointment may have originally required the "advice and consent" of the Senate and even though Congress may have forbidden such removal. [*Compare* Myers v. United States, 272 U.S. 52 (1926)—Congress may ***not*** forbid removal of a postmaster; *with* Morrison v. Olson, *supra*—Congress ***may*** condition removal of independent prosecutor on "good cause"]

(a) **Attempted removal by Congress:** [§177] Congress may not vest executive functions (*e.g.*, exercising discretion in interpreting and implementing the legislative mandate) in an officer who is ***removable only*** by Congress (by means other than impeachment). *Rationale:* If Congress could do so, it would give Congress control over execution of the laws and violate the constitutional separation of powers. [Bowsher v. Synar, 478 U.S. 714 (1986)]

(3) **Officers appointed pursuant to act of Congress:** [§178] On the other hand, officers of administrative bodies created by acts of Congress—where the act specifies the term of office and causes for removal—may be removed by the President only for causes specified in the statute. [Humphrey's Executor v. United States, 295 U.S. 602 (1935)—removal of F.T.C. officer; Weiner v. United States, 357 U.S. 349 (1958)—removal of War Claims Commission officer]

c. **Pardon power:** [§179] Article II, Section 2 grants the President power "to grant reprieves and pardons for offenses ***against the United States***, except in cases of impeachment."

(1) **Scope of power:** [§180] The President's power to pardon is not subject to control by Congress. It includes the power to ***commute a sentence*** on conditions not authorized in the statute (as long as the conditions do not offend some other provision in the Constitution). [Schick v. Reed, 419 U.S. 256 (1974)]

(2) **Contempt:** [§181] A ***criminal*** contempt is deemed an "offense against the United States," and thus can be pardoned by the President. [*Ex parte* Grossman, 267 U.S. 87 (1925)]

d. **"Legislative" power of President:** [§182] Article I, Section 1 vests all legislative powers in the Congress. The President thus has ***no*** general power to enact legislation. In respect to certain matters, however, the President does have limited legislative powers.

(1) **By delegation:** [§183] Congress may, of course, delegate legislative power to the President and other executive agencies, subject to the limits of the separation of powers doctrine (*see supra*, §§126-129). [*See* National Cable Television Association v. United States, 415 U.S. 336 (1974)]

(a) **Exceeding statutory delegation:** [§184] If the President claims a general power to legislate (*i.e.*, to engage in general lawmaking without a congressional delegation of such authority), then the President acts unconstitutionally. But if the Court finds that the President simply has exceeded the statutory authority granted by Congress, this does not ordinarily violate the Constitution. Thus, the President's decision to close a certain shipyard under the Defense Base Closure and Realignment Act of 1990 was not reviewable on constitutional grounds merely because it may have been based on a recommendation using criteria improper under the Closure Act. [Dalton v. Specter, 114 S. Ct. 1719 (1994)]

(2) **Veto power:** [§185] Article I, Section 7 specifies that every act of Congress shall be approved by the President before it can take effect, or being disapproved, must be repassed by a two-thirds vote of each House.

(a) **Congressional veto:** [§186] The President's veto power applies to all legislative action unless explicitly excepted by the Constitution (*e.g.*, Senate ratification of treaties). Thus, acts of Congress that authorize one or both Houses (or a congressional committee) to change decisions or rules delegated by Congress to executive departments or administrative agencies are invalid—such changes are "legislative actions" and must therefore be presented to the President and subject to his veto. [Immigration & Naturalization Service v. Chadha, 462 U.S. 919 (1983)]

(3) **Military powers:** [§187] Although the President has ***no power*** to declare war (*see supra*, §144), Article II, Section 2 makes the President

Commander-in-Chief of the military. This affords the President extensive legislative power in "theaters of war," *e.g.*, to establish military governments in occupied territories. Such actions generally are not subject to judicial review.

(a) **Commitment of armed forces:** [§188] In the event of insurrection or invasion, the President may deploy military forces against any enemy, foreign or domestic, without waiting for a congressional declaration of war. [Prize Cases, 67 U.S. (2 Black) 635 (1863)—upholding seizure of vessels and cargoes belonging to foreign neutrals and residents of southern states pursuant to presidential directive blockading southern ports during Civil War]

(4) **Inherent "emergency" power:** [§189] Even without congressional authorization, the President ***probably*** has some "inherent" power to act in cases of great national emergency. It has been suggested that this derives from the aggregate of the President's constitutional powers and the need created by emergencies. [Youngstown Sheet & Tube Co. v. Sawyer, 343 U.S. 579 (1952)]

(a) **Limitation—congressional denial of authority:** [§190] In the *Youngstown* case, President Truman's executive order seizing the steel mills to keep them operating during the Korean War was held to be a ***legislative*** act and thus beyond his power. Whether he had "inherent emergency power" in this situation was not at issue because some Justices read congressional statutes as ***denying*** the President the power of seizure.

e. **Impoundment:** [§191] The President has ***no power*** to refuse to spend appropriated funds when Congress has ***expressly mandated*** that they be spent. [Kendall v. United States *ex rel.* Stokes, 37 U.S. (12 Pet.) 524 (1838)] The Court has avoided deciding other issues concerning the extent, if any, to which the President has "inherent" power to impound funds authorized by Congress. [Train v. New York, 420 U.S. 35 (1970)—interpreting federal statute as mandating expenditure]

f. **Executing laws:** [§192] Presidential action may also be upheld as an exercise of the President's power to execute the laws—on the theory that it is not unilateral action on the President's part, but action ***implicitly authorized*** by Congress. (Here, the Court simply engages in statutory interpretation.)

3. **Executive Privilege:** [§193] Although not expressly mentioned in the Constitution, a privilege is recognized to protect against the disclosure of presidential communications made in the exercise of executive power. This privilege derives from the doctrine of separation of powers. [United States v. Nixon, 418 U.S. 683 (1974)]

a. **Scope:** [§194] Where the presidential communications relate to military, diplomatic, or sensitive national security secrets, the claim of privilege is given the utmost deference by the courts. However, other presidential communications are only ***presumptively*** privileged. [United States v. Nixon, *supra*]

(1) **Use in criminal trial:** [§195] Thus, although a generalized claim of presidential privilege is accorded considerable respect, it must yield to a demonstrated specific need for essential evidence in a criminal trial. [United States v. Nixon, *supra*] In such cases, the trial court must make an ***in camera*** inspection of the communications, and "scrupulously protect" against disclosure of materials not found to be relevant and admissible in the criminal case. [United States v. Nixon, *supra*]

(2) **Governmental and historical purposes:** [§196] Similarly, the need to preserve presidential material for legitimate governmental and historical purposes has been held to justify legislation requiring that such materials be reviewed and classified by federal archivists—as long as the statute provides safeguards to insure minimal intrusion into executive confidentiality. [Nixon v. Administrator of General Services, 433 U.S. 425 (1977)]

(3) **Other uses:** [§197] It is an open question whether the same considerations would require disclosure of presidential communications in a civil trial, or in response to congressional demands for information.

b. **Civil damages:** [§198] At least absent an expressly created congressional cause of action against him, our "constitutional heritage and structure" affords the President an ***absolute immunity*** from private suits for damages based on any acts within the "outer perimeter" of his constitutional authority. [Nixon v. Fitzgerald, 457 U.S. 731 (1982)]

(1) **Compare—aides:** [§199] This blanket immunity does ***not*** extend to cabinet officers or other presidential aides. They ***may*** be entitled to ***absolute*** immunity in respect to discretionary authority in such sensitive areas as foreign policy, but ordinarily, they have only a ***qualified*** immunity—being shielded from civil damages if their conduct does not violate clearly established statutory or constitutional rights of which a reasonable person would have known. [Harlow v. Fitzgerald, 457 U.S. 800 (1982); Mitchell v. Forsyth, 472 U.S. 511 (1985)]

D. POWER OVER FOREIGN AFFAIRS

1. **Constitutional Provisions:** [§200] Article I, Section 8 grants ***Congress*** the power to regulate commerce with foreign nations (*see infra*, §260), to declare war, to raise and support armies, and to provide and maintain a navy. Article II, Sections 2 and 3 provide that the ***President*** shall be Commander-in-Chief of the Army and Navy, that he has certain powers in regard to treaty-making (*see* below), that he shall receive foreign ambassadors and ministers, and that he shall nominate and appoint U.S. ambassadors and other public ministers, subject to Senate confirmation.

2. **Comparison with Domestic Powers:** [§201] The powers of the federal government concerning foreign or external affairs are different in origin and nature from those involving domestic or internal affairs. [United States v. Curtiss-Wright Export Corp., *supra*, §125]

a. **Domestic affairs—federal power shared with states:** [§202] In regard to internal affairs, the power of the federal government was carved from the general legislative powers originally possessed by the states. Thus, the federal government has only those powers ***specifically granted*** to it by the Constitution and those ***"necessary and proper"*** to exercising those enumerated powers (*see supra*, §§119-121).

b. **Foreign affairs—exclusive federal power:** [§203] However, powers over foreign affairs—such as the power to declare war, conclude peace, make treaties, and maintain diplomatic relations with other nations—were never possessed by the individual states, but passed directly to the federal government from the sovereign nation of Great Britain. Thus, these powers are held ***exclusively*** by the federal government. [United States v. Curtiss-Wright Export Corp., *supra*]

(1) **State regulation:** [§204] Since the federal power is exclusive, no state regulation is permitted to intrude into the area. [Zschernig v. Miller, 389 U.S. 429 (1968)—invalidating state law that sought to prevent aliens from inheriting local property, where their country confiscated property therein inherited by United States citizens]

c. **Greater delegation permitted regarding external affairs:** [§205] Congress may delegate greater powers in respect to foreign affairs to the President—who represents the nation in that realm—than would be permissible in regard to internal affairs. [United States v. Curtiss-Wright Export Corp., *supra*]

3. **Treaty Power:** [§206] As indicated above, the President is empowered to make treaties with foreign nations "with the advice and consent of [two-thirds of] the Senate."

a. **Status of treaties:** [§207] Under the Supremacy Clause (Article VI, Section 2), treaties confirmed by the Senate are ***"the supreme law of the land."***

(1) **Effect on state laws:** [§208] Thus, any state statute or constitutional provision that conflicts with a treaty provision is ***invalid***. [Hauenstein v. Lynham, 100 U.S. 483 (1880)—treaty providing inheritance rights for aliens prevailed over state law disqualifying aliens from inheriting]

(2) **Conflict with act of Congress:** [§209] Where there is conflict between a treaty and an act of Congress, they are of equal weight; thus, the ***last expression*** of the sovereign will control. [Chae Chan Ping v. United States, 130 U.S. 581 (1889)]

(a) **Effect:** Congress can by subsequent statute alter or repeal United States treaty rights and obligations. [Head Money Cases, 112 U.S. 580 (1884)]

(b) **But note:** Although an act of Congress repealing a treaty would preclude enforcement of any rights thereunder in the courts, the nation might still remain accountable to the other parties to the treaty under the "law of nations." [*See* Clark v. Allen, 331 U.S. 503 (1947)]

b. **Types of treaties:** [§210] A treaty may be ***"self-executing"***: *i.e.*, rights and liabilities are created thereunder without the necessity of further action by Congress. Or a treaty may expressly or impliedly require that Congress must pass ***effectuating legislation*** to create rights and liabilities thereunder.

c. **Independent source of power:** [§211] Since the Supremacy Clause places treaties on an equal footing with the Constitution and acts of Congress, the treaty power is an ***independent*** source of federal power, and Congress may legislate pursuant to a treaty under the Necessary and Proper Clause. The treaty power thereby permits federal action over subjects outside the other enumerated federal powers in the Constitution. (The Tenth Amendment reserves to the states only nondelegated powers, and the treaty power is a delegated power.)

(1) **Limitations on treaty power:** [§212] In *Missouri v. Holland*, 252 U.S. 416 (1920), the Court noted that while an act of Congress must be made "in pursuance of the Constitution," a treaty need only be made "under the authority of the United States." This ***suggests*** that the ***only*** limitations on the federal treaty power and congressional legislation pursuant thereto are the formal requirements of presidential proposal and Senate ratification.

(a) **Individual rights:** [§213] But the Court has made clear that treaties may not contravene constitutional prohibitions (*e.g.*, the Bill of Rights) that protect individual rights. [Reid v. Covert, 454 U.S. 1 (1957)]

(b) **"Proper subject of negotiation":** [§214] The Court has also ***suggested*** a further limitation: that the treaty must concern a "proper subject of negotiation between our government and the governments of other nations." [Geofroy v. Riggs, 133 U.S. 258 (1890)] It seems clear that treaties dealing with matters such as control of wildlife that moves between our country and another [Missouri v. Holland, *supra*] concern "proper subjects of negotiation." And the Court has stated that the cession of a portion of a state without its consent is ***not*** a "proper subject of negotiation" with a foreign power. [Geofroy v. Riggs, *supra*] It is unclear what scope of review the Court would give to a determination by the political branches that a treaty involved a "proper subject of negotiation."

4. **Executive Agreements:** [§215] The President has power to enter into agreements or compacts with other countries. This authority is independent of the treaty power and thus may be exercised without the consent of the Senate.

a. **Scope of power uncertain:** [§216] The full scope of the President's power to bypass the Senate, by entering into executive agreements that cover the same subjects as treaties, is uncertain. But the Court has recognized certain bases of the President's authority to do so:

(1) **Executive power over foreign affairs:** [§217] The constitutional powers granted to the President in Article II include the power to make executive agreements. [United States v. Belmont, 301 U.S. 324 (1937)—

President's power of "diplomatic recognition" supports executive agreement with Soviet Union concerning its claims against Americans]

(2) **Implied power from Congress:** [§218] The President, with the implicit approval of Congress, has power to settle claims of United States citizens against foreign governments through an executive agreement. [Dames & Moore v. Regan, 453 U.S. 654 (1981)]

b. **Status:** [§219] Executive agreements have a status and dignity "similar" to treaties in that they prevail over any ***state law*** inconsistent therewith. [United States v. Pink, 315 U.S. 203 (1942)] But it is unclear whether, like treaties, they also prevail over inconsistent acts of Congress.

II. THE FEDERAL SYSTEM— INTERGOVERNMENTAL RELATIONS

chapter approach

This chapter concerns the interrelationship of state and federal powers in our federal system of government. While this topic is not usually a major source of exam questions, you may see a question raising one or more of the following issues:

1. **Nature of Federal and State Powers:** Although the Tenth Amendment states that all powers not delegated by the Constitution to the federal government are reserved to the states, today federal powers are given an expansive interpretation. Thus, if an examination question involves state legislation, to determine whether the legislation is valid you must examine whether the area regulated is exclusively federal. A power may be made exclusively federal by explicit ***constitutional limitations*** on state power (*e.g.*, states are prohibited from coining money), by the ***nature*** of the power (*e.g.*, only the federal government can borrow money on the credit of the United States), or by ***explicit language*** in the Constitution making the power exclusively federal (*e.g.*, legislation over the District of Columbia). Also note that even where the states have concurrent power to regulate, because of the ***Supremacy Clause*** a state may not enact legislation that interferes with federal legislation.

2. **Intergovernmental Privileges and Immunities:** States are prohibited from making or enforcing laws that abridge the privileges or immunities of citizens of the United States, under the Fourteenth Amendment Privileges and Immunities Clause. These "privileges and immunities" are rights that arise out of the ***relationship of the individual and the national government*** (*e.g.*, the right to petition Congress for redress). Perhaps more importantly, for exam purposes, the Interstate Privileges and Immunities Clause of Article IV, Section 2 prohibits states from discriminating against noncitizens or nonresidents in respect to ***essential activities*** (*e.g.*, pursuing a livelihood) or ***basic rights*** (*e.g.*, obtaining an abortion), unless the discrimination is closely or substantially related to a substantial state purpose.

3. **Intergovernmental Immunity:** If an examination question involves ***federal regulation or taxation of state governments,*** be sure to note that the Tenth Amendment limits the federal government's power to interfere with state and local functions, but here again, the Tenth Amendment is a fairly weak argument; the Court generally will not hold an otherwise permissible exercise of congressional power invalid just because it regulates or taxes the states as well as private persons. If a question involves ***state taxation of the federal government*** or state regulation of federal property or activities, be aware that Congress may permit such taxation or regulation; otherwise, it is forbidden. However, be sure to distinguish between a tax on persons dealing with the federal government and a tax on the government itself. A tax on those who deal with the government is permissible as long as the legal incidence of the tax does ***not fall on the United States.***

A. NATURE AND SCOPE OF FEDERAL AND STATE POWERS

1. **In General:** [§220] The powers of government under the federal system may be classified as follows: (i) those given ***exclusively to the federal*** government, (ii) those ***exclusively reserved to the states,*** and (iii) those that can be ***exercised concurrently*** by both the federal and state governments. Difficult questions arise in determining whether a particular federal power is "exclusive" or "concurrent."

2. **Exclusive vs. Concurrent Powers**

   a. **Exclusive state powers:** [§221] The Tenth Amendment reserves to the states all powers not delegated by the Constitution to the federal government. However, federal powers are now given an expansive interpretation.

   b. **Exclusive federal powers:** [§222] Whether a particular federal power is "exclusive" or "concurrent" depends on: (i) ***constitutional limitations on state power*** in the area, (ii) the ***nature of the power*** itself, and (iii) the ***words granting the power.***

      (1) **State action prohibited:** [§223] Certain federal powers are "exclusive" by virtue of express provisions in the Constitution prohibiting any state action.

         (a) **Example:** Article I, Section 10 expressly prohibits various state actions: "No State shall enter into any treaty . . . coin money . . . lay any Imposts or Duties on Imports or Exports . . . lay any duty on Tonnage, keep Troops or Ships of War in time of Peace. . . ."

      (2) **Nature of power:** [§224] Other federal powers are held to be "exclusive" because the nature of the power itself is such that it can be exercised only by the federal government, and any exercise of power by the state government would be inconsistent therewith.

         (a) **Example:** The federal government has the power "[t]o borrow Money on the credit of the United States." [Art. I, §8, cl. 2] While there is no express prohibition in the Constitution on state power to do likewise, such action would obviously be inconsistent with the powers of the national government, and thus federal power in this area is held to be "exclusive." Similar reasoning applies to federal powers concerning naturalization and citizenship, to declare war, provide for national defense, etc.

      (3) **Exclusive grant of power:** [§225] Finally, a few federal powers are considered "exclusive" because the Constitution grants the power in such terms. For example, Congress has the power "[t]o exercise exclusive Legislation in all Cases whatsoever, over the District of Columbia." [Art. I, §8, cl. 17]

   c. **Concurrent federal and state power—effect of Supremacy Clause:** [§226] Article VI, Section 2 (the "Supremacy Clause") provides: "The Constitution and the Laws of the United States which shall be made in pursuance thereof . . . shall be the supreme Law of the Land. . . ." The effect of this clause is that to whatever extent Congress has exercised its powers, any "inconsistent" state laws are prohibited.

(1) **"Inconsistency" of state law:** [§227] A state law will be held void under the Supremacy Clause if it would retard, impede, burden, or otherwise stand as an obstacle to the accomplishment and execution of the full purposes and objectives of Congress in enacting the federal law. [McCulloch v. Maryland, *supra*, §122—state law that sought to impose tax on Bank of United States, created by Congress, held void as burden on federal power to regulate currency under art. I, §8, cl. 5]

(a) **Note:** This is true even where the state law was enacted for some ***valid purpose****—i.e.,* where not intended to frustrate federal law. [Perez v. Campbell, 402 U.S. 637 (1971)]

(b) **Example:** A state law provided for suspension of the driver's license of any person who failed to pay off a judgment against him arising out of an auto accident, regardless of that person's discharge in bankruptcy. The state law had a valid purpose (keeping irresponsible drivers off road), but impeded the purpose of the Federal Bankruptcy Act (giving discharged debtors a new start) by forcing persons to pay off discharged judgments if they wanted to drive a car. [Perez v. Campbell, *supra*]

(2) **Where Congress has not yet acted:** [§228] Normally, the Supremacy Clause applies only where Congress has exercised its power; until then, the states are free to regulate subject matter that is clearly within the federal power. [Sturges v . Crowninshield, 17 U.S. (4 Wheat.) 122 (1819)—upholding state bankruptcy laws, because no federal bankruptcy law had yet been enacted]

(a) **But note:** As to certain federal powers (*e.g.,* the commerce power), the mere existence of the federal power is held to inhibit state power to some degree (*see infra*, §§290-291).

B. INTERGOVERNMENTAL PRIVILEGES AND IMMUNITIES

1. **National Citizenship:** [§229] The Fourteenth Amendment provides in part: "No State shall make or enforce any law which shall abridge the ***privileges or immunities of citizens*** of the United States."

a. **What constitutes "privileges and immunities" of national citizenship:** [§230] These privileges and immunities have been limited to those rights that ***arise out of the relationship of the individual and the national government.*** [Twining v. New Jersey, 211 U.S. 78 (1908)]

(1) **Examples:** Among the rights and privileges of national citizenship that may not be infringed by state action are the right to pass freely from state to state; the right to petition Congress for redress of grievances; the right to vote for national officers; the right to assemble peaceably; and the right to discuss matters growing out of valid national legislation and to communicate with respect to them. [Twining v. New Jersey, *supra*]

(2) **Note:** The right to travel freely from state to state has also been grounded on other sections of the Constitution; *see* below.

b. **Bill of Rights not included:** [§231] However, the Court in the *Slaughter-house Cases,* 83 U.S. (16 Wall.) 36 (1873), held that the fundamental rights protected against federal action by the first eight amendments to the Constitution were ***not*** "privileges and immunities of national citizenship" so as to be protected from state action under the Fourteenth Amendment Privileges and Immunities Clause.

(1) **Effect:** The decision rendered the Fourteenth Amendment Privileges and Immunities Clause largely a dead letter in protecting individual rights from state abridgment. Subsequently, the Court has relied on the Fourteenth Amendment Due Process and Equal Protection Clauses to provide basic protection of individual rights against state action. (*See infra,* §§401 *et seq.*)

c. **Compare—Enabling Clause:** [§232] While the Privileges and Immunities Clause of the Fourteenth Amendment has not in itself proved to be a significant limitation on state power, the same amendment contains an ***Enabling Clause*** (section 5), which authorizes ***Congress*** "to enforce, by appropriate legislation, the provisions of this article." As discussed below, this Enabling Clause is an important ***source of federal power—i.e.,*** to protect the "privileges and immunities" of the citizenry from violation by the states, or even from the acts of other citizens (*see infra,* §§692 *et seq.*).

2. **State Citizenship:** [§233] Article IV, Section 2 (interstate privileges and immunities) provides: "The Citizens of each State shall be entitled to all Privileges and Immunities of Citizens in the several States."

a. **General rule:** [§234] This clause prohibits state discrimination against noncitizens (or nonresidents) of the state in respect to "essential activities" or "basic rights" (such as access to courts), unless the discrimination is ***closely*** or ***substantially related*** to a ***substantial*** state purpose. [Hicklin v. Orbeck, 437 U.S. 518 (1978)] In deciding this question, the Court considers the availability of ***less restrictive means.*** [Supreme Court of New Hampshire v. Piper, 470 U.S. 274 (1985)]

(1) **Municipal residency:** [§235] State action that discriminates against noncitizens (or nonresidents) of a particular municipality within the state is subject to the strictures of this clause. [United Building & Construction Trades Council v. Mayor & Council of Camden, 465 U.S. 208 (1984)]

(2) **Corporations and aliens:** [§236] Corporations and aliens are not "citizens of a state" within the meaning of this clause and thus are ***not*** entitled to its protection. [Bank of Augusta v. Earle, 38 U.S. 519 (1839)]

b. **Examples—invalid discrimination:** [§237] The following have been held invalid by the Court.

(1) ***Statute requiring $2,500 license fee from nonresident*** commercial fishermen seeking shrimp offshore, while residents paid $25, involved essential activity of "pursuing a livelihood" without substantial justification related to state costs or enforcement. [Toomer v. Witsell, 334 U.S. 385 (1948)]

(2) ***Statute giving resident creditors priority*** over nonresident creditors to assets of foreign corporations in receivership proceedings involved basic rights of "ownership and disposition of property." [Blake v. McClung, 172 U.S. 239 (1898)]

(3) ***Statute imposing a residency requirement for abortions*** involved the basic right to seek medical care. [Doe v. Bolton, 410 U.S. 179 (1973)]

(4) ***State law requiring employers to give hiring preference*** to residents involved essential activity of "pursuing a livelihood" and the law was not closely related to solving peculiar state unemployment problems. [Hicklin v. Orbeck, *supra*]

(5) ***Rule limiting bar admission*** to state residents involved basic right to pursue an occupation. [Supreme Court of Virginia v. Friedman, 487 U.S. 59 (1988); Supreme Court of New Hampshire v. Piper, *supra*]

c. **Example—discrimination upheld:** [§238] A statute requiring nonresidents to pay $225 license fee (as opposed to $30 resident fee) for recreational hunting was upheld. [Baldwin v. Fish & Game Commission, 436 U.S. 371 (1978)—no "essential activity" or "basic right" involved]

(1) **State ownership:** [§239] The Court has *stated* that a discrimination against nonresidents will be given special—but not conclusive—weight if its purpose is conservation of ***state-owned*** natural resources. [Hicklin v. Orbeck, *supra*; *and see* Sporhase v. Nebraska, 458 U.S. 941 (1982)—scarce water resources]

d. **Relationship to Commerce Clause:** [§240] Although the Interstate Privileges and Immunities Clause and the Commerce Clause may apply different standards and may produce different results (*see infra*, §302), they do tend to "mutually reinforce" each other. [Hicklin v. Orbeck, *supra*] Consequently, issues arising under Article IV, Section 2 may be decided on the basis of the Commerce Clause limitation on state regulation of interstate commerce. (*See infra*, §§261 *et seq.*)

C. INTERGOVERNMENTAL IMMUNITY

1. **In General:** [§241] The Supremacy Clause places certain implied limitations on state power to regulate and tax the property and activities of the federal government, and the Tenth Amendment places such limitations on federal power to regulate and tax the property and activities of state governments.

a. **Intergovernmental differences:** [§242] Under modern doctrine, federal property and activities enjoy a greater immunity from state regulation and taxation than the states are afforded from federal regulation and taxation.

(1) **Rationale:** The states are represented in Congress and have political voice therein—but the federal government has no similar political representation in state government. Thus, the Court infers a greater immunity for the federal government.

2. **Federal Regulation of State Governments:** [§243] The Tenth Amendment preserves "a significant measure of sovereign authority" for the states and limits the federal government's regulatory power to interfere with state and local functions. But the Court has held that ordinarily these state interests are more properly protected by the inherent restraints of state participation that are built into the structure of the federal system (*e.g.*, state representation in Congress) than by judicial review. Thus—at least absent a showing of "some extraordinary defects" in the procedural safeguards for the states in the national political process—the ***Court*** will ***not*** find that an otherwise permissible exercise of congressional power violates the Tenth Amendment because it regulates the states as well as private persons. [Garcia v. San Antonio Metropolitan Transit Authority, 469 U.S. 528 (1985), *overruling* National League of Cities v. Usery, 426 U.S. 833 (1976)—Congress has power under Commerce Clause to apply federal minimum wage and overtime provisions to state employees]

   a. **Exception—using states to implement regulations:** [§244] The Tenth Amendment ***does place limits***, however, on Congress's power to regulate the ***states alone*** by directing the states to act in a particular way. Congress may hold out ***incentives*** to influence a state's policy choices—*e.g.*, by attaching conditions to the receipt of federal funds [*see* South Dakota v. Dole, *supra*, §141], or by offering states the choice of regulating in accord with federal standards rather than being preempted by federal law. However, Congress may not ***compel*** states to enact or enforce a federal regulatory program. *Rationale:* Federal direction of state regulation will insulate federal officials from political accountability. [New York v. United States, 112 S. Ct. 2408 (1992)—federal statute requiring states to either regulate radioactive waste or take title to the waste is ***compulsion,*** not encouragement, and thus is beyond Congress's power]

3. **Federal Taxation of State Governments:** [§245] Although the Court has not so held, the same general rule seemingly applies to federal taxation of the property and activities of state and local governments. [*See* New York v. United States, 326 U.S. 572 (1946)—sale of mineral waters by state is subject to a general federal excise tax; South Carolina v. Baker, 485 U.S. 505 (1988)—state bond interest may be subject to nondiscriminatory federal tax]

4. **State Taxation of Federal Government**

   a. **When Congress has spoken:** [§246] Pursuant to its delegated powers (and the Necessary and Proper Clause), Congress has complete power to regulate state taxation of federal property and activities. Congress may permit (or consent to) state taxes that, absent federal legislation, would be impliedly forbidden by the Constitution. Or, Congress may immunize federal activities as to which, absent such legislation, state taxes would not be forbidden.

   b. **When Congress has not spoken:** [§247] Absent federal legislation, the Court assumes that Congress intended all implied constitutional limitations on state taxation to apply. In general, the Supremacy Clause impliedly forbids (i) state taxes that ***discriminate*** against federal property or activities, and (ii) nondiscriminatory state taxes that ***"unduly interfere"*** with or place a ***"substantial burden"*** on the federal government. In determining these questions, the Court applies the following rules:

(1) **No tax on federal property or activity:** [§248] States may not tax the property or activities of the federal government itself—or of federal agencies. [McCulloch v. Maryland, *supra*, §227]

(2) **Tax on those dealing with federal government:** [§249] States may tax persons who merely contract or deal with the federal government as long as the tax does not discriminate against such persons by taxing them and not other persons similarly situated. [United States v. Fresno County, 429 U.S. 452 (1977)] *Examples:*

(a) **State income tax:** [§250] The state income tax may be applied to the salaries of federal employees within the state. [Graves v. New York *ex rel.* O'Keefe, 306 U.S. 466 (1939)—tax did not unduly interfere with federal functions; and although there is economic burden on United States because it will have to pay higher salaries, burden is not substantial]

(b) **State sales tax:** [§251] The state sales tax may be applied to purchases made by a person who has a "cost-plus" contract with the United States. [Alabama v. King & Boozer, 314 U.S. 1 (1941)—tax upheld even though cost is passed on to the United States, and it is thus economically burdened]

1) **Legal incidence determinative:** [§252] As long as the legal incidence of the tax does not fall on the United States, the fact that it results in an economic burden on a United States function will not invalidate it.

a) **Note:** If the ***United States*** itself actually purchases the goods to be used by the "cost-plus" contractor, a state sales tax may not be applied to the purchase—since the legal incidence of the tax would fall on the federal government itself. [Kern-Limerick, Inc. v. Scurlock, 347 U.S. 110 (1954)] The rule against taxes on the United States applies even though the economic effect is the same whether the purchase is made by the United States or a "cost-plus" contractor.

b) **And note:** If state law requires that a sales tax be passed on to the purchaser and collected by the vendor, the legal incidence of the tax is on the purchaser. Thus, the tax may not be applied when the United States or its instrumentality is the purchaser. [United States v. Mississippi Tax Commission, 421 U.S. 599 (1975)]

(c) **State property tax:** [§253] Federal property may be used to measure a nondiscriminatory state tax on persons who deal with the United States. [Detroit v. Murray Corp., 355 U.S. 489 (1958)—state property tax measured by value of property upheld as applied to contractor who used property owned by the United States]

1) **Compare—tax on United States property:** [§254] If the property is subject to a lien for unpaid taxes, the tax may be construed as being one on United States property itself—and

thus invalid—even if the state does not seek to hold the United States liable, but attempts to collect from a person who uses or possesses it. [United States v. Detroit, 355 U.S. 466 (1958)]

2) **Considerations:** [§255] The Court will consider all relevant circumstances in determining whether the state tax is on United States property (invalid) or on a person dealing with the United States and merely measured by United States property (valid).

3) **Illustration of nondiscriminatory tax:** [§256] A state tax on all private persons using real property whose owners were tax-exempt is valid as applied to the lessee of federal property. It does not discriminate against those who deal with the United States if it also applies to those who used the property of other tax-exempt owners—*i.e.,* the state and its political subdivisions, churches, charitable organizations, etc. Also, those who use property that is not tax-exempt pay higher rent (because the owner passes on the property tax she pays). [United States v. Detroit, *supra*]

(3) **Discrimination:** [§257] In determining whether a state tax discriminates against those who deal with the federal government, the state's whole tax structure is examined. Thus, a special tax may be imposed on contractors who deal with the federal government as long as the economic burdens that result do not discriminate against the United States. [Washington v. United States, 460 U.S. 536 (1983)—special tax valid; general tax on purchasers from contractors was not imposed on federal government because of its immunity]

5. **State Regulation of Federal Government:** [§258] Congress has complete power to forbid or permit state regulation of federal property or activities. But absent consent by Congress, the Supremacy Clause impliedly immunizes the instrumentalities and agents of the federal government from state regulations that interfere with the performance of federal functions. [Hancock v. Train, 426 U.S. 167 (1976)] The state regulation is also invalid if inconsistent with the policy of a federal statute.

a. **Examples:** A post office employee need not obtain a state driver's license to perform his official duty of driving a mail truck. [Johnson v. Maryland, 254 U.S. 51 (1920)] And a federal contractor need not obtain a state license to construct facilities at an Air Force base pursuant to government contract. [Leslie Miller, Inc. v. Arkansas, 352 U.S. 187 (1956)]

b. **Federal lands:** [§259] Article IV, Section 3, Clause 2 gives Congress power "to dispose of and make all needful rules and regulations respecting" lands of the United States. Thus, federal enclaves (*e.g.,* federal Indian reservations, military bases, post offices) are subject to state regulation only to the extent that the state, when ceding the land to the federal government, reserved jurisdiction, or to the extent that Congress has enacted legislation granting jurisdiction to the state. [United States v. Sharpnack, 355 U.S. 286 (1958)—federal legislation authorizing application of state criminal laws to federal enclaves upheld against challenge of excessive delegation]

III. REGULATION AND TAXATION OF COMMERCE

chapter approach

This chapter focuses on the concurrent power of the states and the federal government to regulate and tax interstate commerce and the power of the states to regulate and tax interstate and foreign commerce.

1. **Regulation of Foreign Commerce:** All you need to know here is that ***only the federal government*** can regulate foreign commerce.

2. **Regulation of Interstate Commerce**

   a. **By federal government:** If your examination question involves federal government regulation of interstate commerce, the exercise is ***most likely valid***. The Commerce Clause grants Congress the power to regulate commerce among the states, and this power has been broadly held to extend to the regulation of the ***channels or facilities*** of interstate commerce (*e.g.*, transmission facilities) and to any ***activity affecting more than one state*** (which includes seemingly local concerns, such as a farmer's production of wheat for home consumption, which affects what he will buy from interstate commerce). The only clear limitations on this power are the specific limitations imposed elsewhere in the Constitution (*e.g.*, in the Bill of Rights).

   b. **By state:** On the other hand, if your examination question involves state regulation of interstate commerce, use the following approach:

      (1) **Where Congress has acted:** First you must review federal legislation in the area, because Congress's acts are controlling. Recall that Congress ***may authorize*** state regulations that otherwise would violate the Commerce Clause (because the regulations discriminate against interstate commerce) or ***may prohibit*** state regulation that would otherwise be valid. However, on an exam, there usually will be no express congressional authorization or prohibition. Thus, if there is federal legislation concerning an area, but Congress was silent as to states' rights to act, look to Congress's intent. A ***conflicting*** state law will be held invalid, and ***any*** state law (whether or not conflicting) will be invalid if Congress is found to have ***preempted*** the field.

      (2) **Where Congress has not acted:** If there is no federal legislation at all in an area, states may regulate local transactions even though the transactions affect interstate commerce. However, watch for state laws that ***discriminate*** against interstate commerce. These are almost always invalid unless (i) they are necessary to protect noneconomic interests (*e.g.*, health and safety) ***and*** there are no reasonable alternative ways to protect those interests or (ii) the state is a market participant. If state regulation does ***not discriminate*** against interstate commerce, but does burden it, the Court will ***balance the burden*** against the strength of the state's interest to determine whether it is reasonable.

3. **State Taxation of Interstate Commerce:** Your approach to state taxation of interstate commerce is basically the same as for state regulation of interstate commerce: First see

whether Congress has acted; recall that Congress has complete power to authorize or forbid state taxation that affects interstate commerce. If there is no federal legislation, watch for ***discriminatory*** state action. Unless authorized by Congress, a state tax that discriminates against interstate commerce is ***invalid***. If the tax is ***nondiscriminatory***, the Court will ***balance*** the state's need for revenue against the burden on interstate commerce. Remember that the Commerce Clause prohibits multiple burdens and the Due Process Clause requires a nexus to the taxing state. Be sure to identify the type of tax levied (*e.g.*, property tax, sales tax, etc.).

4. **State Taxation of Foreign Commerce:** Again, the federal government has the ultimate power over foreign commerce. Thus, a state tax on imported goods, as such, is ***invalid*** without congressional consent, as is a tax on exports that have entered into the stream of exportation.

A. REGULATION OF FOREIGN COMMERCE—EXCLUSIVE FEDERAL POWER [§260]

Regulation of foreign commerce is exclusively a federal power. *Rationale:* The federal government must speak with one voice when regulating commercial relations with foreign governments. [Michelin Tire Corp. v. Wages, 423 U.S. 276 (1976)]

B. REGULATION OF INTERSTATE COMMERCE

1. **Concurrent Power:** [§261] The federal power to regulate interstate commerce is concurrent with state power over transactions within the state. Thus, the Court has frequently been called upon to determine the respective scope of federal power and state power in regulating interstate commerce.

2. **Scope of Federal Power:** [§262] The Commerce Clause [Art. I, §8, cl. 3] grants Congress the power "to regulate commerce . . . among the several states." There are ***two principal theories*** upon which congressional exercise of the commerce power may be upheld: (i) Congress's power over the ***channels or facilities*** of interstate commerce and (ii) Congress's power over activities that have a "***national economic effect***."

   a. **"Channels" or "facilities" of interstate commerce:** [§263] Congress has ***plenary*** power to regulate the "channels" and "facilities" of interstate commerce. This includes power over interstate carriers, roads, and transmission facilities (among other things).

      (1) **Federal "police power":** [§264] This plenary power includes the authority to ***exclude*** from shipment or travel in the channels of interstate commerce any goods, persons, or activities found by Congress to be harmful to the public health, safety, welfare, or morals.

         (a) **Motive irrelevant:** [§265] Congress's motive in enacting the regulation is irrelevant. Thus, Congress may exclude from interstate commerce:

1) ***Goods harmful*** to interstate commerce itself—*e.g.,* diseased animals that might infect other animals in interstate transit.

2) ***Commercial items*** generally—*e.g.,* lottery tickets [Lottery Case, 188 U.S. 321 (1903)], or goods produced under substandard conditions [United States v. Darby Lumber, 312 U.S. 100 (1941)].

3) ***Noncommercial items***—*e.g.,* persons fleeing prosecution or persons kidnapping others. [Gooch v. United States, 297 U.S. 124 (1936)]

(b) **Furthering state law:** [§266] The federal "police power" includes congressional power to further state laws or policies—*e.g.,* a federal statute banning interstate transportation of convict-made goods into a state where their receipt, sale, or possession is unlawful. [Kentucky Whip & Collar Co. v. Illinois Central Railroad, 299 U.S. 334 (1937)]

(2) **Regulation after interstate commerce "ends":** [§267] The federal commerce power is broad enough to allow regulation even after interstate commerce has ended. For example, a congressional requirement that labels on bottles that have been in interstate commerce be retained ***after*** the shipment ends has been upheld. [McDermott v. Wisconsin, 228 U.S. 115 (1913)] *Rationale:* This made inspection convenient; *i.e.,* it assured that the bottles were so labeled while they were ***in*** interstate commerce.

(a) **Note:** This "convenience of inspection" rationale has been extended to a requirement that labels be placed on ***different*** containers into which contents were transferred after interstate shipment—even as to persons who had not directly received the interstate shipment, but had obtained the contents from a local merchant who had received them from interstate commerce. [United States v. Sullivan, 332 U.S. 689 (1948)]

(b) **Power not unlimited:** [§268] The decisions above concern federal statutes governing the ***condition*** of goods. They do not hold that Congress may regulate the ***use*** of such goods after they come to rest within a state (*e.g.,* a statute fixing the price at which such goods may be sold locally).

1) **Activities of persons in interstate commerce:** [§269] Nor do the cases hold that Congress may regulate the activities of persons who have been in interstate commerce once their interstate travel has ended—although Congress may prohibit persons from using the facilities of interstate commerce to accomplish certain ends (and may seek to prove the user's purpose by pointing to acts engaged in shortly after interstate commerce ended).

2) **"Intrastate" commerce:** [§270] There ***may*** be a limit to this basis of congressional power on the theory that, at some point,

the subject of regulation has become local or "intrastate"—although a congressional power to regulate might still be found under the "national economic effect" theory (below).

b. **"National economic effect":** [§271] Congress has the power to regulate all "commerce" or "activity" that ***affects more than one state***. [NLRB v. Jones & Laughlin Steel Corp., 301 U.S. 1 (1937)]

(1) **Scope of power:** [§272] This power to regulate includes the power to ***prohibit*** as well as to ***encourage*** both ***commercial and noncommercial*** activities. And since an activity that takes place ***wholly intrastate*** may still affect other states, it is subject to congressional regulation under this theory. *Examples:*

(a) ***An intrastate railroad*** carrying goods produced and sold locally is subject to the commerce power because local markets compete with markets in other states. Thus, the railroad's rates and services have an effect in those other states, and may be regulated under the commerce power. [Shreveport Rate Case, 234 U.S. 342 (1914)]

(b) ***A factory that produces goods within the state*** may have working conditions regulated by Congress if the goods compete with goods produced in other states, because substandard working conditions may destroy competition, thus having an effect in other states. [United States v. Darby Lumber, *supra*, §265]

(c) ***A factory that produces goods to be sold both locally and interstate*** may have ***all*** of its working conditions regulated by Congress, since labor strife among employees producing local goods may affect employees producing interstate goods, thus having an effect in other states. [Maryland v. Wirtz, 392 U.S. 183 (1968)]

(d) ***A motel that serves interstate travelers*** may be barred from engaging in racial discrimination, since such discrimination may deter persons from traveling, thus having an effect in other states. [Heart of Atlanta Motel, Inc. v. United States, 379 U.S. 241 (1964)]

(e) ***A restaurant that purchases supplies from other states*** may be barred from racial discrimination under the commerce power, since such discrimination may affect the quantity of the restaurant's business, thus having an effect in other states. [Katzenbach v. McClung, 379 U.S. 294 (1964)] *Note:* The Court has observed that racial unrest has a generally depressant effect on business. This indicates a broad power in Congress, under the Commerce Clause, to regulate all forms of racial discrimination, because locally depressed business will affect those in other states who deal with the local business.

(f) ***A farmer who grows wheat for home consumption*** may have production regulated under the commerce power, since the more the farmer produces, the less the farmer will buy, thereby affecting the demand for wheat and its interstate price. [Wickard v. Filburn, 317 U.S. 111 (1942)]

(g) ***Coal companies that strip-mine land previously used for farming*** may be required to reclaim land and comply with other extensive regulations, since strip-mining, rather than farming, may create environmental problems and affect agricultural production in other states. [Hodel v. Virginia Surface Mining & Reclamation Association, 452 U.S. 264 (1981); Hodel v. Indiana, 452 U.S. 314 (1981)]

(2) **Congressional findings:** [§273] If Congress has made findings that the activity in question affects more than one state, the Court will give great deference to the findings, upholding them if they rest on "any rational basis." [Hodel v. Virginia Surface Mining & Reclamation Association, *supra*] However, the Court has ***suggested*** that such findings are ***not*** required and that it will assume what Congress ***could have found***. [Perez v. United States, 402 U.S. 146 (1971)]

(3) **Volume of commerce affected:** [§274] The fact that any single business or individual regulated by Congress has only a small impact on interstate commerce is immaterial. The crucial question is whether there is an ***aggregate*** effect on other states by the ***class of activities*** regulated. [NLRB v. Fainblatt, 306 U.S. 601 (1939)]

(a) **Example:** The intrastate activity of "loan sharking" may affect interstate commerce and thus may be made criminal by Congress—and the courts have no power "to excise, as trivial, individual instances of the class." [Perez v. United States, *supra*]

(4) **Limitless power?** [§275] Virtually every business engages in activity that affects more than one state—whether as a consumer (or source) of goods or services from (or for) interstate commerce (directly or secondarily), or in competing with others offering such goods or services. Thus, the "national economic effect" theory appears to encompass an almost limitless power, permitting congressional regulation of all activities ***except*** those that (i) are ***completely internal*** to a single state [Gibbons v. Ogden, 22 U.S. 1 (1824)], or (ii) so ***remotely*** (or ***trivially***) ***affect*** other states that to uphold congressional regulations would obliterate our concept of federalism [NLRB v. Jones & Laughlin Steel Corp., *supra,* §271].

(a) **"Substantial" effect required?** [§276] A number of more modern opinions have stated that the intrastate activity regulated by Congress must have "a ***substantial relationship*** to interstate commerce" [North American Co. v. SEC, 327 U.S. 686 (1946)], or "a ***substantial effect***" on interstate commerce [Heart of Atlanta Motel, Inc. v. United States, *supra*, §272]. *But note:* Most recently, the Court has stated that "the pertinent inquiry" is ***not how much*** commerce is involved, but whether Congress ***could rationally conclude*** that the regulated activity affects interstate commerce. [Hodel v. Indiana, *supra*, §272]

1) **Comment:** Whether or not a "substantial" effect is required, because Congress's power under the Commerce Clause is extremely broad, the Court's major function respecting federal

statutes enacted under the Commerce Clause is one of ***statutory interpretation***: Did Congress ***intend*** its regulation to apply to the particular activity involved in the case?

(b) **Individual rights limitations:** [§277] The only clear limitations on the commerce power are the specific limits imposed elsewhere in the Constitution (*e.g.,* in the Bill of Rights). For example, if Congress forbade wheat production by Catholics only, the act would violate the First Amendment and would be invalid even though regulation of wheat would generally be valid under the Commerce Clause.

3. **State Regulation of Interstate Commerce:** [§278] Although the federal power over interstate commerce is potentially "all pervasive," it is ***not*** exclusive. The issue to be considered is the extent to which states may exercise regulatory power in this area. This question turns significantly on whether there is relevant federal legislation.

a. **Power of Congress to permit or prohibit state regulation:** [§279] In addition to giving Congress virtually unlimited regulatory power (as noted above), the Commerce Clause gives Congress ***complete*** authority to permit or prohibit state regulation of what is concededly interstate commerce; *i.e.,* the Court judges state regulation of interstate commerce ***under the Commerce Clause*** (*see infra*, §290) only when Congress has ***not*** enacted relevant federal legislation.

(1) **Where Congress expressly authorizes or prohibits state regulation:** [§280] Congress may authorize—or permit, or approve of—state regulations that would otherwise violate the Commerce Clause. Likewise, Congress may prohibit state regulations that could otherwise be upheld under the Commerce Clause.

(a) **Example:** When authorized by Congress, a state statute that actually discriminated against interstate insurance companies has been upheld by the Court. [Prudential Insurance Co. v. Benjamin, 328 U.S. 408 (1946)]

(b) **Equal protection limitation:** [§281] Although state regulations that discriminate against interstate commerce are immune from attack under the Commerce Clause when authorized by Congress, Congress cannot authorize the states to violate the Equal Protection Clause. (*See infra*, §710.) Thus, a congressionally authorized state statute discriminating against interstate commerce by imposing a higher tax on out-of-state insurance companies than on domestic insurance companies has been held to violate equal protection where the state's only purpose was to protect local economic interests; this was ***not*** a "legitimate" state purpose. [Metropolitan Life Insurance Co. v. Ward, 470 U.S. 869 (1985)]

1) **Example of "legitimate" state purpose:** A California statute, authorized by Congress, discriminated against interstate insurance companies whose home states discriminated against California insurance companies. The Court found no equal

protection violation; California had a "legitimate" purpose—*i.e.,* to deter other states from discriminating against interstate commerce. [Western & Southern Life Insurance Co. v. California Board of Equalization, 451 U.S. 648 (1981)]

2) **Scope uncertain:** The reach of the *Metropolitan Life Insurance* case, *supra*, is uncertain. In *Northeast Bancorp, Inc. v. Board of Governors,* 472 U.S. 159 (1985), a Connecticut statute, authorized by Congress, permitted only local companies and out-of-state companies from New England to acquire local banks. Although the statute's purpose seemed no different than that in *Metropolitan Life Insurance*, the Court found no equal protection violation, stressing that banking is "of profound local concern."

(c) **Congressional reversal of Court:** [§282] An "authorizing" or "prohibiting" enactment by Congress can change a prior decision of the Court regarding state regulation of interstate commerce. [*In re* Rahrer, 140 U.S. 545 (1891); Clark Distilling Co. v. Western Maryland Railroad, 242 U.S. 311 (1917)—federal statutes authorizing state regulation of liquor shipped into state from interstate commerce, enacted after such regulations were held invalid in Leisy v. Hardin, 135 U.S. 100 (1890)]

(2) **Where no express congressional authorization or prohibition of state law—"supersession" or "preemption" doctrine:** [§283] When there is relevant federal legislation, but no express authorization or prohibition of state law, the Court determines whether the ***general intent*** of the relevant federal statute authorizes or forbids the state regulation in question. State regulations are invalid under the ***Supremacy Clause*** [Art. VI, §2] where found to be superseded by ***conflicting federal law***, or where federal law is held to ***preempt*** (or occupy) the entire field.

(a) **Rationale:** The issue is one of statutory construction, based on the federal law's ***language*** and ***legislative history***: Does the state regulation conflict with the federal statute? Or if there is no "direct" conflict, did Congress intend to provide complete national regulation of the subject matter, thereby excluding ***any*** state regulation, even one that reinforces or compliments the federal regulation? [Campbell v. Hussey, 368 U.S. 297 (1961)]

(b) **Applicability of doctrine beyond interstate commerce area:** [§284] When Congress properly enacts legislation pursuant to ***any*** of its delegated powers, state regulations that conflict are invalid because of the ***Supremacy Clause***. Similarly, if congressional legislation is found by the Court to be intended to occupy the entire field, state laws are preempted. Thus, the Court has periodically avoided constitutional challenges to a state regulation by finding that a federal statute either conflicts with it or preempts the field.

1) **Example:** A state sedition law, challenged as violating freedom of speech and due process, was held invalid because a series of

federal "anti-communist" statutes "evince a congressional plan . . . as to make reasonable the inference that Congress left no room for the States to supplement it." [Pennsylvania v. Nelson, 350 U.S. 497 (1956)]

(c) **Factors in determining congressional intent:** [§285] The Court examines the entire text of the federal statute(s), legislative history, and administrative interpretations to determine whether Congress intended to occupy the entire field. Significant factors are:

1) **Interest in uniform, national regulation:** [§286] Wherever it finds that the subject matter requires uniform national regulation or is of "inherent national interest" the Court usually holds that Congress intended to occupy the field completely and to supersede state regulation.

a) **Example:** The Alien Registration Act, a federal statute that simply required aliens to register with the government, was held to preempt a state law requiring that aliens register annually and carry a registration card to show to state officials. The Court stressed that the field of aliens and immigration "affects international relations, the one aspect of our government that from the first has been most generally conceded imperatively to demand broad national authority." [Hines v. Davidowitz, 312 U.S. 52 (1941)]

2) **Historical or traditional classification of subject matter as federal or local:** [§287] Where the subject matter has traditionally been the subject of local regulation, the Court is less likely to find federal preemption. [Rice v. Santa Fe Elevator Co., 331 U.S. 218 (1947)—regulation of public warehouses] This is particularly true with respect to state laws designed to protect the public health or safety of local citizens. Congress is not deemed to have intended to supersede such state laws unless the intent is clearly manifested (or the state law actually conflicts with federal law). [Maurer v. Hamilton, 309 U.S. 598 (1940)—safety on highways]

3) **Completeness of federal regulatory scheme:** [§288] The more complete the federal regulation, the more likely it is that Congress will be held to have intended to occupy the entire field and supersede state regulation. [Pennsylvania v. Nelson, *supra*]

4) **Coincidence between federal and state statutes:** [§289] A similarity or identity between federal and state regulations suggests a congressional intent to supersede. However, such similarity is not a controlling factor [California v. Zook, 366 U.S. 725 (1949)], and may be given little weight if the purpose of the federal statute is not frustrated by the identical state statute [Colorado Anti-Discrimination Commission v. Continental

Airlines, Inc., 372 U.S. 714 (1963)], or if it is possible to comply with both regulations [Florida Lime & Avocado Growers, Inc. v. Paul, 373 U.S. 132 (1963)].

b. **Power of states to regulate where Congress has not acted:** [§290] Where Congress has ***not*** enacted legislation regarding the subject matter, states may regulate local transactions even though the transactions affect interstate commerce—subject to certain limitations.

(1) **Discrimination:** [§291] State regulations that discriminate against interstate commerce—*i.e.,* single out such commerce for regulation or impose more burdensome regulations on interstate commerce than on comparable local commerce—are ***almost always*** (*see infra*, §§298, 299) ***invalid*** as an invasion of the federal commerce power. *Rationale:* A primary concern of the Framers was to combat economic protectionism by the states which had led to retaliatory economic warfare among the states.

(a) **Illustrations**

1) **Excluding incoming trade:** [§292] A state statute that excludes entry of products from another state in order to further the economic interests of a local industry violates the Commerce Clause. [*See* Edwards v. California, 314 U.S. 160 (1941)—state statute prohibiting persons from bringing nonresident indigent persons into state violates Commerce Clause]

a) **Protection of environment:** [§293] A state statute that excludes entry of products from another state in order to further the state's environmental goals also violates the Commerce Clause. [Philadelphia v. New Jersey, 437 U.S. 617 (1978)—statute that excluded wastes from outside state to conserve state's remaining landfill space and to reduce pollution held insufficient to justify discrimination against interstate commerce]

2) **Requiring higher price for incoming trade:** [§294] A state statute that requires that a higher price be paid for goods coming from interstate commerce violates the Commerce Clause. [Welton v. Missouri, 91 U.S. 275 (1876)—special license tax on those who sold goods produced outside the state]

3) **Restricting outgoing trade:** [§295] A state statute restricting export of goods or resources from within the state in order to benefit local industries and consumers violates the Commerce Clause. [H.P. Hood & Sons v. DuMond, 336 U.S. 525 (1949)—to protect local supply of milk, state refused to permit company to open a milk receiving depot from which it would ship milk out-of-state]

a) **Conservation of natural resources:** [§296] A state statute restricting export of fish taken from the state's waters violates the Commerce Clause. [Hughes v. Oklahoma, 441 U.S. 322 (1979)—legitimate state interest not enough to justify state discrimination against interstate commerce; *and see* Sporhase v. Nebraska, 458 U.S. 941 (1982)—although public ownership of ground water is "not without significance," state restriction on export of ground water is invalid because it "does not survive the 'strictest scrutiny' reserved for facially discriminatory legislation"]

4) **Requiring performance of business operations locally:** [§297] A state statute requiring that state products be processed within the state before being shipped in interstate commerce violates the Commerce Clause. [Pike v. Bruce Church, Inc., 397 U.S. 137 (1970)—requirement that home-grown cantaloupes be packaged within the state before shipment]

a) **Example:** Similarly, a state statute prohibiting the sale of meat not inspected within the state violates the Commerce Clause because it discriminates against out-of-state slaughterhouses (*i.e.,* it prevents importation of sound meat from animals slaughtered in other states). [Minnesota v. Barber, 136 U.S. 313 (1890)]

(b) **Exception—absence of alternatives:** [§298] Although state regulations that discriminate against interstate commerce ***almost always*** violate the Commerce Clause (unless there is congressional authorization, *see supra,* §280), they are ***not automatically*** invalid. Rather, the Court has said that they may be upheld to protect ***health and safety*** (*i.e.,* ***noneconomic***) interests if there are ***no reasonable and adequate nondiscriminatory alternatives*** available. [Dean Milk Co. v. City of Madison, 340 U.S. 349 (1951)]

1) **Example:** A Maine statute that discriminated against interstate commerce by prohibiting the importation of live baitfish was upheld. The statute served a "legitimate local purpose" (live baitfish from other states posed health threats to Maine's unique and fragile fisheries and there was no developed means of inspection to detect parasites, etc.) and that purpose could not "be served as well by available nondiscriminatory means." [Maine v. Taylor, 476 U.S. 1138 (1986)]

2) **Compare:** A state law made it unlawful to sell milk unless pasteurized within five miles of the city. The law was held ***invalid*** as it discriminated in favor of local pasteurizing businesses and there were nondiscriminatory alternatives available to assure milk's quality. [Dean Milk Co. v. City of Madison, *supra*]

(c) **Exception—state as market participant:** [§299] The Commerce Clause does not prevent a state, when acting as a purchaser (or seller) of goods, from buying only from (or selling only to) local business or from giving subsidies only to its residents. [Hughes v.

Alexandria Scrap Corp., 426 U.S. 794 (1976); Reeves, Inc. v. Stake, 447 U.S. 429 (1980)] Such discrimination merely affects a market created by a state's own purchase (or subsidies), and the state is thus a market participant, rather than a market regulator.

1) **State expenditures:** [§300] A state (or city) acts as a market participant when it funds public construction projects. Thus, it may require contractors to give a hiring preference to local residents for work on such projects—although there are limits on a state's (or city's) ability to impose such preference on private contractors beyond those who are immediate parties to the contract. [White v. Massachusetts Council of Construction Employers, 460 U.S. 204 (1983)]

2) **"Downstream" restrictions:** [§301] It is ***doubtful*** whether a state may impose restrictions on the subsequent use of goods purchased from the state—*e.g.,* that timber from the state must be processed in the state. [South-Central Timber Development, Inc. v. Wunnicke, 467 U.S. 82 (1984)—no holding by a majority of the Court]

3) **Interstate Privileges and Immunities Clause:** [§302] State regulations or expenditures that discriminate against out-of-staters ***are subject*** to the standard of judicial review applied under Article IV, Section 2 (*see supra*, §§233 *et seq.*). [United Building & Construction Trades Council v. Mayor & Council of Camden, *supra*, §235—city ordinance virtually identical to that upheld under Commerce Clause in White v. Massachusetts Council of Construction Employers, *supra*, might nonetheless be invalid under Interstate Privileges and Immunities Clause because "the two clauses have different aims and set different standards for state conduct"]

(d) **Discriminatory impact also improper:** [§303] A state regulation that affects interstate commerce may be neutral on its face but still be discriminatory due to its ***impact***. [Hunt v. Washington State Apple Advertising Commission, *supra*, §58—statute requiring all apple producers to use uniform grading system (or none at all) was discriminatory since local producers (unlike interstate competitors) already used the statutory system]

(e) **Discrimination also against in-state counties:** [§304] A state regulation that discriminates against interstate commerce is ***not*** viewed differently merely because it ***also*** discriminates against certain counties within the state. [Fort Gratiot Sanitary Landfill, Inc. v. Michigan Department of Natural Resources, 112 S. Ct. 2019 (1992)—state law prohibiting landfill of solid waste generated from outside the county invalid]

(2) **Nondiscriminatory regulation:** [§305] State regulations that do not discriminate against interstate commerce are given greater deference by the Court. *Rationale:* If the burden of the state regulation falls ***proportionally***

on local interests as well as those outside the state, ***political restraints*** within the state legislature protect against the abuse of interstate commerce. [South Carolina State Highway Department v. Barnwell Bros., 303 U.S. 177 (1938); *compare* Kassell v. Consolidated Freightways Corp., 450 U.S. 662 (1981)—"disproportionate burden" on interstate commerce because of statute's exemptions makes it less likely that political restraints will serve as check against abuse]

(a) **"Subject matter" test (older approach):** [§306] If the subject matter involved does not require a uniform national rule, but is of local concern and permits diverse regulation, the state regulation has usually been ***upheld***. [Cooley v. Board of Wardens of Philadelphia, 53 U.S. (12 How.) 299 (1851)—requirement that ships receive a pilot while entering or leaving the Port of Philadelphia]

1) **Only "rational basis" required:** [§307] The state regulation has been upheld as long as the state action has some ***rational basis***. [South Carolina Highway Department v. Barnwell Bros., *supra*—upholding maximum weight and width limitations for trucks on state highways because state highways (the subject matter of the regulation) are "peculiarly of local concern"]

2) **Limited use of test:** [§308] The "subject matter" test has not been employed often in modern decisions, although its language has been used occasionally with respect to regulation of interstate transportation facilities on state highways. Even here, however, the Court uses the "balancing" test, below.

(b) **"Balancing" test (modern approach):** [§309] Under the current approach, the fact that the state regulation has some "rational basis" is not enough. Rather, the ***burden on interstate commerce*** imposed by the regulation (*i.e.,* difficulty and cost of compliance, inefficiency involved, etc.) is weighed against the ***strength of the state interest*** in the regulation, with the Court deciding whether the regulation imposes an ***unreasonable burden*** on interstate commerce. [Southern Pacific Co. v. Arizona, 325 U.S. 761 (1945)—statute regulating length of trains held invalid because public safety purpose outweighed by burden on interstate railroads]

(c) **Application of "balancing" test:** [§310] In balancing the burden imposed on interstate commerce against the state interest served, the Court gives greater weight to statutes that further local ***health, safety,*** or ***social welfare*** interests than to statutes that seek to protect local ***economic*** interests. [H.P. Hood & Sons v. DuMond, *supra*, §295]

1) **Judicial role:** [§311] The Court makes its own determination as to the purposes of the state regulation. It is not bound by recitals by the state legislature in enacting the statute, or by state court determinations as to such objectives. However, the Court generally will defer to a state legislative determination of

disputed factual questions on whether the state's purpose is served by the regulation or on the cost of compliance. [Minnesota v. Clover Leaf Creamery Co., 449 U.S. 456 (1981)]

2) **Statutes furthering social welfare, health, and safety**

a) **Social welfare:** [§312] A statute forbidding solicitation by door-to-door sellers without invitation by the homeowner, applied to interstate magazine salespeople, has been upheld. Although the statute burdened interstate commerce by making solicitation much more difficult, this was outweighed by the state interest in protecting privacy. [Breard v. City of Alexandria, 341 U.S. 622 (1951)]

b) **Health:** [§313] A statute requiring that cattle or meat imported from other states be certified as free from disease by the state of origin has been upheld. The burden on interstate commerce involved in supplying such certificate was outweighed by the "public health" objectives of the state law. [Mintz v. Baldwin, 289 U.S. 346 (1933); *but see* Minnesota v. Barber, *supra*, §297—***discriminatory*** statute seeking to protect same state interest held ***invalid***]

c) **Safety:** [§314] A statute requiring that all trains operated within the state carry "full crews" has been upheld. The burden on interstate commerce was outweighed by the "public safety" objective of the regulation. [Brotherhood of Locomotive Firemen v. Chicago, Rock Island & Pacific Railroad, 393 U.S. 129 (1968)]

d) **Unreasonable burden may still be found:** [§315] The fact that a nondiscriminatory state regulation has the purpose of protecting local health, safety, or social welfare interests does not automatically immunize it. Although such a regulation carries a "strong presumption of validity," it is ***invalid*** if, on balance, it furthers the state's interest only ***speculatively or marginally*** and imposes a ***substantial*** burden on interstate commerce. [Kassel v. Consolidated Freightways Corp., *supra*, §305; Raymond Motor Transportation, Inc. v. Rice, 434 U.S. 429 (1978)—state laws limiting length of trucks on local highways]

1/ **Example:** An Illinois statute required all trucks to be equipped with contour mudguards, instead of the flat mudguards permitted in all other states (contour mudguards actually being illegal in one state). The safety benefit of the contour mudguards was found to be minimal at best and was held ***outweighed*** by the costs and inconvenience to interstate carriers in complying (*i.e.,* requiring truckers to change mudguards before entering Illinois). [Bibb v. Navajo Freight Lines, Inc., 359 U.S. 520 (1959)]

e) **Alternative means:** [§316] In determining whether a state interest outweighs the burden on interstate commerce, the Court periodically considers whether there are any alternatives available to the state that could achieve the same objective without imposing as great a burden. [Pike v. Bruce Church, Inc., *supra,* §297]

3) **Economic regulations:** [§317] The fact that a nondiscriminatory state regulation is designed to protect local economic interests does ***not automatically*** invalidate it under the Commerce Clause. The Court has upheld a number of state laws requiring that minimum prices be paid to local producers, thus enhancing local industry, despite the fact that a large amount of the product was sold in interstate commerce. [Milk Control Board v. Eisenberg Farm Products Co., 306 U.S. 346 (1939)—***most*** of the milk subject to minimum price law was sold within state]

a) **Relevance of national policy:** [§318] Several of these cases stressed that the regulation was consistent with certain national policies, even though Congress had not specifically acted in this area. [Parker v. Brown, 317 U.S. 431 (1943)—state marketing program regulating sale of locally grown raisin crop in interstate commerce upheld because state program coincided with congressional policies regulating agriculture]

4) **"Reciprocity agreements":** [§319] Reciprocity agreements between states respecting the sale of products do ***not automatically*** violate the Commerce Clause. *But note:* A ***mandatory*** reciprocity requirement forbidding sale of products from another state unless that state reciprocates is invalid unless there is a substantial state interest (health or welfare, etc.) which cannot be attained by alternative means. [Great Atlantic & Pacific Tea Co. v. Cottrell, 424 U.S. 366 (1976)]

(3) **Permits or licenses for interstate business:** [§320] The traditional rule is that a state cannot require a permit or license for the privilege of engaging in interstate transportation [Buck v. Kuykendall, 267 U.S. 307 (1925)], or of engaging in trade or business that is ***exclusively*** interstate commerce (*e.g.,* an interstate company that ***only*** sends "drummers" into the state who take orders that are accepted and filled outside the state, and the goods for which are sent in from out of state). [*But see* Eli Lilly & Co. v. Sav-On-Drugs, Inc., 366 U.S. 276 (1961)—interstate seller was not engaged ***exclusively*** in interstate commerce because it provided local customers with various services and sales aids]

(a) **Note:** This rule has been qualified by *Complete Auto Transit, Inc. v. Brady, see infra,* §351.

(b) **Exception for permissible noneconomic interests:** [§321] But a state may require and deny a permit to promote safety rather than simply to prevent competition. [Bradley v. Public Utilities Commission, 280 U.S. 92 (1933)]

(4) **Broader state power over liquor regulation:** [§322] The Twenty-First Amendment prohibits "the transportation or importation into any State for delivery or use therein of intoxicating liquors in violation of local laws." This amendment has been held to give the states broader regulatory power over regulation of liquor than over any other type of interstate commerce. By virtue thereof, a state is "unconfined by traditional Commerce Clause limitations" in deciding whether to ***permit importation or sale*** of liquor ***destined for local use*** or consumption and in structuring the liquor distribution system. [Hostetter v. Idlewild Bon Voyage Liquor Corp., 377 U.S. 324 (1964)]

(a) **Power limited to local sale or use:** [§323] But the Twenty-First Amendment does not give the states power to regulate or tax liquor shipments intended for delivery ***overseas, outside the state***, or to federal enclaves (*e.g.,* military posts) within the state. As to such shipments, the federal commerce power is exclusive and supreme. [Hostetter v. Idlewild Bon Voyage Liquor Corp., *supra*; United States v. Mississippi Tax Commission, 412 U.S. 363 (1973)]

1) **Further limitation—noncentral state interests:** [§324] Even those state liquor regulations that concern local sale and use may be subject to Congress's commerce power when the federal policies are particularly strong and the state's central interests in regulating the time, place, and manner of liquor importation and sale are not directly implicated. [California Retail Liquor Dealers Association v. Midcal Aluminum, Inc., 445 U.S. 97 (1980)—state's fair trade law allowing wine wholesalers to set minimum prices violates Sherman Antitrust Act; Capital Cities Cable, Inc. v. Crisp, 467 U.S. 691 (1984)—state ban on alcoholic beverage advertising preempted by federal regulation of cable television]

2) **Discrimination:** [§325] Furthermore, the Twenty-First Amendment does not permit state regulations or taxes on the local sale or use of liquor to discriminate against interstate commerce. A central tenet of the Commerce Clause is to forbid economic protectionism. [Bacchus Imports, Ltd. v. Dias, 468 U.S. 263 (1984)]

3) **Extraterritorial effect:** [§326] Nor does the Twenty-First Amendment permit state regulations or taxes on the local sale or use of liquor if the practical effect is to regulate liquor sales or prices in other states. [Healy v. The Beer Institute, Inc., 491 U.S. 324 (1989), *overruling* Joseph E. Seagram & Sons, Inc. v. Hostetter, 384 U.S. 35 (1966)—state statute requiring sellers of beer to sell at prices no higher than prices in bordering states violates Commerce Clause, because it operates to force sellers to account for this state's price in evaluating market conditions in other states]

(b) **Import-Export Clause:** [§327] Note that the Twenty-First Amendment does not repeal the explicit limitation of the Import-Export Clause (*see infra,* §384). [Department of Revenue v. James B. Beam Distilling Co., 377 U.S. 341 (1964)—state license tax on importers of liquor from abroad invalid]

C. POWER OF STATES TO TAX INTERSTATE COMMERCE

1. General Considerations

a. **Congressional supremacy:** [§328] Pursuant to the Commerce Clause, Congress has complete power to authorize or forbid state taxation that affects interstate commerce. [Prudential Insurance Co. v. Benjamin, 328 U.S. 408 (1946)—upholding Congress's power to authorize state taxes that discriminate against interstate commerce]

b. **When Congress has not spoken**

(1) **Discriminatory taxes:** [§329] Unless authorized by Congress, state taxes that discriminate against interstate commerce violate the ***Commerce Clause***. [Boston Stock Exchange v. State Tax Commission, 429 U.S. 318 (1977)]

(a) **Interstate Privileges and Immunities Clause:** [§330] Such taxes that discriminate against nonresidents of the state may also be held to violate the Interstate Privileges and Immunities Clause [Art. IV, §2]. [Austin v. New Hampshire, 420 U.S. 656 (1975)]

(b) **Equal Protection Clause:** [§331] State taxes that discriminate against interstate commerce may also violate the Equal Protection Clause if the discrimination is not ***rationally*** related to a ***legitimate*** state purpose. [WHYY, Inc. v. Borough of Glassboro, 393 U.S. 117 (1968)—denial of tax exemption solely because taxpayer was incorporated in another state is invalid]

(c) **Finding discrimination:** [§332] If a state tax singles out interstate commerce for taxation, the Court ordinarily will not "save" the tax by finding other state taxes imposed only on local commerce (which might arguably eliminate the "apparent" discrimination against interstate commerce). [Nippert v. City of Richmond, 327 U.S. 416 (1946); *but see* Alaska v. Arctic Maid, 366 U.S. 199 (1961)—tax on freezing salmon if canned in another state is "equalized" by tax on local canneries]

1) **Exception:** [§333] State taxes that single out interstate commerce are considered nondiscriminatory if the particular statutory section or scheme also imposes the same type of tax on local commerce (*e.g.,* sales and use taxes, discussed below).

(2) **Nondiscriminatory taxes:** [§334] In the absence of relevant federal legislation, the Court reviews nondiscriminatory state taxes affecting interstate commerce—under both the Commerce Clause and the Due Process Clause—and ***balances*** the state's need to obtain revenue against the

burden such taxes impose on the free flow of commerce. Interstate commerce is ***not immune*** from such taxation; it must pay its fair share.

(a) **Commerce Clause:** [§335] The Commerce Clause is principally used to prevent state taxes that impose multiple burdens on interstate commerce.

(b) **Due Process Clause:** [§336] The principal focus of the Due Process Clause is "jurisdiction." It is mainly used to require that the benefits and protection afforded by the taxing state have a sufficient relationship to the subject matter taxed ("minimum or adequate contacts") so that the subject matter has a "tax situs" in the taxing state.

(c) **Comment:** The use of these two constitutional provisions is often not sharply delineated and may overlap in many instances.

2. **Ad Valorem Property Taxes:** [§337] Ad valorem property taxes are taxes based upon the value of the property being taxed.

a. **Tax on property used to transport goods interstate:** [§338] The validity of ad valorem property taxes on "instrumentalities of commerce" (airplanes, railroad cars, etc.) depends on: (i) whether the property has acquired a "***taxable situs***" in or "***nexus***" to the taxing state—*i.e.,* whether there are sufficient "contacts" with the taxing state to justify the tax, and (ii) since the property may move from state to state during the year, whether its value has been ***properly apportioned*** according to the amount of "contacts" with each taxing state. (The taxable situs ("nexus") is required by the Due Process Clause to establish the state's power to tax at all, and apportionment is required by the Commerce Clause to prevent an undue or multiple burden on interstate commerce.)

(1) **Taxable situs ("nexus"):** [§339] In general, property has a taxable situs in a state if it receives ***benefits or protection*** from the state. [Braniff Airways v. Nebraska Board of Equalization, 347 U.S. 590 (1954)—airplanes have taxable situs in state where airline company owned no property but made 18 regularly scheduled flights per day from rented depot space, even though same aircraft did not land every day]

(a) **More than one taxable situs:** [§340] An "instrumentality of commerce" may have more than one taxable situs, each of which can impose a tax subject to the required apportionment (below).

(2) **Apportionment:** [§341] Where an "instrumentality of commerce" has more than one taxable situs, a fair apportionment of its value to the taxing state is required—*i.e.,* one that fairly approximates the average physical presence of the property within the taxing state. [Union Tank Line Co. v. Wright, 249 U.S. 275 (1919)]

(a) **Fair apportionment:** [§342] The following methods of apportionment have been upheld by the Court.

1) **Miles in state to total miles:** Using the proportion of miles traveled within the taxing state to the total number of miles

traveled by the instrumentalities in the entire operation. [Ott v. Mississippi Valley Barge Line Co., 336 U.S. 169 (1949)]

2) **Average number in state on any one day:** Computing the average number of instrumentalities (*e.g.,* tank cars) physically present in the taxing state on any one day during the tax year and taxing that portion at full value—*i.e.,* as if in the state all year. [Johnson Oil Refining Co. v. Oklahoma, 290 U.S. 158 (1933)]

3) **Note:** Since different states may use different apportionment formulas to tax the same property, there may still be some multiple taxation of the same property. However, this should be minimal if fair apportionment formulas have been used.

(b) **Unfair apportionment:** [§343] The apportionment formula used must be ***rational***, both on its face and as applied, to property values connected with the taxing state. A state is not permitted to use imprecise formulas resulting in totally unrealistic assessments; this would violate both the Due Process and Commerce Clauses. [Norfolk & Western Railway v. Missouri Tax Commission, 390 U.S. 317 (1968)—apportionment based on track mileage within state, as compared to total track mileage, resulted in apportioning over twice the value of railroad cars actually present in taxing state because railroad had unusually high amount of track in taxing state]

1) **Burden of proof:** [§344] The taxpayer has a heavy burden of showing "gross overreaching." [Norfolk & Western Railway v. Missouri Tax Commission, *supra*]

(c) **Domiciliary state:** [§345] The taxpayer's domiciliary state need not apportion the value of "instrumentalities of commerce" and may tax the ***full value*** of the property—unless the taxpayer can prove that the property has acquired a taxable situs elsewhere.

1) **Proving situs elsewhere:** [§346] Mere proof that the property was absent from the domiciliary state for part of the tax year is not enough. The taxpayer must prove that the property is either: (i) ***permanently located*** or (ii) ***habitually employed*** in some other state, thus acquiring a taxable situs outside the domiciliary state. *But note:* The taxpayer need not prove that the property was actually taxed by a nondomiciliary state. [Central Railroad v. Pennsylvania, 370 U.S. 607 (1962)]

b. **Tax on cargo in transit:** [§347] States cannot levy an ad valorem tax on property being shipped interstate that happens to be in the taxing state on the tax day; otherwise, each state could tax as the property passed through, thus imposing multiple taxation on interstate commerce. [Standard Oil Co. v. Peck, 342 U.S. 382 (1952)]

(1) **When does interstate transit begin?** [§348] Interstate transit begins when (i) the cargo is ***delivered to an interstate carrier*** (the shipper

thereby relinquishing further control) ***or*** (ii) the cargo actually ***starts its interstate journey***. Goods merely being prepared for transit are not immune from state taxation. [Coe v. Errol, 116 U.S. 517 (1886)]

(2) **Effect of a "break" in transit:** [§349] Once started, a shipment remains in interstate transit unless actually diverted. Temporary interruptions for the convenience of transportation do ***not*** destroy the interstate nature of the shipment. [Hughes Bros. Timber Co. v. Minnesota, 272 U.S. 469 (1926)] However, a break intended to end or suspend the shipment (*e.g.*, for possible sale of the property) renders the property subject to state taxation. [Minnesota v. Blasius, 290 U.S. 1 (1933)]

3. **"Doing Business" Taxes:** [§350] "Doing business" taxes are taxes imposed for engaging in business within the state. They may be labeled "privilege," "occupation," "license," or "franchise" taxes—or simply "gross receipts" or "net income" taxes—and may be measured either by a flat annual fee or by a proportional rate based on revenue derived from the taxing state.

a. **Four-part test:** [§351] States may generally impose such taxes on persons doing business in the state—both on companies engaged exclusively in interstate commerce as well as on interstate companies engaged in local commerce—if four criteria are met:

(i) The activity taxed must have a ***"substantial nexus"*** to the taxing state;

(ii) The tax must be ***"fairly apportioned"***;

(iii) It must ***not "discriminate"*** against interstate commerce; and

(iv) It must ***"fairly relate to services provided"*** by the taxing state.

[Complete Auto Transit, Inc. v. Brady, 430 U.S. 274 (1977)—*overruling* Spector Motor Service, Inc. v. O'Connor, 340 U.S. 602 (1951)]

(1) **Example:** A privilege tax for doing business, based on the gross income derived from transporting goods within the state, can be applied to a trucking company that delivers goods coming from outside the state. [Complete Auto Transit, Inc. v. Brady, *supra*]

(2) **Example:** An occupation tax on all business, based on gross income derived within the state, can be applied to a stevedoring company operating within the state that loads and unloads ships carrying goods in interstate commerce. [Washington Revenue Department v. Association of Washington Stevedoring Companies, 435 U.S. 734 (1978)—*overruling* Joseph v. Carter & Weekes Stevedoring Companies, 330 U.S. 422 (1947)]

(3) **Example:** A gross receipts tax on all railroads doing business within the state, apportioned on the basis of track mileage in the taxing state, may be applied to a railroad that operates totally within the state hauling goods in interstate commerce. [Canton Railroad v. Rogan, 340 U.S. 511 (1951)]

(4) **Example:** A "value added tax" on all persons with business activities within the state may be applied on the basis of the traditional "three-factor"

apportionment formula (*see infra,* §355) even though the taxpayer had virtually no property or payroll (but did have substantial sales) in the taxing state. [Trinova Corp. v. Michigan Department of Treasury, 498 U.S. 358 (1991)]

(5) **Burden of proof:** [§352] The taxpayer has the burden of showing that the state's apportionment formula is unfair. [General Motors Corp. v. Washington, 377 U.S. 436 (1964)]

b. **Net income taxes:** [§353] As indicated, a net income tax is another type of "doing business" tax that has been upheld as applied to an interstate company engaged in business within the taxing state. [Northwestern States Portland Cement Co. v. Minnesota, 358 U.S. 450 (1959)]

(1) **Adequate contacts:** [§354] In *Portland Cement*, the taxpayer had several salespeople and a rented office in the taxing state, and the Court found this a sufficient "nexus" for the tax. (*Note:* Congress subsequently enacted a statute [15 U.S.C. §§381-384] prohibiting state net income taxes, irrespective of fair apportionment, on out-of-state businesses whose only contacts with the taxing state are salespeople.)

(2) **Fair apportionment:** [§355] In *Portland Cement*, the state used the approved "three-factor" apportionment formula (ratio of property, payroll, and sales within state to taxpayer's total property, payroll, and sales). The taxpayer could not show that this was unfair given state protection and services for the taxpayer's local activities, and there was no showing of "multiple burden."

(a) **A "single-factor" formula:** [§356] Note that a "single-factor" formula (ratio of sales within state to taxpayer's total sales) has also been upheld as "presumptively valid"—the taxpayer being unable to prove by "clear and cogent evidence" that it "led to a grossly distorted result." The fact that some income may be subject to overlapping taxes because other states (even a majority) use a different formula (the "three-factor" formula) does not prove that the single-factor formula is arbitrary. [Moorman Manufacturing Co. v. Bair, 437 U.S. 267 (1978)]

(b) **Income includible:** [§357] Income from separate corporate divisions, or from subsidiary corporations operating in other states or foreign countries, may be included in the tax base—unless the taxpayer proves that the divisions or subsidiaries were not part of its "single unitary business" [Mobil Oil Corp. v. Vermont Commissioner of Taxes, 445 U.S. 425 (1980); Exxon Corp. v. Wisconsin Department of Revenue, 447 U.S. 207 (1980)], but rather were conducted as "discrete business enterprises" [Asarco, Inc. v. Idaho Tax Commission, 458 U.S. 307 (1982)]. Substantial deference will be given to the judgment of state courts on this issue. [Container Corp. of America v. Franchise Tax Board, 463 U.S. 159 (1983)]

4. **Severance Taxes:** [§358] A nondiscriminatory state tax on extraction of minerals from the state, measured by a percentage of the value of such minerals, is valid

even though most of the minerals are sold in interstate commerce. The tax satisfies the "four-part test" of *Complete Auto Transit, Inc. v. Brady* (*supra*, §351): (i) since the minerals are taken from the taxing state, there is a "substantial nexus"; (ii) since extraction can occur in no other state, there is "fair apportionment"; (iii) if the rate is the same for in-state and out-of-state consumers, there is no "discrimination against interstate commerce"; and (iv) as long as the tax is imposed on activity within the taxing state, the Court will ***not*** inquire into the ***amount*** of the tax or the ***value*** of benefits received by the taxpayer. [Commonwealth Edison Co. v. Montana, 453 U.S. 609 (1981)]

5. **Taxes on Solicitors:** [§359] Flat license fees may not be levied upon solicitors ("drummers") who seek local orders to be filled from goods shipped interstate—even if the same fee is levied on those selling intrastate goods. [Nippert v. Richmond, 327 U.S. 416 (1946)] Otherwise each municipality visited by the drummer could impose such a tax (resulting in a tremendous cumulative burden), while the local retail merchant would be subject to only one local tax—thus, in ***practical effect***, discriminating against interstate commerce.

   a. **Compare—peddlers:** [§360] However, the state ***may*** impose a license tax on a peddler who actually sells and delivers wares within a state (even though the goods are shipped into the state from interstate commerce), provided the tax rates are nondiscriminatory. [Dunbar Stanley Studios, Inc. v. Alabama, 393 U.S. 537 (1969)—transient photographers took the delivered pictures locally but had them developed outside the state]

      (1) **Comment:** As a practical matter, however, such a tax may affect peddlers as severely as it does drummers, thus placing an undue burden on interstate commerce.

6. **Highway Use Taxes:** [§361] License and similar taxes on interstate carriers will be upheld if they are nondiscriminatory and are imposed to compensate states for the costs of maintaining and administering their roads.

   a. **Burden of proof:** [§362] The taxpayer bears the burden of proving that the tax requires more than "fair compensation" for road use. [Capitol Greyhound Lines v. Brice, 339 U.S. 542 (1950)]

   b. **Formula to determine amount of tax:** [§363] The Court has, of course, approved formulas that are reasonably related to road use (*e.g.,* mileage within the state, number and capacity of vehicles), but it has also upheld ***flat fees***, even though not directly related to use, as long as they were not shown to be "unreasonable in amount." [Capitol Greyhound Lines v. Brice, *supra*—flat fee upheld when imposed in addition to mileage tax]

7. **Airport Use Fees:** [§364] Similarly, a one-dollar state or municipal tax, imposed on emplaning commercial airline passengers to help defray airport construction costs, does not violate the Commerce Clause (or the Equal Protection Clause, or the "right to travel"). As long as: (i) the amount of the tax is based on some fair approximation of use and is not excessive in comparison with the government benefit conferred, and (ii) the tax does not discriminate against interstate commerce by taxing all passengers, it is valid even though some other formula might better reflect the relative use of airports by individual users. [Evansville-Vanderburgh Airport Authority District v. Delta Airlines, Inc., 405 U.S. 707 (1972)]

8. **Sales and Use Taxes:** [§365] A sales tax is one imposed on sales consummated ***within the state***. A use tax is imposed on the user of goods purchased ***outside the state***. (Use taxes are designed to prevent residents from purchasing goods outside the state in order to avoid a state sales tax.)

a. **Compensatory use tax by "consumer" state:** [§366] Although use taxes single out interstate commerce for taxation (*i.e.*, they are imposed only on goods purchased outside the state), they do not violate the Commerce Clause. [Henneford v. Silas Mason Co., 300 U.S. 577 (1937)] *Rationale:* As long as the use tax rate is ***not higher*** than the sales tax rate, the purpose is to equalize the tax on goods purchased outside the state with the tax on goods purchased within the state (and subject to the state sales tax).

(1) **Defining "not higher":** [§367] Where sales taxes vary within a state because of differing local tax rates, the Supreme Court will look to the effect of the use tax in each locality rather than compare the use tax rate to the average sales tax rate. The use tax will be held invalid as to those localities where the use tax rate exceeds the sales tax rate. [Associated Industries of Missouri v. Lohman, 114 S. Ct. 1815 (1994)]

(2) **Credit for sales tax paid in "seller" state:** [§368] It has been argued that: (i) if the sale is consummated outside the state and is subjected there to a sales tax, (ii) if the goods are then brought into the consumer state to be used there, and (iii) if the consumer state imposes a use tax, then the consumer state must give credit for the sales tax already paid in the seller state; *i.e.*, if no credit is given, the transaction is subjected to two taxes (a multiple burden) simply because the transaction involved interstate commerce. However, the Court has not decided whether such a credit must be given. [Southern Pacific Co. v. Gallagher, 306 U.S. 167 (1939)]

(a) **Discrimination against nonresidents:** [§369] In the absence of ***some*** "legitimate" purpose, if a consumer state gives such a credit ***only to its own residents*** who pay a sales tax in the seller state, it violates the Equal Protection Clause. [Williams v. Vermont, 472 U.S. 14 (1985)]

b. **Use tax by "seller" state:** [§370] Such taxes do not exist, since use taxes are not imposed by the state where the sale is made. In any case, since the "seller" state has no contact with the use or consumption of the goods, an attempt to impose a use tax would probably violate due process.

c. **Sales tax by "seller" state:** [§371] The issue here concerns sales by local sellers to buyers from outside the state.

(1) **Sale within state:** [§372] If the sale is consummated ***within*** the state (*i.e.*, buyer takes possession within the state), the Commerce Clause does not prohibit a sales tax by the seller state—even though the buyer takes the goods outside the state for use. [International Harvester Co. v. Department of Treasury, 322 U.S. 340 (1944)—tax is one on a "local sale"]

(2) **Sale outside state:** [§373] If the sale is made to a buyer ***outside*** the state (*i.e.*, goods delivered there by the seller or a common carrier), the

Commerce Clause ***prohibits*** a sales tax by the seller state—at least if the tax is ***unapportioned***. [Adams Manufacturing Co. v. Storen, 304 U.S. 307 (1938)—tax is one on "interstate sale"]

(a) **Comment:** The Court has not passed on a ***fairly apportioned*** sales tax sought to be imposed by a "seller" state on goods sold to a buyer outside the state. But such a tax might well be valid if it satisfied the "four-part test" of *Complete Auto Transit, Inc. v. Brady, supra,* §351.

d. **Sales tax by "consumer" state:** [§374] Here, the sales are to local buyers by sellers engaged in interstate commerce.

(1) **Sufficient contacts:** [§375] If the interstate seller has substantial contacts in the consumer state (*e.g.,* office, salesroom, property, etc.), the Commerce Clause does not prohibit a sales tax by the consumer state—even though the goods are delivered from outside the state. [McGoldrick v. Berwind-White Coal Mining Co., 309 U.S. 33 (1940)—tax is on a "local sale," and no multiple burden because no other state may impose sales or use tax]

(2) **"Drummers" insufficient:** [§376] But if the only contact between the interstate seller and the consumer state consists of "drummers" (*i.e.,* solicitation of orders subject to acceptance at seller's out-of-state office, and goods shipped by carrier with payment by mail), both the Commerce Clause and the Due Process Clause prohibit any sales tax by the consumer state. [McLeod v. J. E. Dilworth Co., 322 U.S. 327 (1944)—tax is on an "interstate sale" taking place beyond state jurisdiction]

e. **"Consumer" state's ability to require interstate seller to collect use tax:** [§377] The consumer state may require collection of a use tax if the interstate seller has the "minimum contacts" with the consumer state required by the Due Process Clause ***and*** the "substantial nexus" required by the Commerce Clause. [Quill Corp. v. North Dakota, *infra,* §381—"substantial nexus" may require more than "minimum contacts"]

(1) **"Drummers" sufficient:** [§378] In the situation described in *McLeod, supra* (interstate seller with drummers in consumer state), the consumer state could impose a use tax on the purchaser. [*See* Henneford v. Silas Mason, *supra,* §366] Furthermore, although the consumer state may not impose a sales tax on the interstate seller [*see* McLeod v. J. E. Dilworth Co., *supra*], it may force the interstate seller to collect the use tax from the local purchaser and remit it to the consumer state [General Trading Co. v. Iowa Tax Commission, 322 U.S. 335 (1944)].

(a) **"Independent contractors":** [§379] The same result applies where the seller uses "independent contractors" instead of the seller's own salespeople. [Scripto v. Carson, 362 U.S. 207 (1960)]

(2) **Offices sufficient:** [§380] Where the interstate seller has offices in the consumer state, there is sufficient nexus even though the use tax was imposed on interstate mail order sales of merchandise not solicited by the

local offices. [National Geographic Society v. California Board of Equalization, 430 U.S. 551 (1977)]

(3) **Mail solicitation insufficient:** [§381] If the interstate seller solicits sales by mail, with orders shipped by mail or common carrier, the interstate seller gains the benefit of an economic market in the forum state that constitutes adequate "contacts" to satisfy the Due Process Clause. However, the seller lacks the "substantial nexus" required by the Commerce Clause, and thus the consumer state may ***not*** impose a duty on the interstate seller to collect a use tax on sales to local residents. [Quill Corp. v. North Dakota, 112 S. Ct. 1904 (1992), *modifying* National Bellas Hess, Inc. v. Illinois Department of Revenue, 386 U.S. 753 (1967)]

(a) **And note:** Nor is there sufficient nexus if the interstate seller occasionally advertises and makes truck deliveries in the consumer state. [Miller Bros. v. Maryland, 347 U.S. 340 (1954)]

9. **Taxes on Foreign Corporations:** [§382] A state is not required to admit foreign corporations (those incorporated in other states) to do business locally since a corporation is not a "citizen" within the Interstate Privileges and Immunities Clause [Art. IV, §2]. The extent to which the ***Commerce Clause*** bars burdensome state taxes or regulations on such corporations is uncertain. But, under the ***Equal Protection Clause***, a state may ***not*** impose more onerous taxes or other burdens on foreign corporations than on domestic corporations unless the discrimination is ***rationally related*** to a ***legitimate state purpose***. [Western & Southern Life Insurance Co. v. California Board of Equalization, 451 U.S. 648 (1981)]

a. **Illegitimate purpose:** [§383] A state may ***not*** impose a more onerous tax on foreign corporations simply for the purpose of promoting the business of domestic competitors. [Metropolitan Life Insurance Co. v. Ward, *supra,* §281]

D. POWER OF STATES TO TAX FOREIGN COMMERCE

1. **Import-Export Clause:** [§384] Article I, Section 10, Clause 2 provides: "No state shall, without the Consent of the Congress, lay any Imposts or Duties on Imports or Exports, except what may be absolutely necessary for executing its inspection Laws. . . ."

a. **State taxation of "imports":** [§385] The Import-Export Clause prohibits the states from imposing any tax on imported goods ***as such*** or on commercial activity connected with imported goods ***as such*** (*i.e.*, taxes discriminating against imports), except with congressional consent. [Brown v. Maryland, 25 U.S. (12 Wheat.) 419 (1827)—license tax on importer invalid because it would increase price of his commodities]

(1) **Nondiscriminatory taxes:** [§386] A nondiscriminatory ad valorem property tax on all goods located in the state (including imported goods) is ***not*** prohibited. [Michelin Tire Corp. v. Wages, *supra,* §260] *Rationale:* Such taxes merely apportion the cost of state services among all beneficiaries, and imports must bear their fair share.

(a) **Goods in transit:** The Court has left as an ***open question*** whether a nondiscriminatory ***property tax*** may be imposed on imported goods that are still in transit. But a nondiscriminatory ***occupation tax*** on all businesses operating within the state may be applied to a company that services imported (or exported) goods even when the goods are still in transit. [Washington Revenue Department v. Association of Washington Stevedoring Companies, *supra,* §351]

b. **State taxation of "exports":** [§387] The Import-Export Clause only prohibits the states from taxing exports after they have begun their "***physical entry*** into the stream of exportation." [Kosydar v. National Cash Register Co., 417 U.S. 62 (1974)—goods in warehouse ***pending shipment*** abroad pursuant to completed sale may still be taxed]

2. **Commerce Clause:** [§388] The Commerce Clause gives Congress plenary power to regulate foreign commerce, and thus inherently limits a state's power to tax that commerce.

a. **In general:** As a ***first step***, the Commerce Clause imposes the same limits on state taxation of foreign commerce as it does on state taxation of interstate commerce (*see supra*, §§328 *et seq.*). [Barclays Bank PLC v. Franchise Tax Board, 114 S. Ct. ____ (1994)—sustaining same apportionment formula for corporate franchise tax on foreign businesses as has been upheld for interstate businesses]

b. **Additional considerations:** [§389] In the absence of congressional authorization, there are stricter limits on state taxation of foreign commerce than of interstate commerce because of (i) the enhanced risk of multiple taxation and (ii) the greater need for federal uniformity. [Container Corp. of America v. Franchise Tax Board, *supra*, §357]

(1) **Example—instrumentalities of foreign commerce:** A state may not impose an ad valorem property tax on instrumentalities that are ***foreign owned*** and used ***exclusively in international commerce***. This is true even if the property has a situs in the taxing state and the tax is nondiscriminatory and fairly apportioned (*compare supra,* §338, regarding state taxation of instrumentalities of ***interstate*** commerce). [Japan Line, Ltd. v. County of Los Angeles, 441 U.S. 434 (1979)] In the absence of congressional authorization, there are stricter limits on state taxation of foreign commerce than of interstate commerce because there is a greater need for federal uniformity and a lesser opportunity for the Court to prevent multiple taxation.

(2) **Compare:** But a state ***may*** impose a fairly apportioned sales tax on a lease within its borders of instrumentalities that are ***domestically owned***, even though used exclusively in international commerce. [Itel Containers International Corp. v. Huddleston, 113 S. Ct. 1095 (1993)]

(a) **Government's position:** Although not dispositive, the views expressed by the United States in the litigation on whether the state tax interferes with the need for federal uniformity may help reconcile the results in the *Japan Line* and *Itel* cases, which are otherwise very difficult to distinguish. [*See* Itel Containers International Corp. v. Huddleston, *supra*]

IV. INDIVIDUAL RIGHTS—LIMITATIONS ON THE EXERCISE OF GOVERNMENTAL POWER

chapter approach

This chapter focuses on the limitations on the exercise of governmental power over individuals. The Constitution explicitly provides protections for individuals against certain actions by the federal government and certain actions by state governments. Other limitations have been read into other constitutional provisions; most significantly, most of the Bill of Rights has been held applicable to the states through the Fourteenth Amendment Due Process Clause. You will almost certainly see an exam question concerning one or more of the following topics:

1. **Due Process Clauses:** The Due Process Clauses (in the Fifth and Fourteenth Amendments) provide two types of protection: substantive and procedural.

   a. **Procedural Due Process:** Procedurally, the Due Process Clauses guarantee that liberty and property interests shall not be impaired without some form of ***notice and hearing*** by an unbiased decisionmaker. Whether a prior evidentiary hearing is required is determined by weighing the importance of the interest involved, the value of the safeguards to the interest, and the government interest in fiscal and administrative efficiency.

   b. **Substantive Due Process:** Your approach to determining whether a law violates substantive due process should start with an analysis of whether the law is an economic or social regulation or whether a fundamental right is involved.

      (1) ***If economic or social regulations*** are involved, the court will use the traditional test: The regulations are ***presumed valid***, and thus will be upheld if they bear a ***rational relationship*** to the end sought.

      (2) ***If fundamental rights*** are affected by the regulation, the strict scrutiny test is used: The regulation will be held ***invalid unless*** it is ***necessary*** to achieve a ***compelling*** governmental interest, a much more difficult test.

2. **Equal Protection Clause:** The Equal Protection Clause of the Fourteenth Amendment limits governmental discrimination by the states. The Fifth Amendment Due Process Clause has been held to limit most similar discrimination by the federal government. Your analysis should begin by looking at the classification.

   a. ***If the classification is not based on suspect or quasi-suspect criteria****—i.e.*, almost all ***economic or social regulations***—and does not discriminate against a ***fundamental right***, it will be upheld if it is ***rationally related*** to a ***constitutionally permissible*** state interest. Keep in mind that these classifications will be presumed valid and must be "wholly arbitrary" to be invalid.

   b. ***If the government action intentionally discriminates against a suspect class*** (*i.e.*, race or national origin), ***strict scrutiny*** will be applied and the law will be ***invalid***

unless it is ***necessary*** to promote a ***compelling*** state interest, a much more difficult test. Note too that this test will be used for laws that discriminate against a ***fundamental right***.

c. ***If the classification is based on a quasi-suspect criteria*** (*i.e.*, gender and legitimacy), an intermediate level test is used: To be valid, the regulation must be ***substantially*** related to ***important*** governmental objectives.

3. **State Action:** In analyzing due process or equal protection issues, be sure that governmental action is involved. Private discrimination may not be remediable under these clauses. Finding state action may require a close look at the facts of your question. Remember that state action may include action by individuals under some circumstances (*e.g.*, a private individual performing a function that is traditionally the ***exclusive*** prerogative of the state or where the government has ***required*** or ***significantly encouraged*** private acts of discrimination).

4. **Freedoms of Speech, Press, and Association:** The First Amendment provides protection against abridgment of the freedoms of speech, press, and association. These rights are protected from state abridgment by the Fourteenth Amendment. When the government acts to limit these rights, the Court will usually balance the following factors: (i) the ***importance of the right***; (ii) the ***nature and scope*** of the restraint; (iii) the ***type and strength*** of the government interest involved; and (iv) whether the restraint is a ***narrowly tailored means*** to achieve the interest. Your analysis should do the same. Recall too that the right to speak includes the right to speak in public forums, subject to reasonable content-neutral time, place, and manner restrictions. Also, commercial speech is protected, but to a lesser extent than noncommercial speech; obscenity is not protected at all.

5. **Establishment and Free Exercise Clauses:** The First Amendment also forbids the government from making laws that establish religion or prohibit the free exercise of religion. These prohibitions likewise apply to the states through the Fourteenth Amendment. Consider freedom of religion questions in terms of both the Establishment and Free Exercise Clauses.

a. **Establishment Clause:** To be valid under the Establishment Clause, government action must: (i) have a ***secular purpose***; (ii) have a principal effect that ***neither advances nor inhibits religion***; and (iii) ***not foster excessive government entanglement***. Review the cases to familiarize yourself with permissible government "involvement" with religion (*e.g.*, providing secular textbooks or health services to parochial school students is valid, but "voluntary" prayer in the schools is not).

b. **Free Exercise Clause:** The Free Exercise Clause invalidates government action that singles out religion for adverse treatment or hinders a particular religion. Remember that a statute interfering with ***religious beliefs will always violate*** the Clause, but one dealing with religious ***conduct*** will ***rarely*** be invalidated. If the government action burdening religious conduct is ***neutral*** and ***applies to others*** who engage in the conduct for nonreligious reasons, it will be ***upheld*** despite the burden on religion. The only exceptions involve constitutional protections besides the Free Exercise Clause (*e.g.*, the right of the Amish to educate their children, free speech, or due process concerning unemployment compensation). Finally, keep in mind that the truth of a person's beliefs is never susceptible to judicial inquiry, but sincerity of beliefs is.

6. **Other Limitations on Governmental Power:** Although somewhat less likely to be an exam question, you should be aware of the other limitations on governmental power. Note that these limitations provide for compensation when private property is taken for public use, prohibit the impairment of contracts, prevent retroactive legislation aimed at punishment, and assure persons accused of crimes a number of rights.

A. INTRODUCTION

1. **Bill of Rights—Limitation on Federal Power:** [§390] The first eight amendments to the Constitution (known as the Bill of Rights) as originally enacted protected only against actions of the ***federal*** government; these provisions were not limitations on the states. [Barron v. Baltimore, 32 U.S. (7 Pet.) 243 (1833)]

2. **Fourteenth Amendment—Limitation on State Power:** [§391] Section I of the Fourteenth Amendment, adopted in 1868, provides: "No State shall make or enforce any law which shall abridge the ***privileges or immunities*** of citizens of the United States; nor shall any State deprive any person of life, liberty, or property without ***due process*** of law; nor deny to any person within its jurisdiction the ***equal protection*** of the laws."

   a. **Fourteenth Amendment Privileges and Immunities Clause:** [§392] As already discussed (*see supra*, §231), it was early held that the guarantees in the Bill of Rights were ***not*** privileges and immunities of national citizenship protected from state abridgment through the Fourteenth Amendment Privileges and Immunities Clause. [Slaughterhouse Cases, *supra*, §231]

   b. **Fourteenth Amendment Due Process Clause:** [§393] Thereafter, the Court held that provisions of the Bill of Rights may be sufficiently "fundamental" as to be protected against state abridgment through the Fourteenth Amendment Due Process Clause.

      (1) **"Total incorporation" rejected:** [§394] The view that the Fourteenth Amendment Due Process Clause incorporates all of the Bill of Rights in toto has been rejected by the Court. [Adamson v. California, 332 U.S. 46 (1947)]

      (2) **"Selective incorporation":** [§395] However, most provisions of the Bill of Rights have been held applicable to the states through the Fourteenth Amendment Due Process Clause.

         (a) **Standard for incorporation:** [§396] In determining which provisions of the Bill of Rights are protected from ***both*** federal and state action, the Court has used various criteria, *e.g.*, stating that the Fourteenth Amendment incorporates those principles "implicit in the concept of ordered liberty" [Palko v. Connecticut, 302 U.S. 319 (1947)], or ***"fundamental to the American scheme of justice"*** [Duncan v. Louisiana, 391 U.S. 145 (1968)].

         (b) **Extent of incorporation:** [§397] A majority of the Court has concluded that if a right is incorporated by the Fourteenth Amendment, then ***all aspects and elements*** of the right must be deemed incorporated, so that the right receives the same protection against state action (via the Fourteenth Amendment) that it receives against federal action (under the Bill of Rights).

1) **Dissent:** However, some Justices take the position that there may be some aspects of a provision of the Bill of Rights that are not so "fundamental" that they must be held binding on the states as a matter of due process. Following this view, a right—although incorporated by the Fourteenth Amendment—may not be protected to the same extent against state action as it is against federal action. [*See* Crist v. Bretz, 437 U.S. 28 (1978)—Burger, C.J., Powell and Rehnquist, JJ.]

2) **Example:** In *Apodaca v. Oregon*, 406 U.S. 404 (1972), four Justices concluded that the Sixth Amendment right to a jury trial included the right to a unanimous verdict; and, since the right to a jury trial had been incorporated by the Fourteenth Amendment Due Process Clause, the requirement of a unanimous verdict was binding on the state courts. Four other Justices concluded to the contrary. The deciding vote was cast by the ninth Justice (Powell), who reasoned that even though the right to jury trial was incorporated by the Fourteenth Amendment, the unanimous verdict aspect of this right was not so fundamental as to be required by due process, and hence, although the states must afford a jury trial, they do not have to afford a unanimous verdict. The net result is that the Sixth Amendment right to jury trial receives ***lesser*** protection in state than in federal courts (*see infra*, §§1195-1196).

(c) **Provisions of Bill of Rights incorporated:** [§398] Most provisions of the Bill of Rights have been held to be so fundamental as to be applicable to the states. They are:

1) First Amendment protections for ***religion, speech, assembly,*** and ***petition for grievances***. (*See infra*, §§721 *et seq.*)

2) Fourth Amendment provisions regarding ***arrest***, and ***search and seizure***. [Ker v. California, 374 U.S. 23 (1963)]

3) Fifth Amendment protection against ***double jeopardy*** [Benton v. Maryland, 395 U.S. 784 (1969)], the privilege against ***self-incrimination*** [Malloy v. Hogan, 378 U.S. 1 (1964)], and the bar on taking of property ***without just compensation***.

4) Sixth Amendment rights in criminal prosecutions to ***counsel*** [Gideon v. Wainwright, 372 U.S. 335 (1963)]; ***confrontation*** and cross-examination of witnesses [Pointer v. Texas, 380 U.S. 400 (1965)]; ***speedy trial*** [Klopfer v. North Carolina, 386 U.S. 213 (1967)]; ***public trial*** [*In re* Oliver, 333 U.S. 257 (1948)]; ***jury trial*** [Duncan v. Louisiana, 391 U.S. 145 (1968)]; and ***compulsory process*** for obtaining witnesses [Washington v. Texas, 388 U.S. 14 (1967)].

5) Eighth Amendment prohibition against ***cruel and unusual punishment*** (*see infra*, §§1176 *et seq.*). *But note:* The Court has ***not*** ruled on the applicability to the states of the Eighth Amendment's bar on "excessive bail." [*Cf.* Schilb v. Kuebel, 404 U.S. 357 (1971)]

(d) **Provisions of Bill of Rights not incorporated:** [§399] The following have been held not to be so fundamental as to be applicable to the states:

1) ***Grand jury indictment*** guarantee of the Fifth Amendment. [Hurtado v. California, 110 U.S. 516 (1884)]

2) ***Civil jury trial*** guarantee of the Seventh Amendment for all suits at common law involving more than $20. [Walker v. Sauvinet, 92 U.S. 90 (1876)]

(e) **"Due process" as protecting rights beyond those enumerated in Bill of Rights:** [§400] Modern decisions by the Court indicate that the "due process" guaranteed by the Fourteenth Amendment goes ***further*** than merely incorporating various rights enumerated in the first eight amendments. Rather, it reaches various rights that are ***not*** expressed therein (or anywhere else in the Constitution)—for example, that proof in a criminal prosecution be "beyond a reasonable doubt." [*In re* Winship, 397 U.S. 358 (1970)] (*See infra*, §§1227 *et seq.*)

c. **Fourteenth Amendment Equal Protection Clause:** [§401] The Fourteenth Amendment guarantee of "equal protection of the laws" by its terms limits only actions of the ***states***. There is no similar provision in the Constitution applicable to the federal government. However, it has been held that most acts by the federal government that would deny equal protection constitute a "deprivation of liberty" within the ***Fifth*** Amendment Due Process Clause ("No person . . . shall be deprived of life, liberty, or property without due process of law"). [*See* Bolling v. Sharpe, 347 U.S. 497 (1954)—racial segregation in public schools in District of Columbia held to deprive black children of their "liberty" in violation of Fifth Amendment Due Process Clause]

(1) **But note:** Fourteenth Amendment "equal protection" and Fifth Amendment "equality" are not always coextensive. The Court has indicated that where the federal law has nationwide impact, there may be special national interests that justify discrimination by the federal government that would be unacceptable if imposed by a state. (However, federal discrimination with only local impact, and no special national interest involved, is judged by the same standard as state discrimination.) [Hampton v. Mow Sun Wong, 426 U.S. 88 (1976)—regulation of aliens by Congress]

B. DUE PROCESS

1. **Introduction:** [§402] Both the Fifth and Fourteenth Amendments protect against the deprivation of "life, liberty, or property without due process of law."

The Due Process Clause is most often used to provide procedural safeguards to persons accused of crime (*see supra*, §§398-400; *and see infra*, §§1154 *et seq.*). But due process also protects interests outside the criminal context.

2. **Procedural Due Process:** [§403] In addition to the procedural safeguards afforded persons accused of crime before they may be deprived of "life, liberty, or property," the Due Process Clause of the Fifth and Fourteenth Amendments protects an additional range of ***"liberty"*** and ***"property"*** interests from being impaired without ***some form*** of notice and hearing before an unbiased decisionmaker. The Court uses a two-step analysis in determining whether this procedural due process has been denied: (i) it first determines whether a "liberty" or "property" interest has been impaired; and (ii) ***if so***, it then determines what procedures are due.

a. **Definition of "liberty" and "property":** [§404] The Court has not comprehensively defined what constitutes the "liberty" and "property" that may not be denied without procedural due process.

(1) **Liberty:** [§405] "Liberty" plainly encompasses the right to be free of ***physical restraints*** imposed by government in the noncriminal context as well as by the criminal process. [Vitek v. Jones, 445 U.S. 480 (1980); Addington v. Texas, 441 U.S. 418 (1979)—involuntary commitment of an adult to a mental institution] It also includes the ***right to contract*** and to engage in ***gainful employment***. [Board of Regents v. Roth, 408 U.S. 564 (1972)]

(a) **Defamation by government:** [§406] "Liberty" also includes the right to be free of defamation by a government official, when such defamation is ***made public*** and occurs in connection with denial of some ***significant tangible interest***. [Board of Regents v. Roth, *supra*—failure to renew nontenured public employment; Goss v. Lopez, 419 U.S. 565 (1975)—disciplinary suspension from public school; Wisconsin v. Constantineau, 400 U.S. 433 (1971)—police posted names of "excessive drinkers" in liquor stores, thereby forbidding sales to them for one year]

1) **Compare—defamation alone:** However, defamation resulting ***only*** in damage to one's reputation is not a denial of protected "liberty." [Paul v. Davis, 424 U.S. 693 (1976)]

2) **Compare—loss of employment alone:** And mere loss of public employment without publicity as to the defamatory reasons therefor is ***not*** a denial of "liberty." [Bishop v. Wood, 426 U.S. 341 (1976)]

(b) **Parental interests:** [§407] A parent has a "liberty" interest in a ***developed*** parent-child relationship—*e.g.*, when a father plays a substantial role in his illegitimate child's rearing. But the mere biological fact of parenthood does not merit equivalent constitutional protection. [Lehr v. Robertson, 463 U.S. 248 (1983)—father never had any significant relationship with his illegitimate child]

(2) **Property:** [§408] "Property" denotes more than ownership of realty, chattels, or money. It also includes "entitlements"—*i.e.*, "interests already

acquired in specific benefits." This requires more than an abstract need or desire for (or unilateral expectation of) the benefit: there must be a ***legitimate claim*** to the benefit under applicable local, state, or federal law. [Board of Regents v. Roth, *supra*]

(a) **Examples:** There is a constitutionally protected "property" interest in ***public education*** when school attendance is required [Goss v. Lopez, *supra*]; in ***continued welfare benefits*** where the applicant meets statutory criteria [Goldberg v. Kelly, 397 U.S. 254 (1970)]; in ***retention of a driver's license*** under prevailing statutory standards [Bell v. Burson, 402 U.S. 535 (1971)]; and in ***continued utility service*** where state law only permits a municipal utility company to terminate service "for cause" [Memphis Light, Gas & Water Division v. Craft, 436 U.S. 1 (1978)].

1) **Compare:** But a lawyer licensed in one state has no property interest to appear in the courts of another state in the absence of a state rule or "mutually explicit understanding" to that effect. [Leis v. Flynt, 439 U.S. 438 (1979)]

(b) **Public employment:** [§409] Whether there is a "property" interest in continued public employment is determined by applicable local, state, or federal law. A statute (or ordinance), the employment contract, or some clear practice or understanding must provide that the employee can be terminated only for "cause." [Arnett v. Kennedy, 416 U.S. 134 (1974)] There is ***no*** "property" interest if the position is held "at the will of" the public employer. [Bishop v. Wood, *supra*]

(c) **Causes of action:** [§410] There is a "property" interest in a legislatively or judicially created cause of action, *e.g.*, a state statutory right against employment discrimination. [Logan v. Zimmerman Brush Co., 455 U.S. 422 (1982)]

(3) **Compare—indirect effect:** [§411] Government action that affects a person only ***indirectly or incidentally*** is ***not*** deemed a deprivation of any interest in that person's "liberty" or "property." [O'Bannon v. Town Court Nursing Center, 447 U.S. 773 (1980)—patients of nursing home not entitled to a hearing solely because government revoked nursing home's certification to receive payments; patients had no statutory right to receive benefits at ***that particular*** nursing home]

b. **Definition of "deprivation":** [§412] A "deprivation" of life, liberty, or property without due process requires something more than ***mere negligent conduct*** by government officials, even though such conduct causes injury. It is an open question whether something less than intentional conduct—such as "recklessness" or "gross negligence"—may constitute a deprivation. [Daniels v. Williams, 474 U.S. 327 (1986)]

(1) **"Deprivation" by private persons:** [§413] Failure of a government entity or its agents to adequately protect an individual against being harmed by others does not constitute a deprivation of life, liberty, or property without due process. The purpose of the Due Process Clause is

to protect people from government, not to ensure that government protects people from each other. [DeShaney v. Winnebago County Department of Social Services, 489 U.S. 189 (1989)]

c. **Timing and scope of required hearing:** [§414] An ***adversary, judicial-type*** hearing—whether before or after deprivation of a protected liberty or property interest—is ***not*** required in all circumstances. Rather, whether a ***prior*** evidentiary hearing is required, and the ***extent*** of procedural requirements, is determined by weighing:

(i) The importance of the individual interest involved;

(ii) The value of specific procedural safeguards to that interest; and

(iii) The government interest in fiscal and administrative efficiency.

[Mathews v. Eldridge, 424 U.S. 319 (1976)]

(1) **Civil forfeiture of real property used in connection with crime:** [§415] Due process requires notice and an adversary hearing ***prior*** to government seizure and forfeiture of ***real property*** allegedly used in connection with crime. The private interest in possession of a home (even when rented to others), for example, is of historic and continuing importance, and a subsequent hearing may not recompense losses caused by an erroneous seizure. In the absence of exigent circumstances—such as easy removal of personal property [*see* Calero Toledo v. Pearson Yacht Leasing Co., 416 U.S. 663 (1974)]—the government has no pressing need for an ex parte seizure. [United States v. James Daniel Good Real Property, 114 S. Ct. 492 (1993)]

(2) **Termination of welfare benefits:** [§416] Due process ***requires an evidentiary*** hearing ***before*** termination of welfare benefits. It need not be a judicial or quasi-judicial trial if there is adequate post-termination review; but the recipient must have timely and adequate ***notice*** of the reasons for the proposed termination, the right to ***confront and cross-examine*** adverse witnesses, and the right to ***present his own arguments*** and evidence orally. ***Counsel*** need ***not*** be provided, but must be permitted. Finally, the decision must be based ***solely on evidence*** adduced at the hearing and must be rendered by an ***impartial decisionmaker***. [Goldberg v. Kelly, *supra*]

(3) **Termination of disability benefits:** [§417] ***No prior evidentiary hearing*** is required for termination of disability benefits, provided there is prior ***notice*** to the recipient, an ***opportunity to respond*** in writing, and a ***subsequent evidentiary hearing*** (with retroactive payment of benefits if the recipient prevails). *Rationale:* Disability benefits (unlike welfare benefits) are not based on financial need, and thus are not deemed "vital." [Mathews v. Eldridge, *supra*]

(a) **Limit on attorneys' fees:** [§418] Because of Congress's desire that the proceedings be "as informal and nonadversarial as possible" and that claimants' benefits not be unnecessarily diverted to lawyers, a federal law limiting to $10 the fee that may be paid an attorney or agent who represents a veteran seeking service-connected disability benefits does ***not*** violate due process, absent a ***strong*** showing of likely errors under the existing system that would likely be cured by the presence of lawyers. [Walters v. National Association of Radiation Survivors, 468 U.S. 1323 (1985)]

(4) **Termination of public employment:** [§419] A public employee subject to removal only for "cause" may be removed ***without a prior evidentiary*** hearing on "cause," at least if there is ***some form of pretermination notice and opportunity to respond*** (to determine whether there are reasonable grounds to believe the charge), and a ***subsequent evidentiary*** hearing (with reinstatement and back pay if the employee prevails). [Arnett v. Kennedy, *supra,* §409]

(a) **Suspension:** [§420] If there is a ***significant hazard*** perceived in keeping the employee on the job, he may be suspended (with pay) without notice and a prior hearing. [Cleveland Board of Education v. Loudermill, 470 U.S. 532 (1985)]

(5) **Public education—disciplinary suspension:** [§421] Although ***no formal evidentiary*** hearing is required before a student may be ***temporarily*** suspended (for 10 days or less), due process usually requires ***some notice of*** the charges and ***some opportunity to explain***. But if the student's presence poses a danger to persons or property or threatens to disrupt the academic process, such notice and hearing may ***follow*** removal as soon as practicable. [Goss v. Lopez, *supra,* §406]

(a) **Corporal punishment in public school:** [§422] This may involve constitutionally protected liberty. However, the traditional common law remedies for excessive punishment satisfy procedural due process and ***no prior hearing*** is required. [Ingraham v. Wright, 430 U.S. 651 (1977)]

(6) **Public education—academic dismissal:** [§423] ***No*** prior ***evidentiary*** hearing is required when a student is dismissed for "academic" deficiencies rather than for "disciplinary" reasons. Due process is satisfied if the student is ***adequately informed*** of the deficiency and given an ***opportunity to respond***. [Board of Curators v. Horowitz, 435 U.S. 78 (1978)]

(7) **License suspension:** [§424] If there is ***probable cause*** to believe that the conditions of a license have been violated, the state's interest may ***sometimes*** be important enough to permit suspension of the license ***without*** any ***prior*** hearing—but there must be a ***prompt*** post-suspension hearing and decision on any disputed issues. [Barry v. Barchi, 443 U.S. 55 (1979)—horse trainer's license suspended regarding drugging of horse; Mackey v. Montrym, 443 U.S. 1 (1979)—driver's license suspended for refusing to submit to breathalyzer test]

(a) **"Promptness":** [§425] The permissible length of time between suspension and a decision after a hearing is determined by weighing: (i) the importance of the interest and the harm occasioned by delay; (ii) the government's justification for delay; and (iii) the likelihood that the interim decision may have been mistaken. [Federal Deposit

Insurance Corp. v. Mallen, 486 U.S. 232 (1988)—upholding procedure for decision within 90 days of suspension of bank official who is indicted]

(8) **Creditor remedies:** [§426] Due process ***requires*** notice and a hearing ***prior*** to any prejudgment ***garnishment of wages***. [Sniadach v. Family Finance Corp., 395 U.S. 337 (1969)] But in other commercial settings, creditors can cause prejudgment seizures of their debtors' property (or a conditional seller can seize or sequester the asset sold), ***without*** prior notice and hearing to the debtor ***if*** the following requirements are met:

(i) ***Application for the prejudgment seizure is made to a judge*** (rather than a court clerk or other ministerial official);

(ii) ***The application contains an affidavit based on personal knowledge*** setting forth ***"specific facts"*** (not mere conclusions) establishing the creditor's right to issuance of the writ ("narrowly confined facts susceptible of a summary disposition");

(iii) ***The creditor posts an adequate surety bond*** prior to issuance of the writ; and

(iv) ***Provision is made for an early hearing***, at which the creditor must prove "probable cause for the seizure."

[*See* Mitchell v. W. T. Grant Co., 416 U.S. 600 (1974); Fuentes v. Shevin, 407 U.S. 67 (1972); North Georgia Finishing, Inc. v. Di-Chem, Inc., 419 U.S. 601 (1975)]

(9) **Attachment of real property:** [§427] Prejudgment attachment of real property without prior notice and hearing is not permitted unless the plaintiff's factual allegations demonstrate a likelihood of recovery. This is more easily shown in uncomplicated matters that lend themselves to documentary proof (*e.g.*, the existence of a debt or delinquent payments) than cases of a factually valid complaint that is subject to dispute (*e.g.*, for assault and battery). The risk of erroneous deprivation of significant property interests (*e.g.*, cloud on title) is too great in the latter instances. [Connecticut v. Doehr, 501 U.S. 1 (1991)]

(10) **Commitment to a mental institution:** [§428] The Court has not detailed the procedural safeguards required by due process prior to the involuntary commitment of an adult to a mental institution. But it has held that, although the standard of proof of the criteria for such commitment need ***not*** be "beyond a reasonable doubt," it must at least require ***"clear and convincing"*** evidence. [Addington v. Texas, *supra*, §405]

(a) **Children:** [§429] Parents, or a governmental agency acting on behalf of a child, can institutionalize a child for mental treatment ***without*** a ***prior*** adversary hearing if:

(i) ***Prior to admission, an inquiry is made by a neutral fact finder*** (who may be a physician) to determine whether the statutory requirements for admission are satisfied;

(ii) ***The inquiry carefully probes the child's background***; and

(iii) ***The child's continued need for institutionalization is subject to periodic review*** by a similarly independent procedure.

[Parham v. J.R., 442 U.S. 584 (1979)]

1) **Note:** The Court has left open the question of whether the periodic review required when a governmental agency commits a ward should differ from the review required when parents commit their child.

(11) **Antipsychotic drugs for prison inmates:** [§430] Due process does not require a trial-type hearing before a judicial officer or outside psychiatrist prior to a state's treating a mentally ill prisoner with antipsychotic drugs against his will. Nor does the mentally ill prisoner have a right to counsel with respect to such treatment. [Washington v. Harper, 494 U.S. 210 (1990)—pretreatment notice and hearing before staff medical professionals who are not institutionally biased is sufficient]

(12) **Termination of parental status:** [§431] Procedural due process does ***not*** require appointment of counsel for indigent parents in ***every*** hearing to terminate parental status, but only when "fundamental fairness" demands it. [Lassiter v. Department of Social Services, 452 U.S. 18 (1981)]

(a) **Burden of proof:** [§432] Procedural due process requires that the state establish its allegations of parental unfitness by at least ***"clear and convincing evidence."*** [Santosky v. Kramer, 455 U.S. 745 (1982)]

1) **Compare—paternity:** [§433] However, due process does ***not*** require "clear and convincing evidence" in a civil action to establish paternity. The "preponderance of the evidence" standard is constitutional. [Rivera v. Minnich, 483 U.S. 574 (1987)]

3. Substantive Due Process

a. **Economic and social regulations:** [§434] In the first third of the twentieth century, the Court often reviewed the ***substance*** of legislation and used the Due Process Clause to invalidate economic and social regulations. The basic rationale was that the legislation ***unreasonably*** interfered with "liberty" and "property" interests protected by the Due Process Clause. The Justices made their own ***personal judgments*** as to whether the ***means*** used by the regulation were ***reasonably related*** to a ***legitimate*** end. [*See, e.g.*, Allgeyer v. Louisiana, 165 U.S. 578 (1897)—"liberty" protected by Due Process Clause includes ***right to contract***, which was abridged by state insurance regulation]

(1) ***Lochner*** **case:** [§435] The most famous decision of this era was *Lochner v. New York*, 198 U.S. 45 (1905), which held that a law limiting the number of hours that bakers could work unreasonably interfered with "the freedom of master and employee to contract in relation to their employment."

Rationale: The freedom to contract may be restricted through the state's police power to protect public health, safety, welfare, or morals, but the ***means*** used by this statute (limiting baker's hours) were ***not reasonably related*** to such ends. Rather, this was "purely a labor law," and government had ***no legitimate purpose*** in this type of regulation ("We do not believe in the soundness of the views which uphold this law").

(2) **Modern approach:** [§436] Since the mid-1930s, the Court has adopted a different approach; it defers to legislative judgments in respect to economic and social regulations unless they are "demonstrably ***arbitrary*** or ***irrational***." [Duke Power Co. v. Carolina Environmental Study Group, Inc., 438 U.S. 59 (1978)] Such laws are ***presumed*** valid and will be upheld unless no reasonable state of facts can be conceived to support them, or unless they bear no rational relationship to the end sought—the burden of proof being on the person challenging the law. [United States v. Carolene Products Co., 304 U.S. 144 (1938)] The Court will ***not*** "weigh the wisdom" of such legislation or substitute its own judgment for that of the legislative body. [Ferguson v. Skrupa, 372 U.S. 726 (1963)]

(a) **Effect:** [§437] Under this approach, public health and safety measures—as well as various regulations of business such as price controls [*see* Nebbia v. New York, 291 U.S. 502 (1934)], trade practices [*see* North Dakota Board of Pharmacy v. Snyder's Drug Stores, 414 U.S. 156 (1973)], wage and hour laws [*see* West Coast Hotel Co. v. Parrish, 300 U.S. 379 (1937)], bans on discrimination against union or nonunion employees [*see* Lincoln Federal Labor Union v. Northwestern Iron & Metal Co.. 335 U.S. 525 (1949)], and limitations on engaging in certain occupations [*see* Williamson v. Lee Optical Co., 348 U.S. 483 (1955)]—are effectively ***immune*** from a general Due Process Clause attack.

(b) **Punitive damages:** [§438] Jury-awarded punitive damages must be ***reasonable***. The Due Process Clause requires that: (i) the jury be given adequate guidance and its discretion be constrained by standards that are rationally related to determining an award no greater than reasonably necessary to punish and deter; and (ii) there be meaningful review by the trial judge and appellate courts [Pacific Mutual Life Insurance Co. v. Haslip, 499 U.S. 1 (1991)], including review as to whether the ***amount*** of punitive damages is too great [Honda Motor Co. v. Oberg, 114 S. Ct. ____ (1994)].

1) **Amount:** [§439] "Grossly excessive" damages are invalid. But the Court has not agreed on a "test" to determine excessiveness. [TXO Production Corp. v. Alliance Resources Corp., 113 S. Ct. 2711 (1993)—upholding $10 million punitive damages in a case with $19,000 compensatory damages]

2) **Excessive fines:** [§440] The Eighth Amendment's prohibition of "excessive fines" places limits only on ***government*** and thus does not apply to punitive damages in civil litigation. [Browning Ferris Industries of Vermont, Inc. v. Kelso Disposal, Inc., 492

U.S. 257 (1989)] But the "excessive fines" prohibition ***does apply*** to government-imposed civil forfeiture if intended to serve as punishment. [Austin v. United States, 113 S. Ct. 2801 (1993)—law providing for forfeiture of property used in drug-related crimes]

b. **Fundamental personal rights:** [§441] Since the mid-1960s, the Court has revived substantive due process review as a means of protecting certain ***fundamental*** personal rights not specifically enumerated in the Constitution. If a government regulation impinges upon such a fundamental right, it is subjected to essentially the same type of strict scrutiny applicable to "fundamental rights" issues under the Equal Protection Clause (*see infra*, §§582 *et seq.*); *i.e.*, the regulation is invalid unless found to be ***necessary*** (narrowly drawn) to a ***compelling*** government interest.

(1) **Right of privacy:** [§442] The right of privacy is nowhere mentioned in the Constitution. Nevertheless, the Court has recognized that a right of personal privacy, or at least a guarantee of certain areas or zones of privacy, ***is*** constitutionally protected. Some Justices have found the right recognized by the ***Ninth Amendment*** ("The enumeration of certain rights shall not be construed to deny or disparage others retained by the people"), while other Justices felt it was within the ***"penumbras"*** or ***"emanations"*** of various provisions of the Bill of Rights [Griswold v. Connecticut, 381 U.S. 479 (1965)]. More recently, the Court has simply held that the right of personal privacy is implicit in the concept of "liberty" within the protection of the Due Process Clause; *i.e.,* it is one of those ***basic human rights*** which are of "fundamental" importance in our society. [Roe v. Wade, 410 U.S. 113 (1973)]

(a) **Scope:** [§443] The right of personal privacy encompasses the following:

1) **Marriage:** [§444] The right to marry has been referred to as a "basic civil right." [Loving v. Virginia, 388 U.S. 1 (1967); *and see infra*, §602]

2) **Procreation:** [§445] The right to procreate has been referred to as "one of the basic civil rights of man." [Skinner v. Oklahoma, 316 U.S. 535 (1942); *and see infra*, §604]

3) **Contraception:** [§446] In *Griswold v. Connecticut, supra*, the Court invalidated a state law that made it a crime for any person to use contraceptives, including married persons. The Court held that the statute infringed on a constitutionally protected "zone of ***marital privacy***."

a) **Note:** In *Eisenstadt v. Baird*, 405 U.S. 438 (1972), the Court reasoned that the decision whether to use contraceptives was one of ***individual*** privacy, and thus the right belonged to ***single*** as well as married persons.

b) **And note:** In *Carey v. Population Services International*, 431 U.S. 678 (1977), the Court held that a state could not prohibit distribution of nonmedical contraceptives to adults except through licensed pharmacists, nor prohibit sales of such contraceptives to persons under age 16 who did not have approval of a licensed physician.

4) **Abortion:** [§447] A woman's decision whether to terminate her pregnancy is encompassed within the right of privacy. [Roe v. Wade, *supra*—state law permitting abortion only to save mother's life invalid]

a) **Before fetal viability:** [§448] Prior to viability (*i.e.*, when there is no realistic possibility of maintaining the fetus's life outside the womb) the state's interests in protecting the mother's health and the life of the fetus that may become a child are outweighed by the woman's right to have an abortion without imposition of "undue burdens" (or "substantial obstacles") by the state. [Planned Parenthood of Southeastern Pennsylvania v. Casey, 112 S. Ct. 2791 (1992)]

1/ **Undue burden:** [§449] The Court did not specifically define what will constitute an undue burden. However, the Court did state that a law that serves a valid purpose (*i.e.*, "is not a law designed to strike at the right itself") does ***not*** impose an undue burden simply because it has the incidental effect of making it more difficult or expensive to procure an abortion. Neither does a law designed to persuade a pregnant woman to choose childbirth over abortion impose an "undue burden" unless it has the effect of placing a "substantial obstacle" in her path. [Planned Parenthood of Southeastern Pennsylvania v. Casey, *supra*]

2/ **Informed consent:** [§450] Requiring informed consent to an abortion is not necessarily an undue burden. Thus, the state ***may*** require a woman to give written, informed consent to the abortion, and that she be of a certain age or maturity in order to consent. [Planned Parenthood v. Danforth, 428 U.S. 52 (1976)] Furthermore, the state may require that a physician provide the woman with truthful information about the nature of the abortion procedure, the health risks of abortion and childbirth, and the probable gestational age of the fetus. [Planned Parenthood of Southeastern Pennsylvania v. Casey, *supra*]

3/ **Waiting period:** [§451] A state-required 24-hour waiting period between the time the woman gives her informed consent and the time of the abortion does ***not*** amount to an undue burden. [Planned Parenthood of Southeastern Pennsylvania v. Casey, *supra*]

4/ **Data collection:** [§452] Recordkeeping and reporting provisions that are reasonably directed to preserving maternal health and that properly respect a patient's privacy do ***not*** impose an undue burden. [Planned Parenthood v. Danforth, *supra*]

5/ **Husband's consent:** [§453] A state may not require the consent of the pregnant woman's husband to an abortion during the first trimester. Since the state itself cannot proscribe during this period, it cannot delegate such authority to some person other than the woman's physician. [Planned Parenthood v. Danforth, *supra*]

6/ **Unmarried minors:** [§454] For the same reasons, the state may not require parental consent for an abortion during the first trimester of an unmarried minor (who is old enough and mature enough to give effective consent). [Planned Parenthood v. Danforth, *supra*] Nor, where a mature minor is involved, may the state require the consent of a judge. [Bellotti v. Baird, 443 U.S. 622 (1979)]

a/ **Parental consent:** [§455] A state may require parental or judicial consent for an immature minor—as long as she has the opportunity to demonstrate that she is mature or that, despite her immaturity, an abortion would be in her best interests. [Planned Parenthood v. Ashcroft, 462 U.S. 476 (1983)]

b/ **Parental notification:** [§456] A state may, require that notice be given to ***a*** parent of an unemancipated minor, and that she wait up to 48 hours thereafter before an abortion—at least when the minor has an opportunity to obtain a court order permitting the abortion to proceed. [Ohio v. Akron Center for Reproductive Health, 497 U.S. 502 (1990)] But a requirement that ***both*** parents be notified, whether or not both wish to be notified or have assumed responsibility for the upbringing of the child, does not reasonably further the state interest in giving the benefit of parental advice to the minor. The two-parent notice requirement is thus invalid, unless combined with a judicial bypass procedure. [Hodgson v. Minnesota, 497 U.S. 417 (1990)]

7/ **Other regulations uncertain:** [§457] Prior to *Planned Parenthood of Southeastern Pennsylvania v. Casey*, the Court had invalidated requirements that abortions be performed only in specially accredited hospitals or health facilities, or that they be approved by more than one physician or a hospital committee. [Doe v. Bolton, 410 U.S. 179 (1973)] It is unclear whether these types of regulations will now be held to impose an "undue burden."

b) **When fetus viable:** [§458] Once the fetus has become viable, the state may prohibit abortion unless it is shown to be necessary for the preservation of the mother's life or health. [Roe v. Wade, *supra*] However, viability itself is a medical question. A state cannot unduly interfere with the attending physician's judgment, on the particular facts of the case, as to whether there is a reasonable likelihood of the fetus's survival outside the womb, with or without artificial support. [Colautti v. Franklin, 439 U.S. 379 (1979)]

1/ **Determining viability:** [§459] The state's compelling interest in the potential life of a viable fetus renders its interest in determining the point of viability equally compelling. Thus, the state may require the performance of tests that are ***medically prudent*** and ***useful*** in determining whether a fetus is viable. [Webster v . Reproductive Health Services, 492 U.S. 490 (1989)]

c) **Public benefits:** [§460] The right to terminate a pregnancy does not carry with it the right to receive public funds for such termination. [Harris v. McRae, 448 U.S. 297 (1980)] Nor must the state permit public employees or the use of public facilities to perform abortions. [Webster v. Reproductive Health Services, *supra*]

5) **Right to educate children as one chooses:** [§461] Although the state may prescribe reasonable educational standards, it may ***not*** require that all children be educated in public schools. [Pierce v. Society of Sisters, 268 U.S. 510 (1925)] Nor may the state forbid education in a language other than English. [Meyer v. Nebraska, 262 U.S. 390 (1923)]

6) **Familial rights:** [§462] The Court has recognized the right of ***related persons*** to live together in a single household. [Moore v. City of East Cleveland, 431 U.S. 494 (1977)]

(b) **Interests not protected by right of privacy:** [§463] The right of privacy does ***not*** protect:

1) ***The right to engage in consensual homosexual sodomy***—the right to privacy decisions encompassing family, marriage, and procreation do not extend this far. [Bowers v. Hardwick, 478 U.S. 573 (1986)]

2) ***The right not to have the state publicize a record*** of an official act, such as an arrest. [Paul v. Davis, 424 U.S. 693 (1976)]

3) ***The right of parents to send their children to private schools that refuse to admit blacks***. [Runyon v. McCrary, 427 U.S. 160 (1976)]

4) ***The right of a large and basically unselective organization to exclude women from full membership***. [Roberts v. United States Jaycees, 468 U.S. 609 (1984)]

5) ***The right of the father of an illegitimate child to veto the child's adoption***—at least where the father has never sought custody and adoption is found to be in the child's "best interests" because the child would continue to live in the same family unit (with its mother and her husband). [Quilloin v. Walcott, 434 U.S. 246 (1978)]

6) ***The right of police officers to have their hair length unregulated***. Assuming that the general public has some Fourteenth Amendment "liberty" with respect to personal appearance, the state interest in public safety requires only that regulations concerning the organization of a police force be "rational." [Kelley v. Johnson, 425 U.S. 238 (1976)]

7) ***The right not to have the state accumulate and computerize the names and addresses of patients for whom dangerous drugs are prescribed*** (at least where there are appropriate precautions against indiscriminate public disclosures). [Whalen v. Roe, 429 U.S. 589 (1977)—leaving open the questions of ***unwarranted*** disclosures, or the accumulation of such data ***without*** security measures]

8) ***The right of a United States President to protect personal communications from review and screening*** by federal archivists, when such communications are commingled with other materials of important public interest and cannot be segregated from the private communications without comprehensive screening. [Nixon v. Administrator of General Services, 433 U.S. 425 (1977)]

(2) **Right to interstate travel:** [§464] The right to travel freely from state to state is constitutionally protected and is ***virtually unqualified***. [United States v. Guest, 383 U.S. 745 (1966)]

(a) **Source of right uncertain:** [§465] This right is not specifically mentioned in the Constitution, and the Court has not clearly placed it under any specific provision.

1) **Historical view:** [§466] Some of the earliest cases held it was protected under the Commerce Clause. [Passenger Cases, 48 U.S. (7 How.) 283 (1849)] Later, it was regarded as a right

of state citizenship protected under the Interstate Privileges and Immunities Clause [Paul v. Virginia, 75 U.S. (8 Wall.) 168 (1869)]; or as a right of national citizenship, protected under the Fourteenth Amendment Privileges and Immunities Clause [Twining v. New Jersey, *supra*, §230]; or as a right having its source in the Due Process Clause.

2) **Modern view:** [§467] More recently, the Court has refrained from attempting to pinpoint the source of the right, but simply acknowledges that it is constitutionally protected. [Shapiro v. Thompson, 394 U.S. 618 (1969)]

(b) **Limits:** [§468] The right to travel interstate is ***not*** violated by a law that forbids a person who has committed a crime within the state from leaving that state—at least if such departure would aggravate the consequences of the original crime. [Jones v. Helms, 452 U.S. 280 (1981)—law increased penalty of those who leave state after abandoning their children]

(3) **Right to international travel:** [§469] The right to travel abroad has been held to be part of the "liberty" guaranteed by due process. [Kent v. Dulles, 357 U.S. 116 (1958)]

(a) **Scope of right:** [§470] The right of international travel is not as unqualified as the right to travel interstate and ***may be regulated*** within the bounds of due process.

1) **Examples—valid restrictions:** [§471] Denial of social security benefits when recipients are outside the country has been upheld as being "rationally based." [Califano v. Aznavorian, 439 U.S. 170 (1978)] And it is "reasonable" to revoke the passport of a person whose conduct in foreign countries presents a serious danger to national security and foreign policy. [Haig v. Agee, 453 U.S. 280 (1981)] Reasonable "area restrictions" for passports (prohibiting travel to certain countries or danger zones) have also been upheld because of a substantial justification of national security and foreign policy. [Zemel v. Rusk, 381 U.S. 1 (1965)—Cuban passport denied]

a) **Judicial deference:** In reviewing federal restrictions on international travel, the Court defers to the judgment of the political branches on matters of foreign policy. [Regan v. Wald, 468 U.S. 222 (1984)]

2) **Example—"overbroad" restriction:** [§472] A provision of the Subversive Activities Control Act that authorized the denial of passports to ***all*** members of the Communist Party or front groups was held invalid as too broad in scope. It applied to members who had neither knowledge nor intent, and it authorized the Secretary of State to prohibit ***all*** travel by such persons, even for legitimate purposes (*e.g.*, to receive medical treatment). [Aptheker v. Secretary of State, 378 U.S. 500 (1964)]

(4) **Right to vote:** [§473] The Constitution generally empowers the states to set the requirements for voting in both state and federal elections. [*See* Art. I, §2—House of Representatives; Seventeenth Amendment—Senate] However, even beyond several amendments to the Constitution that forbid government denial of the right to vote on specified grounds (*see infra*, §607), the Court has held that voting is a "fundamental" right at the heart of our constitutional system, and thus there is a constitutionally protected right to participate in elections on an equal basis. (*See infra*, §§607 *et seq.*)

(5) **Rights of mentally ill:** [§474] The Court has held that commitment to a mental hospital is a deprivation of liberty subject to protection by the Due Process Clause. [O'Connor v. Donaldson, 422 U.S. 563 (1975)]

(a) **Standards for commitment:** [§475] A finding that an adult is "mentally ill" is not enough to justify involuntary deprivation of his right to liberty. No legitimate state interest is served by involuntarily confining a mentally ill adult unless it appears that the person is ***dangerous*** to himself or others, or ***incapable of surviving*** safely outside an institution either through his own efforts or through the help of willing friends and relatives. [O'Connor v. Donaldson, *supra*]

1) **Two conditions required:** [§476] Even though an adult may be found to be dangerous to himself or others, he may not be involuntarily confined unless he is also found to be "mentally ill." [Foucha v. Louisiana, 112 S. Ct. 1780 (1992)—defendant who is found not guilty by reason of insanity may not be held in a psychiatric hospital after it is determined that he is no longer mentally ill]

2) **Prisoners:** [§477] A prison inmate who has a serious mental illness may be treated with antipsychotic drugs against his will, ***if*** the inmate is dangerous to himself or others and the treatment is in the inmate's medical interest. [Washington v. Harper, *supra*, §430]

(b) **Conditions of confinement:** [§478] The constitutional right to liberty of involuntarily committed, mentally retarded persons includes rights of adequate food, shelter, clothing, and medical care. It also requires reasonably safe conditions, freedom from bodily restraint, and minimally adequate training to ensure these rights, but an appropriate professional's judgment that these obligations have been satisfied (given all relevant circumstances) is entitled to a presumption of correctness. [Youngberg v. Romeo, 457 U.S. 307 (1982)]

(6) **Right to reject medical treatment:** [§479] The liberty protected by the Due Process Clause guarantees a competent person the right to refuse unwanted medical treatment. [Cruzan v. Director, Missouri Department of Health, 497 U.S. 261 (1990)]

(a) **Standard of proof:** [§480] A state may apply a clear and convincing evidence standard to determine an individual's actual wishes in the matter and need not accept the "substituted judgment" of others (including close family). [Cruzan v. Director, Missouri Department of Health, *supra*]

C. EQUAL PROTECTION

1. **Constitutional Provision:** [§481] The Fourteenth Amendment provides: "No ***State*** shall . . . deny to any person within its jurisdiction the equal protection of the laws."

   a. **Federal government:** [§482] As previously discussed (*see supra*, §401), although there is no comparable provision in the Constitution that expressly limits the federal government, the Court has held that, in ***most instances*** (*see infra*, §714), the Fifth Amendment Due Process Clause applies the same prohibition to the federal government.

2. **In General:** [§483] It must be recognized that almost all statutes and other forms of government regulation classify (or discriminate among) people; virtually none treats all persons in the same manner.

   a. **Examples:** The income tax laws apply different rates to persons in different income brackets; wage and hours laws do not apply to persons in certain occupations; etc.

   b. **Need for permissible classifications:** In recognition of the fact that the operation of government requires regulations that classify (or discriminate), the Court has established several different tests for determining their permissibility under the Equal Protection Clause. Each of these tests, including the three major ones—(i) the "traditional" (or "rational basis") test, (ii) the "strict scrutiny" (or "compelling interest") test, and (iii) the "intermediate level of scrutiny" (or "quasi-suspect class") test—is discussed below.

3. **Traditional Test—Economic and Social Regulations:** [§484] When the statutory classification is not based on "suspect" or "quasi-suspect" criteria (*see infra*, §§489 *et seq.*), the Court reviews it under the "traditional" equal protection test. Thus, this approach is used for virtually all economic and social regulations.

   a. **Extreme judicial deference:** [§485] This test is ***usually*** stated as follows: The classification (or discrimination) is valid if it is ***rationally related*** to a ***proper*** (or ***constitutionally permissible***) ***state interest***. Under this test, a classification is ***presumed valid*** and will be upheld unless the person challenging it proves that it is "invidious," "wholly arbitrary," or "capricious." Moreover, the legislative body enacting the classification need not articulate its reasons for the classification—*i.e.*, the challenger must show that ***no reasonable state of facts*** can be conceived to justify it. [Lindsley v. Natural Carbonic Gas Co., 220 U.S. 61 (1911); McGowan v. Maryland, 366 U.S. 420 (1961); United States Railroad Retirement Board v. Fritz, 449 U.S. 166 (1980)]

      (1) **Over- and under-inclusion:** [§486] The line drawn by the legislature may be imperfect, resulting in some over- or under-inclusiveness, and the statute may still be valid. [Vance v. Bradley, 440 U.S. 93 (1979)]

Legislatures may proceed one step at a time and may partially eliminate a perceived evil, deferring complete regulation to the future. [Williamson v. Lee Optical Co., 348 U.S. 483 (1955); New Orleans v. Dukes, 427 U.S. 297 (1976)]

(2) **Effect:** [§487] By employing this test, the Court gives legislative bodies "wide latitude" in drawing classifications when enacting economic and social regulations pursuant to the police power. [New York City Transit Authority v. Beazer, 440 U.S. 568 (1979)—upholding rule denying employment to persons receiving methadone treatment] ***Only rarely*** will the Court find a violation of equal protection.

(a) **Example:** The federal food stamp program excluded any household containing unrelated persons. The Court found the classification "wholly without any rational basis." The legislative history indicated that the provision was aimed at excluding "hippie communes" from the program. The Court found that discrimination against this "politically unpopular group" was ***not*** a ***constitutionally permissible*** government interest. [United States Department of Agriculture v. Moreno, 413 U.S. 528 (1973)]

(b) **Example:** A county tax assessor valued real property at its sale price but made only minor modifications for property that had not been recently sold. As a result, some property was assessed at as much as 35 times more than comparable neighboring property. The Court held that this practice was not "rationally related" to the state policy of assessing all property at its estimated market value. [Allegheny Pittsburgh Coal Co. v. County Commission, 488 U.S. 386 (1989)]

1) **Compare:** Although California's Proposition 13 (which adopted an acquisition valuation system of taxation whereby property is reassessed to new value at construction or change of ownership) produced similar disparities in property valuation, it did not violate equal protection. California had deliberately adopted a policy of assessing largely on the basis of "acquisition value" (rather than "market value") and Proposition 13 ***rationally*** furthered ***legitimate*** interests served by the policy. [Nordlinger v. Hahn, 112 S. Ct. 2326 (1992)]

b. **Less deferential formulation:** [§488] Occasionally, the Court states the "traditional" test in a way that suggests a slightly less deferential judicial standard of review: The classification "must rest upon some ground of difference having a ***fair and substantial*** relation to the object of the legislation." [Royster Guano Co. v. Virginia, 253 U.S. 412 (1920)] But even when using this formulation, the Court ***almost always sustains*** the classification. [Johnson v. Robison, 415 U.S. 361 (1974)—upholding federal law denying veterans' education benefits to conscientious objectors who performed alternate civilian service]

4. **Suspect Classifications—"Strict Scrutiny":** [§489] Government action that ***intentionally*** (*see infra*) discriminates against racial or ethnic minorities is "suspect" and thus subject to "strict scrutiny."

a. **Test:** [§490] A regulation discriminating against a suspect class will be held to violate equal protection unless found to be ***necessary*** to promote a ***compelling state interest.***

(1) **"Necessary" to promote compelling state interest:** [§491] A classification is "necessary" when it is narrowly drawn so that ***no alternative, less burdensome means*** is available to accomplish the state interest.

(a) **Effect:** Under this test, almost all intentional government discrimination against the following groups has been held ***invalid:***

1) ***Blacks*** [Strauder v. West Virginia, 100 U.S. 303 (1880)—law forbidding blacks from serving on grand or petit juries];

2) ***Persons of Chinese ancestry*** [Yick Wo v. Hopkins, 118 U.S. 356 (1886)—denial of laundry licenses only to Chinese]; and

3) ***Persons of Mexican ancestry*** [Hernandez v. Texas, 347 U.S. 475 (1954)—discrimination against Mexican-Americans in respect to jury service].

(b) **Exception:** [§492] Such discrimination has sometimes been upheld. During World War II, curfew orders and forced relocation applicable only to persons of Japanese ancestry was held not violative of equal protection. [Hirabayashi v. United States, 320 U.S. 81 (1943); Korematsu v. United States, 323 U.S. 214 (1944)—"pressing public necessity may sometimes justify racial restrictions"]

(2) **Requirement of intentional discrimination:** [§493] The "strict scrutiny" test for "suspect" criteria requires that the government action have a discriminatory purpose; *i.e.*, intentional or deliberate discrimination must be shown. [Washington v. Davis, 426 U.S. 229 (1976)] Such "de jure" discrimination may be found in three ways:

(a) **On its face:** [§494] Government action (*e.g.*, a statute, executive or administrative order, judicial decree, etc.) that explicitly—by its written or spoken terms—discriminates is the most obvious form of de jure discrimination.

(b) **Unequal administration:** [§495] Laws or other official actions that are racially ***neutral on their face*** may be purposefully applied on the basis of suspect criteria and thereby become subject to the strict equal protection standard of review.

1) **Example:** In *Yick Wo v. Hopkins, supra*, a statute provided that laundries could not be operated in wooden buildings without a license. The classification itself was racially neutral, but the licensing authority consistently refused licenses to Chinese applicants while granting them to others. Since the authority could offer no "racially neutral" explanation, this was held to be de jure discrimination violative of the Equal Protection Clause.

2) **Burden of proof:** [§496] A person who alleges this form of discrimination must prove that it is intentional or purposeful. [Snowden v. Hughes, 321 U.S. 1 (1944)] The claimant may establish a prima facie case by showing a ***substantial disproportionate racial impact*** as a result of the law's administration. [*Cf.* Mayor of Philadelphia v. Educational Equality League, 415 U.S. 605 (1974)—proof was "too fragmentary and speculative"] Then, the ***burden shifts to the state*** to show that this impact was caused by constitutionally permissible (*i.e.*, nonracial) factors. [Castaneda v. Partida, 430 U.S. 482 (1977)]

a) **Example—peremptory challenges:** [§497] If a black defendant claims that the prosecution used its peremptory challenges to exclude all blacks from the jury and shows facts or circumstances that raise an inference that the exclusions were based on race, the burden shifts to the state to come forward with a neutral explanation—*i.e.*, something other than that the prosecutor believed that black jurors would be partial to the defendant because of their shared race. [Batson v. Kentucky, 476 U.S. 79 (1986)]

1/ **Note:** Subsequent cases have expanded *Batson* so that defendants and civil plaintiffs are also prohibited from using peremptory challenges to exclude jurors on the basis of race or sex. (*See infra*, §§559, 688.)

b) **Example—capital sentencing:** [§498] Note that statistics showing that the death sentence is most frequently imposed on black defendants who kill white victims do ***not*** produce an inference of intentional discrimination because: (i) each death sentence is made by a unique jury and is based on innumerable special facts, and (ii) it is contrary to public policy to require jurors and prosecutors to defend their necessarily discretionary decisions. [McCleskey v. Kemp, 481 U.S. 279 (1987)]

c) **Deference to fact finder:** [§499] The trial court's decision on the ultimate question of discriminatory intent represents a finding of fact of the sort accorded great deference on appeal, particularly on issues of credibility. [Hernandez v. New York, 500 U.S. 1 (1991)]

3) **Invalid on face:** [§500] In certain special areas, state action that is racially neutral by its terms may be held invalid on its face; *i.e.*, the Court may enjoin future operation of the statute at the behest of one who cannot show that it has been applied to him in an intentionally or purposefully discriminatory fashion.

a) **Application:** This has been done in the case of statutes (i) that by their terms give the administrator an "uncontrolled discretion" to engage in intentional racial discrimination, (ii) that have in the past been used to discriminate on the basis of race, and (iii) as to which the courts are not fully capable of remedying further discriminatory applications. [Louisiana v. United States, 380 U.S. 145 (1965)—literacy test for voting]

(c) **Impermissible motive:** [§501] Finally, laws that are racially ***neutral*** by their terms may constitute de jure discrimination violative of equal protection if the challenger proves that the ***legislative "motive" was to discriminate*** against racial or ethnic minorities. [Washington v. Davis, *supra*, §493]

1) **Effect as establishing motive:** [§502] Establishing an impermissible motive is relatively easy if the effect of a law (or administrative action) bears heavily on a racial or ethnic minority and cannot be explained on permissible grounds.

a) **Example:** In *Gomillion v. Lightfoot*, 364 U.S. 339 (1960), city boundaries were changed with the effect of removing nearly all black voters from the city. Since there was no constitutionally permissible explanation, this was held to violate the Fifteenth Amendment.

2) **Judicial inquiry:** [§503] If the impermissible motive is not obvious from the effect of the law, the Court conducts a "sensitive inquiry" into such other factors as:

(i) ***The historic background*** of the state action (*e.g.*, whether it was preceded by other racially discriminatory laws);

(ii) The ***sequence of events*** leading up to the action (*e.g.*, abrupt departures from normal substantive or procedural rules); or

(iii) ***Statements by members of the decision-making body***. (In some instances, such members may be required to testify as to their motives—unless the testimony is barred by legislative or executive privilege.)

[Village of Arlington Heights v. Metropolitan Housing Development Corp., 429 U.S. 252 (1977)]

3) **Effect of showing of impermissible motive:** [§504] If the state action is shown to be motivated ***in part*** by a forbidden purpose, the burden of proof shifts to the state. However, the state can prevail if it shows that the same decision would have resulted despite the impermissible purpose. [Village of Arlington Heights v. Metropolitan Housing Development Corp., *supra*]

a) **Example:** The motive of a provision adopted by the Alabama Constitutional Convention in 1901 that disenfranchised persons convicted of crimes involving "moral turpitude" was found to discriminate against blacks. The Court examined the convention's proceedings and historical studies and testimony. An ***additional*** purpose to discriminate against poor whites did ***not*** save the provision because it would not have been enacted ***"but for"*** the purpose of discriminating against blacks. [Hunter v. Underwood, 471 U.S. 222 (1985)]

4) **Standard of review:** [§505] The Court will not ordinarily disturb a federal district court's factual finding of discriminatory motive that is upheld by the court of appeals as being not "clearly erroneous." [Rogers v. Lodge, 458 U.S. 613 (1982)]

(3) **Compare—"de facto" discrimination:** [§506] Laws or other official actions that are racially neutral on their face, in their administration, and in their motivation may, nonetheless, be discriminatory in effect; *i.e.*, they may have a ***racially disproportionate impact*** (affect racial or ethnic minorities more adversely than whites). Such "de facto" discrimination is judged by the "traditional" test; it will be upheld if it is ***rationally related*** to a ***constitutionally*** permissible state interest. [Washington v. Davis, *supra*, §501]

(a) **Example:** A requirement that police officer applicants undergo a test of verbal skills has been upheld under the traditional equal protection test despite its racially discriminatory impact. [Washington v. Davis, *supra*]

(b) **De facto school segregation:** [§507] On the above theory, the fact that many schools in a district are either predominantly white or predominantly black has been found ***not*** to be a violation of equal protection, absent a showing of intentional acts of segregation by the school board. [Dayton Board of Education v. Brinkman, 433 U.S. 406 (1977)]

(c) **Thirteenth Amendment:** [§508] The Court has not decided whether a racially "discriminatory purpose" is required for a violation of the Thirteenth Amendment's bar against imposing "a badge or incident of slavery" on blacks. [Memphis v. Greene, 451 U.S. 100 (1981)]

(d) **Fifteenth Amendment:** [§509] Nor has the Court specifically decided whether a "discriminatory purpose" is required for a violation of the Fifteenth Amendment's bar against government racial discrimination in voting. [City of Mobile v. Bolden, 446 U.S. 55 (1980)]

b. **What is "suspect" classification?**

(1) **Racial (or ethnic) "classifications":** [§510] Some government action merely "classifies" on the basis of race (or national origin); *i.e.*, it does

not simply impose burdens on racial or ethnic minorities, but does draw lines on the basis of a racial criterion. For example, the prohibition of interracial cohabitation [McLaughlin v. Florida, 379 U.S. 184 (1964)—invalid] or of racial intermarriage [Loving v. Virginia, 388 U.S 1 (1967)—invalid] ostensibly does not discriminate against members of one race; it appears to treat both races equally.

(a) **In general—strict scrutiny:** [§511] The Court has ***generally*** treated racial "classifications" the same as "discriminations"; *i.e.*, they are prohibited unless ***necessary*** to a ***compelling*** state interest. [McLaughlin v. Florida, *supra*; Loving v. Virginia, *supra*]

1) **Example:** In *Anderson v. Martin*, 375 U.S. 399 (1964), the Court invalidated a state law requiring that a candidate's race be designated on the election ballot on the ground that this "induces racial prejudice at the polls." [*Cf.* Tancil v. Woolls, 379 U.S. 19 (1964)—state ***may***, for statistical purposes, require designation of parties' race on divorce decrees]

2) **Example:** In *Palmore v. Sidoti*, 466 U.S. 429 (1984), the Court invalidated denial of child custody to a mother because her new spouse was of a different race—the racial prejudice of others cannot justify a government racial classification.

(b) **Racial segregation:** [§512] Segregation by race is a "classification" that appears to treat both races equally. However, deliberate ("de jure") racial segregation in public schools violates equal protection. [Brown v. Board of Education, 347 U.S. 483 (1954)—separate facilities are "inherently unequal"; Bolling v. Sharpe, *supra*, §401—racial segregation in District of Columbia public schools violates Fifth Amendment due process]

1) **Scope of application:** [§513] This principle has been applied to public facilities of all types—*e.g.*, public beaches and bathhouses, municipal golf courses, public transportation, stadiums and theaters, courtrooms, and public office buildings.

2) **Proving school segregation:** [§514] Although the existence of schools segregated in fact, without more, will not establish a constitutional violation (*supra*, §507), evidence for the necessary finding of ***segregative intent*** may be drawn from actions having foreseeable and anticipated disparate impact. [Columbus Board of Education v. Penick, 443 U.S. 449 (1979)]

a) **"Segregated":** [§515] In determining whether a school is "segregated," courts must consider the number of all minority groups therein (not just blacks) who have suffered unequal treatment in education. [Keyes v. School District No. 1, 413 U.S. 189 (1973)—segregation of Hispanics]

b) **Presumptions:** [§516] The Court uses several presumptions in the school segregation area [Keyes v. School District No. 1, *supra*]:

1/ **Dual system in entire district:** [§517] A finding that school authorities intentionally segregated a ***significant portion*** of the school district creates a presumption that the ***entire school district***—*i.e.*, even schools with mixed racial composition—is being operated on a segregated basis. This is because of the "substantial reciprocal effect" that segregation of some schools may have on others.

2/ **Uniracial schools:** [§518] A finding that school authorities have intentionally segregated a ***meaningful portion*** of the school district creates a presumption of intentional segregation for all other schools in the district that are in fact segregated. This is because a showing of segregative intent as to some schools suggests that all other schools in the system that are in fact segregated were also intentionally segregated.

c) **Rebuttal:** [§519] If a presumption of segregative intent exists, the burden shifts to the school authorities to prove that (i) irrespective of any racially neutral explanations for their policies (such as maintenance of neighborhood schools), segregative intent was not among their motivations, or (ii) if they were motivated at all by segregative intent, past intentional segregative actions did not create or contribute to the current condition of segregation, or (iii) because of natural geographic boundaries, the school district is in fact divided into separate and unrelated units. [Keyes v. School District No. 1, *supra*]

3) **Remedying segregation:** [§520] School boards have an affirmative duty to eliminate intentional racial segregation of schools. The burden is on the school authorities to produce a plan that promises "immediate progress," and to explain why seemingly more effective methods have not been employed. [Green v. New Kent County School Board, 391 U.S. 430 (1968)]

a) **Scope of remedy:** [§521] The remedy in any given case must be determined by the nature and scope of the constitutional violation. It may not extend beyond the conditions produced by that violation. A system-wide remedy may be imposed only if a system-wide violation has been found. [Dayton Board of Education v. Brinkman, *supra*, §507]

1/ **Interdistrict remedies:** [§522] Thus, the remedy may not extend beyond the boundaries of the school district that has engaged in de jure segregation, unless it is shown that district lines were discriminatorily drawn, or that the discrimination has produced a "significant segregative effect" in the other districts included in the desegregation plan. [Milliken v. Bradley, 418 U.S. 717 (1974)]

a/ **Compare—housing:** [§523] But a metropolitan-area remedy for public housing segregation may be imposed even though the segregation took place only within the city—***if*** (i) the government agency that engaged in the segregation can act outside city boundaries, ***and*** (ii) the remedy does not "impermissibly interfere" with innocent suburban governmental units. [Hills v. Gautreaux, 425 U.S. 284 (1976)]

b) **Scope of duty:** [§524] If a school system is found to have been intentionally segregated at the time of the *Brown* decision in 1954 (or thereafter), the school board may not take any action (irrespective of its purpose) that has the ***effect*** of continuing the dual school system—unless the school board satisfies its "heavy burden" that such action serves "important and legitimate ends." [Dayton Board of Education v. Brinkman, 443 U.S. 526 (1979); Columbus Board of Education v. Penick, *supra*, §514]

c) **Guidelines for school authorities and courts:** [§525] The Court has held that conditions in different localities vary so widely that ***no rigid rules*** can be laid down for all situations. The first obligation is that of the school authorities. Their interest in managing their own affairs must be taken into account, but if they default, a court's ***equitable powers*** to remedy past wrongs are broad. "The task is to correct, by a ***balancing*** of the individual and collective interests, the condition that offends the Constitution." [Swann v. Charlotte-Mecklenburg Board of Education, 402 U.S. 1 (1971)]

1/ ***Ordering some busing***, and ***assigning students on a racial basis*** irrespective of compactness or contiguousness of school zones may be used by school boards and the courts. Also, they may ***use mathematical ratios*** of black and white students in the district as a starting point in fashioning a remedy. Furthermore, they need not be "color-blind" in ***assigning teachers*** in order to achieve faculty desegregation.

2/ ***If a plan leaves some schools containing all or predominantly one race***, the school board has the burden of showing that assignments are genuinely nondiscriminatory.

3/ ***New school construction and abandonment of old schools*** may ***not*** be used to perpetuate or restore segregation.

4/ ***Optional "majority-to-minority" transfer provisions*** are valid—and they must provide free transportation to, and space available in, the school to which transfer is sought.

5/ ***State laws that forbid such remedial measures*** violate the Fourteenth Amendment. [Swann v. Charlotte-Mecklenburg Board of Education, *supra*]

6/ ***Remedial programs*** may be ordered if necessary to restore the victims of discrimination to the educational position they would otherwise have enjoyed. [Milliken v. Bradley, 433 U.S. 267 (1977)]

d) **New school districts:** [§526] Courts have discretion to enjoin carving out new school districts from existing districts if the ***effect***—irrespective of a permissible purpose—would be to hinder the dismantling of a dual school system. Although disparity in the racial composition of the two systems is not enough per se to enjoin the creation of a separate district, it is significant. [Wright v. Council of Emporia, 407 U.S. 451 (1972)]

e) **Termination of duty:** [§527] Once a racially neutral attendance pattern has been established by student assignment, the federal court ***cannot*** require a school district to rearrange its attendance zones annually in order to insure the desired racial mix (absent further segregative actions by the district). [Pasadena Board of Education v. Spangler, 427 U.S. 424 (1976)]

1/ **Partial withdrawal of judicial supervision:** [§528] If a district has achieved unitary status with respect to one aspect of school administration (*e.g.*, student assignments), the court ***may*** withdraw supervision over this category even though the vestiges of segregation may exist in respect to another category (*e.g.*, faculty assignments). Judicial discretion should particularly be informed by whether the school district has shown its good faith commitment to desegregate all aspects of the dual system and whether continued ***full*** judicial control is needed to achieve compliance in ***all*** categories. [Freeman v. Pitts, 112 S. Ct. 1430 (1992)]

f) **No application beyond schools:** [§529] The ***affirmative duty*** to eliminate intentional racial segregation does not extend beyond schools to such ***voluntary*** associations as 4-H Clubs or Homemaker Clubs operated by a state agricultural agency. [Bazemore v. Friday, 478 U.S. 385 (1986)]

g) **Higher education:** [§530] However, the affirmative duty to eliminate intentional racial segregation ***does apply*** to public colleges and universities. Any policy (*e.g.*, admissions) that is traceable to the prior dual system and that continues to have segregative effects is invalid unless the state proves that it has "sound educational justification" and that it is "impractical to eliminate." [United States v. Fordice, 112 S. Ct. 2727 (1992)]

h) **Aid to segregated private schools:** [§531] Despite a nondiscriminatory purpose, state provision of textbooks (or tuition grants) to students of private schools that "practice racial or other invidious discrimination" violates equal protection. These are "basic educational tools" that significantly aid the schools themselves—and are distinguishable from generalized services (electricity, water, police and fire protection), which the government might provide to schools in common with other users. [Norwood v. Harrison, 413 U.S. 455 (1973)]

1/ **And note:** State provision to private segregated schools of periodic exclusive access to recreational facilities likewise violates equal protection—at least where such schools were formed in response to a court desegregation order. [Gilmore v. City of Montgomery, 417 U.S. 556 (1974)]

i) **Closing of facilities:** [§532] The Court found no equal protection violation where a city closed its public swimming pools after a court order to desegregate, "to preserve peace and order and because the pools could not be operated economically on an integrated basis." [Palmer v. Thompson, 403 U.S. 217 (1971)]

1/ **Rationale:** The Court in *Palmer* concluded that the city's purposes were legitimate, and that there was no showing of "state action affecting Blacks differently from Whites." *Griffin v. County School Board*, 377 U.S. 218 (1964), which ordered the reopening of public schools closed to avoid a desegregation order, was distinguished. There, the state was covertly aiding and maintaining "private" segregated schools that were private in name only.

(c) **"Benign" discrimination:** [§533] Since all classifications based on race carry a danger of stigmatic harm, government action that ***favors*** racial or ethnic minorities is subject to the same standard of "strict scrutiny" review as is government action that discriminates

against racial or ethnic minorities. [City of Richmond v. J.A. Croson Co., 488 U.S. 469 (1989)]

1) **Remedying past discrimination against minorities:** [§534] The government has a "compelling" interest in remedying past discrimination against racial or ethnic minority groups and, under some circumstances, it may give preference to members of such groups (even if the persons benefited are not themselves the actual victims of the discrimination). However, the past discrimination must be identified by a properly authorized government body as a constitutional or statutory violation. A race-based plan cannot be used to remedy ***general*** past "***societal*** discrimination." [City of Richmond v. J.A. Croson Co., *supra*]

    a) **Findings required:** [§535] An affirmative action plan need ***not*** be preceded by a ***formal finding*** that there has been past discrimination by the government body instituting the plan or by other private parties. But when nonminorities challenge the plan, the court must make a ***factual determination*** that there was a ***strong basis*** for the government body's conclusion that remedial action was necessary. [Wygant v. Jackson Board of Education, 476 U.S. 267 (1986)]

    b) **Numerical goals:** [§536] ***Flexible*** numerical goals may be used to remedy past discrimination. However, they must be "narrowly tailored," *e.g.*: (i) of limited duration, (ii) based on pertinent racial percentages in the relevant population, (iii) impose relatively light burdens on nonminorities, and (iv) there are no effective "race neutral" remedies. [Sheet Metal Workers' International Association v. Equal Employment Opportunity Commission, 478 U.S. 421 (1986)—no majority opinion]

    c) **Deference to trial judge:** [§537] Although a judicial order to remedy past discrimination should be "narrowly tailored" substantial respect should be accorded a district judge's choice of remedies. The least restrictive means is ***not*** always required. [United States v. Paradise, 480 U.S. 149 (1987)]

    d) **School desegregation:** [§538] As noted previously, the Court has held that racial criteria may be used in assigning students and teachers to remedy prior ***de jure*** school segregation. [Swann v. Charlotte-Mecklenburg Board of Education, *supra*, §525]

2) **Student diversity in higher education:** [§539] Apart from the government's interest in remedying past discrimination against minorities (*see supra*, §533), five Justices have held that equal protection permits a state university to take race or

ethnicity into account—*i.e.*, to ***deem it a "plus"***—in order to achieve diversity in its admissions. [Regents of University of California v. Bakke, 438 U.S. 265 (1978)—no majority opinion]

a) **De facto school segregation:** [§540] It is also an open question whether school boards may use racial criteria for assignment in a voluntary effort to remedy de facto school segregation—but lower courts have upheld it.

3) **Congressional power:** [§541] Deference to congressional judgment is appropriate in this area in light of Congress's institutional competence as the national legislature. Thus, benign race-conscious measures that have been specifically approved by Congress under its delegated powers—particularly its broad power to enforce equal protection (*see infra*, §§704-715)—are valid if "substantially" related to "important" government objectives, even if those measures are not designed to remedy past governmental or societal discrimination. [Metro Broadcasting, Inc. v. Federal Communications Commission, 497 U.S. 547 (1990)—upholding FCC preferences for minorities in granting radio and television licenses in order to achieve greater diversity in programming; ***and see*** Fullilove v. Klutznick, 448 U.S. 448 (1980)—upholding set aside for minority businesses of 10% of federal grants for public works projects]

a) **Preference for Native Americans:** [§542] A federal statute granting employment preference in the Bureau of Indian Affairs to qualified American Indians has been upheld on grounds that it was not a "racial" preference because it applied only to members of "federally recognized" tribes. [Morton v. Mancari, 417 U.S. 535 (1974)]

4) **Legislative apportionment:** [§543] Racial or ethnic criteria may be used for drawing voting district boundaries (*e.g.*, to create or preserve the strength of minority groups) as long as (i) no racial group has its overall voting strength minimized [United Jewish Organizations v. Carey, 430 U.S. 144 (1977)]; or (ii) the shape of districts is not so bizarre as to be explainable only on grounds of race [Shaw v. Reno, 113 S. Ct. 2816 (1993)]. In the latter instances, the reapportionment will violate equal protection unless shown to be narrowly tailored to further a compelling government interest.

(d) **Repeal of remedies for discrimination or segregation:** [§544] A state's simple repeal (or modification) of antidiscrimination laws (or remedies for de facto segregation) that are not required by the Constitution in the first place is ***not*** racial discrimination in violation of equal protection. [Crawford v. Los Angeles Board of Education, 458 U.S. 527 (1982)—state law providing that state courts may no longer order busing to remedy ***de facto*** school segregation upheld] But a state ***does*** violate equal protection if it reallocates decision-making authority in respect to ***racial issues*** between levels of government so as to make it more difficult for racial minorities to get favorable laws passed.

1) **Example:** A city charter that required the electorate to approve (by referendum) any city council ordinance aimed at racial or ancestral discrimination in housing, while voter approval was not required as to other kinds of ordinances, was held to violate equal protection. (The effect was to "freeze" the power of the city council to legislate in this field—to the obvious disadvantage of racial and ancestral minorities.) [Hunter v. Erickson, 393 U.S. 385 (1969)]

2) **Example:** A state law forbidding school boards, which had general authority over school matters (including busing), to order busing to remedy ***de facto*** school segregation was held to violate equal protection. (The effect was to make it harder for those seeking to end de facto segregation than for persons seeking comparable legislation.) [Washington v. Seattle School District, 458 U.S. 457 (1982)]

(2) **Discrimination against aliens:** [§545] Because Congress has plenary power over the admission or exclusion of aliens (*see supra*, §150), ***federal*** classifications based on alienage are ***not*** subject to strict equal protection scrutiny. [Mathews v. Diaz, 426 U.S. 67 (1976)—upholding congressional denial of Medicare to certain classes of aliens, using "traditional" equal protection test] However, ***most state*** discrimination against lawfully admitted aliens is "suspect" since aliens are precisely the kind of "discrete and insular" minority—with no direct vote in the political process—for whom judicial solicitude is appropriate. [Graham v. Richardson, 403 U.S. 365 (1971)]

(a) **Examples of invalid state laws**

1) **Welfare:** [§546] Since aliens as well as citizens pay taxes from which welfare benefits are derived, there is no compelling state interest justifying denial of welfare to resident aliens. [Graham v. Richardson, *supra*]

2) **Bar admission:** [§547] Since the fact that a person is an alien does not mean he would be unqualified to practice law, such discrimination is not necessary to a compelling state interest. [*In re* Griffiths, 413 U.S. 717 (1973); *and see* Examining Board of Engineers v. de Otero, 426 U.S. 572 (1976)—law denying civil engineer's license to aliens held invalid; Bernal v. Fainter, 467 U.S. 216 (1984)—law precluding aliens from being notaries public held invalid]

3) **Civil service:** [§548] Similarly, there is no compelling state interest in excluding aliens from ***all*** civil service employment; such a law "sweeps indiscriminately." [Sugarman v. Dougall, 413 U.S. 634 (1973)]

4) **Land ownership:** [§549] Some earlier cases upheld state laws barring aliens from land ownership [Terrace v. Thompson, 263 U.S. 297 (1923)], or from exploiting natural resources [Patsone v. Pennsylvania, 232 U.S. 138 (1914)]. However, these decisions are questionable in light of the more recent cases discussed above. [*See also* Takahashi v. Fish & Game Commission, 334 U.S. 410 (1948)—state law denying commercial fishing licenses to persons ineligible for citizenship held invalid]

(b) **Effect of eligibility for citizenship:** [§550] The fact that the state discriminates only against aliens who are eligible for U.S. citizenship but choose not to become citizens is irrelevant; the discrimination is still "suspect." [Nyquist v. Mauclet, 432 U.S. 1 (1977)—denial to such aliens of state financial assistance for higher education held invalid]

(c) **Participation in process of self-government—"traditional" test:** [§551] A state has "historical power to exclude aliens from participation in its democratic political institutions." Thus, as long as the state acts "rationally," aliens ***may*** be excluded from voting, jury service, elective office, and nonelective offices that formulate, execute, or review important public policy—*e.g.*, police officers [Foley v. Connelie, 435 U.S. 291 (1978)] or probation of officers [Cabell v. Chavez-Salido, 454 U.S. 432 (1982)]. Furthermore, aliens may be denied positions as public elementary and secondary school teachers (since they influence the attitudes of students toward government, the political process and citizenship, as well as promote and provide an example for civic virtues). [Ambach v. Norwick, 441 U.S. 68 (1979)]

(d) **Illegal aliens:** [§552] State discrimination against illegal aliens is ***not*** "suspect." However, denial of free public education to the children of illegal aliens imposes an enormous and lasting burden based on a status over which the children have no control. Thus, absent a congressional policy favoring the state rule, the discrimination violates equal protection unless it furthers a "substantial" state goal. [Plyler v. Doe, 457 U.S. 202 (1982)]

(e) **Supremacy Clause:** [§553] Apart from the Equal Protection Clause, state laws that discriminate against lawfully admitted aliens, by imposing burdens not contemplated or authorized by Congress, conflict with Congress's plenary power over the admission of aliens. [Toll v. Moreno, 458 U.S. 1 (1982)—state university denial of in-state tuition to nonimmigrant aliens who are children of employees working for international organizations held invalid]

5. **Quasi-Suspect Classifications—Intermediate Level of Scrutiny:** [§554] Classifications based on gender or legitimacy are not "suspect," but neither are they judged by the "traditional" (or "rational basis") test.

a. **Test:** [§555] Intentional discriminations against members of a ***"quasi-suspect"*** class violate equal protection unless they are ***substantially related*** to ***important*** government objectives. [Craig v. Boren, 429 U.S. 190 (1976)—law that authorized serving of beer to females over 18 years old but to males only over 21 held invalid]

(1) **"De facto" discrimination:** [§556] As is true in respect to race and national origin (*see supra*, §506), laws or other official actions that do not ***intentionally*** discriminate on the basis of gender but nonetheless have a sexually disproportionate impact are judged by the ***"traditional"*** test; they will be upheld if ***rationally*** related to a constitutionally permissible state interest. [Personnel Administrator of Massachusetts v. Feeney, 442 U.S. 256 (1979)—veteran's preference law upheld even though it severely restricted public employment opportunities for women]

b. **Gender discrimination**

(1) **Discrimination against women:** [§557] All recent decisions have held that laws discriminating against women are ***not*** substantially related to an important government objective and thus violate equal protection. [*See, e.g.*, Reed v. Reed, 404 U.S. 71 (1972)—preferring men over women as between persons equally qualified under state law to administer estates; Frontiero v. Richardson, 411 U.S. 677 (1973)—federal statute limiting servicewoman's right to dependency benefit for her husband by requiring proof of actual dependency upon her for support, whereas a serviceman could obtain similar benefits for his wife without such proof]

(a) **Definition of sex discrimination:** [§558] A law excluding pregnancies from state disability insurance benefits has been upheld as "rational." The provision was held ***not*** to discriminate against women, but merely to exclude certain physical conditions from coverage so as to make the program (which covered both sexes) self-supporting. [Geduldig v. Aiello, 417 U.S. 484 (1974)]

(2) **Discrimination against men:** [§559] Several decisions have held that laws that discriminate against men violate equal protection. [*See, e.g.*, Craig v. Boren, *supra*] For example, the Court invalidated a law providing that a husband, but not a wife, may be required to pay alimony because it did not serve the important state objective of assisting needy spouses; rather, this could be accomplished by treating men and women equally. [Orr v. Orr, 440 U.S. 268 (1979)] Also, the Court struck down a law permitting an unwed mother, but not an unwed father, to block the adoption of their child by withholding consent. [Caban v. Mohammed, 441 U.S. 380 (1979)] The Court also found the exclusion of males from a state nursing school was invalid as it perpetuated the stereotype of nursing as an exclusively women's job. [Mississippi University for Women v. Hogan, 458 U.S. 718 (1982)] Most recently, the Court found that using peremptory challenges to exclude males from a jury violates equal protection. [J.E.B. v. Alabama *ex rel.* T.B., 114 S. Ct. 1419 (1994)]

(a) **Compare—valid discrimination against men:** [§560] But laws that discriminate against men have been upheld when found to be substantially related to an important government objective. Thus, for example, the Court has upheld statutory rape laws, which punish the male but not the female partner to the intercourse, because of the important state interest in preventing teenage pregnancy. [Michael M. v. Sonoma County Superior Court, 450 U.S. 464 (1981)] The Court has also upheld draft registration of males only because of Congress's considered conclusion, pursuant to its military powers, that this was needed to further the important government interest of preparing for a draft of combat troops. [Rostker v. Goldberg, 453 U.S. 57 (1981)] And a state law precluding an unwed father, but not an unwed mother, from suing for the child's wrongful death unless the father has legitimated the child has been upheld because this promotes the important state objective of avoiding proof of paternity problems, which are more difficult to resolve for fathers. [Parham v. Hughes, 441 U.S. 347 (1979)]

(3) **Compensating women for past discrimination:** [§561] Laws that purport to compensate for past discrimination against women have been upheld as being substantially related to an important government objective.

(a) **Example:** State law granting a property tax exemption to widows, but not widowers, has been held to further the state policy of cushioning the financial impact of spousal loss upon the sex for whom that loss usually imposes a heavier burden. [Kahn v. Shevin, 416 U.S. 351 (1974)]

(b) **Example:** A Social Security Act formula entitling female wage earners to preference over males has been held to reduce the disparity in economic condition between men and women, caused by the long history of discrimination against women. [Califano v. Webster, 430 U.S. 313 (1977)]

(c) **Example:** The Navy's mandatory discharge procedure, which accords different treatment for male and female line officers (*i.e.*, male officers are automatically discharged if twice denied promotion, whereas women officers are not), was upheld because the promotional opportunities offered by the Navy for men had been greater than for women. [Schlesinger v . Ballard, 419 U.S. 498 (1975)]

c. **Discrimination against illegitimate children:** [§562] Discrimination against illegitimate children is not "suspect," but neither is it subject to the "toothless" traditional standard. [Mathews v. Lucas, 427 U.S. 495 (1976)] It is judged by a ***"quasi-suspect"*** standard, the same as that used for gender discrimination (*supra*, §554). [Clark v. Jeter, 486 U.S. 456 (1988)—"***substantially*** related to an ***important*** state interest"]

(1) **Prohibition against "punishing" innocent children:** [§563] Most state laws that discriminate against illegitimate children have been invalidated to assure that a state's concern over illicit relationships is not the basis for punitive measures against the product of such a relationship.

(a) **Example:** The Court found state laws excluding illegitimate children from sharing equally with natural children in workers' compensation death benefits payable on their father's death to be invalid. [Weber v. Aetna Casualty & Surety Co., 406 U.S. 164 (1972)]

(b) **Example:** State laws permitting legitimate children (but not illegitimate children) to maintain wrongful death actions on account of their parents' death were also struck down by the Court. [Levy v. Louisiana, 391 U.S. 68 (1968)]

(c) **Example:** The Court has also struck down state laws creating a support right in favor of legitimate children, but not illegitimate children. [Gomez v. Perez, 409 U.S. 535 (1973)]

(2) **Compare—some discrimination valid:** [§564] However, some discrimination against illegitimate children has been upheld. For example, a Social Security Act provision treating some classes of illegitimate children differently from all legitimate children has been upheld as a "reasonable effort to serve administrative convenience." [Mathews v. Lucas, *supra*—excluding certain classes of illegitimate children from presumption of dependency on deceased or disabled parent]

(a) **Example—probate:** Similarly, a state may promote the just and expeditious disposition of property at death by denying intestate succession to an illegitimate child unless the paternity of the father is formally proved sometime before the death of the father. [Lalli v. Lalli, 439 U.S. 259 (1978)]

(b) **Example—immigration:** And immigration provisions excluding an illegitimate child and the natural father from receiving preferences accorded to the "child" or "parent" of U.S. citizens have been upheld because of the broad plenary power of Congress over immigration legislation (*see supra*, §150). [Fiallo v. Bell, 430 U.S. 787 (1977)]

6. **Classifications that Are Not Suspect or Quasi-Suspect**

a. **Discrimination against the poor:** [§565] The Court has ***said*** that "poverty standing alone is not a suspect classification" [Harris v. McRae, *supra*, §460], and has ***upheld*** an explicit state classification adversely affecting poor people [James v. Valtierra, 402 U.S. 137 (1971)—state constitutional provision requiring a local referendum as a prerequisite to construction of low-rent public housing projects in the community].

(1) **Compare—discrimination invalid:** [§566] In *Turner v. Fouche*, 396 U.S. 346 (1970), the Court employed the "traditional" test in holding that a law making only freeholders eligible to be school board members violated equal protection. The classification was found to be "wholly irrelevant" to achievement of the state's asserted objectives.

(2) **De facto discrimination:** [§567] The major developments concerning discrimination against the poor have involved state laws or other official

practices that have a disproportionate impact on poor people. Several decisions have held that a state's refusal to (i) waive a fee, or (ii) provide certain services free of charge for poor people in the course of criminal or civil litigation violates the Equal Protection Clause (or the Due Process Clause).

(a) **Criminal appeals:** [§568] To assure "adequate and effective appellate review" of a criminal conviction, the state must provide indigents with a free trial transcript [Griffin v. Illinois, 351 U.S. 12 (1956)] and appointed counsel for the first appeal granted as a matter of right under state law [Douglas v. California, 372 U.S. 353 (1963)].

1) **Compare—discretionary appeals:** [§569] The right to appointed counsel does ***not*** extend to discretionary appeals from criminal convictions. [Ross v. Moffit, 417 U.S. 600 (1974)]

(b) **Fine or imprisonment:** [§570] State laws imposing imprisonment for nonpayment of fines have the effect of discriminating against indigents. Thus, equal protection prohibits the state from imposing a fine as a sentence and then ***automatically*** converting it into a jail term solely because the defendant cannot immediately pay the fine in full. [Tate v. Short, 401 U.S. 395 (1971)]

1) **Probation revocation:** [§571] If the defendant is given probation on condition that he pay the fine (or make restitution), the "fundamental fairness" required by equal protection and due process forbid revocation of probation for failure to pay—absent evidence and findings that defendant was somehow responsible for the failure or that alternative forms of punishment (*e.g.*, public service work) were inadequate. [Bearden v. Georgia, 461 U.S. 660 (1983)]

(c) **Divorce:** [§572] Under the Due Process Clause, states may not require the payment of court fees as a condition for judicial dissolution of marriage as to indigents who in good faith seek a divorce. The Court has limited the potential scope of this decision by noting (i) the "basic position of the marriage relationship" in society, and (ii) "state monopolization of the means for legally dissolving this relationship." [Boddie v. Connecticut, 401 U.S. 371 (1971)]

(d) **Paternity actions:** [§573] Similarly, under the Due Process Clause, a state must pay for blood tests that may exculpate indigent defendants in paternity actions—at least where the state is itself requiring the mother to bring the paternity suit. [Little v. Streater, 452 U.S. 1 (1981)]

(e) **Compare—bankruptcy:** [§574] However, the state ***may*** require payment of a fee (or a promise to pay in installments) as a condition for discharge in a voluntary bankruptcy proceeding. The *Boddie* case (*supra*) was distinguished because the "marital relationship" is of "fundamental importance"; also, a state judicial proceeding is ***not***

the only method available for adjustment of the legal relationship—since a debtor may also settle with creditors by negotiated agreement. [United States v. Kras, 409 U.S. 434 (1973)]

(f) **Compare—welfare appeal:** [§575] On somewhat similar reasoning—particularly the fact that, unlike the marital relationship, which has "constitutional significance," welfare falls "in the area of economics and social welfare"—the Court has held that a state filing fee applied to an indigent seeking judicial review of an adverse welfare decision does not violate due process or equal protection. [Ortwein v. Schwab, 410 U.S. 656 (1973)]

(g) **Compare—abortion:** [§576] Furthermore, states may deny indigents Medicaid for nontherapeutic abortions. Again (unlike *Boddie*), the state has not monopolized the means to terminate pregnancies. [Maher v. Roe, 432 U.S. 464 (1977)] Similarly, the state may deny Medicaid for abortions even if "medically necessary"—at least where the mother's life is not threatened. [Harris v. McRae, *supra*, §565]

(h) **Voting:** [§577] Cases invalidating payment requirements for the right to vote, as discriminating against poor people, are discussed below. [Harper v. Virginia Board of Elections, 383 U.S. 663 (1966)—poll tax; Bullock v. Carter, 405 U.S. 134 (1972)—high filing fees to get on primary election ballot]

b. **Discrimination against the elderly:** [§578] Laws or other official actions that discriminate against the elderly are neither "suspect" nor "quasi-suspect." They are judged by the ***"traditional"*** ("rational basis") test.

(1) **Rationale:** Although the Court has not authoritatively defined the criteria that make a classification "suspect" (or "quasi-suspect"), it has noted that important indicia are (i) a ***class determined by characteristics that are unalterable***; and (ii) a class subjected to such a ***history of purposefully unequal treatment***, or relegated to a position of such ***political powerlessness***, as to command extraordinary protection from majority rule. [*See* Johnson v. Robison, 415 U.S. 361 (1974)] It has been held that the aged do ***not*** satisfy the second criterion. [Massachusetts Board of Retirement v. Murgia, 427 U.S. 307 (1976)—police officer can be compelled to retire at age 50]

c. **Discrimination against nonresidents:** [§579] A bona fide residence requirement—living in the place with an intention to remain—creates no "suspect" classification. It is judged by the "traditional" ("rational basis") test. [Martinez v. Bynum, 461 U.S. 321 (1983)—free public education may be denied children who, apart from their parents and guardians, come to a school district solely to attend public schools]

d. **Discrimination against the mentally retarded:** [§580] Laws that discriminate against mentally retarded persons are neither "suspect" nor "quasi-suspect." *Rationale:* Government may legitimately take mental retardation into account for a wide range of decisions. And recent laws that benefit the mentally retarded demonstrate that there is ***no history of prejudice*** against them and that they are ***not politically powerless***. [Cleburne v. Cleburne Living Center, Inc., 470 U.S. 1002 (1985)]

(1) **"Invidious" discrimination:** [§581] But discriminatory government action that is not rationally related to a legitimate purpose is "invidious" and thus violates equal protection. [Cleburne v. Cleburne Living Center, Inc., *supra*—ordinance requiring special permit for mentally retarded group home, but not for most other kinds of multiple dwellings (including hospitals, nursing homes, dormitories) rests on irrational prejudice against the mentally retarded and violates equal protection]

7. **Fundamental Rights—Strict Scrutiny:** [§582] Government action that discriminates against (or "penalizes," or "unduly burdens") a "fundamental right"—*i.e.*, a right ***explicitly or implicitly guaranteed by the Constitution***—is subject to "strict scrutiny" and violates equal protection unless found to be ***necessary*** to a ***compelling*** state interest. [*See* San Antonio Independent School District v. Rodriguez, 411 U.S. 1 (1973)]

a. **Freedom of association:** [§583] A state law that imposed ***burdensome*** requirements for new political parties to get their candidates on the election ballot (while exempting established political parties from such requirements) was held violative of equal protection because it impaired the freedom of association of the members of the new parties, and no "compelling state interest" was shown to justify the discrimination. [Williams v. Rhodes, 393 U.S. 23 (1968)]

(1) **Nonburdensome classification:** [§584] However, state laws imposing different, but not burdensome, requirements for small or new political parties to get their candidates' names printed on the ballot—such as using a convention process rather than a primary election—do ***not*** violate equal protection. [American Party of Texas v. White, 415 U.S. 767 (1974)]

(2) **"Compelling" state interest:** [§585] State requirements that candidates of new political parties demonstrate public support to get on the ballot have been upheld. Such requirements further a "compelling" state interest—*i.e.*, preserving the integrity of the electoral process by preventing the ballot from becoming unmanageable and confusing. [American Party of Texas v. White, *supra*]

(a) **How much support:** [§586] Persons or parties seeking to get on the ballot may be required to demonstrate a "significant, measurable quantum of community support." [Jenness v . Fortson, 403 U.S. 431 (1971)—upholding requirement of nominating petitions signed by at least 5% of registered voters; groups unable to muster the 5% could still conduct "write-in" campaign]

(b) **"Disaffiliation" requirement:** [§587] A law barring independent candidates in general elections if they were registered with a political party within one year prior to the immediately preceding primary has been upheld. The law did not discriminate against independents, because other provisions imposed similar disqualifications on regular political party candidates. The state's interest in "the stability of its political system" was held to be "compelling"—and the Court found "no reason for concluding that the [law] was not an essential part of [the state's] overall mechanism to achieve its acceptable goals." [Storer v. Brown, 415 U.S. 724 (1974)]

(c) **Early filing deadlines:** [§588] But a law requiring an independent candidate for President to file more than seven months before the November general election, was held to violate the fundamental rights of voters and candidates. The state's interest in regulating ***presidential*** elections is less important than for state and local elections because the former will be largely determined by voters in other states. The state's interests here (*e.g.*, having an informed electorate, promoting political stability) are "minimal" when compared to the significant restriction imposed by the seven-month rule on the ability of independent candidates and their supporters to take advantage of campaign developments occurring closer to the general election. [Anderson v. Celebrezze, 460 U.S. 780 (1983)]

(3) **Funding presidential campaigns:** [§589] The provision by Congress of more public funds to the two "major" political parties than to "minor" or "new" parties for presidential campaigns (*i.e.*, based on the ratio of the vote the latter receive to that of the major parties) does not violate equal protection. The general interest of Congress in "eliminating the proper influence of large contributions" is vital, and the interest in "not funding hopeless campaigns" with substantial public monies justifies withholding assistance from candidates without significant public support. Finally, those who accept public funds suffer a countervailing restriction—in that they must agree to limit their total expenditures. [Buckley v. Valeo, 424 U.S. 1 (1976)]

b. **Right to travel interstate:** [§590] State ***durational*** residence requirements, which impose ***waiting periods*** before new residents may receive ***vital*** government benefits or services, have been held to "penalize" those who have recently exercised their constitutional right to travel interstate (*see infra*, §696), and thus violate equal protection unless found to be "necessary to promote a compelling state interest."

(1) **Welfare:** [§591] A one-year residency requirement to qualify for public welfare has been held invalid because (i) budgetary and record-keeping considerations are ***not*** "compelling," and (ii) deterring indigents from entering the state or limiting welfare to those who have paid taxes are constitutionally impermissible objectives. [Shapiro v. Thompson, 394 U.S. 618 (1969)]

(2) **Medical care:** [§592] Similarly, a one-year residency requirement in order to qualify for free nonemergency medical care has been held invalid. Like welfare, it is a "basic necessity of life." [Memorial Hospital v. Maricopa County, 415 U.S. 250 (1974)]

(3) **Voting:** [§593] State durational residence requirements of one year in the state and three months in the county in order to vote have failed to survive "strict scrutiny." [Dunn v. Blumstein, 405 U.S. 330 (1972)]

(a) **Permissible limits:** [§594] Voting ***registration*** requirements of some sort are permissible. The Court has observed that a 30-day residency and registration requirement should be sufficient to prepare voters lists, etc.; it has upheld even longer requirements (*e.g.*, 50 days) where there was a positive showing that the longer period was actually necessary. [Marston v. Lewis, 410 U.S. 679 (1973)—"approaches outer constitutional limits"]

(4) **Other rights and benefits:** [§595] However, not all state durational residence requirements are invalid. Where neither "necessities of life" nor "constitutional rights" (such as voting, *infra*, §§607 *et seq.*) are denied, the right to travel from state to state is held not to be "penalized."

(a) **Reduced tuition:** [§596] The Court has upheld durational residence requirements for students to qualify for reduced tuition rates at state colleges and universities. [Starns v. Malkerson, 401 U.S. 985 (1971)]

(b) **Divorce:** [§597] A one-year residency requirement in order to obtain a divorce has also been upheld. Obtaining a divorce is not a "necessity of life" in the same sense as welfare or medical care. Moreover, the residency requirement served "momentous" government purposes: (i) it assured a "modicum of attachment" to the state where important interests such as alimony and child custody are litigated; and (ii) it avoided collateral attack on the state's divorce decrees for lack of domicile. [Sosna v. Iowa, 419 U.S. 393 (1975)]

(5) **"Length of residence" requirements:** [§598] It is "impermissible" for states to apportion benefits and services according to length of residency. [Zobel v. Williams, 457 U.S. 55 (1982)—Alaska dividends from oil revenue to residents based on length of residency violates equal protection]

(a) **"Date of residence" requirements:** [§599] Nor may a state prefer those who are residents as of a certain date over new residents in the allocation of economic benefits. [Hooper v. Bernalillo County Assessor, 472 U.S. 612 (1985)—property tax exemption only for those Vietnam veterans who were state residents as of a certain date not "rationally related" to the state's goals and thus violates equal protection; *and see* Attorney General v. Soto-Lopez, 476 U.S. 898 (1986)—state employment preference only for those veterans who were state residents when they entered military service violates equal protection]

(6) **Compare—continuing residency requirement:** [§600] An appropriately defined and uniformly applied requirement of residency at the time of (and during) receipt of governmental benefits, services, etc., has been held ***not*** to impair the right to travel interstate. *Rationale:* The person is free to move to the state and establish residence there. [McCarthy v. Philadelphia Civil Service Commission, 424 U.S. 645 (1976)—requiring personal residence at place of governmental employment; Martinez v. Bynum, *supra*, §579]

(a) **Note:** Under this approach, a state need not continue to afford benefits to persons who are no longer residents. [Califano v. Torres, 435 U.S. 1 (1978)—Social Security benefits available in United States, but not Puerto Rico, may be lost when person moves from United States to Puerto Rico]

c. **Right of privacy:** [§601] A right of personal privacy has been recognized as implicit in the "liberty" protected by the Due Process Clause. (*See supra*, §§442 *et seq.*) Hence, statutory classifications that "penalize" or unduly burden this right are subject to "strict scrutiny" under the Equal Protection Clause.

(1) **Right to marry:** [§602] Laws that "interfere ***directly and substantially***" with the right to marry violate equal protection unless they can withstand "rigorous scrutiny." [Zablocki v. Redhail, 434 U.S. 374 (1978)—law forbidding marriage by person not complying with court order to support minor children is invalid]

(a) **Some regulation of marriage valid:** [§603] The strict scrutiny standard does not apply to all laws regulating marriage, as where the law does not "significantly interfere" with the decision to marry. Such laws are valid if they are "rational." [Califano v. Jobst, 429 U.S. 1089 (1977)—terminating Social Security to person who marries is valid because it places "no direct obstacle" to marriage]

(2) **Right to procreate:** [§604] The Court has invalidated a statute providing for the sterilization of "habitual criminals," because the statute was written so as to provide for sterilization of persons convicted of larceny but not embezzlement. The right to procreate is "one of the basic civil rights of man" and classifications affecting it are judged by the strict equal protection test. [Skinner v. Oklahoma, *supra*, §445]

(3) **Right to abortion:** [§605] Government refusal to give Medicaid for abortions, while providing it for childbirth, does ***not*** penalize or unduly burden the constitutional right of a woman to terminate a pregnancy; the state does not thereby create any obstacles to an indigent's obtaining an abortion that were not already present. Thus, such regulations are subject to the traditional equal protection test. [Maher v. Roe, 432 U.S. 464 (1977); Harris v. McRae, *supra*, §576] Likewise, providing public hospital services for childbirth but not for abortions does not violate equal protection. [Poelker v. Doe, 432 U.S. 519 (1977)]

d. **Freedom of speech:** [§606] When government restricts speech or speech-related activities, the legislation must be ***finely tailored*** to serve ***substantial*** state interests and the justification offered for any distinctions it draws must be carefully scrutinized. [Carey v. Brown, 447 U.S. 455 (1980)—holding unconstitutional a statute that prohibited picketing of dwellings, but exempted from its prohibition peaceful picketing of a residence that was a place of employment involved in a labor dispute; Chicago Police Department v. Mosley, 408 U.S. 92 (1972)—holding unconstitutional an ordinance barring all picketing near schools, but exempting such picketing of a school involved in a labor dispute]

e. **Right to vote:** [§607] Several amendments to the Constitution forbid government (state and federal) denial of the right to vote on specified grounds: "race, color, or previous condition of servitude" [Fifteenth Amendment]; "sex" [Nineteenth Amendment]; "failure to pay any poll tax or other tax" to vote in federal elections [Twenty-Fourth Amendment]; and "age" if more than 18 years old [Twenty-Sixth Amendment]. Apart from these specific prohibitions, however, there is no general right to vote mentioned in the Constitution. Nonetheless, the Court has held that government discriminations with respect to voting are subject to strict scrutiny under the Equal Protection Clause; unless they are necessary to a ***compelling*** interest, such discriminations violate the "constitutionally protected right to participate in elections on an equal basis with other citizens in the jurisdiction." [Dunn v. Blumstein, *supra*, §593]

(1) **Denial of the vote:** [§608] A number of cases have considered state laws granting the right to vote to some ***bona fide residents*** of requisite ***age*** and ***citizenship*** while denying it to others. Most such laws have been held to deny equal protection—either because the discrimination could not be justified by a "compelling" state interest, or because the classification was "overbroad" (in that it was not "necessary" to promote a compelling state interest). *Examples:*

(a) **Armed forces:** [§609] A state law that required bona fide residence as a qualification to vote, but which prohibited military service personnel stationed within the state from ever acquiring such residence, was held to violate equal protection. [Carrington v. Rash, 380 U.S. 89 (1965)]

(b) **Poll tax:** [§610] A law conditioning the right to vote upon payment of a poll tax was held to violate the Equal Protection Clause—because wealth bears no relation to voter qualification. [Harper v. Virginia Board of Elections, *supra*, §577]

(c) **School board elections:** [§611] A law limiting the vote in school district elections to those who have children in local public schools, or who own or lease real property, was held to violate equal protection. Even if voters could be limited to those "primarily interested in school affairs," the classification was ***overbroad***—since it excluded some types of people who were interested and included others who were not. [Kramer v. Union Free School District, 395 U.S. 622 (1969)]

(d) **Federal enclaves:** [§612] Persons who live on a federal enclave (*e.g.*, National Institutes of Health) located within a state cannot be denied the right to vote in state elections—since these persons are subject to important aspects of state power and are as interested in electoral decisions as those outside the enclave. [Evans v. Cornman, 398 U.S. 419 (1970)]

(e) **Bond elections:** [§613] Nor can the right to vote on the issuance of municipal bonds be limited to local property taxpayers—because nonproperty owners also have a substantial interest in the improvements to be financed by such bonds. And even if the bonds are to be paid from property taxes alone, the costs thereof inevitably will be passed on to nonproperty owners (as tenants or purchasers of goods and services from property owners). [City of Phoenix v. Kolodziejski, 399 U.S. 204 (1970); Hill v. Stone, 421 U.S. 289 (1975)]

(f) **Waiting periods for existing residents:** [§614] Waiting periods have been held to discriminate against the right to vote as well as the right to interstate travel. (*See supra*, §§593-594.)

(g) **Exceptions:** [§615] In several situations, the Court has upheld laws denying certain persons the vote.

1) **Felons:** [§616] State laws denying the vote to persons convicted of a felony do ***not*** violate equal protection. Such laws are not subject to strict scrutiny.

a) **Rationale:** Disenfranchising felons is "affirmatively sanctioned" by Section 2 of the Fourteenth Amendment (which mentions that those convicted of crimes may be excluded in computing who is eligible to vote); therefore, the Equal Protection Clause of Section 1 "could not have been intended" as applicable thereto. [Richardson v. Ramirez, 418 U.S. 24 (1974)]

2) **"Special purpose" elections:** [§617] Laws denying persons the right to vote in elections for officials who do not exercise "normal government authority," but rather deal with matters of "special" interest to a limited group within the community, are not subject to strict scrutiny; they are judged by the "traditional" equal protection test.

a) **Water storage districts:** [§618] Thus, a law restricting the vote in elections for a "water storage district" (dealing with conservation and distribution of water and flood control) to landowners does not violate equal protection. The district's powers disproportionately affect landowners. Thus, the restriction on the franchise was "rational." [Salyer Land Co. v. Tulare Water Storage District, 410 U.S. 719 (1973)] Nor is this result changed by the fact that the water district is a major supplier of electricity in the state and that almost all its income comes from such sales. [Ball v. James, 451 U.S. 355 (1981)]

3) **Nonresidents:** [§619] Laws denying the right to vote in a governmental entity's election to nonresidents do not violate equal protection—even when those outside the entity's boundaries are subject to that entity's limited extraterritorial powers, such as its police, sanitary, and business-licensing regulations. Such laws are subject only to the traditional "rational basis" standard. [Holt Civic Club v. City of Tuscaloosa, 439 U.S. 60 (1978)]

4) **Limiting "effectiveness" of the vote:** [§620] Some laws that ***substantially*** impair the effectiveness of the right to vote have also been subject to ***fairly*** strict scrutiny under the Equal Protection Clause.

(a) **Registration for primary elections:** [§621] State laws requiring a voter to register as a member of a particular party at least 30 days before a general election in order to be eligible to vote in that party's next primary election (the following year) have been upheld. Such laws serve an ***important*** purpose (preventing "raiding"—whereby one party's members vote in the other party's primary to distort the results). [Rosario v. Rockefeller, 410 U.S. 752 (1973)]

1) **Compare—reasonable time period:** [§622] But this time period may not be so long as to effectively prevent a person who wants to change registration from voting in the next primary—*e.g.*, a state law that prevented voting in the primary election if the voter had changed his party registration within the preceding 23 months was held invalid, because a voter would have to forgo voting in at least one primary in order to change his party registration. [Kusper v. Pontikes, 414 U.S. 51 (1974)—state interest in preventing "raiding" could be "attained by less drastic means"]

(b) **Absentee ballots:** [§623] A law granting only certain classes of persons the right to vote by absentee ballot has been upheld using the "traditional" test. *Rationale:* The right to vote was ***not*** involved, since the record did not show that the state precluded appellants from voting. [McDonald v. Board of Elections, 394 U.S. 802 (1969)]

1) **Compare:** However, a law denying absentee ballots to persons being held for trial and to convicted misdemeanants violated equal protection because it was "wholly arbitrary"; it discriminated between those held in their home county and those held outside their county of residence. This law effectively ***denied*** the right to vote. [O'Brien v. Skinner, 414 U.S. 524 (1974)]

(c) **Ballot qualification restrictions:** [§624] State laws that impose burdensome requirements on small or new political parties attempting to get their candidates on the election ballot have been held to discriminate against the "right of qualified voters, regardless of their political persuasion, to cast their votes effectively"—as well as to discriminate against the freedom of association (*see supra*, §§583-589). Such laws are thus subject to strict scrutiny under the Equal Protection Clause.

(2) **"Dilution" of the vote—apportionment:** [§625] For many years. the Court refused jurisdiction of cases challenging the fairness of the representation in state legislatures, on the ground that the issue was a "political question." [*See, e.g.*, Colegrove v. Green, 328 U.S. 549 (1946)]

However, the Court abandoned this position in *Baker v. Carr*, 369 U.S. 186 (1962), which held that the courts have jurisdiction to determine the validity of state legislative apportionment plans, in order to assure to each voter the equal protection guaranteed by the Fourteenth Amendment.

(a) **Congressional districts:** [§626] The provision in Article 1, Section 2—that members of Congress be chosen "by the People of the several States"—requires that congressional districts contain ***equal population*** "as nearly as is practicable." [Wesberry v. Sanders, 376 U.S. 1 (1964)] "Precise mathematical equality" is the goal. Departures are permissible only if "unavoidable despite a good faith effort," or if proper "justification is shown."

1) **Justifications:** [§627] If challengers show that population deviations were not "unavoidable despite a good faith effort," the state then has the burden to prove with ***specificity*** that each significant deviation was necessary to achieve a "legitimate goal—such as "making districts compact, respecting municipal boundaries, preserving the cores of prior districts, or avoiding contests between incumbents." [Karcher v. Daggett, 462 U.S. 725 (1983)]

2) **Projected population shifts:** [§628] Since districting plans are usually based upon census figures, which are taken only every 10 years, projected population shifts among the districts may be considered if adequately documented. [White v. Weiser, 412 U.S. 783 (1973)—inadequate documentation]

3) **Preserving seats of incumbents:** [§629] The Court has left open the question of whether deviation can be justified so as to maintain existing relationships between incumbents and their constituents and to preserve seniority rights in Congress—interests that ***may perhaps*** be considered in the context of ***state*** districting (*see* below). [White v. Weiser, *supra*]

4) **Apportionment of districts among states:** [§630] Article I, Section 2 requires that Congress apportion representatives among the states "according to their respective numbers." Congress's good faith choice of method commands "far more deference" than state districting decisions and is ***not*** subject to the same precise mathematical standard. [United States Department of Commerce v. Montana, 112 S. Ct. 1415 (1992)]

(b) **State legislative districts:** [§631] In *Reynolds v. Sims,* 377 U.S. 533 (1964), the Court held that equal protection requires representation in both houses of a state legislature to be based on population as nearly as practicable. Each voter is entitled to have an equally weighted vote. The fact that malapportionment is the result of a popular referendum is irrelevant because the majority cannot deny the minority the right to an undiluted vote. [Lucas v. 44th General Assembly, 377 U.S. 713 (1964)]

1) **Permissible deviations:** [§632] Mathematical exactness is not required, since small deviations may be unavoidable. A maximum deviation between any two districts ***under 10%*** requires no state explanation and is valid even though there may be other plans with even lower deviations. [Gaffney v. Cummings, 412 U.S. 735 (1973); White v. Regester, 412 U.S. 755 (1973)] However, larger deviations ***cannot*** be upheld unless ***explained*** by some acceptable state policy. [Swann v. Adams, 385 U.S. 440 (1967)]

    a) **Preserving city or county boundaries:** [§633] Existing boundaries of political subdivisions may be taken into account by the state as long as it is done in a consistent and nondiscriminatory fashion and the final apportionment is substantially based on population. *Rationale:* Preserving the integrity of local subdivisions facilitates the enactment of legislation on matters of purely local concern, and it gives local voters a more effective voice on such matters in the state legislature. [Mahan v. Howell, 410 U.S. 315 (1973)—16.4% deviation justified by state to maintain political subdivison lines; *and see* Brown v. Thomson, 462 U.S. 835 (1983)—larger deviation justified under special circumstances]

        1/ **Local government districts:** [§634] Because flexibility is needed for viable local government, ***slightly greater*** percentage deviations are allowed for local government apportionment than for state and congressional apportionment—as long as justifying factors exist. [Abate v . Mundt, 403 U.S. 182 (1971)]

    b) **Balance between two houses:** [§635] Both houses of the state legislature may be considered together, so that a slight population disparity in one may be balanced by an offsetting disparity in the other.

    c) **Preserving seats of incumbents:** [§636] Although considerations based on history, area size, group interests, or preservation of an incumbent's seat are ***not*** generally legitimate [Reynolds v. Sims, *supra*], the Court has held that a plan "acceptable populationwise" is not rendered invalid because its purpose was to "achieve a rough approximation of the statewide political strengths of the . . . two parties in the state large enough to elect legislators from discernible geographic areas" [Gaffney v. Cummings, *supra*].

2) **Multi-member districts:** [§637] Multi-member districts have been held to be ***not*** per se violative of the "one person-one vote" rule. But they ***do*** violate equal protection if, "designedly or otherwise," it is shown that they operate to minimize the voting strength of a particular racial or political group. [*Compare*

Whitcomb v. Chavis, 403 U.S. 124 (1971)—valid, *with* White v. Regester, *supra*—invalid]

a) **Residency requirements:** [§638] A multi-member district's representatives may be required to live in particular subdistricts irrespective of their population. *Rationale:* The representative's residence does not mean that he will not effectively represent the voters of the entire district. [Dusch v. Davis, 387 U.S. 112 (1967)]

3) **Gerrymandering:** [§639] State districting plans that disadvantage an identifiable racial or political group on a statewide basis ***may*** violate equal protection. For ***political*** gerrymanders, the challengers must prove (i) an ***intent*** to discriminate ***and*** (ii) a discriminatory ***effect*** of a kind that, either in actual fact or by projection, ***consistently*** degrades the political group's influence on the political process as a whole (*i.e.*, more than the loss of a single election). [Davis v. Bandemer, 478 U.S. 109 (1986)—plurality opinion] As for ***racial*** gerrymanders, it is unclear whether a showing of an intent to discriminate is enough.

4) **Relevant population:** [§640] Districting need not be based on ***total*** population—*e.g.*, aliens, transients, and convicts may be excluded. But distributing representation on the basis of registered or actual voters is suspect because these are not criteria for state citizenship and lend themselves to improper political influences; this will be upheld ***only*** if the result is not substantially different from that obtained by the use of a permissible basis. [Burns v. Richardson, 384 U.S. 73 (1966)]

5) **Relevant officials:** [§641] The "one person-one vote" rule applies to the ***election*** of ***all*** officials who perform "normal governmental functions." Thus, it applies not only to legislators, but also to administrative and executive officials who are elected by popular vote. [Hadley v. Junior College District, 397 U.S. 50 (1970)—trustees of junior college district]

a) **"Special purpose" officials:** [§642] The duties of some officials are so far removed from "normal governmental activities" and so disproportionately affect different groups that their election can be on some basis other than population. [Salyer Land Co. v. Tulare Water Storage District, *supra*, §618—upholding apportionment of votes on basis of ***assessed value of land*** owned for election of directors of water storage district which had limited governmental powers, all relating to water servicing activities, and its costs and charges were assessed solely against the land in proportion to benefits received]

b) **Nomination of officials:** [§643] The "one person-one vote" rule applies to nomination procedures. Thus, the

Court has invalidated a state law that required independent candidates for statewide office to be nominated by petitions signed by at least 200 voters from each of at least 50 of the 102 counties in the state. This procedure in effect discriminated against the residents of the more populous counties, because even if all the people in these counties wished to nominate, they would be unable to do so. [Moore v. Ogilvie, 394 U.S. 814 (1969)]

c) **Appointed officials:** [§644] But the "one person-one vote" rule does ***not*** apply where a state provides for ***appointment*** of administrative or other nonlegislative state or local officers. [Sailors v. Board of Education, 387 U.S. 105 (1967)—upholding appointment of county school board members by local school boards serving unequal populations]

1/ **Appointment vs. election:** [§645] The Court has found "no constitutional reason" why government officials—at least ***nonlegislative*** officials—may not be appointed rather than elected. [Sailors v. Board of Education, *supra*] Thus, a state's ***governor*** may be chosen by the state legislature when no candidate received a majority vote in the election. [Fortson v. Morris, 385 U.S. 231 (1966)] And the Court has upheld ***temporary*** appointments of ***legislators*** to fill vacancies caused by death, resignation, etc.—even when the appointment is made by the political party with which the previous incumbent was affiliated. [Rodriguez v. Popular Democratic Party, 457 U.S. 1 (1982)]

(c) **Supermajority requirements:** [§646] Provisions requiring enactments—either by the legislature or by referendum—to be approved by more than majority vote have been held ***not*** to violate equal protection as long as they do not discriminate against (or authorize discrimination against) any identifiable class. (*Rationale:* The Constitution does not require "that a majority always prevail on every issue.") The Court ***did not pass*** on (i) a requirement of "unanimity or giving a veto power to a very small group," or (ii) a requirement of "extraordinary" majorities for the election of public officers. [Gordon v. Lance, 403 U.S. 1 (1970)— upholding 60% requirement in state referendum for bond issue; Town of Lockport v. Citizens for Community Action, 430 U.S. 259 (1977)—upholding requirement that new county charter be approved by separate majorities of city and noncity voters]

(d) **Remedies for malapportionment:** [§647] The federal courts have been instructed to remedy malapportionment according to general ***equitable*** principles. If the problem is being dealt with in the state judicial system, the federal court should usually defer. Likewise, the federal court should give the state legislature an adequate opportunity to remedy the situation. [Scott v. Germano, 381 U.S. 407 (1965)]

1) **Limited flexibility:** [§648] If the state or local body fails to act, the federal court will draw up a plan. However, federal courts do not have as much flexibility as these bodies; also, the plans so fashioned are held to stricter standards on appellate review both in respect to deviation from the goal of population equality [Chapman v. Meier, 420 U.S. 1 (1975)], and in the use of multi-member districts [Connor v. Finch, 431 U.S. 407 (1977)].

f. **Right to be a candidate:** [§649] The Court has ***not*** recognized a "fundamental right" to be a candidate for public office. But state laws that impose burdensome requirements on candidates are subject to ***fairly*** strict scrutiny under the Equal Protection Clause because of their impact on the right to vote. (*See supra*, §§583-589.)

(1) **Filing fees:** [§650] The requirement of a fee to get on the election ballot is ***not*** per se invalid. As applied to indigent candidates, however, such fees do not survive "close scrutiny" and thus violate equal protection. *Rationale*: Selection of candidates solely on the basis of ability to pay a fixed fee, "without providing any alternative means of ballot access," is not "reasonably necessary" to accomplish the state's "legitimate" election interests. [Lubin v. Panish, 415 U.S. 709 (1974); Bullock v. Carter, *supra*, §577]

(2) **Existing officials:** [§651] Laws placing various limits on the ability of certain public officeholders to run for ***other*** elective office during their terms as incumbents are ***not*** subject to "strict" scrutiny and do not violate equal protection. [Clements v. Fashing, 457 U.S. 957 (1982)—no majority opinion]

8. **"Nonfundamental" Rights:** [§652] To be deemed a "fundamental right"—and thereby subject to "strict scrutiny"—the right must be "explicitly or implicitly guaranteed by the Constitution." [San Antonio Independent School District v. Rodriguez, *supra*, §582] Pursuant to this doctrine, the Court has held that many important interests are ***not*** "fundamental" and thus discriminations affecting them are reviewable under the ***traditional "rational basis" test.***

a. **Welfare:** [§653] There is no constitutional right to receive public welfare. Classifications respecting welfare benefits are therefore subject only to the traditional equal protection test. [Dandridge v. Williams, 397 U.S. 471 (1970)—state "maximum grant" law, imposing an upper limit on the total amount of welfare assistance any one family could receive and thereby discriminating against large families, upheld as "rational"; law dealt only with "economics and social welfare"]

(1) **Disability benefits:** [§654] Similarly, a provision of the Social Security Act reducing disability benefits for those receiving state workers' compensation, but not for those who received compensation from private insurance or tort claim awards, was upheld under the "traditional" test. [Richardson v. Belcher, 404 U.S. 78 (1971)]

b. **Housing:** [§655] There is ***no*** constitutional right to "decent, safe and sanitary" housing. Thus, a state law giving landlords a special cause of action to evict tenants was upheld as drawing a "rational" classification. [Lindsey v. Normet, 405 U.S. 56 (1972)]

(1) **Unrelated persons living together:** [§656] Similarly, a zoning law restricting land use to "one family dwellings"—and defining "family" to mean one or more persons related by blood, adoption, or marriage but not more than two unrelated persons living together—was upheld under the "traditional" equal protection test. [Village of Belle Terre v. Boraas, 416 U.S. 1 (1974)]

c. **Education:** [§657] There is no constitutional right to a particular quality of education. Thus, a state system of public school financing that relied on property values was upheld as "rational." [San Antonio Independent School District v. Rodriguez, *supra*, §652]

(1) **Bus transportation:** [§658] Nor is there any constitutional right to free bus service to public schools. [Kadrmas v. Dickinson Public Schools, 484 U.S. 1000 (1988)]

d. **Bankruptcy:** [§659] There is no constitutional right to discharge one's debts through bankruptcy proceedings. [United States v. Kras, *supra*, §574—filing fee requirement upheld as serving a "rational" basis to make bankruptcy proceedings self-supporting, and thus not a denial of equal protection to indigents]

e. **Compare—important rights:** [§660] In a few cases involving important—but ***not*** "fundamental"—rights, the Court has found equal protection violations under the "traditional" rational basis test.

(1) **Housing:** [§661] A law requiring a special "double bond" only for evicted tenants who wished to appeal has been held "arbitrary and irrational." [Lindsey v. Normet, *supra*]

(2) **Welfare:** [§662] A law denying food stamps to "any household containing an individual who is unrelated to any other member of the household was held to be "wholly without rational basis." [United States Department of Agriculture v. Moreno, *supra*, §487]

9. **"Irrebuttable Presumptions" and the Right to a Hearing:** [§663] During the early 1970s, in several cases involving "important" interests, the Court—although declining to find a "fundamental" right—nonetheless invalidated ***over-inclusive*** state classifications (*see supra*, §486) on the ground that they created improper "irrebuttable" (or "conclusive") presumptions. The Court, usually relying on the Due Process Clause rather than the Equal Protection Clause, reasoned that since all persons within the statutory classification did not satisfy the criteria on which the classification were based, ***procedural due process*** required that individuals be given some opportunity to show that they should be treated differently.

a. **Parental custody:** [§664] A state law provided that a father automatically lost his illegitimate children upon the death of their mother. The effect was to create an irrebuttable presumption that unwed fathers are unfit parents, which is neither "necessarily nor universally true." The Court noted that a father's interest in retaining custody of his children warranted protection, "absent a powerful countervailing interest," and held that procedural due process requires that the father be given a hearing as to his fitness as a parent. [Stanley v. Illinois, 405 U.S. 645 (1972)]

b. **Residency status:** [§665] A state law required that nonresidents pay higher fees to attend the state university and created an irrebuttable presumption of nonresidency for the entire period of education if the applicant filed from outside the state. The Court held that since the state had reasonable alternative means of determining residency, procedural due process required that applicants be afforded a hearing to present evidence of their bona fide residency. [Vlandis v. Kline, 412 U.S. 441 (1973)]

c. **Pregnancy and employee fitness:** [§666] Where school board rules required pregnant teachers to leave work at least four or five months before the date of anticipated childbirth, the effect was to create an irrebuttable presumption that every teacher five months pregnant is physically incapable of continuing her duties. The Court noted that since this is neither "necessarily nor universally true," due process requires a case-by-case determination (*e.g.*, through medical exams). [Cleveland Board of Education v. LaFleur, 414 U.S. 632 (1974)] (A similar rule making a teacher ineligible to return to work until her child was three months old was also held invalid.)

d. **Food stamps:** [§667] A federal statute excluded (as "not needy") any household containing a person over 18 who was claimed as a tax dependent by a taxpayer who was not himself eligible for food stamps. In effect, this operated as an irrebuttable presumption that the household was not needy. Due process was held to require that the household be given the opportunity to present evidence as to whether it was needy. [United States Department of Agriculture v. Murry, 413 U.S. 508 (1973)]

e. **Disability benefits for illegitimate children:** [§668] A Social Security Act provision denied benefits to some (but not all) illegitimate children born after their parent's disability, irrespective of their dependency. The Court held that this denied ***equal protection*** (rather than due process), since it "conclusively excludes some illegitimates who are, in fact, dependent upon their disabled parent" without giving them "an opportunity to establish their dependency." [Jiminez v. Weinberger, 417 U.S. 628 (1974)]

f. **Decline of the doctrine:** [§669] In *Weinberger v. Salfi*, 422 U.S. 749 (1975), a provision of the Social Security Act denied benefits to wives and stepchildren who were such for less than nine months prior to the wage earner's death, thus creating a conclusive presumption that marriages within this time were undertaken simply to secure benefits. The Court recognized that the presumption might prove "over-inclusive" or "under-inclusive" in particular cases, but upheld it since "Congress could rationally have concluded that any imprecision . . . was justified by its ease and certainty of operation." The Court has not since used the irrebuttable presumption approach to invalidate any government regulations.

D. THE "STATE ACTION" REQUIREMENT

1. **Introduction:** [§670] The language of the Fourteenth and Fifteenth Amendments (including those provisions of the Bill of Rights applicable to the states) restricts only

governmental action. The acts of mere private individuals were early held ***not*** to fall within their prohibition; only "state action" is restricted. [Civil Rights Cases, 109 U.S. 3 (1883)] However, "state action" includes ***more*** than action taken by the legislative, executive, judicial, and administrative branches of the federal and state governments and their subdivisions; it also includes certain actions taken by ostensibly private individuals or organizations (*see* below).

2. **Acts of Government "Agents":** [§671] State action includes conduct of government officials acting in their official capacity—*i.e.*, "under color of law"—even though the specific action they take may be forbidden by law.

    a. **Example:** When a state ***jury commissioner discriminates*** against blacks in selecting jury panels, this is "state action" even though state and federal law may bar such discrimination. [*Ex parte* Virginia, 100 U.S. 339 (1879)]

    b. **Example:** When a state ***police officer beats a prisoner to death*** in an effort to obtain a confession, or stands aside while someone else beats a prisoner to death, this is "state action" since the officer, acting in his official capacity, has deprived the prisoner of life without due process of law. [Screws v. United States, 325 U.S. 91 (1945)]

3. **"Public" or "Government" Functions:** [§672] In a few instances, the Court has found that activities undertaken by private individuals or organizations are ones that are "traditionally the ***exclusive*** prerogative of the State." The Court has characterized such an activity as a "public" or "government" function, and therefore treated it as "state action" subject to the Fourteenth and Fifteenth Amendments.

    a. **Elections:** [§673] The Court has held that conducting elections is an exclusively state function, and thus has invalidated racial discrimination by groups with effective control over the selection of candidates.

        (1) **Primaries:** [§674] A political party cannot exclude blacks from voting in primary elections from which the party nominee for the general election is chosen. [Smith v. Allwright, 321 U.S. 649 (1944)]

        (2) **Pre-primaries:** [§675] County political groups cannot exclude blacks from a pre-primary election when the winner almost always runs unopposed in the party primary and general election. [Terry v. Adams, 345 U.S. 461 (1953)]

    b. **Company towns:** [§676] A private corporation owned a town that had "all the characteristics of any other American town." The corporation caused the trespass conviction of a distributor of religious literature who refused to leave the town's business district sidewalk. The Court held this to be "state action" violating the First and Fourteenth Amendments because the town's streets, although privately owned, were the ***functional equivalent*** of city streets and the residents of the company town had as great an interest in receiving information as did those of an "ordinary" town. [Marsh v. Alabama, 326 U.S. 501 (1946)]

    c. **Limits of doctrine:** [§677] In most instances, however, the Court has ***not*** found the privately conducted activity to be a "public" or "government" function.

(1) **Shopping centers:** [§678] Although a large, self-contained shopping center is in many ways similar to the business district of an ordinary town, it is ***not*** the "functional equivalent" of a municipality because it does not possess ***all*** the attributes of a town. [Hudgens v. NRLB, 424 U.S. 507 (1976)—*overruling* Amalgamated Food Employees Union v. Logan Valley Plaza, Inc., 391 U.S. 308 (1968)]

(2) **Monopoly businesses:** [§679] A heavily regulated electric company that had been granted a monopoly by the state was held ***not*** to have engaged in "state action" when it terminated a user's service without notice or hearing. The Court reasoned that "the supplying of utility service is not traditionally the exclusive province of the state." [Jackson v. Metropolitan Edison Co., 419 U.S. 345 (1974)]

(3) **Regulated businesses:** [§680] Similarly, the fact that nursing homes or specialized private schools are almost wholly funded and extensively regulated by the state does not make their conduct state action. Again, the Court reasoned that these enterprises are not "the exclusive province of the state." [Blum v. Yaretsky, 457 U.S. 991 (1982); Rendell-Baker v. Kohn, 457 U.S. 830 (1982)]

(4) **Creditors' remedies:** [§681] A warehouseman authorized by state statute to sell goods stored with him for unpaid charges is ***not*** engaged in state action. Although resolution of private disputes ***is*** a traditional "state function," the bailor had state law remedies to check abuse by the warehouseman and thus the state had not delegated an "exclusive public function" to the warehouseman. [Flagg Bros., Inc. v. Brooks, 436 U.S. 149 (1978)]

4. **Significant State "Involvement":** [§682] A larger number of cases have found state action by private individuals (usually racial discrimination in violation of the Equal Protection Clause) because the government has ***required*** or ***significantly encouraged*** the acts of discrimination. Note that government is not constitutionally required to outlaw private discrimination—merely permitting private conduct to occur is not enough for "state action"; the state must ***compel*** or ***significantly participate*** in the private conduct. Whether such state involvement exists requires a case-by-case determination, based on the particular facts before the Court. [Burton v. Wilmington Parking Authority, 365 U.S. 715 (1961)]

a. **Government compulsion of private discrimination:** [§683] When a city ordinance (or an official policy announced by the police) required racial segregation in restaurants, the action of a private restaurateur who caused blacks to be prosecuted for trespass when they refused to leave was held to be state action. Even though the private restaurateur would have wished to discriminate wholly apart from the ordinance, by enacting the ordinance, the state had made the choice for private persons. [Peterson v. City of Greenville, 373 U.S. 244 (1963); Lombard v. Louisiana, 373 U.S. 267 (1963)]

b. **Government administration of private discrimination:** [§684] When state officials acted as trustees under a private will, which devised property for use as a school (or a park) and required racial discrimination, this was held to be state action. [Pennsylvania v. Board of Trusts, 353 U.S. 230 (1957)] Furthermore, a state court's appointment of private trustees, replacing the state officials, who had resigned as trustees to facilitate the appointment, constituted state action where the obvious purpose was to perpetuate racial discrimination which the state officials themselves could no longer implement. [Evans v. Newton, 382 U.S. 296 (1966)]

(1) **Compare:** In subsequent litigation, the state court held that since the settlor of the trust was absolutely opposed to integration, the trust failed because its purpose had become illegal; the property therefore reverted to the settlor's heirs (the state court refusing to apply cy pres doctrine to save the trust). The Supreme Court found no discriminatory state action; the state law as to interpretation of the will and application of cy press doctrine was "neutral with regard to race," and there was no evidence that the state judges were "motivated by racial animus" in construing the will. [Evans v. Abney, 396 U.S. 435 (1970)]

c. **Joint action by government officials and private persons—creditors' remedies:** [§685] When creditors act pursuant to statutes that authorize the property of their debtors to be attached or sequestered with the aid of a state official (such as the sheriff), the private person's "joint participation with state officials is sufficient to characterize that person as a 'state actor' for purposes of the Fourteenth Amendment." [Lugar v. Edmondson Oil Co., 457 U.S. 922 (1982)]

d. **Judicial enforcement of private discrimination—restrictive covenants:** [§686] If state courts enforce racial restrictive covenants by all homeowners in an area by (i) enjoining a black person who purchased from a white owner from taking possession, and (ii) awarding damages against the white seller to other signatories, there is "state action." While ***voluntary*** adherence to the covenants does ***not*** involve state action, ***judicial enforcement*** does. [Shelley v. Kraemer, 334 U.S. 1 (1948); Barrows v. Jackson, 346 U.S. 249 (1953)]

(1) **Comment:** The implications of this doctrine (*i.e.*, that judicial enforcement of private discrimination makes it subject to the Fourteenth Amendment) are ***very broad***, and logically extend to converting all private action into state action if the private discriminator seeks aid from the courts to carry out his purpose. However, the Court has made ***almost*** no use of this doctrine beyond racial restrictive covenants.

(2) **Possible limitation—forcing otherwise unwilling discrimination:** [§687] The "restrictive covenant" cases involved judicial enforcement of private discrimination that had the effect of forcing a white homeowner (the seller) to discriminate against his wishes. This is distinguishable from the usual situation in which the discriminator seeks judicial assistance to carry out his discriminatory desires without forcing anyone else to discriminate, *e.g.*, restaurateur who refuses to serve blacks and brings a trespass action against those who refuse to leave. [*See* Bell v. Maryland, 378 U.S. 226 (1964)—several Justices so limiting the doctrine of the "restrictive covenant" cases]

(a) **Example:** A state liquor regulation required that private clubs granted liquor licenses must adhere to their constitutions and bylaws. The Court, relying on the doctrine of the "restrictive covenant" cases, held that if a court were to enforce a club's bylaw that denied membership to blacks (*e.g.*, in a suit filed by some members against the club for admitting a black), this would "invoke the sanctions of the state to enforce discrimination." The effect would be forcing the club to engage in racial discrimination against its wishes. [Moose Lodge v. Irvis, 407 U.S. 163 (1972)]

e. **Peremptory challenges:** [§688] Use of peremptory challenges by a private litigant in a civil trial significantly involves the state and places the court's power and prestige behind the resulting racial discrimination. [Edmonson v. Leesville Concrete Co., 500 U.S. 614 (1991)] The same rule applies to the use of peremptory challenges by a criminal defendant. [Georgia v. McCollum, 112 S. Ct. 2348 (1992)] Thus, neither civil litigants nor criminal defendants may base peremptory challenges on race.

f. **Government approval of private conduct:** [§689] When a state regulatory agency affirmatively approves a practice of a regulated business (*e.g.,* after a full investigation), the practice has been held to be state action. [Public Utilities Commission v. Pollak, 343 U.S. 451 (1952)—involving a challenge to a licensed bus company's practice of broadcasting radio programs in its buses]

(1) **Compare:** But the mere fact that the practice has been filed with and accepted by the regulatory agency does ***not*** make the practice state action. [Jackson v. Metropolitan Edison Co., *supra*] And it follows that the mere fact an extensively regulated business engages in certain practices does ***not*** make these practices state action, as long as the state does not ***require*** or ***significantly encourage*** the practices. [Blum v. Yaretzsky, *supra,* §680; Rendell-Baker v. Kohn, *supra,* §680] Similarly, the fact that a regulated business is licensed by the state (or receives state services such as electricity and water, and police and fire protection) does ***not*** make its conduct state action. [Moose Lodge v. Irvis, *supra*—liquor license; *and see* CBS v. Democratic National Committee, 412 U.S. 94 (1973)—opinion of three Justices regarding broadcast licenses]

(2) **State policy of approval:** [§690] Where a state constitutional amendment repealed existing antidiscrimination-in-housing statutes and prevented the legislature from regulating the sale or rental of residential property in the future, and when an apartment owner then refused to rent to a black tenant, the Court held this to be state action. The Court reasoned that the state constitutional amendment did more than merely repeal antidiscrimination laws; its purpose was seen as ***encouraging*** racial discrimination, since discriminators were freed from any official censure as a matter of basic state policy. [Reitman v. Mulkey, 387 U.S. 369 (1967)]

g. **"Symbiotic" relationship:** [§691] State action has also been found where the private discriminator was a ***lessee of public property*** (restaurant operated as "integral part" of public parking structure in which it was located). The private restaurant benefited from cars parking in the public building and vice versa. [Burton v. Wilmington Parking Authority, *supra*, §682]

E. CONGRESSIONAL POWER TO ENFORCE CONSTITUTIONAL RIGHTS

1. **In General:** [§692] Pursuant to the Necessary and Proper Clause (*see supra*, §123) and the Enabling Clauses of the Thirteenth, Fourteenth, and Fifteenth Amendments (which empower Congress to enforce those amendments by "appropriate legislation"), Congress is authorized to protect the exercise of (and remedy interference with) constitutional rights. To some extent, Congress has the power to legislate against policies and practices that the Court itself would not find unconstitutional (*see* below).

   a. **Government action:** [§693] If the constitutional right operates only against government action (as most do; *see supra*, §670), Congress may impose criminal or civil remedies against one who interferes when "acting ***under color of law***"—generally a synonym for "government action."

   b. **Private action:** [§694] If the constitutional right operates against private individuals as well as government action (*see infra*, §§702 *et seq.*), Congress may legislate remedies against anyone who interferes.

2. **Necessary and Proper Clause:** [§695] The Court has held that there are several ***constitutional rights of national citizenship*** which, although not enumerated in the Constitution, "arise from the relationship of the individual and the federal government." These rights are secured against ***private*** as well as ***government*** action. Thus, under the Necessary and Proper Clause, Congress has power to pass laws protecting these rights from interference by ***anyone***. [United States v. Williams, 341 U.S. 70 (1951)]

   a. **Right to travel interstate:** [§696] Since this is a right of national citizenship, a federal statute making it a crime to interfere with another person's use of interstate highways was upheld as a valid exercise of Congress's power to protect a citizen's right to travel freely from state to state. [United States v. Guest, *supra*, §464]

      (1) **Federal provision for civil damages:** [§697] Similarly, a federal statute authorizing ***civil damages*** for interference with constitutional rights of others, as applied in a suit for harassment on interstate highways, was upheld as a proper exercise of federal power to protect the right to travel interstate. [Griffin v. Breckenridge, 403 U.S. 88 (1971)]

      (2) **Federal limitation on state statutes:** [§698] And a federal statute ***banning*** state ***residency requirements*** in presidential elections was upheld as a proper exercise of federal power to protect the right to travel freely from state to state—since Congress could find that the residency requirements unreasonably burdened the right. [Oregon v. Mitchell, 400 U.S. 112 (1970)]

   b. **Right to vote in federal elections:** [§699] Since the right to vote in federal elections is a right of national citizenship, Congress has been held to have power to regulate age requirements for voting in federal elections. [Oregon v. Mitchell, *supra*—some Justices relying on Section 5 of the Fourteenth Amendment, discussed below]

      (1) **Federal primary elections:** [§700] This power also applies to congressional regulation of ***primary elections*** for federal officials. [United States v. Classic, 313 U.S. 299 (1941)]

c. **Right to petition national government:** [§701] The final important right of national citizenship is the right "peaceably to assemble for the purpose of petitioning Congress for redress of grievances." [United States v. Cruikshank, 92 U.S. 542 (1876)]

3. **Thirteenth Amendment:** [§702] The Thirteenth Amendment's prohibition of slavery applies to private as well as government action. Therefore, under the Enabling Clause in Section 2, Congress has power to remedy interference by ***anyone***. This power has been broadly construed. The test is whether Congress could ***rationally*** determine that the conduct it is making criminal (or providing civil remedies against) imposes on the victim a ***"badge or incident" of slavery***. [Jones v. Alfred H. Mayer Co., 392 U.S. 409 (1968)]

a. **Examples:** Congress has been held to have the power to create a statutory cause of action against private persons who deprive blacks of "basic rights that the law secures to all free men"—*e.g.*, freedom from racial discrimination in the sale or rental of real and personal property [Jones v. Alfred H. Mayer Co., *supra*]; in the making of contracts for admission to private schools [Runyon v. McCrary, *supra*, §463]; and in respect to "rights such as free speech, assembly, association and movement" [Griffin v. Breckenridge, *supra*].

b. **Scope:** [§703] It would seem that, under the Thirteenth Amendment's Enabling Clause, Congress may prohibit ***virtually*** all racial discrimination ***against blacks***. Moreover, Congress may also prohibit racial discrimination ***against whites***. [McDonald v. Santa Fe Trail Transportation Co., 427 U.S. 273 (1976)] It is an ***open question*** whether Congress may forbid other forms of discrimination pursuant to this power.

4. **Fourteenth Amendment:** [§704] Under the Enabling Clause in Section 5, Congress has power to remedy state discrimination that it finds denies someone equal protection (and, seemingly, state action that it finds violates due process)—and the Court will uphold such federal legislation as long as it can "perceive a basis" for the congressional determination. [Katzenbach v. Morgan, 384 U.S. 641 (1966)—congressional ban on state English literacy tests for voting held to be a valid exercise of power even though the Court itself, unaided by this congressional judgment, would ***not*** have found that the literacy tests violated equal protection; ***and see*** Oregon v. Mitchell, *supra*—although fairly administered literacy tests had been held to be constitutionally permissible, Congress is empowered under the Enabling Clause to ban such tests altogether by finding that such tests are ***inherently*** discriminatory against blacks]

a. **"Remedial" power:** [§705] In addition to the power to "define" the substantive terms of the Fourteenth Amendment (*supra*), Congress also has the power under the Enabling Clause to ***remedy*** Fourteenth Amendment violations by prohibiting conduct that is ***not itself*** unconstitutional.

(1) **Preventing future violations:** [§706] In *Katzenbach v. Morgan, supra*, Congress was held to have the power to forbid state English literacy tests for voting—even though the Court would not find such tests to be unconstitutional—since the Court was able to "perceive a basis" for Congress's judgment that the racial minorities thereby enfranchised

would prevent the state from unconstitutionally discriminating against them in the allocation of public services.

(2) **Remedying prior violations:** [§707] Even though state action that has only a racially disproportionate impact (but is not intentionally discriminatory) does not violate the Equal Protection Clause (*see supra*, §§506-509), Congress has the power under the Enabling Clause to prohibit such state action if it reasonably concludes that this is "an appropriate method of attacking the perpetuation of prior purposeful discrimination." [Fullilove v. Klutznick, *supra*, §541]

b. **Limitations:** [§708] The power of Congress to determine ***whether*** the Fourteenth Amendment has been violated, and to determine the ***appropriate remedies*** for constitutional violations, is potentially very extensive. But it is ***not unlimited***—although the full limits are as yet unclear.

(1) **Conflict with other constitutional provisions:** [§709] One limitation exists when a federal statute enacted to enforce the Fourteenth Amendment comes into conflict with another provision of the Constitution. For example, Congress has no power under Section 5 to lower the voting age in ***state and local*** elections as a means of enforcing equal protection, since Article I, Section 2 reserves to the states the power to prescribe qualifications of voters in state and local elections and no constitutional provision has narrowed this state power. [Oregon v. Mitchell, *supra*—no majority opinion]

(2) **Dilution:** [§710] "Congress's power under Section 5 is limited to adopting measures to ***enforce*** the guarantees of the amendment; Section 5 grants Congress ***no power to restrict, abrogate, or dilute*** these guarantees. Thus, for example, an enactment authorizing the states to establish racially segregated systems of education would not be—as required by Section 5—a measure 'to enforce' the Equal Protection Clause since that clause of its own force prohibits such state laws." [Katzenbach v. Morgan, *supra*]

(3) **Expansion vs. dilution:** [§711] The Court has not clearly indicated the extent to which it will defer to congressional judgment when Congress passes a law that expands one constitutional right apparently at the expense of another—*e.g.*, if Congress were to restrict First Amendment freedom of the press to protect the Fifth Amendment right of a criminal defendant to a fair trial.

c. **Government vs. private action:** [§712] As noted previously (*see supra*, §670), violation of Fourteenth Amendment rights requires some element of state action. Nonetheless, the conduct of private individuals ***may*** sometimes interfere with the exercise of such rights—and Congress has broad powers to remedy this situation.

(1) **State officials:** [§713] In a number of decisions, the Court has relied upon the Enabling Clause to sustain federal statutes authorizing civil damage judgments or criminal convictions against state or local officials who misuse their authority so as to violate the rights protected by the Fourteenth Amendment.

(a) **Examples:** Federal legislation punishing persons who, under color of state law, deprive another of any right, privilege, or immunity secured or protected by the Constitution has been upheld as applied to law enforcement officers who knowingly deprived a prisoner of his life without due process of law. [Screws v. United States, *supra*, §671—police beat prisoner to death in effort to obtain a confession] Also, it has been applied to city council members. [Owen v. City of Independence, 445 U.S. 622 (1980)]

(2) **Compare—federal officials:** [§714] No comparable federal statute provides redress against federal officials who violate the constitutional rights of individuals. But the Court has held that the ***Constitution itself*** empowers federal courts to recognize a cause of action against federal agents who violate the constitutional rights of others. [Bivens v. Six Unknown Named Agents, 403 U.S. 388 (1971)—violation of Fourth Amendment; Davis v. Passman, 442 U.S. 228 (1979)—violation of Fifth Amendment based on sexual bias which denied equal protection]

(3) **Private individuals:** [§715] Where private individuals engage in a "joint activity" with government officials to infringe the constitutional rights of others over whom state power has been exerted, the private individuals, as well as the government officers, are subject to sanctions under federal law. Having gained the benefit of official state power, the private individuals are also subject to the responsibilities of the state. [United States v. Price, 383 U.S. 787 (1966)—private citizens killed civil rights workers pursuant to plan joined in by local police]

(a) **Example:** In *United States v. Guest, supra*, §696, private individuals prevented black persons from using ***state-owned facilities*** because of their race. Six Justices (in two separate opinions) expressed the view that "the right to use state facilities without discrimination on the basis of race" is a right secured by the Equal Protection Clause. Thus, Congress could penalize private interference with that right.

5. **Fifteenth Amendment:** [§716] Under the Enabling Clause in Section 2, Congress has similarly broad power to prevent government racial discrimination in voting. The test is whether Congress could ***rationally*** find that the conduct or practice it seeks to prohibit or regulate has been or may be used to deny voting rights to blacks. [South Carolina v. Katzenbach, *supra*, §61—Congress has power to provide a range of remedies (including suspension of literacy tests and appointment of federal voting examiners) in states where Congress has found government racial discrimination in voting]

a. **Discriminatory effect:** [§717] Even though voting regulations that have only a disproportionate racial impact (but are not intentionally discriminatory) ***might*** not violate the Fifteenth Amendment (*see supra*, §509), Congress may prohibit such regulations in areas "with a demonstrable history of racial discrimination" in voting—since Congress could rationally find that they create the "risk of purposeful discrimination." [City of Rome v. United States, 446 U.S. 156 (1980)]

6. **Other Sources of Power:** [§718] In addition to its power under the Necessary and Proper Clause and the Enabling Clauses, Congress has other sources of power that may be used to protect constitutional rights against both private and government conduct.

   a. **Commerce power:** [§719] Provisions of the Civil Rights Act of 1964 (prohibiting racial discrimination in interstate transportation or in restaurants, hotels, and other places of public accommodation) have been upheld as a valid exercise of Congress's power under the Commerce Clause. [Heart of Atlanta Motel, Inc. v. United States, *supra*, §272]

   b. **Taxing and spending powers:** [§720] The federal government may indirectly, through its taxing or spending powers, compel persons to recognize the constitutional rights of others (*e.g.*, governmental contracts may be conditioned on the supplier's not discriminating in hiring, etc.). [Fullilove v. Klutznick, *supra*, §707]

F. FREEDOM OF SPEECH, PRESS, AND ASSOCIATION

1. In General

a. **Constitutional provision:** [§721] The First Amendment provides: "Congress shall make no law . . . abridging the freedom of ***speech***, or of the ***press***; or the right of people peaceably to ***assemble***, and to petition the government for a redress of grievances." This provision has been held applicable to the states through the Due Process Clause of the Fourteenth Amendment. [Gitlow v. New York, 268 U.S. 652 (1925)]

(1) **Includes freedom to believe:** [§722] The First Amendment plainly protects the freedom to hold beliefs. [Dawson v. Delaware, 112 S. Ct. 1093 (1992)—admitting evidence that convicted defendant was a member of a racist group in order to enhance his punishment violated the First Amendment because it penalized him for his abstract beliefs]

(2) **Includes freedom not to speak:** [§723] The First Amendment protects not only the right to speak freely but also the right to ***refrain*** from speaking at all. These are complementary components of the broader concept of "individual freedom of mind." [Wooley v. Maynard, 430 U.S. 705 (1977)—state may not require person to disseminate ideological message (the motto "Live Free or Die" on a license plate) by displaying it on his private property]

(a) **Compare—property open to public:** [§724] The freedom not to speak does not prohibit a state's requiring a large shopping center (that is open to the public) to permit persons to exercise their speech rights on shopping center property—at least as long as the particular message is not dictated by the state and is not likely to be identified with the owner of the shopping center. [Pruneyard Shopping Center v. Robins, 447 U.S. 74 (1980)]

(b) **Required disclosures as a condition of speech:** [§725] Mandating speech that a speaker would not otherwise make necessarily alters the content of the speech. Therefore, it is subject to the same close scrutiny as a law that forbids speech. [Riley v. National Federation of the Blind of North Carolina, 487 U.S. 781 (1988)—state may not require that professional fundraisers disclose their fees to potential donors before an appeal for funds]

(3) **Includes freedom to associate and not to associate:** [§726] The First Amendment protects the "freedom to associate and privacy in one's associations." [NAACP v. Alabama, *supra*, §56—state cannot compel NAACP to disclose its membership list] This extends to some right to ***refuse*** to associate. [Abood v. Detroit Board of Education, 431 U.S. 209 (1977)—state cannot require employees to contribute for support of ideological causes with which they disagree; *see infra*, §985]

(a) **"Expressive association" and "intimate association":** [§727] The freedom of association includes the right to associate for the purpose of engaging in First Amendment activities—speech, assembly, and religious exercise. It also includes the right to enter into and maintain certain intimate human relationships—to share ideals and beliefs. [Roberts v. United States Jaycees, *supra*, §463] These freedoms of "expressive association" and "intimate association" do not include a general right of "societal association." [City of Dallas v. Stanglin, 409 U.S. 19 (1989)—no right of association in coming to dance hall for recreational dancing]

(4) **Includes freedom to receive information:** [§728] The First Amendment protects both the right to communicate and the right to receive information. [Lamont v. Postmaster General, 381 U.S. 301 (1965)—government may not require that addressee specifically request post office to deliver "communist political propaganda"]

(5) **Includes solicitation of funds:** [§729] The First Amendment protects seeking financial support for particular causes and views because this is often necessary to the flow of information and advocacy. [Village of Schaumburg v. Citizens for a Better Environment, 444 U.S. 620 (1980)]

(6) **Compare—does not include right to be heard:** [§730] The First Amendment right of free speech does not include the right to have public decision making bodies listen or respond to the views communicated. [Minnesota State Board for Community Colleges v. Knight, 465 U.S. 271 (1984)]

(7) **Includes some conduct:** [§731] Freedom of expression and association encompasses certain ***action*** or ***conduct*** in addition to purely verbal or visual expression.

(a) **Necessary incidents of freedom:** [§732] Distributing membership applications, setting up facilities for a meeting, hanging signs announcing a point of view, and similar conduct are among the numerous actions incidental to the freedoms protected by the First Amendment—and thus not subject to the ordinary state power to regulate conduct.

(b) **Action to acquire information:** [§733] But the First Amendment does ***not*** protect conduct simply because it is undertaken to acquire information to be used in connection with the freedoms of speech, press, or association. [Zemel v. Rusk, *supra*, §471—travel to Cuba not within ambit of First Amendment]

(c) **Action motivated by beliefs:** [§734] Nor does the First Amendment protect conduct simply because it happens to be motivated by a person's point of view or beliefs. [Wisconsin v. Mitchell, 113 S. Ct. 2194 (1993)—upholding law enhancing punishment for crime of aggravated battery when defendant selects victim because of race]

(d) **"Symbolic" conduct:** [§735] The First Amendment affords ***some*** protection to action undertaken to communicate an idea. (*See infra*, §861.)

b. **Rights not absolute:** [§736] First Amendment rights do not unqualifiedly protect all verbal or visual expression. The government may punish utterances that impose such undesirable results on society as to outweigh the value of free speech. For example, disclosure of U.S. intelligence operations and names of intelligence personnel for the purpose of obstructing intelligence operations is "clearly not protected" speech. [Haig v. Agee, *supra*, §471] It is often repeated that "the most stringent protection of free speech would not protect a person in falsely shouting 'Fire!' in a crowded theater." Other examples of verbal and visual expression held to be outside the protection of the First Amendment include "obscenity" (*see infra*, §§781 *et seq.*) and "fighting words" (*see infra*, §806).

(1) **Example—freedom not to associate:** A state's compelling interest in eradicating race and sex discrimination justifies the state's forbidding the denial of membership to minorities and women by organizations that are large and basically unselective or that are often used for business contacts—when it is not shown that this would impede the individuals' ability to engage in First Amendment activities. [New York State Club Association, Inc. v. New York City, 484 U.S. 811 (1988); Board of Directors of Rotary International v. Rotary Club of Duarte, 481 U.S. 537 (1987); Roberts v. United States Jaycees, *supra*, §727]

c. **General approach to validity of restrictions:** [§737] When the government acts to limit speech, press, or association, the Court will usually ***weigh*** (i) the great ***importance of these rights*** in a democratic society, (ii) the ***nature and scope of the restraint*** imposed on the individual, (iii) the ***type and strength of the government interest*** sought to be served, and (iv) whether the restraint is a ***narrowly tailored means*** to achieving that interest.

(1) **Content-based regulations:** [§738] It is presumptively unconstitutional for government to place burdens on speech because of its content. To justify such differential treatment of speech, the government must show that the regulation (or tax) is ***necessary*** to serve a ***compelling*** state interest and is narrowly drawn to achieve that end. [Simon & Schuster, Inc. v. Members of the New York State Crime Victims Board, 112 S. Ct.

501 (1991)—striking a law requiring that proceeds of criminals from books and other productions describing their crime be placed in escrow for five years to pay claims of victims of the crime]

(a) **Definition:** Regulations are ***not*** content-neutral if—either by their ***terms*** or their ***manifest purpose***—they distinguish favored speech from disfavored speech on the basis of the ideas or views expressed. [Turner Broadcasting System v. FCC, 114 S. Ct. ____ (1994)]

d. **"Overbreadth" and "vagueness":** [§739] In the free speech area, the Court sometimes permits regulations to be challenged "on their face" if they are "overbroad" or "vague." *Rationale:* The very existence of such regulations may "chill" the exercise of First Amendment rights—*i.e.*, may cause others not before the Court to refrain from constitutionally protected expression. [Broadrick v. Oklahoma, 413 U.S. 601 (1973)]

(1) **Consequences of facial invalidity:** [§740] A law held to be "void on its face" is ***totally invalid***; *i.e.*, it is held incapable of any valid application. Thus, persons are immune from regulation thereunder even though their speech or association is ***not*** constitutionally protected—*i.e.*, even if they could be regulated by a statute drawn with the requisite specificity. In effect, the Court (i) permits litigants to raise the First Amendment rights of third parties not before the Court, (ii) penalizes the government for permitting such statutes to remain on the books (because of their chilling effect), and (iii) forces enactment of a new statute—or an interpretation of the existing one (*see infra*, §748)—to eliminate the overbreadth or vagueness.

(2) **Overbreadth:** [§741] An overbroad law is one that regulates "a substantial amount of constitutionally protected" expression or association (as well as speech or conduct that is not constitutionally protected). [Village of Hoffman Estates v. Flipside, Hoffman Estates, Inc., 455 U.S. 489 (1982)] Overbreadth may be more readily found if the law is "directed at speech as such"; *i.e.*, it covers ***only*** verbal and visual expression rather than ***any*** conduct. [Broadrick v. Oklahoma, *supra*]

(a) **Limitation—substantial overbreadth:** [§742] A "facial challenge" will not be permitted if only ***marginal applications*** of the statute would infringe upon First Amendment rights—*i.e.*, if the statute mainly covers a wide range of easily identifiable and constitutionally proscribable conduct. [United States Civil Service Commission v. National Association of Letter Carriers, 413 U.S. 548 (1973)]

(b) **Limitation—proper party before court:** [§743] If those challenging the law desire themselves to engage in protected speech that the overbroad law proscribes, only that part of the law that reaches too far will be declared invalid. *Rationale:* Since the proper parties are before the court, there is no concern that an attack on the law will be unduly delayed or that protected speech will be chilled. [Brockett v. Spokane Arcades, Inc., 472 U.S. 491 (1985)]

(3) **Explicit overbreadth:** [§744] Regulations may be explicitly overbroad—*e.g.*, a statute prohibiting ***"all"*** membership in groups that engage in unprotected advocacy. Some such membership is protected by the First Amendment (*i.e.*, membership without specific intent—*see infra*, §§963-965), while other membership may not be constitutionally protected.

(4) **Overbreadth due to vagueness:** [§745] Alternatively, a regulation may contain imprecise language that, because of vagueness or uncertainty, may be read by persons "of common intelligence" as proscribing or regulating speech or association that is protected by the First Amendment. Such "standardless" statutes likewise permit arbitrary and discriminatory law enforcement by police, prosecutors, and juries. Because of their "chilling effect," ***special precision*** is required of statutes that proscribe or regulate speech or association.

(a) **Example:** A state law requiring teachers to take the oath, "That I have not and will not lend aid, support, advice, counsel, or influence to the Communist Party," was held impermissibly vague; the language might embrace anyone who ever supported a candidate supported by the Communist Party, who supported any cause that the Party had supported, or who (as a journalist or otherwise) had supported the constitutional rights of the Communist Party. [Cramp v. Board of Public Instruction, 368 U.S. 278 (1961)]

(b) **Example:** An ordinance making it a crime for "three or more persons to assemble on any of the sidewalks and there conduct themselves in a manner annoying to persons passing by" was held to violate the general due process standard of vagueness, because people of "common intelligence must necessarily guess at its meaning." It also violated the First Amendment "right of free assembly and association" because "mere public intolerance or animosity" cannot be the basis for its abridgment, and because the ordinance "contains an obvious invitation to discriminatory enforcement" against those whose association is "annoying" due to their ideas or physical appearance. [Coates v. Cincinnati, 402 U.S. 611 (1971)]

(5) **Vagueness alone:** [§746] A statute regulating expression or association may also be impermissibly vague even though not overbroad—*e.g.*, "It shall be unlawful to make any speech not protected by the First and Fourteenth Amendments."

(6) **Exceptions to facial challenges**

(a) **"Hard core" violator:** [§747] Sometimes (but not always) the Court will refuse to permit a person to attack a statute on its face—if the person's conduct is not even arguably constitutionally protected but is "the sort of hard-core conduct that would be prohibited under any construction of the statute." [NAACP v. Button, 371 U.S. 415 (1963)]

(b) **Saving judicial interpretation:** [§748] If an overbroad or vague statute is authoritatively construed (*i.e.*, a state statute by the state courts, a federal statute by the federal courts) to cure the overbreadth or vagueness—so that it proscribes or regulates ***only*** expression or association ***not*** protected by the First Amendment—it may be applied to unprotected conduct occurring ***prior*** to the limiting construction as long as the person had ***fair warning*** that the conduct was covered. [Osborne v. Ohio, 495 U.S. 103 (1990)]

1) **Legislative repeal or amendment:** [§749] However, an overbreadth defense continues to be available even if the overbroad statute under which a person is charged is subsequently repealed or amended to cure its overbreadth. *Rationale:* Legislators who can cure their mistakes by amendment or repeal without significant cost might not be careful to avoid passing overbroad laws. [Massachusetts v. Oakes, 491 U.S. 576 (1989)]

2. **Advocacy of Unlawful Action**

a. **Speech that is vituperative, abusive, or contemptuous of government or public officials:** [§750] As long as this type of expression does not incite others to perform unlawful acts or involve breach of the peace (*see infra*, §§805 *et seq.*), it is protected by the First Amendment—even though "unpatriotic," "disrespectful," "defiant," or "patently offensive to the community." [Watts v. United States, 394 U.S. 705 (1969)—"If they ever make me carry a rifle the first man I want to get in my sights is [the President]"; Street v. New York, 394 U.S. 576 (1969)—"We don't need no damn American flag"] *Rationale:* The right of uninhibited debate on public issues is an essential ingredient of our political system.

(1) **Example:** A federal statute making it a crime to engage in a theatrical production while wearing an army uniform if the portrayal "tends to discredit" the armed forces violates the First Amendment. [Schacht v. United States, 398 U.S. 58 (1970)]

b. **Criminal penalties for advocacy of illegal action**

(1) **Background:** [§751] In the first three decades of this century, the Court held that speech (or writing) advocating ***forceful overthrow*** of the government may be penalized; that a legislative finding that such speech was inherently dangerous—even though the speech might not succeed in stimulating the action advocated—was presumptively valid; that it was reasonable for the legislature to punish such speech before the conduct being advocated was imminent; and that the Court would not make an independent determination as to whether the speech posed a danger of the advocated conduct's taking place. [Gitlow v. New York, 268 U.S. 652 (1925)]

(a) **Holmes-Brandeis view:** [§752] In concurring and dissenting opinions in these early cases, Justices Holmes and Brandeis took a different position. They contended that government may punish only speech that ***produces, or is intended to produce, a clear and imminent danger of a serious substantive evil***; *i.e.*, speech advocating illegal action may be punished only when the advocated action is serious and there is no time for further discussion before the advocated action will take place. Furthermore, whether these elements exist in a given case must be determined according to federal constitutional standards, and ultimately, by the Supreme Court—not by a legislature, jury, or trial court.

1) **Contemporary influence:** The Holmes-Brandeis "clear and present danger" test has great influence today, even though (as noted below) it has not been adopted in every respect by the modern Court.

(2) **The *Dennis-Yates* "test":** [§753] In *Dennis v. United States*, 341 U.S. 494 (1951), and *Yates v. United States*, 354 U.S. 298 (1957), leaders of the American Communist Party were charged with conspiring to advocate forceful overthrow of the government and were prosecuted under the Smith Act. In *Dennis*, the Court affirmed the convictions, rejecting the argument that defendants' activities were protected by the First Amendment. In *Yates*, the Court reversed the convictions, interpreting the Smith Act as not making unlawful the particular activities in which the defendants had engaged. Thus, *Yates* did not involve a ***constitutional*** interpretation.

(a) **Significance of *Yates*:** Since the Smith Act was a federal statute, the Court had final judicial authority to construe it. In doing so, the Court used the common technique of interpreting the federal statute so as to ***avoid the constitutional question*** of whether the statute violated the First Amendment. Nevertheless, the Court's discussion had constitutional significance, and the *Yates* interpretation on the limits of the Smith Act has since been referred to in defining the limits of the First Amendment. [Communist Party of Indiana v. Whitcomb, 414 U.S. 441 (1974)]

(b) **Rationale:** The rationale of *Dennis* and *Yates* is as follows:

1) **Must be substantial governmental interest:** Government must have a ***substantial*** interest before it may punish speech—and this must be independently determined by the courts, not by the legislature or a jury.

2) **Call to action punishable:** Advocacy aimed at promoting the forceful overthrow of government—*i.e.*, a ***call to action***, urging that people ***act*** (rather than ***merely believe***)—can be punished without violating the First Amendment. [Dennis v. United States, *supra*]

a) **But note:** Advocating or justifying the forceful overthrow of government as an ***abstract principle***—*i.e.*, urging that people ***believe*** this ***ought*** to be done (rather than that they do it)—is ***not*** punishable. [Yates v. United States, *supra*] And this is true even when such advocacy is urged as a moral necessity, and/or when the advocate has evil intent.

3) **Gravity and imminence weighed:** Government need not wait until the last moment before it punishes advocacy of illegal action: The ***graver*** the evil being advocated, the ***less imminent*** its actually happening need be before the speaker can be punished. Thus, imminence is ***not*** an independent factor, but one to be ***weighed*** with the ***gravity*** of the evil.

(3) **The *Brandenburg* "test":** [§754] More recently, the Court has held that a state may not penalize advocacy of the use of force or of law violation except where such advocacy is ***"directed to inciting or producing imminent lawless action and is likely to incite or produce such action."*** [Brandenburg v. Ohio, 395 U.S. 444 (1969)]

(a) **Note:** This test makes ***imminence*** an independent requirement, and appears to make ***evil intent*** on the part of the speaker ("directed to . . . ") an independent requirement as well.

(b) **But note:** *Brandenburg* cites *Dennis* and *Yates* (in which imminence was ***not*** an independent factor) with approval. The cases may perhaps be squared on the ground that when the evil advocated is ***very*** grave or serious (*e.g.*, forceful overthrow of government, as in *Dennis*, or widespread riot), imminence is only one factor to be weighed; but when the evil advocated is a mere legal violation (*e.g.*, peaceful civil disobedience) or the ***use*** of ***some*** force (minor property damage), imminence is an independent requirement.

3. **Defamation:** [§755] Speech or writing that is defamatory is ***generally*** not protected by the First Amendment and may therefore be subject to criminal libel laws or civil laws awarding damages. [Beauharnais v. Illinois, 343 U.S. 250 (1952)]

a. **Group libel laws:** [§756] Group libel laws punish false statements or vilification of a group—if likely to cause violence or disorder. *Note:* Truth here may not be a defense if the utterance is made with bad motive or for unjustifiable ends. In the 1950s, the Court upheld a group libel law as applied to circulation of anti-black literature [Beauharnais v. Illinois, *supra*], but doctrinal developments under the First Amendment have cast significant doubt on the continued validity of the decision.

b. **Matters of public interest:** [§757] There is an inherent conflict between the need for full disclosure and debate on matters of public interest (protected by the First Amendment), and the need to protect personal reputations against injurious falsehoods (through state laws against libel). The Court has resolved this conflict by creating a constitutional privilege protecting freedom of expression as to ***certain kinds*** of defamations.

(1) **Defamation of "public officials":** [§758] Freedom of speech and press bars a civil libel judgment for criticism of "***public officials***" in respect to their "***official conduct***," unless the plaintiff shows "***malice***" by clear and convincing evidence. [New York Times v. Sullivan, 376 U.S. 254 (1964)—reversing large civil libel judgment awarded in Alabama courts based on newspaper's publishing paid advertisement critical of conduct of Alabama officials in handling of racial matters]

(a) **Rationale:** To allow recovery in such cases could lead to self-censorship on matters of public concern; *i.e.*, persons might well avoid expressing justified criticisms of official conduct for fear of being held liable for "erroneous statements honestly made" or because of the costs of defending legal actions arising therefrom. Furthermore, public officials may protect their reputations through their opportunity for public rebuttal and thus are not greatly in need of legal remedies. [New York Times v. Sullivan, *supra*]

(b) **"Malice":** [§759] "Malice" requires a showing that the publication was ***known to be false or*** was published with ***reckless disregard*** as to its truth or falsity. Mere negligence is not enough—even if the publication was made with ill will or the intent to injure. Since there is no public interest in protecting calculated falsehoods, First Amendment protection does not extend to speech made with "malice." [New York Times v. Sullivan, *supra*; Garrison v. Louisiana, 379 U.S. 64 (1964)]

1) **Inaccurate quotations:** [§760] Even if an author deliberately misquotes a person, there is no "malice" unless the false quotation results in a material change in the meaning of the actual statement. [Masson v. New Yorker Magazine, Inc., 501 U.S. 496 (1991)]

2) **Reference to individual required:** [§761] Even if "malice" is shown, no damages will be awarded to an individual member of a group ***if only a large group is defamed***. To recover, the individual must prove particular reference to himself—or that a relatively small group was defamed and that he is a ***clearly identifiable*** member thereof. [Rosenblatt v. Baer, 383 U.S. 75 (1966)] Thus, a criticism of "the police" does not give the commissioner of police a cause of action. [New York Times v. Sullivan, *supra*]

3) **Discovery:** [§762] In attempting to prove knowing or reckless falsehood, plaintiff may inquire (i) into the state of mind of those who edit, produce, or publish (*i.e.*, about their thoughts, opinions, and conclusions concerning the accuracy of the material gathered), and (ii) as to what took place in the editorial process (*i.e.*, conversations with editorial colleagues). [Herbert v. Lando, 441 U.S. 153 (1979)]

4) **Summary judgment:** [§763] If the defendant moves for summary judgment on the ground that there is no "genuine issue as to any material fact," the plaintiff must show that the quality or quantity of the documentary evidence would allow the fact finder to find "malice" by "clear and convincing evidence." [Anderson v. Liberty Lobby, Inc., 477 U.S. 242 (1986)]

5) **Appellate review:** [§764] As noted, "malice" must be shown by clear and convincing evidence. Appellate courts

must exercise independent judgment when reviewing a finding of "malice"; they are ***not*** restricted by the usual "clearly erroneous" standard of review for questions of fact. [Bose Corp. v. Consumers Union, 467 U.S. 1267 (1984)]

(c) **"Official conduct":** [§765] The *New York Times* rule applies only to criticism of "official conduct"—although, of course, such criticism may also damage private reputation. "Official conduct" extends to anything touching on an official's fitness for office. [Monitor Patriot Co. v. Roy, 401 U.S. 265 (1971)—official accused of being "former small-time bootlegger"]

(d) **"Public officials":** [§766] "Public officials" include both elected officials and candidates for public office. The rule also applies to those public employees who have substantial responsibility for the conduct of government affairs—*i.e.*, those who hold ***positions of public interest***, not merely employees who happen to do something of public interest. [Rosenblatt v. Baer, *supra*]

(e) **Criminal libel:** [§767] The *New York Times* rule applies to prosecutions for criminal libel as well as in civil defamation suits. [Garrison v. Louisiana, *supra*]

(2) **Defamation of "public figures":** [§768] The *New York Times* rule likewise applies to defamation actions by persons who are "public figures," although not "public officials." *Rationale:* Like public officials, such persons have significant access to channels of communication in order to counteract false statements, and they invite the attention and comment to which they have usually exposed themselves. [Gertz v. Robert Welch, Inc., 418 U.S. 323 (1974)]

(a) **Definition:** [§769] A citizen may become a "public figure" in two ways: (i) he may be such for ***"all purposes and in all contexts"*** if he achieves "general fame or notoriety in the community and pervasive involvement in the affairs of society"; or (ii) he may "voluntarily inject himself or be drawn into a ***particular*** controversy, thus becoming a public figure for a limited range of issues." [Gertz v. Robert Welch, Inc., *supra*]

1) **Note:** In *Gertz*, the Court indicated that it might be possible for a person to become a public figure through no purposeful action of his own, but considered such instances to be "exceedingly rare." It also underlined the fact that when a citizen participates in ***some*** community and professional affairs, that does ***not*** make him a public figure for ***all*** purposes.

(b) **Examples—"public figures":** [§770] "Public figures" has been held to include the following persons: a ***former football coach*** reported to have "thrown" a football game [Curtis Publishing Co. v. Butts, 388 U.S. 130 (1967)] and a ***retired army general and political commentator*** reported to have participated in race riots [Associated Press v. Walker, 388 U.S. 130 (1967)].

(c) **Examples—not "public figures":** [§771] A person is not a "public figure" simply because she is extremely wealthy and engaged in divorce proceedings of interest to the reading public. The fact that she files for divorce (and even holds press conferences during the proceedings) does not mean she voluntarily chooses to publicize her married life—since going to court is the only way she can legally dissolve her marriage. [Time, Inc. v. Firestone, 424 U.S. 448 (1976)] Nor is a person a "public figure" simply because he is charged with a crime [Wolston v. Reader's Digest Association, 443 U.S. 157 (1979)]; or applies for federal grants and publishes in professional journals [Hutchinson v. Proxmire, *supra*, §168]; or is counsel in a case that receives extensive media exposure [Gertz v. Robert Welch, Inc., *supra*].

(3) **Defamation of "private individuals":** [§772] The *New York Times* rule does ***not*** apply to private individuals who, unlike "public officials" or "public figures," have no significant access to the media to counteract false statements and have not voluntarily exposed themselves to an increased risk of defamation. [Gertz v. Robert Welch, Inc., *supra*] Even so, there are still constitutional limitations in defamation actions by private individuals:

(a) **Standard of liability:** [§773] The states may define liability standards in defamation actions by private individuals, as long as (i) they do not impose ***liability without fault*** (*i.e.*, the defendant must at least be negligent); (ii) the factual misstatement ***warns*** a ***reasonably prudent*** editor or broadcaster of its defamatory potential; and (iii) damages are limited to compensation for ***actual*** injury—including impairment of reputation, personal humiliation, and mental suffering.

1) **Presumed or punitive damages:** [§774] These are not permitted, absent knowledge of falsity or reckless disregard for the truth, when the defamation of the private individual involves ***"matters of public concern."*** This approach accommodates "the strong and legitimate state interest in compensating private individuals for injury to reputation" with "the danger of media self-censorship." [Dun & Bradstreet, Inc. v. Greenmoss Builders, Inc., 472 U.S. 749 (1985)]

a) **"Matter of public concern":** [§775] This is determined by the statement's ***content, form,*** and ***context***—considering all the relevant circumstances. [Dun & Bradstreet, Inc. v. Greenmoss Builders, Inc., *supra*—credit report sent only to a few subscribers is ***not*** of public concern]

(b) **Nonmedia defendants:** [§776] A majority of the Justices have stated that the *New York Times* and *Gertz* protections for media defendants apply as well to defamation suits against nonmedia defendants. [Dun & Bradstreet, Inc. v. Greenmoss Builders, Inc., *supra*]

(c) **Falsity:** [§777] In a suit for ***damages*** by a private individual for a defamation involving a "matter of public concern," the plaintiff must bear the burden of proving that the defamatory statements are false—at least against a media defendant. [Philadelphia Newspapers, Inc. v. Hepps, 475 U.S. 767 (1986)]

(4) **"Fact" vs. "opinion":** [§778] There is no separate "opinion" privilege. Any statement (including a statement of "opinion") that may be reasonably interpreted as stating actual facts about an individual may be actionable under the *New York Times* rule. [Milkovich v. Lorain Journal Co., 497 U.S. 1 (1990)]

(5) **Intentional infliction of emotional distress:** [§779] The *New York Times* requirement of a "false statement of fact" made with "malice" applies to damage actions by public figures for the tort of intentional infliction of emotional distress for publications that are parodies of the plaintiff, even if the publication is "patently offensive" or "outrageous." [Hustler Magazine v. Falwell, 485 U.S. 46 (1988)]

(6) **Invasion of privacy suits:** [§780] Prior to the *Gertz* decision, the Court held that the *New York Times* rule ***applies*** to damage actions for invasion of privacy (for false reporting) if the matter reported was of ***substantial public interest***—even though the plaintiff is neither a "public official" nor a "public figure." [Time, Inc. v. Hill, 385 U.S. 374 (1967)] There is serious question whether this principle in ***right of privacy*** (false reporting) suits by private individuals survives after *Gertz* (which held that the *New York Times* rule does ***not*** apply to ***defamation*** suits by private individuals).

4. **Obscenity:** [§781] Obscene expression is ***not*** protected by the First Amendment. It is "not an essential part of the exposition of ideas, is of slight social value, and the benefits therefrom are outweighed by the social interest in morality." [Chaplinsky v. New Hampshire, 315 U.S. 568 (1942)] Obscenity is "not communication and is, by definition, utterly without social value." [Roth v. United States, 354 U.S. 476 (1957)] Obscenity is "assumed to be harmful to society and is, by definition, without serious literary, artistic, political, or scientific value." [Miller v. California, 413 U.S. 15 (1973); Paris Adult Theatre I v. Slaton, 413 U.S. 49 (1973)]

a. **Definition:** [§782] Sex and obscenity are not synonymous. The discussion of "sex" may be of public concern and is thus entitled to First Amendment protection. "Obscenity" is a description or depiction of sexual conduct which, taken as a ***whole***, by the ***average person***, applying ***contemporary community standards***—(i) appeals to the ***prurient interest*** in sex and (ii) portrays sex in a ***patently offensive*** way; ***and*** (iii) using a ***reasonable person standard*** (rather than the contemporary community standard) does not have ***serious*** literary, artistic, political, or scientific value when taken as a whole. [Roth v. United States, *supra, as modified by* Miller v. California, *supra*]

(1) **Elements of "obscenity":** [§783] Under the *Miller* modification of the prior *Roth* definition, several separate elements must be found before matter can be held to be "obscene":

(a) **Prurient interest:** [§784] The ***dominant*** theme of the material—considered as a ***whole***—must appeal to prurient interest in sex to the ***average (normal) person***. [*Compare* Cohen v. California, 403 U.S. 15 (1971)—protestor's jacket emblazoned "Fuck the Draft" was not obscene because it was in no way erotic]

1) **Prurience:** [§785] This identifies speech that appeals to a ***shameful*** or ***morbid***—rather than ***normal***—interest in sex. [Brockett v. Spokane Arcades, Inc., *supra*, §743]

2) **Average person:** [§786] Both "sensitive" and "insensitive" adults may be included in determining contemporary community standards, but children may not be considered part of the relevant community. [Pinkus v. United States, 436 U.S. 293 (1978)]

a) **Example:** A statute prohibiting the sale of any book "tending to the corruption of the morals of youth" is invalid. *Rationale:* The effect of the statute was to reduce the adult population to reading only what was fit for children. [Butler v. Michigan, 352 U.S. 380 (1959)]

b) **Example:** Similarly, government cannot impose a ***total ban*** on "indecent" commercial telephone messages ("dial-a-porn") in order to prevent children from gaining access to such messages. [Sable Communications of California, Inc. v. FCC, 492 U.S. 115 (1989)]

3) **Material designed for deviant group:** [§787] Where the allegedly obscene material is designed for and primarily disseminated to a clearly defined deviant sexual group (*e.g.*, sadists), rather than to the public at large, the "prurient appeal" requirement is satisfied if the dominant theme of the material, taken as a whole, appeals to the prurient interest of ***that group***. [Mishkin v. New York, 383 U.S. 509 (1966)]

(b) **Patently offensive:** [§788] The material must be "patently offensive" in affronting contemporary community standards regarding the description or portrayal of sexual matters.

(c) **Contemporary community standards:** [§789] A "national" standard is ***not*** required. A statewide standard is permissible, but not mandatory. A juror may draw on knowledge of the vicinity from which she comes; and the court may either direct the jury to apply "community standards" without specifying what "community," or to define the standard in more precise geographic terms. [Hamling v. United States, 418 U.S. 87 (1974); Jenkins v. Georgia, 418 U.S. 153 (1974)]

1) **Note:** The "community standards" criterion applies only to the "prurient interest" and "patently offensive" parts of the *Miller* definition. A "reasonable person" standard applies to the third part (*supra,* §782). [Pope v. Illinois, 481 U.S. 497 (1987)]

(d) **Lacking in serious social value:** [§790] The fact that the material may have ***some*** redeeming social value will ***not*** necessarily immunize it from a finding of obscenity. [Miller v. California, *supra*]

(e) **"Pandering":** [§791] In ***close cases***, evidence of "pandering" on the part of the defendant (commercial exploitation for the sake of prurient appeal) may be probative on whether the material is obscene. Such evidence may be found in the defendant's advertising, his instructions to authors and illustrators of the material, or his intended audience. In effect, this simply accepts the purveyor's own estimation of the material as relevant. [Ginzburg v. United States, 383 U.S. 643 (1966)]

1) **Profit purpose irrelevant:** [§792] But the mere fact that a publisher may have profited from the sale of particular publications is entitled no weight in determining whether his publication is "obscene." [Ginzburg v. United States, *supra*]

b. **"Obscenity" as question of fact and law:** [§793] What is "obscene" is a question of ***fact*** for the ***jury***, "accompanied by the safeguards that judges, rules of evidence, presumption of innocence, and other protective features provide." [Miller v. California, *supra*] But juries do not have unbridled discretion in determining what is "patently offensive," even if they are properly charged. Appellate ***courts*** will conduct an ***independent review*** of constitutional claims, when necessary, to assure that the proscribed materials "depict or describe patently offensive 'hard core' sexual conduct." [Jenkins v. Georgia, *supra*]

(1) **Evidence:** [§794] The prosecution need not produce "expert" testimony. And evidence that similar materials are available on community newsstands, or that the publication has acquired a second-class mailing privilege, does not necessarily show that the material is not obscene and hence, that evidence is not automatically admissible. Nor is there any automatic right to have other materials held not to be obscene admitted into evidence. [Hamling v. United States, *supra*]

(2) **Scienter requirement:** [§795] In the prosecution of a bookseller, it must be shown that he had ***knowledge*** that the contents of the material were obscene. *Rationale:* Strict or absolute criminal responsibility might well cause booksellers to be exceedingly careful as to what materials they would sell; the resulting ***self-censorship*** might deprive the public of access to constitutionally protected materials. [Smith v. California, 361 U.S. 147 (1959)]

(a) **Proof of "knowledge":** [§796] Scienter need not be shown by direct proof. It is probably enough that a ***reasonable*** seller or distributor should have shown the contents of the materials and their nature and character. [Smith v. California, *supra*; Hamling v. United States, *supra*]

c. **Special rules for minors:** [§797] A state may afford minors a more restricted access to sex materials than that allowed to adults. The state can adopt a ***specific*** definition of "obscenity" in terms of the sexual interests of such minors, since it is rational to conclude that minors' exposure to such material might be harmful. [Ginsberg v. New York, 390 U.S. 629 (1968)]

(1) **Child pornography:** [§798] Because of the strong interest in preventing child abuse, a state may prohibit distribution of pictures, even though not "obscene," that depict children engaging in sexual acts or lewdly displaying genitalia. However, serious educational or scientific use of such pictures as in medical textbooks or *National Geographic* is probably constitutionally protected. [New York v. Ferber, 456 U.S. 942 (1982)]

(a) **Private possession:** [§799] Similarly, in contrast to *Stanley v. Georgia* (below), the strong interest in protecting the victims of child pornography permits the state to make its possession a crime, ***even within the privacy of the home***. [Osborne v. Ohio, *supra*, §748]

d. **Private possession of obscenity at home:** [§800] A person's possession of obscene materials in his home ***cannot*** be made a crime because of the "constitutional right of personal privacy." [Stanley v. Georgia, 394 U.S. 557 (1969)] But the zone of privacy does not extend beyond the home. Thus, ***distribution*** of obscene material may be made a crime even as to willing recipients who state that they are adults [United States v. Reidel, 402 U.S. 351 (1971)], as may ***exhibition*** of obscene materials in places of public accommodation, including theaters for consenting adults only [Paris Adult Theatre I v. Slaton, *supra*, §781].

(1) **Transportation and importation:** [§801] Transportation and importation of obscene material for either ***public*** or ***private*** use may be prohibited. [United States v. Orito, 413 U.S. 139 (1973); United States v. 12 200-Ft. Reels, 413 U.S. 123 (1973)]

(a) **Note—procedures:** Any such seizure is a form of prior restraint, and therefore adequate procedural safeguards must be afforded (*see infra*, §§845 *et seq.*).

e. **Regulation of sites and display of "near" obscene material:** [§802] A zoning ordinance, whose predominant purpose is for legitimate land-use purposes, which regulates the location of "adult" theatres (presenting material not obscene under *Miller* but emphasizing "specified sexual activities or anatomical areas") is permissible if its effect does not suppress or greatly restrict access to such material. [Young v. American Mini Theatres, Inc., 427 U.S. 50 (1976); City of Renton v. Playtime Theatres, Inc., 475 U.S. 41 (1986)]

(1) **Limits on zoning:** [§803] But a municipality that permits a ***broad range*** of commercial establishments may ***not*** prohibit all live entertainment (including nonobscene, nude dancing) from its commercial district—at least if such entertainment is not available in reasonably nearby areas. [Schad v. Borough of Mount Ephraim, 452 U.S. 61 (1981)]

(2) **Display:** [§804] The display of nonobscene (but sexually related) material may be regulated to prevent it from being so obtrusive that the unwilling viewer cannot avoid exposure to it. [Redrup v. New York, 386 U.S. 767 (1967)]

5. **"Fighting Words" and "Hostile Audiences":** [§805] Certain types of expression used in connection with public speeches, parades, meetings, demonstrations, and the like may be prohibited under "breach of the peace" or "disorderly conduct" statutes—provided such statutes are ***narrowly drafted*** or ***narrowly construed*** (*i.e.*, are neither "overbroad" nor "vague").

   a. **"Fighting words":** [§806] "Fighting words" are words, usually intended as a personal insult to the person addressed, which by their very utterance inflict injury or tend to incite an ***immediate*** breach of the peace. "Fighting words" are ***not*** protected by the First Amendment, their slight social value being outweighed by the public interest in order. [Chaplinsky v. New Hampshire, 315 U.S. 568 (1942)—"You God-Damned Fascist"]

      (1) **Compare—offensive language:** [§807] The fact that certain words are generally offensive does ***not*** make them "fighting words." Thus, the First Amendment forbade a conviction of "disturbing the peace by offensive conduct" of a peace demonstrator for wearing a jacket bearing the words "Fuck the Draft" in a courthouse corridor. *Rationale:* The underlying content of the message was clearly protected, and it did not incite immediate violence, it was in no way erotic, and it was not directed as a personal insult to any person. [Cohen v. California, *supra*, §784]

      (2) **Note:** The regulation of "fighting words" may not ordinarily be limited to speech of a certain ***content*** that would otherwise be protected. The First Amendment forbids special prohibitions on speakers who express views on disfavored subjects. [R.A.V. v. City of St. Paul, 112 S. Ct. 2538 (1992)—ordinance that applies only to those "fighting words" that insult or provoke violence on the basis of race, religion, or gender is invalid]

   b. **"Hostile audience":** [§808] If the speaker does not use "fighting words" but is nonetheless convicted for "breach of the peace" or "disorderly conduct," the Court will independently examine the record to determine whether the speaker's activities produced ***imminent danger*** of ***uncontrolled violence*** by those onlookers or addressees of the speaker. If so, the exercise of First Amendment rights is outweighed by the public interest in order.

      (1) **Example:** A speaker on a city street used very inflammatory language about public officials; the crowd was angry and pushing—one member threatened violence—and two police officers arrived. Believing a fight was imminent, the police twice asked the speaker to leave. He refused and was arrested for disorderly conduct. His conviction was ***upheld***. [Feiner v. New York, 340 U.S. 315 (1951)]

      (2) **Compare:** A civil rights leader led an orderly protest of black students who urged store boycotts and sang songs. The leader urged nonviolence and sit-ins at segregated lunch counters. Although onlookers grumbled, ample police were present. The leader's conviction for "disturbing the peace" was ***reversed***. The Court found no imminent danger of uncontrollable violence. "Mere expression of unpopular views cannot be held to be a breach of the peace." [Cox v. Louisiana, 377 U.S. 288 (1965)]

(3) **Overbreadth or vagueness:** [§809] Breach of the peace and disorderly conduct statutes are frequently drafted or interpreted in an overbroad or vague manner, and are thereby subject to attack "on their face" (*see supra*, §§739 *et seq.*). [Gooding v. Wilson, 405 U.S. 518 (1972)—statute prohibiting "abusive language . . . tending to cause a breach of the peace" is overbroad; *i.e.*, not limited to "fighting words"; Lewis v. City of New Orleans, 415 U.S. 130 (1974)—statute prohibited "opprobrious language"]

6. **Commercial Speech:** [§810] Commercial speech is protected by the First Amendment but is subject to ***greater regulation*** than other forms of protected speech. [Bigelow v. Virginia, 421 U.S. 809 (1975)]

a. **Definition:** [§811] Commercial speech is whose ***dominant theme*** simply ***proposes a commercial transaction***. [Bolger v. Youngs Drug Products Corp., 463 U.S. 60 (1983)]

(1) **Advertisements:** [§812] The fact that a communication appears as an advertisement does ***not*** automatically make it commercial speech. [New York Times v. Sullivan, *supra*, §759—paid advertisement critical of official conduct]

(2) **Economic motivation:** [§813] The fact that a communication is economically motivated or refers to a specific product does ***not*** automatically make it commercial speech. [Bigelow v. Virginia, *supra*—advertisement by abortion referral service contained substantial information of significant public interest]

(a) **But note:** If a communication's ***dominant theme*** is to propose a commercial transaction, it is commercial speech despite ***some discussion*** of important public issues. Advertisers may not immunize themselves from public regulation "simply by including references to public issues." [Bolger v. Youngs Drug Products Corp., *supra*—advertisement for contraceptives was commercial speech despite discussion of venereal disease and family planning]

b. **Regulation of content permissible:** [§814] Because commercial advertising has greater potential for deception and confusion than noncommercial speech, its content may be more readily regulated.

(1) **False or misleading:** [§815] Commercial speech that is false or misleading may be prohibited.

(a) **Example—trade names:** Since practicing optometry under a trade name has only an incidental effect on the content of commercial speech and may be used to mislead the public, it can be prohibited. [Friedman v. Rogers, 440 U.S. 1 (1979)]

(2) **Illegal transactions:** [§816] Commercial speech that proposes illegal transactions may be prohibited (*e.g.*, advertisements of narcotics or prostitution, or help-wanted ads that foster discrimination in employment).

[Pittsburgh Press Co. v. Pittsburgh Human Relations Committee, 413 U.S. 376 (1973)—newspaper enjoined from running help-wanted columns headed "male" or "female" because such classifications constituted illegal sex discrimination under local ordinance]

(a) **Example:** Similarly, speech that furthers illegal price-fixing may be prohibited if this "represents a reasonable method of eliminating the consequences of the illegal conduct." [National Society of Professional Engineers v. United States, 435 U.S. 679 (1978)]

c. **Overbreadth:** [§817] The First Amendment "overbreadth" doctrine (*see supra*, §§739 *et seq.*) does ***not*** apply to commercial speech. Thus, the person seeking to use commercial speech must demonstrate that the speech actually used is protected by the First Amendment. [Ohralik v. Ohio State Bar Association, 436 U.S. 447 (1978)]

d. **Prior restraint:** [§818] The Court has suggested that the usual prohibition on prior restraints (*see infra*, §832) ***may*** not apply to commercial speech. [Virginia State Board v. Virginia Citizens Consumer Council, 425 U.S. 748 (1976); *and see* Pittsburgh Press Co. v. Pittsburgh Human Relations Committee, *supra*, §816]

e. **Scope of protection:** [§819] Truthful commercial speech concerning a lawful activity has an informational function and cannot be prohibited unless (i) a ***substantial*** government interest is served by the restriction, (ii) the restriction ***directly advances*** that government interest, and (iii) the restriction is ***no more extensive than necessary*** to serve that interest. [Central Hudson Gas & Electric Corp. v. Public Service Commission, 447 U.S. 557 (1980)—ban on ***all*** promotional advertising by electric utility directly serves substantial state interest in energy conservation but is nonetheless invalid because it is not drawn sufficiently narrowly]

(1) **Burden on state:** [§820] The state must show that the harms attributable to the truthful commercial speech are real and will be alleviated by the state restriction imposed. [Ibanez v. Florida Department of Business & Professional Regulation, 114 S. Ct. ____ (1994)—ban on lawyer's use in advertising of CPA and CFA designations is invalid]

(2) **"No more extensive than necessary":** [§821] This part of the test does ***not*** require that the "least restrictive means" be used. Rather, the regulation must be "narrowly drawn" and there must be a "reasonable fit" between the legislature's ends and the means chosen. [Board of Trustees of State University of New York v. Fox, 492 U.S. 469 (1989)]

(3) **"For sale" signs:** [§822] An ordinance prohibiting the posting of "for sale" signs on real estate has been held invalid even though deemed by the township to be in the best interests of the community (to prevent "white flight" from racially integrated neighborhoods). [Linmark Associates, Inc. v. Township of Willingboro, 431 U.S. 85 (1977)]

(4) **Mailed contraceptive advertisements:** [§823] A law prohibiting the mailing of unsolicited advertisements for contraceptives has been held invalid. The government's interest in protecting recipients from mail

they find "offensive" is ***insubstantial***. And although the interest in aiding parents to discuss birth control with their children ***is*** substantial, the law serves that interest only marginally. [Bolger v. Youngs Drug Products Corp., *supra*]

(5) **Casino advertising:** [§824] A regulation prohibiting any advertisement of casino gambling aimed at residents (rather than tourists) has been upheld. It directly advances the substantial interest in reducing gambling by residents and is no more extensive than necessary. [Pasadas de Puerto Rico Associates v. Tourism Company of Puerto Rico, 478 U.S. 328 (1986)]

(6) **Interstate advertising of state lottery:** [§825] Congress may prohibit the broadcasting of lottery advertising by stations licensed in nonlottery states—even as applied to a station that has most of its listeners in an adjoining lottery state, and even when broadcasters in the lottery state reach many listeners in the nonlottery state. The law directly advances, albeit only marginally, the substantial government interest in limiting (though not eliminating) advertising in the nonlottery state. [United States v. Edge Broadcasting Co., 113 S. Ct. 2696 (1993)]

(7) **Differential treatment of commercial speech:** [§826] A ban on all newsracks that dispense commercial handbills is invalid. The city may not achieve its interests in safety and aesthetics by a prohibition that distinguishes between commercial and noncommercial publications when they are ***equally responsible*** for the problems. [City of Cincinnati v. Discovery Network, Inc., 113 S. Ct. 1505 (1993)]

(8) **Billboards:** [§827] To advance its interests in traffic safety and aesthetics, a state may prohibit all billboards carrying commercial advertising, except those advertising the business of the property's occupant. [Metromedia, Inc. v. City of San Diego, 453 U.S. 490 (1981)]

(9) **Legal services:** [§828] Truthful advertising of the ***availability*** and ***price*** of ***routine*** legal services cannot be prohibited. The Court has ***left open*** the issue of advertising the ***quality*** of legal services. [Bates v. State Bar of Arizona, 433 U.S. 350 (1977)] Furthermore, in the absence of evidence that it is misleading or potentially misleading, a lawyer cannot be prohibited from stating that a bona fide national organization has "certified" him as a specialist in a certain area [Peel v. Illinois Attorney Registration & Disciplinary Commission, 496 U.S. 91 (1990)]; nor from advertising specific areas of practice and the jurisdictions in which licensed; nor from mailing cards to the general public that announce the opening of a law office [Matter of R.M.J., 455 U.S. 191 (1982)]; nor from including illustrations in advertisements; nor from mailing letters to potential clients known to have particular legal problems [Shapero v. Kentucky Bar Association, 486 U.S. 466 (1988)], or including accurate information or advice regarding the legal rights of potential clients [Zauderer v. Office of Disciplinary Counsel, 471 U.S. 626 (1985)].

(a) **Required disclosures:** [§829] Since commercial speech is protected mainly because of its value to consumers, an advertiser's First Amendment interest in ***not*** providing information is minimal.

Thus, required disclosures are permissible if they are not unduly burdensome and are reasonably related to the state's interest in preventing deception. [Zauderer v. Office of Disciplinary Counsel, *supra*—lawyers who advertise representation for a contingent ***fee*** may be required to state that client may have to pay ***costs***]

(b) **In-person solicitation for pecuniary gain:** [§830] But a state may discipline lawyers for ***in-person*** solicitation of clients for ***pecuniary*** gain—at least under circumstances likely to present dangers such as misrepresentation, overreaching, invasion of privacy, or stirring up litigation. Unlike advertising legal services, such solicitation may pressure clients without providing time for reflection. [Ohralik v. Ohio State Bar Association, *supra*]

1) **Compare—accountants:** [§831] A state ban on in-person, uninvited solicitation of business clients by accountants does ***not*** directly and materially advance state interests. While a lawyer may be soliciting an unsophisticated, injured, or distressed lay person, a CPA's typical prospective client is a sophisticated and experienced business executive who has an existing professional relation with a CPA, who selects the time and place for their meeting, and for whom there is no expectation or pressure to retain the CPA on the spot. [Edenfield v. Fane, 113 S. Ct. 1792 (1993)]

7. **Censorship and Prior Restraint:** [§832] As seen above, some kinds of speech (obscenity, "fighting words," certain defamations, etc.) are not protected by the First Amendment. Thus, government may impose various sanctions—including criminal punishment—on those who engage in such unprotected speech. But even in dealing with unprotected expression, the government generally may not establish a system of ***censorship*** to regulate ***in advance*** what may be uttered or published, or ***enjoin*** speech, or employ other "***prior restraints***." [Near v. Minnesota, 283 U.S. 697 (1931); New York Times Co. v. United States, 403 U.S. 713 (1971)]

a. **"Informal" government action:** [§833] The prohibition against prior restraints applies to acts of government that have the ***effect*** of preventing speech in advance. Thus, even "informal" sanctions taken by state agencies may be invalid.

(1) **Example:** A state juvenile delinquency commission was empowered to make "informal recommendations" to book distributors as to which publications were objectionable for sale to youths. The recommendations were followed up by threats of court action, visits from police, etc., and the distributors were given no notice or hearing (*see* below) before their publications were listed as objectionable. The Court held compliance with the commission's directives by distributors was not voluntary and represented unconstitutional censorship. [Bantam Books, Inc. v. Sullivan, 372 U.S. 58 (1963)]

(2) **Compare—speech of foreign governments:** [§834] However, foreign governments may be required to label as "foreign propaganda" any expressive materials disseminated in this country that are intended to

influence U.S. foreign policy. The Court found that the word "propaganda" (as defined in the statute) was a neutral (not a pejorative) term ***and*** that there was no evidence that public reaction had actually interfered with distribution of the foreign materials. [Meese v. Keene, 481 U.S. 465 (1987)]

b. **Exceptional situations:** [§835] Although prior restraints of speech bear a heavy presumption of unconstitutionality, in a few exceptional situations, injunctions or censorship may be allowed; basically, where the unprotected speech is so inimical to the public welfare that normal remedies (such as subsequent criminal punishment) are inadequate.

(1) **National security:** [§836] For example, the First Amendment would not bar an injunction against publishing the date of sailing for troop ships in ***time of war***. [Near v. Minnesota, *supra*]

(a) **And note:** The First Amendment does not forbid agreements between the CIA and an employee that require ***prepublication review*** by the CIA of any writing related to his employment, even if it does not contain classified material. (A constructive trust on all profits from publishing is an appropriate remedy for violation of such agreement.) [Snepp v. United States, 444 U.S. 507 (1980)]

(2) **Preserving a "fair trial":** [§837] The strong presumption against prior restraints applies especially where an injunction against media reporting of criminal proceedings is sought to preserve a fair trial for the accused (*see infra*, §§906-917). Before such an injunction may issue, the court must find that (i) there is a clear and present danger that pretrial publicity ***would*** (not merely could) threaten a fair trial, (ii) alternative measures are inadequate, and (iii) an injunction would effectively protect the accused. [Nebraska Press Association v. Stuart, 427 U.S. 539 (1976)]

(a) **Public proceedings:** [§838] An injunction against media reporting is especially inappropriate if the proceedings are open to the public and press. [Oklahoma Publishing Co. v. District Court, 430 U.S. 308 (1977)]

(3) **Pretrial discovery:** [§839] A court may issue a protective order against dissemination of information gained through the pretrial discovery process and not yet admitted at trial. There is a substantial government interest in preventing abuse of information that would not have been obtained from other sources. [Seattle Times Co. v. Rhinehart, 467 U.S. 20 (1984)]

(4) **Obscenity:** [§840] Certain forms of censorship and prior restraint have also been upheld in the area of obscenity (*see* below).

(5) **Regulation of public property:** [§841] A city may require a license for the use of its property for the exercise of First Amendment rights if certain requisites are satisfied (*see infra*, §§898-905).

c. **Procedural safeguards:** [§842] Even in those exceptional situations where prior restraints are permissible, adequate procedural and judicial safeguards are constitutionally required.

(1) **General requirement of notice and hearing:** [§843] Unless time is of the essence, an adversary hearing, after notice to all interested parties, is normally essential to any procedure by which freedom of speech is burdened by prior restraints. [Carroll v. Princess Anne County, 393 U.S. 175 (1969)—invalidating ex parte injunctions restraining members of political party from holding rallies]

(2) **Injunctions:** [§844] Thus, a state procedure permitting an injunction against further distribution of a publication found to be "obscene" after a ***full judicial hearing*** may be upheld. Such an injunction, after the publication has had some distribution, may even be a lesser deterrent to free speech than "subsequent punishment" since it does not put the bookseller in the predicament of not knowing whether the sale of a book may subject him to criminal prosecution. The civil procedure assures him that such consequences will not follow unless he ignores a court order specifically directed to him and based on a ***carefully circumscribed*** determination of obscenity. [Kingsley Books, Inc. v. Brown, 354 U.S. 436 (1957)]

(3) **Seizure of books and films:** [§845] "Large scale" seizures of allegedly obscene books and films—"to destroy them or block their distribution or exhibition"—constitute a prior restraint and must be ***preceded*** by a ***full adversary hearing*** and a ***judicial determination of obscenity***. [Marcus v. Search Warrant, 367 U.S. 717 (1961)] But the seizure of copies of a film (or book) to preserve them as evidence need only be made "pursuant to a warrant issued after a determination of probable cause by a neutral magistrate." Even here, however, a ***prompt*** judicial determination of obscenity in an adversary proceeding must be available ***after*** the seizure. [Heller v. New York, 413 U.S. 483 (1973)]

(a) **Jury trial:** [§846] A jury trial is not required in a civil forfeiture proceeding for obscene materials. [Alexander v. Virginia, 413 U.S. 836 (1973)]

(b) **Standard of proof:** [§847] The Court has not set the standard of proof in a civil proceeding involving obscene material. But it has held that the First Amendment does ***not*** require proof beyond a reasonable doubt. [Cooper v. Mitchell Brothers' Santa Ana Theater, 454 U.S. 90 (1981)]

(c) **Forfeiture after criminal conviction:** [§848] The First Amendment does not forbid forfeiture and destruction of an adult bookstore chain's entire inventory of films and books (including some held not to be obscene) after the owner's conviction for sale of obscene material and a finding that the chain's assets were related to violation of the federal racketeering act. This is permissible criminal punishment with only an "incidental effect" on First Amendment activities. [Alexander v. United States, 113 S. Ct. 2766 (1993)]

(4) **Movie censorship:** [§849] Although government may not establish licensing or censorship boards to examine publications in advance for approval of content (*see* above), some such system of prior submission is permissible for motion pictures ***if*** it contains the following procedural safeguards: (i) the standards for denial of a license or permit must be "narrowly drawn, reasonable, and definite," so as to include only unprotected films; (ii) if the censor does not wish to issue a permit, the censor must ***promptly*** seek an injunction; (iii) in such judicial proceedings, the ***censor*** must bear the ***burden of proof*** that the film is unprotected; and (iv) there must be ***prompt judicial*** determination. [Freedman v. Maryland, 380 U.S. 51 (1965)]

(a) **Rationale—movies are different:** In upholding such censorship systems for movies, the Court has noted that "films differ from other forms of expression," and that the time delays incident to censorship are less burdensome for movies than for other forms of expression. [Times Film Corp. v. City of Chicago, 365 U.S. 43 (1961)]

(b) **Narrow and definite standards:** [§850] A number of decisions involve the banning of movies by censor boards under standards that were vague or overbroad.

1) **Vagueness:** [§851] A film may not be banned because the censor concludes it is "sacrilegious" [Joseph Burstyn, Inc. v. Wilson, 343 U.S. 495 (1952)] or "immoral" [Commercial Pictures Corp. v. Regents, 346 U.S. 587 (1954)].

2) **Overbreadth:** [§852] Nor may a film be banned because it "portrays adultery alluringly and as proper behavior." The Court reasoned that protected speech "is not confined to the expression of ideas that are conventional or shared by a majority. [The First Amendment] protects advocacy of the opinion that adultery may sometimes be proper, no less than advocacy of socialism or the single tax." [Kingsley International Pictures Corp. v. Regents, 360 U.S. 684 (1959)]

(5) **Use of municipal theaters:** [§853] A public agency's denial of the use of publicly owned theaters dedicated to expressive activities must conform to the procedural safeguards of *Freedman v. Maryland* (*supra*, §849). [Southeastern Promotions, Ltd. v. Conrad, 420 U.S. 546 (1975)]

(6) **Licensing businesses that deal in potentially obscene books and films:** [§854] An ordinance requiring that "sexually oriented businesses" obtain a license is subject to the *Freedman v. Maryland* procedural safeguards concerning a decision within a reasonable period of time, because undue delay results in suppression of constitutionally protected speech. However, the city need ***not*** bear the burden of going to court or the burden of proof once in court—the businesses affected have adequate incentive to assume this burden themselves. [FW/PBS Inc. v. City of Dallas, 493 U.S. 215 (1990)]

(7) **Licensing charitable solicitors:** [§855] Raising money on behalf of charitable causes is protected by the First Amendment (*see supra*, §729),

and therefore a law requiring that professional fundraisers obtain a license is subject to the *Freedman v. Maryland* procedural safeguards. [Riley v. National Federation of the Blind of North Carolina, *supra*, §725]

(8) **Use of the mails:** [§856] Use of the mails is a part of freedom of expression, and consequently any restrictions on a citizen's use thereof are subject to constitutional limitations.

(a) **"Obscene" mail:** [§857] The government is not permitted to deny a citizen the right to mail materials (or to detain incoming mail) on the ground they are "obscene," unless it affords adequate procedural safeguards. [Blount v. Rizzi, 400 U.S. 410 (1971)]

1) **Procedure:** [§858] The procedural safeguards required are basically those stipulated in *Freedman v. Maryland, supra:* the government must promptly initiate proceedings to obtain a final judicial determination of "obscenity" (administrative hearings invalid); it must bear the burden of proving the mail "obscene"; and any restraint in advance of a final judicial determination for preserving the status quo must be for "the shortest fixed period compatible with sound judicial resolution." [Blount v. Rizzi, *supra*]

(9) **Importation:** [§859] Similarly, the government may exclude "obscene" materials from import into this country, provided, again, that adequate procedural safeguards are afforded. [United States v. Thirty-Seven Photographs, 402 U.S. 363 (1971)—construing federal statute for seizure and confiscation of obscene imports requiring prompt proceedings, in accord with Freedman v. Maryland, *supra*]

d. **Challenging invalid injunctions:** [§860] If persons seeking to exercise First Amendment rights are enjoined from doing so, they usually may ***not*** violate the injunction and then defend a contempt prosecution on the ground that the injunction violated their constitutional rights. (*But note:* There is a possible exception where the court has no jurisdiction, or the injunction is "transparently invalid.") They must seek reasonably available judicial relief; *i.e.*, they must appeal the injunction unless the time is such that an appeal would effectively frustrate exercise of their rights. [Walker v. City of Birmingham, 388 U.S. 307 (1967)—expedited appellate procedure available even though permit denied only ***two days*** before scheduled parade]

8. **Symbolic Conduct:** [§861] The First Amendment does not automatically protect conduct simply because the person engaging in it shows that it is undertaken to communicate an idea. If there is an important state interest ***independent*** of the speech aspects of the conduct, it may be regulated despite the incidental limitation on speech—***especially*** if the state does not have less restrictive means available to accomplish its regulatory purpose. [United States v. O'Brien, 391 U.S. 367 (1968)]

a. **Draft card burning:** [§862] A prohibition on draft card burning was upheld. The government's interest was not simply to suppress speech aspects of the conduct; it had an independent interest of facilitating the smooth functioning of the draft system. [United States v. O'Brien, *supra*; *and see* Clark v. Community for Creative Non-Violence, 468 U.S. 288 (1984)—upholding prohibition on sleeping in national parks, applied to demonstrators calling attention to plight of the homeless]

b. **Armbands:** [§863] But a prohibition on students wearing black armbands in schools (to protest the Vietnam War) was found to be invalid. The government had no independent regulatory interest; its interest was ***only*** in prohibiting the communication. Thus, the conduct was "akin to pure speech" within the First Amendment ambit. [Tinker v. Des Moines Independent Community School District, 393 U.S. 503 (1969)]

c. **Flag desecration:** [§864] A prohibition on burning the American flag is likewise invalid—at least as applied to a situation where the conduct was intended (and understood by those who viewed it) as expressive and there was no actual or imminent breach of the peace. Government may not prohibit expression of an idea merely because society finds it offensive or disagreeable, even when the government's interest is preserving the flag as a symbol of nationhood and national unity. [United States v. Eichman, 496 U.S. 310 (1990); Texas v. Johnson, 491 U.S. 397 (1989)] A prohibition on displaying the flag with the peace symbol attached similarly violates the First Amendment. A person may not be punished "for failing to show proper respect for our national emblem." [Spence v. Washington, 418 U.S. 405 (1974)]

d. **Nudity:** [§865] Although "totally nude" dancing as entertainment is expressive conduct "within the outer perimeter" of the First Amendment, it may be prohibited under a state law against public nudity. Government has a "substantial" interest in protecting societal order and morality unrelated to the suppression of free expression; public nudity, not erotic expression, is the evil sought to be prevented. [Barnes v. Glen Theatre, Inc., 501 U.S. 560 (1991)]

e. **Conviction for conduct and protected speech:** [§866] Irrespective of whether the conduct engaged in is protected by the First Amendment, a conviction must be reversed if constitutionally protected ***speech*** is made ***part of the offense*** or ***may have been relied upon*** by the fact finder to convict.

(1) **Example:** Defendant was convicted of flag burning. The Court reversed, finding it unnecessary to determine whether flag burning was symbolic conduct akin to pure speech because defendant's statements while burning flag ("We don't need no damn flag") were introduced into evidence and may have been relied upon to convict. [Street v. New York, 394 U.S. 576 (1969)]

f. **Regulation of nonexpressive conduct:** [§867] A general regulation of conduct which itself has no communicative element is ***not*** invalid simply because the regulation incidentally burdens First Amendment activities. [Arcara v. Cloud Books, Inc., 478 U.S. 697 (1986)—upholding closure of adult bookstore because it was used for acts of prostitution]

9. **First Amendment Rights in Public Places:** [§868] The right to express one's views in public places is fundamental to a free society; however, it is ***not absolute*** and is subject to valid regulation.

a. **Public forum:** [§869] Certain public property is so historically associated with the exercise of First Amendment rights that it cannot be totally closed to protected expression—such as speeches, meetings, parades, and demonstrations.

(1) **Examples:** Streets, sidewalks, and parks fall within this category [Hague v. CIO, 307 U.S. 496 (1939)], including the public sidewalks abutting the Supreme Court building and grounds [United States v. Grace, 461 U.S. 171 (1983)], as apparently do the grounds around a statehouse [Edwards v. South Carolina, 372 U.S. 229 (1963)].

(2) **Designated public forum:** [§870] Other public property, although not a "traditional" public forum, may become a public forum for such time as the state "by policy or by practice" opens it for use by the public as a place for expressive activity. [Perry Education Association v. Perry Local Educators' Association, 460 U.S. 37 (1983)—public school internal mail system]

b. **Time, place, and manner regulations:** [§871] Both types of "public forums" are subject to valid "time, place, and manner" regulations which:

(i) Are ***content-neutral*** (*see* below);

(ii) Are ***narrowly tailored*** (*see infra*, §§886-889);

(iii) Serve a ***significant government interest*** (*see infra*, §§877-885); and

(iv) Leave open ***ample alternative*** forums or channels of communication for protected expression.

[Heffron v. International Society for Krishna Consciousness, 452 U.S. 640 (1981)]

(1) **Content-neutral:** [§872] The regulation may not be based on the content or subject matter of the speech unless "necessary to serve a compelling state interest and narrowly drawn to achieve that end." [Perry Education Association v. Perry Local Educators' Association, *supra*; *and see* Chicago Police Department v. Mosley, *supra*, §606—ordinance permitting peaceful labor picketing near schools but forbidding all other peaceful picketing discriminated in respect to the content of the expression and was a denial of ***equal protection***] *Examples:*

(a) **Drive-in theaters:** [§873] A law may ***not*** single out nudity in regulating films shown by drive-in theaters whose screens are visible from the highway. [Erznoznik v. Jacksonville, 422 U.S. 205 (1975)]

(b) **Foreign embassies:** [§874] A law may not forbid only those picket signs within 500 feet of a foreign embassy that are critical of the foreign government. [Boos v . Barry, 485 U.S. 312 (1988)]

(c) **Billboards:** [§875] A city may regulate billboards for purposes of traffic safety and aesthetics. But it may ***not*** permit billboards with commercial messages while prohibiting those with noncommercial messages; nor may it distinguish between different types of noncommercial messages. [Metromedia, Inc. v. City of San Diego, *supra*, §827—also upholding prohibition on commercial advertising]

(d) **State university facilities:** [§876] A state university that creates a forum open to students may not exclude a group that wants to use the facilities for religious discussion and worship unless the university shows that this is necessary to a compelling state interest. [Widmar v. Vincent, 454 U.S. 263 (1981)]

(2) **Significant government interest**

(a) **Example—insignificant interest:** [§877] The state has an inadequate interest in ascertaining the identity of ***every*** person who wishes to distribute handbills in public to justify requiring disclosure of the name and address of the author of all such handbills. [Talley v. California, 362 U.S. 60 (1960)]

(b) **Examples—significant interests:** [§878] The following have been found by the Court to be significant government interests.

1) **Orderly movement of crowds:** [§879] State interest in orderly movement of crowds at the state fair justifies restricting organizations' distribution and sale of literature and solicitation of donations to assigned booths at fixed locations. [Heffron v. International Society for Krishna Consciousness, *supra*—emphasizing that "alternative channels for communication of the information" had been left open]

2) **Privacy**

a) **Home:** [§880] State interest in protecting residential privacy justifies a ban on picketing that takes place solely in front of a particular residence. Usually in such instances, the information is not directed to the public but is narrowly directed only at the resident, who has no ready means of avoiding the unwanted speech. [Frisby v. Schultz, 487 U.S. 474 (1988)]

b) **Door-to-door solicitation:** [§881] State interest in protecting citizens from crime and undue annoyance justifies requiring door-to-door solicitors or canvassers to identify themselves to local officials. [Hynes v. Mayor of Oradell, 425 U.S. 610 (1976)—ordinance nevertheless ***invalid*** because of vagueness]

c) **Sound trucks:** [§882] State interest in protecting privacy justifies prohibiting the operation on public streets of sound trucks that emit messages amplified to a "loud and raucous volume." [Kovacs v. Cooper, 336 U.S. 77 (1949)—unwilling listener has no reasonable way of protecting himself]

1/ **But note:** As will be discussed (*infra*, §§898-905), an ordinance that required that anyone seeking to use a sound truck or other amplifiers on public streets must first obtain a permit from the chief of police was held unconstitutional where ***no standards*** were established for the granting or denial of the permit. Vesting complete discretion in the chief made him a censor of what could be broadcast on the public streets. [Saia v. New York, 334 U.S. 558 (1948)]

d) **Unwanted mail:** [§883] Similarly, the government interest in protecting privacy justifies the Post Office, upon a householder's request, to order a mailer to stop ***all future mailings*** to that householder and to remove her name from the mailing list. [Rowan v. United States Post Office, 397 U.S. 728 (1970)—mailer's First Amendment right to communicate must give way to householder's "right to be let alone"]

e) **Compare:** [§884] A person's interest in privacy does ***not*** justify the state's preventing public dissemination of information about that person, urging that pressure be put on him to cease certain business practices (real estate "blockbusting"). [Organization for a Better Austin v. Keefe, 402 U.S. 415 (1971)]

3) **Zoning:** [§885] Zoning laws may properly be used to restrict the locations in which "adult" movies can be shown because the state interest in regulating the secondary land use effects of commercial property outweighs the "less vital" First Amendment interest in uninhibited exhibition of material "on the borderline between pornography and artistic expression." [Young v. American Mini Theatres, Inc., *supra*, §802; City of Renton v. Playtime Theatres, Inc., *supra*, §802]

(3) **Narrowly tailored:** [§886] The regulation must be narrowly tailored; *i.e.,* it may not burden substantially more speech than is necessary to further the significant government interest. However, the regulation need ***not*** be the least restrictive or least intrusive means of doing so. Courts should respect the government's reasonable determination that the regulation best serves its interest. [Ward v. Rock Against Racism, 491 U.S. 781 (1989)—upholding regulation that performers at amphitheater in city park use city's sound-amplification equipment and sound technician]

(a) **Littering:** [§887] Significant state interest in keeping streets clean does ***not*** justify barring all distribution of handbills—because this would suppress a great quantity of speech that does not cause the evils sought to be prevented. [Schneider v. State, 308 U.S. 147 (1939)]

(b) **Door-to-door solicitation:** [§888] Significant state interest in protecting homeowner's privacy does ***not*** justify a ***total*** prohibition on knocking at door or ringing of bell to distribute handbills—because the city has other effective means, such as having unwilling homeowners post a "No Solicitors" sign. [Martin v. Struthers, 319 U.S. 141 (1943)]

1) **Note:** Significant state interest in preventing fraudulent charitable solicitations does ***not*** justify prohibiting such solicitations by ***all*** organizations (including groups engaged in advocacy on matters of public concern) whose overhead exceeds either a specified or a "reasonable" percent of receipts—because the state has other effective means of preventing fraud that will burden substantially less speech. [Riley v. National Federation of the Blind of North Carolina, *supra*, §725]

c. **Total ban:** [§889] Laws that foreclose an entire medium of expression pose a danger of suppressing too much speech. The state may impose a "total ban" on a particular medium of communication only if it satisfies the criteria for a valid time, place, and manner regulation; *i.e.*, the ban must be ***"content-neutral"***; it must further a ***"significant government interest"***; it must be ***"narrowly tailored"***; and there must be ***alternative media*** available for the protected expression. [Metromedia, Inc. v. City of San Diego, *supra*, §875] *Examples:*

(1) **Sound amplification:** [§890] It is unclear whether the state interest in protecting privacy justifies an absolute prohibition on any kind of sound amplification in public places in connection with First Amendment activities. [Kovacs v. Cooper, *supra*]

(2) **Temporary signs:** [§891] State aesthetic interest in eliminating "visual blight" justifies a total ban on posting signs on ***public*** property such as sidewalks, utility poles, etc. [Los Angeles City Council v. Taxpayers for Vincent, 466 U.S. 789 (1984)]

(3) **Residential signs:** [§892] Residential signs are an important, inexpensive, and convenient form of communication. The state's need to regulate all such speech from the home is not sufficiently strong to justify a near-total ban. [City of Ladue v. Gilleo, 114 S. Ct. ____ (1994)]

d. **Not a public forum:** [§893] Certain types of public property—that which is ***not*** traditionally or by government designation ***open to the general public***, or where the state concludes that First Amendment activities would be ***incompatible with the normal use to which the property is put***—may be closed to the exercise of First Amendment rights if the regulation is reasonable and not meant to suppress expression merely because officials oppose it.

(1) **Reasonableness:** [§894] Although the prohibition may not discriminate on the basis of the speaker's ***viewpoint*** (by seeking to discourage one and advance another), it may draw distinctions on the basis of the ***type of subject*** or the ***speaker's status***—as long as the distinction is reasonable in light of the purpose that the property serves. [Perry Education Association v. Perry Local Educators' Association, *supra*, §870]

(a) **Example—nonpublic forum:** An internal mail system among schools within a district is not a "public forum." Thus, the school district may provide access to the union that is the exclusive bargaining representative of the teachers and not to a rival union—because this is a reasonable distinction based on status. [Perry Education Association v. Perry Local Educators' Association, *supra*]

(b) **Example—nonpublic forum:** A government-created charity drive for federal employees, which has not traditionally been open to all charitable organizations, is not a "public forum." Thus, it is permissible to limit participation to traditional health and welfare charities and to exclude groups that engage in political advocacy, lobbying, and litigation. This is reasonable in light of the government's purposes of minimizing disruption to the federal workplace, insuring the success of the fundraising, and avoiding the appearance of political favoritism. [Cornelius v. NAACP Legal Defense & Education Fund, 473 U.S. 788 (1985)]

(c) **Example—nonpublic forum:** Airport terminals operated by a public authority have not historically been available for speech activities, nor have they been intentionally opened by their operators to such activities. Thus, they are not "public forums." It is reasonable to ban ***solicitation*** within the terminals that presents risks of fraud and duress to hurrying and vulnerable travelers and impedes the normal flow of traffic, and limit it to the outside sidewalk areas. [International Society for Krishna Consciousness, Inc. v. Lee, 112 S. Ct. 2701 (1992)] However, it is ***not*** reasonable to ban ***leafletting***, which does not pose these types of problems, in those terminals that are multipurpose facilities much like shopping malls. [Lee v. International Society for Krishna Consciousness, Inc., 112 S. Ct. 2709 (1992)—no majority rationale]

(d) **Example—"viewpoint neutrality":** School property when not in use for school purposes is not a "public forum." But to permit it to be used for presentation of all views about family issues except those from a religious perspective does not satisfy the requirement of "viewpoint neutrality." [Lamb's Chapel v. Center Moriches Union Free School District, 113 S. Ct. 2141 (1993)]

(2) **Examples of property that is not "public forum":** [§895] The following public property has been held ***not*** to be "public forum":

(a) ***Jailhouse*** grounds [Adderley v. Florida, 385 U.S. 39 (1966)];

(b) ***Area immediately surrounding a courthouse while a trial is being held*** [Cox v. Louisiana, *supra*, §808];

(c) ***Military bases*** may be closed to political speeches and distribution of leaflets—if done even-handedly. And this is true even when the public is generally permitted to visit the base, because of the strong government interest in keeping the military free of partisan political entanglements [Greer v. Spock, 424 U.S. 828 (1976)];

1) *Note:* Even if a military base is temporarily opened to the public for expressive activities, persons who have been validly barred for prior misconduct may continue to be excluded—as long as this is done on a "content-neutral" basis. [United States v. Albertini, 472 U.S. 675 (1985)]

(d) ***Area immediately surrounding a school during school sessions*** may be closed to expressive activity that disrupts (or is about to disrupt) normal school activities [Grayned v. City of Rockford, 408 U.S. 104 (1972)];

(e) ***A private letter box*** approved by the Postal Service for receipt of mail is ***not*** a public forum. The deposit of unstamped communications in such boxes would interfere with the safe and efficient delivery of mail and may be prohibited [United States Postal Service v. Council of Greenburgh Civic Associations, 453 U.S. 114 (1981)];

(f) ***A city transit system*** which sold advertising space for "car cards" did not constitute a "public forum." Thus the city's refusal to accept any political advertising by candidates did not violate the First Amendment—the city's policy was "reasonable" in order to minimize chances of abuse, the appearance of favoritism, and the risk of imposing upon a captive audience. Four Justices disagreed. [Lehman v. City of Shaker Heights, 418 U.S. 298 (1974)]; and

(g) The Court has split on whether a ***postal sidewalk leading from the parking area*** to the post office door is a traditional "public forum," akin to ordinary public sidewalks that facilitate the daily commerce and the life of the neighborhood or city [United States v. Kokinda, 497 U.S. 720 (1990)].

(3) **Private property:** [§896] The First Amendment does not require the owner of private property to allow access thereto for the purpose of picketing or distributing handbills. [Hudgens v. NLRB, 424 U.S. 507 (1976)—shopping center] On the other hand, the First Amendment does not prohibit a state from requiring the owner of private property to permit access thereto for the purpose of distributing handbills unrelated to the business conducted on the private property. [Pruneyard Shopping Center v. Robins, *supra*, §724]

(a) **Compare—"equivalent to a public place":** However, privately owned property may in some cases be held to be the functional ***equivalent of a public place***—in which event neither criminal nor civil trespass rules may be applied to limit the ***reasonable*** exercise of First Amendment rights thereon. [Marsh v. Alabama, *supra*, §676—distribution of religious literature in privately owned "company town"]

e. **Licensing:** [§897] One method of reasonably regulating public areas for protected speeches, meetings, parades, demonstrations, etc., is to require a permit or license for such use, specifying the time, place, manner, and duration of the activity. Furthermore, the state may require a reasonable fee for the use in order to defray public expenses. [Cox v. New Hampshire, 312 U.S. 569 (1941)]

(1) **Censorship forbidden:** [§898] In providing for the issuance of such permits, however, the state may ***not*** vest the licensing official (mayor, police chief, etc.) with ***unlimited discretion*** to determine who may receive permits [Lovell v. City of Griffin, 303 U.S. 444 (1938)] or how much to charge for police protection or administrative time [Forsyth County, Georgia v. Nationalist Movement, 112 S. Ct. 2395 (1992)]. To do so would limit the exercise of First Amendment rights to what the official approved of, and would vest the official with censorship power over the content of what is said.

(a) **Requirement of defined standards:** [§899] The licensing authority must therefore contain ***clearly defined standards*** as to time, place, manner, and duration.

(b) **Denial based on content:** [§900] The Court has ***suggested*** that, in certain ***special circumstances***, a permit may be denied because of the content of speech (*e.g.*, a speech that would present the clear and present danger of a riot)—but such a "prior restraint" could take place only under narrowly and clearly defined standards. [Kunz v. New York, 340 U.S. 290 (1951)] Moreover, the Court has ***never upheld*** a licensing system based on the content of the speech.

1) **Licensing organizations:** [§901] Before a state college may deny official recognition and use of college facilities to a student group, a "heavy burden" rests on the college to justify this form of "prior restraint." Neither the group's general affiliation with a national organization nor its philosophy (even if one of violence) will justify denial of recognition, but denial ***may*** be justified if the group poses a ***substantial threat of material disruption*** or refuses to affirm its willingness to adhere to reasonable campus rules respecting conduct. [Healy v. James, 408 U.S. 169 (1972)—denial to Students for a Democratic Society chapter of use of facilities is invalid]

2) **Fees:** [§902] The amount of the fee charged to maintain public order may not be based on actual expense if this would result in greater costs because of the need to control those who might oppose the speech, parade, etc. Listeners' reaction to speech is not a content-neutral basis for regulation. [Forsyth County, Georgia v. Nationalist Movement, *supra*]

(2) **Effect of unlimited discretion:** [§903] If the statute gives licensing officials undue discretion, it is ***"void on its face"***; *i.e.*, applicants need not even apply for a permit. (Note the similarity to facial invalidity because of "overbreadth" or "vagueness," *supra*, §740.) Even if they could properly have been denied a permit under a narrowly drafted statute, they may exercise their First Amendment rights on the public property ***without a permit*** and may not be convicted for violating the licensing statute. [Staub v. Baxley, 355 U.S. 313 (1958)]

(a) **Example:** A city ordinance that vested in local licensing officials the power to grant parade permits on the basis of their judgment as to the effect of such parade on the "welfare" or "morals" of the community was held unconstitutional ***on its face***—for lack of adequate standards. [Shuttlesworth v. City of Birmingham, 394 U.S. 147 (1969)]

(b) **Example:** A city ordinance that gave the mayor complete discretion to grant annual permits for placement of newsracks on public property was held unconstitutional ***on its face***. [Lakewood v. Plain Dealer Publishing Co., 486 U.S. 750 (1988)]

(3) **Statutes valid on their face:** [§904] If the licensing statute is valid on its face—*i.e.*, if it contains clearly defined standards as to time, place, manner, and duration—it may not be ignored. The applicant ***must seek a permit***, and if the permit is refused for any reason—even arbitrarily or unconstitutionally—the applicant must seek ***reasonably available administrative or judicial relief***. The applicant may not speak without a permit and then defend prosecution for violating the statute on the ground that the permit was improperly denied or that his speech was constitutionally protected. [Poulos v. New Hampshire, 345 U.S. 395 (1953)]

(a) **Note:** In *Shuttlesworth v. City of Birmingham, supra*, the licensing statute was void on its face (inadequate standards)—but on appeal of the conviction, the state courts gave the statute a narrow (and probably constitutional) construction. The Supreme Court reversed the conviction for parading without a permit on the ground that the applicants had no reason to anticipate such a limiting construction and, in any case, were told by the officials that they would not get a permit under any circumstances. The Court ***left open*** the question of whether applicants must generally seek a narrowing construction if "expeditious judicial review" is available.

f. **Injunctions:** [§905] A slightly more rigorous degree of scrutiny governs content-neutral injunctions that impose "time, place, and manner" restrictions on the exercise of First Amendment rights in public forums: an injunction is valid if it burdens no more speech than ***necessary*** to serve a ***significant*** government interest. [Madden v. Women's Health Center, Inc., 114 S. Ct. ____ (1994)—upholding injunction against focused picketing near entrance to abortion clinic so as to ensure ingress and egress]

10. **First Amendment Freedoms and Special Government Interests**

a. **Administration of justice:** [§906] Statutes and rules of court restricting the freedoms of speech and press will be sustained to the extent necessary to ensure the orderly administration of justice.

(1) **In court:** [§907] Disruptive or obviously disrespectful statements directed to the ***judge*** or an ***officer of the court*** during the course of a trial are punishable by contempt.

(2) **Out of court:** [§908] Speech or publications by the news media about pending judicial proceedings are not punishable unless they pose a ***clear and present danger of serious interference*** with the administration of

justice—and this issue is ultimately determined by the Supreme Court. [Bridges v. California, 315 U.S. 252 (1941)]

(a) **Freedom of the press:** [§909] The Court has noted that "freedom of the press must be allowed in the ***broadest*** scope compatible with the supremacy of order" [Pennekamp v. Florida, 328 U.S. 331 (1946)], and the strong presumption against prior restraints applies [Nebraska Press Association v. Stuart, *supra,* §837].

(b) **Pending proceedings:** [§910] If the judicial proceedings are ***over***, there is no danger that the utterances or publications will interfere with the administration of justice. But close issues may arise as to whether the proceedings are really complete (*i.e.*, whether there can be an appeal, new trial, etc.).

(c) **Compare—lawyers:** [§911] Speech of lawyers representing clients in pending cases may be regulated under a less demanding standard than for the news media. These lawyers are "officers of the court" and may be sanctioned for speech having ***"substantial likelihood of materially prejudicing"*** the jury venire or the actual outcome of the proceedings. [Gentile v. State Bar of Nevada, 501 U.S. 1030 (1991)]

(d) **Type of proceeding:** [§912] The permissible amount of restriction on speech and press also depends substantially on the ***type*** of judicial proceeding involved.

1) **Trial by jury:** [§913] The greatest restrictions are seemingly permitted to protect the impartiality of a petit jury. [Sheppard v. Maxwell, 384 U.S. 333 (1966)]

2) **Trials without a jury:** [§914] Freedom of speech and press are given ***more leeway*** in trials without a jury, on the theory that judges are better trained than juries to withstand criticism and intimidation. [Craig v. Harney, 331 U.S. 367 (1947)]

3) **Grand jury proceedings:** [§915] Still greater leeway is afforded speech and press in respect to grand jury proceedings, because of their nonfinal nature. And there is even more liberality where the grand jury is engaged in a general investigation. Commentary ***criticizing this process*** may be curtailed only if it is manifestly unjust and likely to impede the outcome of the investigation. This will be an extremely rare situation, since full and free discussion generally furthers, rather than impedes, a grand jury investigation. [Wood v. Georgia, 370 U.S. 375 (1962)]

4) **Confidential proceedings:** [§916] A state may have a legitimate interest in maintaining confidentiality about some proceedings (*e.g.*, inquiries into the fitness of judges). The Court has ***not decided*** whether a state may punish disclosures about such proceedings by (i) participants or (ii) persons who secure the information by illegal means. But criminal sanctions may

not be imposed on other persons (including the press) for divulging truthful information regarding such confidential proceedings, absent substantial interests that justify encroachment on freedom of speech and press. [Landmark Communications, Inc. v. Virginia, 435 U.S. 829 (1978)]

a) **Grand jury testimony:** [§917] The secrecy of what transpires in grand jury proceedings serves a number of important interests. However, on balance, these interests do not justify a ***permanent ban*** on disclosure by a witness of ***any*** of his ***own*** testimony, even after the grand jury has been ***discharged***. [Butterworth v. Smith, 494 U.S. 624 (1990)]

b. **Electoral process:** [§918] Election laws inevitably impose some burdens on individuals' right to vote, which has protection under the First Amendment freedoms of speech and association. The degree of scrutiny that the Court will apply to such laws depends on how great a restriction the regulation imposes on the right to vote. [Burdick v. Takushi, 112 S. Ct. 2059 (1992)—discussed *infra,* §922]

(1) **Campaign activity restrictions:** [§919] Thus, a state law prohibiting any campaigning on election day has been held invalid as applied to a newspaper editorial urging voters to vote a certain way. There was no showing of any clear and present danger to conducting the election, and the right to comment on political issues is one of the most essential elements of free speech. [Mills v. Alabama, 384 U.S. 214 (1966)]

(a) **Exception—campaigning near polling place:** [§920] However, a state law forbidding campaign activity within 100 feet of a polling place is valid. Even though the law bars only political speech in a public forum (and is thus not content-neutral, *see supra*, §872), it is ***necessary*** to serve the ***compelling*** interest of preventing voter intimidation and election fraud in regard to the fundamental right to vote. [Burson v. Freeman, 112 S. Ct. 1846 (1992)]

(b) **Campaign promises:** [§921] Some kinds of campaign promises may be illegal (*e.g.*, a promise to pay for a vote). But a ***publicly made*** promise to benefit the public fisc (*e.g.*, a promise to serve at reduced salary) is constitutionally protected political speech. [Brown v. Hartladge, 456 U.S. 45 (1982)—no compelling state interest to justify voiding election of candidate who makes a good faith promise to serve at reduced salary even when promise cannot be kept because state law forbids reduced salary]

(2) **Write-in voting:** [§922] A state may prohibit write-in voting when the state's overall election scheme provides adequate ballot access. [Burdick v. Takushi, *supra*—"slight" burden on right to vote outweighed by states' "legitimate" interest in avoiding unrestrained party factionalism and related matters]

(3) **Restrictions on political parties:** [§923] Laws that greatly burden the freedom of speech or freedom of association rights of political parties

and their members must be "narrowly tailored" to serve a "compelling state interest." [Eu v. San Francisco County Democratic Central Committee, 489 U.S. 214 (1989)—state cannot prohibit a political party from endorsing candidates in its primary]

(a) **Internal party organization:** [§924] A political party's freedom of association right includes discretion in how to organize itself, conduct its affairs, and select its leaders. [Eu v. San Francisco County Democratic Central Committee, *supra*—state cannot regulate composition and criteria of state central committee members, nor time and place of their meetings]

(b) **Closed primaries:** [§925] A state may not require that voters in a party's primary be registered in the party if the party itself wishes to permit independent voters to participate. [Tashjian v. Republican Party of Connecticut, 479 U.S. 208 (1986)]

(4) **Limits on contributions:** [§926] Laws limiting the amount of money that a person or group may ***contribute*** to a political candidate are ***valid***, since the government has a sufficiently important interest in stopping the fact (or appearance) of corruption which may result from large contributions. Moreover, such laws do not substantially restrict freedom of expression or freedom of association (as long as the contributor may spend her money ***directly*** to discuss candidates and issues). [Buckley v. Valeo, *supra*, §589]

(a) **Political action groups:** [§927] Laws limiting the amount of money that an incorporated or unincorporated organization may contribute to a committee that itself makes contributions to political candidates are similarly valid. [California Medical Association v. Federal Election Commission, 453 U.S. 182 (1981)] So, too, are laws that forbid incorporated or unincorporated organizations from making campaign contributions with funds solicited from the public generally rather than from their members. [Federal Election Commission v. National Right to Work Committee, 456 U.S. 914 (1982)]

(b) **Compare—ballot measures:** [§928] But laws limiting the amount that persons may contribute to a committee that supports or opposes a ballot measure are invalid—at least absent a showing that the restriction is needed to preserve voter confidence in the ballot measure process. In this context, there is no state interest in stopping the fact (or appearance) of corruption of officials. [Citizens Against Rent Control v. Berkeley, 454 U.S. 290 (1981)]

(5) **Limits on expenditures:** [§929] Laws limiting the amount that an individual or group (including a candidate) may ***spend*** on a political campaign are ***invalid***. Such laws impose "direct and substantial restraints" on political speech and do not satisfy the "exacting scrutiny applicable to limitations on core First Amendment rights of political expression." Government may not restrict the speech of wealthy persons in order to enhance the voice of others. [Buckley v. Valeo, *supra*] However, such

expenditures may not be prearranged or coordinated with the candidate (otherwise they would be "contributions").

(a) **Political action groups:** [§930] Laws that limit the amount that an organization of persons may spend on a political campaign are similarly invalid. [Federal Election Commission v. National Conservative Political Action Committee, 470 U.S. 480 (1985)]

(b) **Petition circulators:** [§931] A law that prohibits paying persons to obtain signatures for a ballot initiative is also invalid because its effect is to reduce the quantum of "core political speech." [Meyer v. Grant, 484 U.S. 414 (1988)]

(c) **Corporations:** [§932] Laws prohibiting corporate expenditures to influence the vote on a ***referendum*** violate the First Amendment. Such speech is "indispensable to decision-making in a democracy." [First National Bank v. Bellotti, 435 U.S 765 (1978)—law limiting corporate expenditures to referenda that "materially affect" corporate business or property are invalid] A law forbidding a corporation from using bill inserts to express its views on controversial issues of public policy also violates the First Amendment. [Consolidated Edison Co. v. Public Service Commission, 447 U.S. 530 (1980)]

1) **Candidate elections:** [§933] The Court has acknowledged the legitimate concern that organizations that amass great wealth in the economic marketplace through state-conferred legal advantages not gain unfair advantage in the political marketplace through the corruption of elected officials, and has upheld limitations on corporations making expenditures to influence partisan candidate elections. However, any restriction that may be placed on corporations generally may not be applied to an organization (even though incorporated) that (i) is formed exclusively (or mainly) to promote political ideas, (ii) has no shareholders with claims on its assets or members who wish to benefit from its nonpolitical programs, and (iii) does not serve as a conduit for campaign spending by business corporations or labor unions. Voluntary political associations of this kind do not present the problem of actual or apparent corruption of the political process through concentrated corporate wealth. [Federal Election Commission v. Massachusetts Citizens for Life, Inc., 479 U.S. 238 (1986); Austin v. Michigan Chamber of Commerce, 494 U.S. 328 (1990)]

a) **Corporate treasury funds:** [§934] State laws may prohibit corporate expenditures for state political candidates except from funds segregated to be used for political purposes. [Austin v. Michigan Chamber of Commerce, *supra*]

(6) **Disclosure requirements:** [§935] Laws requiring political parties to disclose information concerning campaign ***contributions*** and ***expenditures***

may be justified by such substantial government interests as enhancement of voter knowledge, deterrence of corruption, and enforcement of contribution limitations. [Buckley v. Valeo, *supra*]

(a) **Minor parties:** [§936] But such laws are ***invalid*** when applied to a minor political party that shows a "reasonable probability" that the disclosure will subject those identified to "threats, harassment, or reprisals from either government officials or private parties." (For further discussion, *see infra*, §§966-967.) In these circumstances, the government interests described above are diminished and the threat to political and associational freedom is much greater. [Brown v. Socialist Workers '74 Campaign Committee, 454 U.S. 1122 (1982)]

c. **Subsidies:** [§937] The First Amendment does ***not*** require government to subsidize exercise of the right of speech. [Regan v. Taxation with Representation of Washington, 461 U.S. 540 (1983)—Congress may deny tax benefits (which amount to government subsidies) for lobbying activities of organizations] Moreover, the government may subsidize lobbying activities of some groups and not others as long as it does not do so on the basis of the ***content*** of their speech. [*Id.*—Congress may rationally decide to subsidize lobbying by veterans' groups]

(1) **Funded programs:** [§938] Government may fund programs to encourage certain activities and not others. In doing so, it may prohibit employees within the funded programs from giving certain kinds of information to program beneficiaries. This is ***not*** government discrimination on the basis of content of speech (as would be so if government restricted fund recipients from certain kinds of speech outside the scope of the funded programs). Rather, the government is just assuring that its funds are used only to further the purposes of its program. [Rust v. Sullivan, 500 U.S. 173 (1991)—upholding federal regulations prohibiting federally funded family planning programs from counseling or giving information about abortion] Similarly, Congress's refusal to give food stamps to persons who meet the low income test because they are on strike does not abridge the strikers' First Amendment right of expression. [Lyng v. International Union, 485 U.S. 360 (1988)]

(2) **Funding political campaigns:** [§939] Government ***may*** provide funds for political campaigns subject to various restrictions (discussed *supra*, §589).

d. **Public schools:** [§940] Students in public schools do not shed their First Amendment rights at the schoolhouse gate. Student speech that happens to occur on school premises may not be prohibited unless "necessary to avoid material and substantial interference with school work, discipline, or the rights of others." [Tinker v. Des Moines Independent Community School District, *supra*, §863]

(1) **Classrooms:** [§941] The First Amendment rights of students in public classrooms or assemblies (where other students are a captive audience) are not coextensive with the rights of adults in other settings. Thus, schools may prohibit the use of lewd, indecent, vulgar, and offensive

speech in this context when it would undermine the school's basic educational mission. [Bethel School District v. Fraser, 478 U.S. 675 (1986)]

(2) **Publications:** [§942] Similarly, as long as their actions are reasonably related to legitimate pedagogical concerns, school officials may regulate the style and content of school-sponsored publications, theatrical productions, and other expressive activities that are part of the educational curriculum (whether or not in a traditional classroom setting) or that are perceived to bear the school's imprimatur. Thus, schools may prohibit speech that is ungrammatical, poorly written, inadequately researched, biased or prejudiced, or unsuitable for immature audiences. [Hazelwood School District v. Kuhlmeier, 484 U.S. 260 (1988)]

(3) **Libraries:** [§943] A school board has broad discretion in respect to school affairs. Pursuant to its authority to promote fundamental civic and cultural values, it may remove books from the school library that it finds to be "pervasively vulgar" or "educationally unsuitable." But the Court has not clearly decided the extent to which the First Amendment rights of students deny a school board the discretion to remove books because the board disapproves of their ideas on narrow partisan or political grounds. [Board of Education v. Pico, 457 U.S. 853 (1982)]

e. **Academic freedom:** [§944] The First Amendment includes an academic freedom right against government attempts to influence the content of academic speech. However, the right does not protect confidential peer review materials from disclosure in appropriate proceedings, because it is unlikely that such disclosure will deter candid evaluations. The Court has not, however, resolved whether certain information in the materials may be redacted. [University of Pennsylvania v. Equal Employment Opportunity Commission, 493 U.S. 182 (1990)—EEOC subpoena of tenure review file in connection with dismissed teacher's claim of discrimination]

f. **Prison administration:** [§945] Prison inmates retain constitutional rights that are consistent with their status as prisoners. Prison regulations impinging on those rights are valid if "reasonably related to legitimate penological interests," but should not represent an "exaggerated response" to those concerns. Courts must ordinarily give ***broad deference*** to the ***reasonable*** judgments of prison administrators. [Turner v. Safley, 482 U.S. 78 (1987)—upholding prison ban on most inmate-to-inmate mail correspondence, but invalidating requirement of superintendent's permission for inmate to marry]

(1) **Interviews by news media:** [§946] For example, prison inmates can be prohibited from being interviewed by the news media as long as alternative means of communication are still available (*e.g.*, inmates can communicate by mail or through visitors). [Pell v. Procunier, 417 U.S. 817 (1974)]

(2) **Prison unions:** [§947] Prison inmates may be prohibited from soliciting other inmates to join a union, from holding union meetings, and from receiving bulk union mailings. [Jones v. North Carolina Prisoners' Labor Union, 433 U.S. 119 (1977)]

(3) **Mail searches:** [§948] Incoming mail to prisoners (even from their attorneys) may properly be opened in the presence of the prisoners, but not read, in order to insure that contraband is not smuggled into the prison. [Wolff v. McDonnell, 418 U.S. 539 (1974)]

(4) **Incoming publications:** [§949] Prison officials may reject incoming publications reasonably found to be detrimental to prison security. [Thornburgh v. Abbott, 490 U.S. 401 (1989)]

(5) **Outgoing correspondence:** [§950] Outgoing mail presents a lesser threat to prison security. Thus, the Court has invalidated prison regulations that authorized censorship of prisoner mail that "unduly complains" or "magnifies grievances," that expresses "inflammatory political, racial, religious or other views," or that is deemed "defamatory or otherwise inappropriate." Such regulations are ***too broad*** for First Amendment purposes. [Procunier v. Martinez, 416 U.S. 396 (1974)]

g. **Military personnel:** [§951] Members of the military do have First Amendment protection, but speech on their part that "undermines the effectiveness of response to command" may be limited even if it could not in a civilian setting. Thus, "facial invalidity" is found less readily because of "significant differences between military law and civilian law." [Parker v. Levy, 417 U.S. 733 (1974)]

(1) **Example:** "Protest" expressions by military personnel have been held punishable as undermining the effectiveness of command, even though similar expressions by civilians are constitutionally protected. [Parker v. Levy, *supra*—upholding court-martial conviction of officer who urged soldiers to refuse to obey orders to go to Vietnam]

(2) **Example:** Also, because of the military's interest in maintaining discipline and respect for duty, a requirement that members of the military obtain their commander's approval before circulating petitions on bases is not void on its face. [Brown v. Glines, 444 U.S. 348 (1980)]

h. **Practice of law:** [§952] Statutes regulating the professional conduct of attorneys in soliciting cases, or in accepting employment or referrals from groups, cannot be applied in a manner that interferes with the group's "freedom of expression and association"—*e.g.*, freedom to band together to advise each other and use counsel in their common interest.

(1) **Requirement of substantial state interest:** [§953] To overcome the group's exercise of First Amendment rights, the state must show a ***substantial*** interest—*i.e.*, evidence of objectionable practices actually occurring, or an actual or clearly threatened conflict of interest between lawyer and client. [Brotherhood of Railroad Trainmen v. Virginia, 377 U.S. 1 (1964)]

(a) **Example:** The NAACP encouraged, instructed, and offered to represent parents of black children to litigate against school segregation. *Held:* Such litigation was a form of political expression and political association; and since the NAACP sought no monetary gain, there was no danger of conflict of interest, which was the purpose of the state ban on solicitation of legal business. [NAACP v. Button, *supra*, §747]

1) **Monetary gain:** Even where politically motivated groups (such as the NAACP or ACLU) seek a court award of counsel fees in such litigation, solicitation by their lawyers is protected as long as they have no personal pecuniary gain at stake. [*In re* Primus, 436 U.S. 412 (1978)] (Compare solicitation for personal gain, discussed *supra*, §830.)

(b) **Example:** Likewise, a union has the right to hire an attorney on a salary basis to represent its members on their workers' compensation claims in state tribunals absent any evidence of abuse or conflict of interest. [United Mine Workers v. Illinois Bar Association, 389 U.S. 217 (1967)]

i. **Labor picketing:** [§954] The dissemination of information regarding a labor or other economic dispute by means of ***peaceful picketing*** is a type of expression protected by the First Amendment and may not be ***absolutely*** prohibited. [Thornhill v. Alabama, 310 U.S. 88 (1940)]

(1) **Violence:** [§955] Even peaceful picketing may be enjoined if it is enmeshed with violence or a justifiable fear that violence will ensue. [Milk Wagon Drivers' Union v. Meadowmoor Dairies, Inc., 312 U.S. 287 (1941)]

(2) **Current doctrine:** [§956] When peaceful economic picketing involves more than "publicity" and seeks to pressure the subject of the picketing to take action that is contrary to lawful state policy—*i.e.*, a state policy not barred by federal statute or the Constitution—it may be enjoined (or otherwise prohibited) without abridging the First Amendment. [International Brotherhood of Teamsters v. Vogt, Inc., 354 U.S. 284 (1957)]

(a) **Lawful state policy:** [§957] State policy may be reflected in a statute making the action sought to be induced by the picketing a crime or civil wrong; or a state court may determine that the action sought is contrary to public policy.

1) **Example:** A state court enjoined peaceful picketing for the purpose of inducing the picketed wholesaler to refrain from selling to nonunion peddlers; the state court found this to be a restraint of trade in violation of state antitrust laws. *Held:* Valid—the state statute reflected a lawful state policy not contrary to any federal statute or the Constitution. [Giboney v. Empire Storage & Ice Co., 336 U.S. 490 (1949)]

2) **Example:** A state court enjoined peaceful picketing for the purpose of forcing the picketed business to hire employees in percentage of the race of its customers; the state court reasoned that employment on racial lines was contrary to public policy as determined by state court. *Held:* Valid—the state policy is

lawful and not contrary to any federal statute or the Constitution. [Hughes v. Superior Court, 339 U.S. 460 (1950)]

(b) **Illustration of unlawful state policy:** [§958] However, if peaceful picketing were used to induce the business picketed to cease racial discrimination in hiring, and a state court enjoined such picketing on the ground that state policy ***favored*** racial discrimination in hiring (and the picketing thus sought to induce the business to violate state policy), the picketing could not be enjoined since the state policy would be unlawful.

j. **Boycotts:** [§959] Nonviolent, politically motivated boycotts (including threats of social ostracism for nonparticipation) that seek to secure ***constitutional rights*** (in contrast to goals prohibited by valid state laws) are protected by the First Amendment and cannot be prohibited—at least absent a narrowly tailored statute prohibiting certain forms of anticompetitive conduct. [NAACP v. Claiborne Hardware Co., 458 U.S. 886 (1982)]

(1) **Money damages:** [§960] Damages may be imposed only for consequences of a boycott that specific ***findings*** show to be ***proximately caused*** by unlawful conduct (*e.g.*, violence). They may not be imposed merely because defendant belonged to a group, some of whose members acted unlawfully. [NAACP v. Claiborne Hardware Co., *supra*]

k. **Trademarks:** [§961] When a word acquires value through the special efforts of a person (or entity), Congress may, consistent with the First Amendment, grant that person (or entity) a "limited property right" in the word, thus enabling the person (or entity) to prevent others from using the word without authorization. [San Francisco Arts & Athletics, Inc. v. United States Olympic Committee, 483 U.S. 522 (1987)—U.S. Olympic Committee may prevent another group from calling its athletic competition "Gay Olympic Games"]

l. **Copyright:** [§962] Similarly, Congress may grant authors (including those who are important public figures) exclusive control over publication of their writing for a limited period. [Harper & Row v. Nation Enterprises, 471 U.S. 539 (1985)—magazine published article with 300 words from former President Ford's forthcoming memoirs] For related discussion, *see infra*, §1008.

11. **Freedom of Association—Special Rules**

a. **Association with groups engaging in unprotected advocacy or activities:** [§963] Even though an individual does not himself engage in unprotected advocacy or other constitutionally unprotected activities, he may be punished for being a member of a certain type of group—but only if ***both*** of the following criteria are met:

(1) **Culpability of group:** [§964] The group or organization itself must engage in advocacy (as defined *supra*, §§753-754) or activities that are not constitutionally protected.

(2) **Culpability of individual member:** [§965] In addition, the individual must have (i) ***knowledge*** of the group's illegal advocacy or activities, and (ii) the ***specific intent*** that its illegal aims be accomplished. [Scales v. United States, 367 U.S. 203 (1961)]

(a) **Example:** Mere attendance at a meeting or assistance in the holding of a meeting may not be proscribed; the government's interest in penalizing such conduct is too weak, and the inhibition on freedom of association is too broad. [DeJonge v. Oregon, 299 U.S. 353 (1937)]

(b) **Rationale:** A prohibition against membership that is knowledgeable but without specific intent is ***overbroad***; it would encompass persons (i) who might belong to the organization only to pursue certain of its lawful aims, or (ii) who might wish to change the organization's unlawful aims. Such persons pose no threat to any substantial government interest. [Elfbrandt v. Russell, 384 U.S. 11 (1966)]

b. **Compulsory disclosure of membership or association:** [§966] Several cases have dealt with the power of government to require an individual to disclose her organizational memberships—or, conversely, to compel an organization to disclose the names of its members. The Court has recognized that disclosure of the fact that a person is a member of (or contributes to) a particular group or organization may ***deter*** her from becoming a member or contributing—especially if the group espouses unpopular views—and therefore may deter freedom of association. [NAACP v. Alabama, *supra*, §726]

(1) **General standard:** [§967] The Court will ***closely scrutinize*** such compulsory disclosure (or compelled registration of membership) to determine whether it "***directly*** serves ***substantial*** government interests," thus ***outweighing*** the individual's need for anonymity (or privacy) in exercising the First Amendment right of association. [Buckley v. Valeo, *supra*, §926]

(2) **Examples**

(a) ***Alabama sought to compel disclosure of NAACP membership lists*** to determine whether the NAACP was engaged in intrastate activities and thus subject to a state registration statute for foreign corporations "doing business" in the state. *Held:* State interest was insufficient to overcome substantial deterrent effect on freedom of association that disclosure in Alabama would have (as demonstrated by threats, harassment, etc.). [NAACP v. Alabama, *supra*]

(b) ***Federal statute required registration of Communist Party membership.*** *Held:* Strong government interest in identifying membership of Communist Party—which depended on secrecy for forceful overthrow of government—outweighs individual interest. The Court noted that the requirement became operative only after specific findings about the Communist Party following notice and hearing, which were subject to judicial review. [Communist Party v. Subversive Activities Control Board, 367 U.S. 1 (1967)]

(3) **Privilege against self-incrimination:** [§968] Although the government interest in compelling disclosure of membership may be sufficient to outweigh the individual's First Amendment freedom of association,

if—because of other criminal statutes—the admission of membership may be used to prosecute the registrant, the registration statute may violate the individual's Fifth Amendment privilege against self-incrimination. [Albertson v. Subversive Activities Control Board, 382 U.S. 70 (1965)]

c. **Disclosures required in legislative investigations**

(1) **Investigatory powers:** [§969] The power of Congress (or a state legislature) to conduct investigations in aid of proposed legislation is inherent in its legislative functions, and is implied under the Necessary and Proper Clause. (*See* discussion *supra*, §160.) Thus, a legislative body may compel the attendance of witnesses, order that they answer questions, and punish as a contempt any refusal by a witness to appear or testify (*see supra*, §162).

(2) **Limitations:** [§970] There are important limitations on the power of a legislative investigating committee to compel a witness appearing before it to answer questions:

(a) **Due process:** [§971] Where a witness is cited for contempt for refusing to answer a question, due process requires that the person be given fair notice of the prohibited conduct. Thus, the ***nature of the legislative inquiry*** and the ***pertinency of the question*** must be made clear to the witness, or the contempt conviction cannot stand. [Watkins v. United States, 354 U.S. 178 (1957)]

(b) **First Amendment:** [§972] Regardless of pertinency, a legislative investigating committee cannot abridge First Amendment rights which protect the privacy of one's views or associations.

1) **Requirement of overriding legislative interest:** [§973] Therefore, a legislative committee may require disclosure of an individual's political beliefs or associations only upon the showing of a valid legislative interest in the information sought that is so ***compelling*** that it ***outweighs*** the individual's right to privacy in his associations. [Gibson v. Florida Legislative Investigation Committee, 372 U.S. 539 (1963)]

a) **Example:** In *Barenblatt v. United States*, 360 U.S. 109 (1960), the witness refused to answer questions about past or present Communist Party membership. His conviction was upheld because the strong government interest in Communist infiltration of education (the matter being investigated) outweighed the relatively slight deterrence on freedom of association resulting from disclosure.

b) **Rationale:** The First Amendment, unlike the Fifth Amendment privilege against self-incrimination, does not specifically protect the right of silence. Congress may inquire beyond the specific elements of what may be made criminal. And while exposure cannot be required simply for the sake of exposure, the Court will generally not question congressional motives in making the inquiry when it appears that Congress is pursuing a valid legislative goal.

2) **"Nexus" requirement:** [§974] To establish an overriding legislative interest in the information sought, a ***substantial connection*** ("nexus") between the information sought and the subject matter of the legislative inquiry must be shown. Without this, disclosure cannot be compelled. [Gibson v. Florida Legislative Investigation Committee, *supra*]

a) **Example:** In the *Gibson* case, the Court reversed a contempt conviction for a witness's refusal to disclose to a state legislative committee the names of members of local chapters of the NAACP. The committee was investigating local Communist activities (a valid legislative interest) and sought to determine whether certain named Communists were NAACP members. However, there was no "nexus" between the local NAACP and Communist activities where the evidence showed only that a few Communists were NAACP members. The *Barenblatt* case was distinguished: It involved inquiry about membership in an ***unlawful*** group (Communist Party), whereas the NAACP was a ***lawful*** group.

d. **Civil penalties for unprotected association (or advocacy):** [§975] Government may also impose civil penalties (*e.g.*, denial of governmental benefits, such as tax exemptions) on those who engage in constitutionally unprotected association (or speech).

(1) **Burden of proof:** [§976] If the civil disability is imposed to ***penalize*** (*i.e.*, to punish or deter) the association (or speech), rather than to serve some important government interest (below), the government has the burden of showing that the individual has engaged in unprotected association (or advocacy). [Speiser v. Randall, 357 U.S. 513 (1958)]

(2) **Overriding government interest:** [§977] Some civil disabilities (*e.g.*, denial of certain kinds of public employment, or of licenses to practice certain professions) may not be "penalties." Rather, they may be imposed only to satisfy an independent state interest, such as assuring that public employees loyally and faithfully carry out their duties. The Court has not held that the government must bear the burden of persuasion in connection with imposition of these disabilities.

(3) **Liability of organization:** [§978] Organizations may be held responsible (*e.g.*, for damages) for acts of their representatives only if undertaken within the scope of actual or apparent authority, or if specifically ratified. [NAACP v. Claiborne Hardware Co., *supra*, §959]

e. **Restrictions on public employment, licensed professions, and other public benefits:** [§979] Federal and state government may prohibit certain types of persons (*e.g.*, the disloyal or dishonest) from being public employees, lawyers, government contractors, or the like. To this end, it may (i) impose certain ***standards*** concerning past or future conduct, and require ***oaths*** in respect thereto; and (ii) require certain ***disclosures*** concerning past or present conduct.

(1) **Standards of conduct and loyalty oaths**

(a) **Support of the Constitution:** [§980] Government ***may*** require an oath from public employees and lawyers to "support the Constitution of the United States" and the state constitution. This type of oath does not relate to political beliefs or protected First Amendment rights. [Connell v. Higginbotham, 403 U.S. 207 (1971); Law Students Civil Rights Research Council v. Wadmond, 401 U.S. 154 (1971)]

(b) **Vagueness:** [§981] Neither standards of conduct requirements, nor loyalty oaths with respect thereto, may be vague. When First Amendment rights may be affected, precision is required because of the potential "chilling effect." (*See supra*, §739.)

1) **Example:** A loyalty oath for public employees that they "promote respect for the flag and . . . reverence for law and order" is void for vagueness, since a refusal to salute the flag on religious grounds might be found in breach thereof. [Baggett v. Bullitt, 377 U.S. 360 (1964)]

2) **Example:** A statute providing for removal of public school teachers for "treasonable or seditious" utterances or acts is void for vagueness; "it would be a bold teacher who would not stay as far as possible from utterances or acts which might jeopardize his living." [Keyishian v. Board of Regents, 385 U.S. 589 (1967)]

3) **Compare—valid oath:** An oath required of all state employees "to ***oppose the overthrow*** of the government . . . by ***force, violence or*** by an ***illegal*** or unconstitutional method" has been upheld. The Court read this oath as akin to those requiring the taker simply to "support" the Constitution, *i.e.*, "to commit themselves to live by the constitutional processes of our system." Moreover, the oath provided fair notice, because its violation could be punished only by a prosecution for perjury (which required proof of knowing falsity). [Cole v. Richardson, 405 U.S. 676 (1972)]

(c) **Substantive content:** [§982] As a ***general rule***, government may not restrict public employment, licensed professions, or other public benefits for specific speech or association unless the speech or association is ***not*** constitutionally protected and ***could be made criminal***. [Bond v. Floyd, 385 U.S. 116 (1966)—state legislature could not exclude duly elected legislator for expressing unpopular political views] Nor may government require loyalty oaths that public employees or licensees will not engage in such types of speech or association. [Elfbrandt v. Russell, *supra*, §965] *Examples:*

1) **Government employees**

a) **Membership in groups:** [§983] Public employment cannot be denied to persons who are simply ***members*** of the Communist Party, or who refuse to take an oath that they are not ***members*** of a "communist front or subversive organization." Such regulations are "overbroad" because only "knowing" membership with "specific intent to further unlawful aims" is not constitutionally protected. [Keyishian v. Board of Regents, *supra*; Wieman v. Updegraff, 344 U.S. 183 (1955)]

b) **Compulsory unionism:** [§984] A government employee cannot be compelled (*e.g.*, by threat of loss of employment) to pay union dues that go to support political or ideological ideas and beliefs with which the employee disagrees.

1/ **Exclusive bargaining agent:** [§985] But if a majority of government employees in an appropriate bargaining unit elect an exclusive representative, the public employer may negotiate exclusively with that representative on matters of collective bargaining, contract administration, and adjustment of grievances. And nonunion members of the bargaining unit may be required to pay the representative union a service fee for reasonable expenses connected with labor-management issues—*e.g.*, cost of union's national convention. *Rationale:* This is justified by the important contribution to peaceful labor relations made by exclusive bargaining agents. [Abood v. Detroit Board of Education, *supra*, §726; Ellis v. Brotherhood of Railway, Airline & Steamship Clerks, 466 U.S. 435 (1984)]

2/ **Procedural safeguards:** [§986] Since nonunion employees' First Amendment rights of freedom of speech and association are at stake, procedural safeguards are necessary to assure that the service fee is not excessive—*i.e.*, that the employees' funds will not be used for political or ideological activities unrelated to collective bargaining. Thus, although the employee may have the burden of objecting, the union must provide an adequate explanation of the propriety of the fee and has the burden of proving that it was not excessive. Furthermore, the procedure must provide for a reasonably prompt decision by an impartial decisionmaker and an escrow for the amount reasonably in dispute while a challenge is pending. [Chicago Teachers Union v. Hudson, 475 U.S. 292 (1986)]

2) **Integrated bar:** [§987] Compulsory state bar membership presents issues similar to compulsory unionism. Lawyers may be required to pay state bar dues for reasonable costs connected with improving legal services and regulating the legal profession (*e.g.*, disciplining lawyers). However, mandatory dues may not be used for political or ideological activities (*e.g.*, endorsing a gun control or nuclear freeze initiative). [Keller v. State Bar of California, 496 U.S. 1 (1990)]

c) **"Patronage":** [§988] The First Amendment forbids the hiring, promotion, transfer, firing, or recall of a public employee because of political party affiliation unless the hiring authority demonstrates that party affiliation is an appropriate requirement for the effective performance of the public office involved, *e.g.*, "policymaking" or "confidential" nature of work. [Rutan v. Republican Party of Illinois, 497 U.S. 62 (1990); Branti v. Finkel, 445 U.S. 507 (1980); Elrod v. Burns, 427 U.S. 347 (1976)]

1/ **Example:** Supervision of a state's election laws may be based on party affiliation if the state requires such supervision by persons of different political parties.

2/ **Example:** Appointees of a governor who are used to write speeches, explain views to the press, or communicate to the legislature may properly be required to share the political beliefs and party commitments of the governor.

3/ **Compare:** However, continued employment of an assistant public defender cannot be properly conditioned upon allegiance to the political party in control of the county government, since whatever policymaking occurs in a public defender's office must relate to the needs of its clients, not to partisan political interests. [Branti v. Finkel, *supra*]

d) **Expression of views:** [§989] Public employment cannot be denied for speech on a "matter of public concern." Thus, in *Pickering v. Board of Education*, 391 U.S. 563 (1968), a teacher was dismissed for publishing a letter falsely criticizing board of education proposals to raise revenue for schools. The Court held that, in the absence of knowing falsity (*see supra*, §§757-767), the teacher could not be dismissed for this exercise of First Amendment rights on a "matter of public concern" (in contrast to mere discussion complaining about employment conditions).

e) **When public employment may be denied:** [§990] The *Pickering* case did ***not*** involve: a situation where the need for confidentiality was great; criticism of a close superior that might undermine the working relationship; harmful and false criticism related to daily school operations where the teacher presumably had greater access to the facts, thus making it difficult for others to counter them; criticism that impeded the teacher's performance of daily classroom duties or that interfered with daily school operation; or statements that were so without foundation as to call into question the teacher's fitness. If these factors are present, the Court will ***balance*** the public employee's First Amendment rights against the government's significant interest as an employer in efficient performance of public service. [Connick v. Myers, 461 U.S. 138 (1983)]

1/ **Procedural requirements:** The public employer must conduct a ***reasonable*** investigation to determine whether the employee's speech was on a "matter of public concern" or, if it was, whether it was outweighed by the government's interest in accomplishing its mission as an employer. [Waters v. Churchill, 114 S. Ct. ____ (1994)]

2/ **Note:** A statute denying ***all*** employment in a defense facility to ***any*** member of a "communist-action organization" was held invalid. The statute was "overbroad" in two ways: (i) it applied to members who might be ***unaware*** of the organization's aims or who were without ***specific intent to*** further those aims; and (ii) it applied even to ***nonsensitive*** positions in defense facilities. [United States v. Robel, 389 U.S. 258 (1967)] There is thus the ***possible suggestion*** that, if a ***sensitive*** position were involved, the government's strong interest in national security might permit denial of employment to a knowing member who had no specific intent—even though such membership could not be criminally punished.

f) **Political activities:** [§991] Government may place ***some*** limits on a public employee's right to engage in political activities. In contrast to the regulation of ***specific*** kinds of speech and association (*see infra*, §§995 *et seq.*), the Court has upheld the Hatch Act provision barring federal executive employees from all "partisan political activity" in respect to "political management" and "political campaigning," ***irrespective of political party*** (*i.e.*, "in an evenhanded and neutral manner"). [Broadrick v. Oklahoma, *supra*, §739] While such activity clearly could not be made criminal, it could be made a condition of federal employment because of the overriding government interest in ***efficient, nonpartisan*** employees and in protecting employees from being forced to work for the election of their superiors.

2) **State university students:** [§992] A student may not be expelled from a public university for "indecent" speech, as long as it was not constitutionally obscene (*see supra*, §§781 *et seq.*) or otherwise unprotected. [Papish v. Board of Curators, 410 U.S. 667 (1973)]

3) **Ballot position:** [§993] A political party may not be denied a place on the ballot for refusing to take a loyalty oath that it does not advocate violent overthrow of the government as an ***abstract doctrine*** (*see supra*, §983). [Communist Party of Indiana v. Whitcomb, *supra*, §753]

4) **Procedural rules:** [§994] When the complainant shows that her speech or association was constitutionally protected and that it was a "substantial factor" in her being denied the benefit in question, the denial may still be upheld if the government shows by a preponderance of the evidence that it would have taken the same action regardless of the protected conduct. [Mt. Healthy Board of Education v. Doyle, 429 U.S. 274 (1977)]

(2) **Disclosure:** [§995] As mentioned previously (*see supra*, §§966, 968), government requirements that disclosure be made of beliefs or associational memberships present issues under both the First Amendment freedom of association and the Fifth Amendment privilege against self-incrimination.

(a) **Freedom of association:** [§996] Government may require disclosure of ***certain*** past or present organizational affiliations that are relevant to loyalty, fitness, and suitability for the position of public employees, lawyers, and recipients of other public benefits. [Garner v. Los Angeles Board of Public Works, 341 U.S. 716 (1951)]

1) **Overbroad inquiries:** [§997] But requiring disclosure of First Amendment activities may have a "chilling effect" (*see supra*, §739). Persons may be deterred from engaging in constitutionally protected activity for fear of displeasing those who control their professional livelihood, or for fear of public disclosure and consequent social obloquy. Thus, such inquiries—even though relevant to a proper state interest—may not be "overbroad." [Shelton v. Tucker, 364 U.S. 479 (1960)—state cannot force every teacher to disclose ***every*** organizational membership; state has "less drastic means" available to achieve its purpose]

2) **Obstructing investigation:** [§998] Government may deny public employment, bar membership, or other public benefits for obstructing a proper investigation by ***refusing to answer relevant inquiries***—even though the required disclosures touch on First Amendment activities. [Konigsberg v. State Bar, 366 U.S. 36 (1961); *In re* Anastaplo, 366 U.S. 82 (1961)—bar admission denied for refusal to answer questions on First Amendment grounds regarding Communist Party membership, even

though such membership (absent knowledge and specific intent) could not be made a substantive ground for denial of bar admission]

a) **Impermissible questions:** [§999] More recent decisions appear to have qualified *Konigsberg* and *Anastaplo* (at least as to their facts). The Court has held that the First Amendment forbids a state to require bar applicants (or public employees) to disclose (i) whether they were ***merely members*** in organizations that advocate violent or forceful overthrow of the government, or (ii) whether they ***merely believe*** in such action. Although there was no majority opinion, the decisions appear to hold that such inquiry must be confined to ***knowing*** membership, and that a state may not act against any person "merely because of his beliefs." (In these cases, the record was "wholly barren" of evidence that the applicants were not "morally and professionally fit" to become members of the bar.) [Baird v. State Bar, 401 U.S. 1 (1971); *In re* Stolar, 401 U.S. 23 (1971)]

b) **Permissible questions:** [§1000] At the same time, the Court has made clear that a state may require bar applicants (and public employees) to disclose (i) whether they had ever organized or become a member of a group with ***knowledge*** that the group advocated or taught violent or unlawful overthrow of the government, ***and*** (ii) whether they had the ***specific intent*** to further such aims of the group. *Rationale:* Dividing the questions in this way is permissible because it "narrows the class of applicants as to whom the Committee is likely to find further investigation appropriate." [Law Students Civil Rights Research Council v. Wadmond, *supra*, §980]

1/ **Effect:** While ***both*** knowledge and specific intent are clearly necessary to deny bar admission (or public employment), ***refusal to disclose either*** may be proper grounds for denial.

(b) **Privilege against self-incrimination**

1) **Claim of privilege as basis for disqualification:** [§1001] Denial of public employment, bar membership, or other public benefits simply because an individual refuses to answer questions on a claim of the privilege against self-incrimination violates the Fifth Amendment. [Spevack v. Klein, 385 U.S. 511 (1967)] For further discussion, *see* the Evidence Summary.

12. **Freedom of Press—Special Problems:** [§1002] As a general matter, the press's First Amendment rights are no greater than the First Amendment freedom of speech afforded to other members of the public.

a. **"News reporter's privilege":** [§1003] Thus, freedom of the press does not afford reporters a privilege to refuse to answer relevant and material questions asked during a ***good faith*** grand jury investigation. In such proceedings, the reporters may be forced to disclose their sources and other information within their possession. However, "official harassment of the press undertaken not for purpose of law enforcement but to disrupt a reporter's relationship with news sources would have no justification." [Branzburg v. Hayes, 408 U.S. 665 (1972)]

b. **Access to government information:** [§1004] The First Amendment guarantees neither the public nor the press access to prisoners or prisons (or to other information controlled by government). [Houchins v. KQED, 438 U.S. 1 (1978)—no majority opinion] Thus, prison rules that forbid interviews with inmates designated by media members do not violate freedom of the press. [Pell v. Procunier, *supra*, §946] But if the government voluntarily grants such access, then the public and the press must be treated equally. And where limitations that might be reasonable as to individual members of the public would impede effective reporting (*e.g.*, prohibition on cameras), such limitations may not—consistent with reasonable prison rules—be used to hamper effective media presentation of what is seen by individual visitors. [Houchins v. KQED, *supra*]

(1) **Access to criminal proceedings:** [§1005] The press may be excluded from some kinds of pretrial hearings (such as a hearing to suppress illegally seized evidence) if there are no reasonable alternatives to protect the defendant's right to a fair trial (which could be jeopardized if the press were present at the pretrial hearings and reported prejudicial evidence that would be inadmissible at the subsequent criminal trial). [Gannett Co. v. DePasquale, 443 U.S. 368 (1979)] However, the First Amendment guarantees the public ***and*** press a right to attend criminal (and ***probably*** civil) trials. But the right may be outweighed by a compelling and narrowly tailored interest articulated in findings by the trial judge. [Richmond Newspapers, Inc. v. Virginia, 448 U.S. 555 (1980)—no majority opinion]

(a) **Example:** A state may not ***automatically*** exclude the press and public during the testimony of a minor victim in a sex-offense prosecution. Rather, there must be particularized, case-by-case determinations. [Globe Newspaper Co. v. Superior Court, 457 U.S. 596 (1982)]

(b) **Preliminary hearings:** [§1006] The First Amendment right extends to elaborate preliminary hearings (which resemble an actual criminal trial) to determine whether probable cause exists to bring the defendant to trial. Such hearings often lead to guilty pleas and may be the sole occasion for public observation of the criminal justice system. [Press-Enterprise Co. v. Superior Court, 478 U.S. 1 (1986)]

(c) **Voir dire:** [§1007] The First Amendment right also extends to the voir dire examination of potential jurors. [Press-Enterprise Co. v. Superior Court, 464 U.S. 501 (1984)—one method for trial judge to protect privacy interests of prospective jurors is to inform them that they may request questioning in camera]

(d) **Defendant's right to public trial:** The Sixth Amendment right of the defendant is discussed *infra*, §§1154 *et seq.*

(2) **Publication of truthful information:** [§1008] Publication of truthful information, which has been ***lawfully obtained*** by the media, concerning a matter of public significance may be prohibited only by a sanction that is "narrowly tailored" to further a state interest of the highest order. [Smith v. Daily Mail Publishing Co., 443 U.S. 97 (1979)—making it a crime to publish name of juvenile delinquent was held invalid; Landmark Communications, Inc. v. Virginia, *supra*, §916—making it a crime to publish information lawfully obtained regarding confidential state proceedings was held invalid; Cox Broadcasting Co. v. Cohn, *supra*, §69—awarding damages for publishing name of rape victim obtained in official court records open to public inspection also held invalid; Florida Star v. B.J.F., 491 U.S. 524 (1989)—same result when name was obtained from police report that inadvertently included full name of rape victim]

(a) **Compare—publication of private performance:** [§1009] However, the First Amendment does not immunize the media from an action for damages when a performer's entire act (for which compensation is usually paid) is published or broadcast without the performer's consent. This is the functional equivalent of broadcasting copyrighted material or a sporting event. [Zacchini v. Scripps-Howard Broadcasting Co., 433 U.S. 562 (1977)—human cannonball act filmed]

(b) **Compare—breach of promise of confidentiality:** [§1010] Similarly, the First Amendment does not immunize the media from a generally applicable law that provides for an award of damages against persons who breach a promise of confidentiality given in exchange for information. [Cohen v. Cowles Media Co., 501 U.S. 663 (1991)—any restriction placed on newspaper's ability to publish truthful information was self-imposed by newspaper's promise of confidentiality]

c. **Search of newspaper office:** [§1011] If there is reason to believe that there is evidence of a crime on the premises of a newspaper, the First Amendment does not forbid the issuance of a search warrant. However, courts must apply the warrant requirements—reasonableness, probable cause, and specificity with respect to the place to be searched and things to be seized—with "particular exactitude" to protect First Amendment interests. [Zurcher v. Stanford Daily, 436 U.S. 547 (1978)]

d. **Broadcasting:** [§1012] Although radio and television broadcasting fall within the ambit of the First Amendment [Los Angeles v. Preferred Communications, Inc., 476 U.S. 488 (1986)], they may be more closely regulated than the press. *Rationale:* Due to the limited number of frequencies available, broadcasters have a special privilege, and consequently, a special responsibility to give suitable time to matters of public interest and to present a suitable range of programs. The paramount right is the ***right of viewers and listeners*** to receive information of public concern, rather than the right of broadcasters to broadcast what they please. [Red Lion Broadcasting Co. v. FCC, 395 U.S. 367 (1969)]

(1) **Right to reply:** [§1013] Accordingly, the Court has upheld FCC orders, under a statutory "fairness doctrine," requiring a radio station to offer ***free*** broadcasting time (i) to ***opponents*** of political candidates or views endorsed by the station; and (ii) to any person who has been ***personally attacked*** in the course of a broadcast, for reply to the attack. [Red Lion Broadcasting Co. v. FCC, *supra*] And under a statutory right of access, the FCC may require licensed broadcasters to sell reasonable amounts of time to legally qualified candidates for federal office. [CBS v. FCC, 453 U.S. 367 (1981)]

(a) **Compare—newspapers:** But a statute requiring a ***newspaper*** to print a reply to its editorials by political candidates criticized in such editorials violates the First Amendment. The government ***cannot*** dictate decisions respecting the content and size of newspapers or require them to disseminate messages with which they disagree. [Miami Herald Publishing Co. v. Tornillo, 418 U.S. 241 (1974)]

(b) **Compare—billing envelopes:** Similarly, privately owned utilities may not be required to insert in their billing envelopes speech of third parties with which they disagree. To require them to do so is not "content neutral," and it forces the utility to associate with the views of others; furthermore, it might deter the utility from stating its own views (for fear of an adverse response from the third party) thereby reducing the flow of information to the public. [Pacific Gas & Electric Co. v. Public Utilities Commission, 475 U.S. 1 (1986)]

(2) **Political campaign advertising:** [§1014] The First Amendment does ***not*** require broadcasters to accept political advertisements. Congress and the FCC, in seeking to assure balanced coverage of public issues, could appropriately conclude that licensed broadcasters subject to the "fairness doctrine" should generally determine what should be broadcast, rather than having affluent persons monopolize air time. [CBS, Inc. v. Democratic National Committee, 412 U.S. 94 (1973)]

(3) **Editorializing by noncommercial broadcasters:** [§1015] But the First Amendment is violated by a congressional ban on editorials by noncommercial educational broadcasters. (And the government may not impose such a ban on those broadcasters who receive government subsidies.) The expression of editorial opinion on controversial issues of public importance lies at the heart of the First Amendment. The public's interest in receiving a "reasonably balanced and fair presentation of controversial issues" may be insured by the "fairness doctrine." [FCC v. League of Women Voters, 468 U.S. 364 (1984)]

(4) **Common ownership:** [§1016] Similarly, to promote the diversity of information received by the public, the FCC may forbid ownership of a

radio or television station by a daily newspaper located in the same community. [FCC v. National Citizens Committee for Broadcasting, 436 U.S. 775 (1978)]

(5) **Indecent speech:** [§1017] Because a broadcast has the ability to invade the privacy of the home, the First Amendment does not forbid imposing civil sanctions on a broadcaster for airing a full monologue (in contrast to isolated use of a few words) of "patently offensive sexual and excretory speech" even though the speech is not obscene—at least during those times when children are likely to be listening. [FCC v. Pacifica Foundation, 438 U.S. 726 (1978); *compare supra*, §786]

e. **Taxation:** [§1018] The First Amendment does not prohibit application to the press of regulations and taxes of general applicability. But a special tax that applies only to the press (or that targets only some types of publications) can operate to censor criticism of government and is invalid unless necessary to a compelling interest. Furthermore, in this area (*compare supra*, §§329-333), the Court will ***not*** examine the state's whole tax structure to determine whether the special tax is just a substitute for another tax that applies generally except to the press. [Minneapolis Star & Tribune Co. v. Minnesota Commissioner of Revenue, 460 U.S. 575 (1983); Arkansas Writers' Project v. Ragland, 481 U.S. 221 (1987)]

(1) **Intermedia discrimination:** A tax of general applicability may impose different burdens on certain segments of the media as long as the discrimination (i) is not content-based, and (ii) is not structured or intended to suppress particular ideas. [Leathers v. Medlock, 499 U.S. 439 (1991)—general sales tax that exempted all media except cable TV upheld]

(a) **Regulation:** A similar rule governs regulations that apply to one medium (or a subset thereof) but not to others. [Turner Broadcasting System v. FCC, *supra*, §738—regulation of cable television justified by "special characteristics" of that medium]

f. **Cable television:** [§1019] Because of technological differences between broadcasting and cable transmission, there is no practical limitation on the number of cable channels. Thus, the relaxed standard of First Amendment scrutiny applicable to broadcasting is inapplicable to cable. [Turner Broadcasting System v. FCC, *supra*]

(1) **Different from newspapers:** [§1020] The physical connection to the viewer's television set gives cable operators special power over what the viewer sees. This distinguishes cable from newspapers, which cannot prevent access to competing newspapers. Thus, the same strict First Amendment scrutiny does not apply to cable. [Turner Broadcasting System v. FCC, *supra*]

G. FREEDOM OF RELIGION

1. **Constitutional Provisions:** [§1021] The principal provisions of the Constitution that deal with the subject of freedom of religion are the "religion clauses" of the First Amendment, which provide: "Congress shall make no law respecting an

establishment of religion, or prohibiting the *free exercise* thereof." (In addition, Article VI provides that "no religious test shall ever be required as a qualification to any office or public trust under the United States.")

2. **Application to States:** [§1022] Both the Establishment Clause and the Free Exercise Clause of the First Amendment protect fundamental personal liberties and apply to the states under the Fourteenth Amendment. [Everson v. Board of Education, *supra*, §49; Cantwell v. Connecticut, 310 U.S. 296 (1940)]

3. **Scope of Establishment Clause:** [§1023] The Establishment Clause does more than forbid a state church or a state religion—but it does not forbid every action by government that results in benefit to religion. The goal is a "benevolent neutrality" by government in respect to religion. [Walz v. Tax Commission, 397 U.S. 664 (1970)]

   a. **Main concerns of Establishment Clause:** [§1024] As a general matter, the Establishment Clause bars government sponsorship of religion, government financial support of religion, and active involvement of government in religious activities. [Walz v. Tax Commission, *supra*]

      (1) **Preference:** [§1025] The Establishment Clause also bars official preference of one religious denomination over another. Any law that grants a denominational preference is subject to strict scrutiny. [Larson v. Valente, 456 U.S. 228 (1982)]

         (a) **Example—advantage:** A state law that creates a special school district for the purpose of enabling one religious group to provide state-funded education for its handicapped children violates the Establishment Clause. [Board of Education of Kiryas Joel Village School District v. Grumet, 114 S. Ct. _____ (1994)]

         (b) **Example—disadvantage:** A state law that imposes registration requirements only on those religious organizations that get more than half their funds from nonmembers is not "closely fitted" to a "compelling government interest." [Larson v. Valente, *supra*]

   b. **Three-pronged "test":** [§1026] To be valid under the Establishment Clause, a statute (or other governmental action) must:

      (i) Have a ***secular purpose***;

      (ii) Have a principal or primary ***effect that neither advances nor inhibits*** religion; and

      (iii) ***Not foster excessive government entanglement*** with religion.

      [Lemon v. Kurtzman, 403 U.S. 602 (1971)] But, as the difficulty of reconciling a number of the cases discussed below will reveal, "the test is inescapably one of degree." [Walz v. Tax Commission, *supra*]

   c. **Aid to parochial school students:** [§1027] Some government programs providing assistance to ***all*** elementary and secondary school students—including those attending parochial schools—have been held to satisfy the three-pronged "test," above, and thus do not violate the Establishment Clause.

(1) **Transportation:** [§1028] The government may reimburse bus fares to and from school of all students, including those attending parochial schools. The purpose and effect is secular—protecting children from traffic hazards. [Everson v. Board of Education, *supra*]

(a) **Compare—field trips:** [§1029] But government payment of field trip transportation is invalid, since the parochial schools control the timing of such trips and the teachers play an integral part in making such educational experiences meaningful. [Wolman v. Walter, 433 U.S. 229 (1977)]

(2) **Textbooks:** [§1030] The government may lend state-approved secular textbooks to all students, including those attending parochial schools. The purpose and effect is to improve secular education. [Board of Education v. Allen, 392 U.S. 236 (1968)]

(a) **Compare—other instructional materials:** [§1031] But lending students instructional materials and equipment (maps, films, lab equipment, etc.) for use in parochial schools is invalid. The primary effect is to advance religion, because of the impossibility of separating their use in secular vs. religious education. [Wolman v. Walter, *supra*—refusing to extend to such materials the Allen case's "unique" presumption that since the textbooks were used in public schools there is assurance that they will not be used for religious purposes in parochial schools]

(3) **Health services:** [§1032] Public health services are religiously neutral and may be provided by government to all students, including those attending parochial schools. [Lemon v. Kurtzman, *supra,* §1026—also stating that a school lunch program is valid]

(a) **Diagnostic services:** [§1033] Similarly, nonparochial school personnel may provide diagnostic speech, hearing, and psychological services to students on the premises of the parochial school. [Wolman v. Walter, *supra*]

(b) **Sign-language interpreter:** [§1034] Government may provide all deaf students with sign-language interpreters, including those students attending parochial schools. The interpreters neither add to nor subtract from the religious environment of parochial schools. [Zobrest v. Catalina Foothills School District, 113 S. Ct. 2462 (1993)]

(4) **Remedial, guidance, and therapeutic services:** [§1035] A government program for "auxiliary services" to parochial school students—with public school personnel providing such things as remedial reading, accelerated instruction, guidance counseling, etc.—is valid if done ***outside*** the parochial school. [Wolman v. Walter, *supra*]

(a) **Compare—on premises:** [§1036] But this type of government program is invalid if done ***within*** the parochial school. The continuing surveillance needed to ensure that the public school personnel remained religiously neutral (and thus avoid a primary effect that advances religion) would produce "excessive government entanglement with religion." [Meek v. Pittenger, 421 U.S. 349 (1975); Grand Rapids School District v. Ball, 473 U.S. 373 (1985); Aguilar v. Felton, 473 U.S. 402 (1985)]

(5) **Tuition grants and tax credits:** [§1037] Government reimbursement to parents whose children attend nonpublic (and predominantly parochial) schools of a percentage of the tuition paid—or the state's giving tax deductions or tax credits for the tuition of such parents—***violates*** the Establishment Clause. Despite a secular purpose, the effect was to advance religion in the schools—since there was no limitation on the purpose for which the funds might be used. [Committee for Public Education v. Nyquist, 413 U.S. 756 (1973)]

(a) **Deductions for all parents:** [§1038] But the Court has upheld a state income tax deduction to ***all*** taxpayers for expenses of tuition, transportation, textbooks, instructional materials, and other school supplies in public ***and*** nonpublic schools. The purpose and primary effect of this "facially neutral" law are secular—despite the fact that the great bulk of deductions may be taken only by parents of children in parochial schools. [Mueller v. Allen, 463 U.S. 388 (1983)]

(b) **General assistance:** [§1039] Similarly, five Justices have stated that any governmental educational assistance to a neutrally defined class (*e.g.*, vouchers to ***all*** students that may be used in public and nonpublic schools) is valid. Any aid to religion results from individual choices. [Witters v. Washington Department of Services for the Blind, 474 U.S. 481 (1986)]

d. **Direct aid to church-related institutions:** [§1040] Some government programs that provide assistance to institutions irrespective of their religious affiliation have been held to satisfy the three-pronged "test" and thus do not violate the Establishment Clause.

(1) **Hospitals:** [§1041] Federal grants to church-related hospitals for construction of new wards and care of indigent patients have a secular purpose and effect and are therefore valid. [Bradfield v. Roberts, 175 U.S. 291 (1899)]

(2) **Colleges and universities:** [§1042] Government grants (or tax benefits) for construction of buildings to be used exclusively for secular education at church-related colleges have been upheld. [Tilton v. Richardson, 403 U.S. 672 (1971); Roemer v. Board of Public Works, 426 U.S. 736 (1976)] The program's "purpose" and "effect" were secular (expanding facilities for secular education). Furthermore, since the ***record did not show*** that the secular education provided by the recipient colleges was "permeated with religion," there was no need for intensive government surveillance, and therefore there was no "excessive government entanglement with religion."

(a) **But note:** There must be assurance of a secular purpose and effect. Thus, in *Tilton v. Richardson, supra*, the Court invalidated a provision limiting the prohibition against religious use of buildings to 20 years, reasoning that the buildings would still have value at that point and their use at that time for religious purposes would have the effect of advancing religion.

(3) **Counseling agencies:** [§1043] Similarly, government funds to religious organizations along with other public and private agencies to counsel against adolescent sexual relations and to care for teenage pregnancies have been upheld. There was a secular purpose (dealing with problems of teenage pregnancy) and the record ***did not show***: (i) that a significant percentage of the funds would be granted to "pervasively sectarian" institutions; or (ii) that the religiously affiliated grantees could not perform their functions in a secular manner without intensive government surveillance. [Bowen v. Kendrick, 487 U.S. 589 (1988)]

(4) **Elementary and secondary schools:** [§1044] Most government programs providing assistance directly to parochial schools have been held ***invalid***—most often because they have been found to involve "excessive government entanglement with religion."

(a) **Teacher salaries:** [§1045] Grants for salaries of teachers of secular subjects have been held invalid. Even though they may have a "secular legislative purpose," the state's efforts to assure a "principal or primary effect that neither advances nor inhibits religion" run afoul of the third criterion—"excessive government entanglement." [Lemon v. Kurtzman, *supra*, §1026]

1) **Rationale:** Unlike church-related colleges, elementary and secondary parochial school education involves substantial religious indoctrination—thus risking government support of religion, and requiring continuing surveillance of the schools' teachers and records (to ensure that teachers paid with public funds do not teach religion, and to determine how much of the schools' expenditures are religious rather than secular). Thus, while some state contact with the church-related institution may be required to assure a secular purpose and effect, excessive state involvement will invalidate the program.

2) **Political divisiveness:** The Court has also considered this to be an aspect of the "excessive government entanglement" criterion. Thus, unlike grants to colleges where most of the recipients are not church-related institutions, the teacher salary statutes involved annual appropriations primarily benefiting religious groups—so that "political fragmentation and divisiveness on religious lines was likely to be intensified." [Committee for Public Education v. Nyquist, *supra*]

(b) **Maintenance and repair:** [§1046] Grants for maintaining school facilities have been held invalid. Despite a secular purpose, since there was no limitation on the facilities for which the funds might be used, the aid might have a "primary effect that advanced religion." [Committee for Public Education v. Nyquist, *supra*]

(c) **Instructional materials:** [§1047] Lending instructional materials to parochial schools (along with all nonpublic schools) has been held invalid. The primary effect is to advance religion, since it is impossible to separate secular educational functions from the predominantly religious role performed by the schools. [Meek v. Pittenger, *supra,* §1036]

(d) **Testing:** [§1048] Reimbursing parochial schools for costs of administering teacher-prepared tests (although the testing is required by state law) has been held invalid because such testing is an integral part of the teaching process, and there is no way of assuring that such tests are kept entirely free of religious instruction. [Levitt v. Committee for Public Education, 413 U.S. 472 (1973)]

1) **Compare:** But the government may supply parochial schools with achievement tests used in public schools, as long as the tests are not prepared or scored by parochial school personnel (*i.e.*, parochial school personnel do not control the content or results). And the government may reimburse the parochial school for the administration and grading of such tests even if the tests are graded by parochial school personnel—as long as objective standards are used and there are ample safeguards, easily applicable, to assure that reimbursement covers only secular services without excessive government entanglement. [Committee for Public Education v. Regan, 444 U.S. 646 (1980)]

(e) **Recordkeeping:** [§1049] Reimbursing parochial schools for recordkeeping required by state law is also permissible—if there is a "straightforward" audit procedure to assure that only costs of secular services are covered without excessive government entanglement. [Committee for Public Education v. Regan, *supra*]

(f) **Other general government benefits**: [§1050] The Court has also said that general benefits—such as police protection, fire protection, or general municipal services (*e.g.*, sewage, garbage, etc.)—may also be afforded to church-related institutions. [Everson v. Board of Education, *supra*, §1022]

e. **Tax exemption for religious property:** [§1051] An exemption from property taxation for "real or personal property used exclusively for religious, educational or charitable purposes" does not violate the Establishment Clause. Neither the purpose nor the effect is the advancement or the inhibition of religion; and it constitutes neither personal sponsorship of, nor hostility to, religion. Not to grant the exemption would ***increase*** church-state entanglement on such issues as valuation of the property, tax liens, etc. Moreover, the exemption "does not transfer . . . revenue to churches"; rather, government "simply abstains from demanding that the church support the state." Finally, the "unbroken practice of according this exemption to churches [cannot] be lightly cast aside." [Walz v. Tax Commission, *supra*, §1026]

(1) **Preference:** [§1052] However, a tax exemption that is ***limited*** to religious organizations is too narrow and violates the Establishment Clause. [Texas Monthly, Inc. v. Bullock, 489 U.S. 1 (1989)]

f. **Use of public facilities:** [§1053] The state's permitting groups to use facilities generally open to the public for "religious worship and discussion" does ***not*** violate the Establishment Clause because: (i) there is a ***secular purpose*** in providing a public forum for the exchange of ideas; (ii) if nonreligious groups also use the public forum, the benefit to religion would be ***"incidental,"*** with no ***primary*** effect of advancing religion; and (iii) there would be greater ***entanglement*** of government and religion if the state sought to exclude "religious" groups. [Widmar v. Vincent, *supra*, §876]

g. **Religion and public schools:** [§1054] A number of public school practices conducted on ***premises*** as part of the school's program, whose purpose and effect is to ***aid religion***, have been held to violate the Establishment Clause.

(1) **Prayers and Bible-reading:** [§1055] The government may not prescribe any particular form of prayer to be used in schools (or other government-sponsored activities). [Engel v. Vitale, 370 U.S. 421 (1962)—invalidating state rule requiring the following prayer composed by a government agency be said aloud in public school classes each day: "Almighty God, we acknowledge our dependence on Thee, and we beg Thy blessings upon us, our parents, our teachers, and our country"] Similarly, reading from the Bible and recitation by students of the Lord's Prayer at the beginning of the school day were found to be "religious" practices and thus invalid. [Abington School District v. Schempp, 374 U.S. 203 (1963)]

(a) **Coercion:** [§1056] The fact that such programs are "voluntary"—*i.e.*, that children not wishing to participate are excused—does not save them. "The Establishment Clause, unlike the Free Exercise Clause, does not depend upon any showing of direct governmental compulsion, and is violated by the enactment of laws which establish an official religion, whether those laws operate directly to coerce nonobserving individuals or not." [Engel v. Vitale, *supra*]

(2) **Silent prayer:** [§1057] A law setting aside a time of silence in public schools for "meditation or voluntary prayer" violates the Establishment Clause when its ***sole purpose*** (as evidenced by its text and legislative history) is to endorse a religious exercise, and it thus has ***no secular*** purpose. [Wallace v. Jaffree, 472 U.S. 38 (1985)]

(3) **Anti-evolution laws:** [§1058] Laws prohibiting the teaching of Darwinian evolution in public schools have been held invalid. The statute's purpose was found to be religious—to placate fundamentalist sectarian convictions concerning the origins of humanity. The statute was not religiously "neutral," since it did not forbid discussion of all theories on the origin of humanity but merely evolution. [Epperson v. Arkansas, 393 U.S. 97 (1968)]

(a) **"Creation-science" laws:** [§1059] Similarly, a law requiring that the scientific evidence supporting the theory of creation be taught whenever evolution is taught has been held invalid. The statute had "no clear secular purpose"; rather, its primary purpose was found to be "to provide persuasive advantage to a particular religious doctrine that rejects the factual basis of evolution." [Edwards v. Aguillard, 482 U.S. 578 (1987)]

(4) **Released time—on premises:** [§1060] Programs in which regular classes end an hour early one day a week and religious instruction is given ***in public school classrooms*** to those students who so request (other students remaining in study halls, etc.) are invalid. They constitute a "utilization of the tax-established and tax-supported public school system to aid religious groups to spread their faith." [McCollum v. Board of Education, 333 U.S. 203 (1948)]

(5) **Posting the Ten Commandments:** [§1061] Displaying the Ten Commandments on the walls of public school classrooms plainly serves a religious purpose and is invalid despite the legislature's statement that it was for a secular purpose. [Stone v. Graham, 449 U.S. 39 (1980)]

(a) **Free Exercise Clause issues:** [§1062] In respect to the public school religious practices held invalid, *supra*, no Free Exercise Clause considerations call for a contrary result (*i.e.*, there is no right under the Free Exercise Clause to have religious exercise or instruction in the public schools—no religion demands it, and the Establishment Clause forbids it). [Abington School District v. Schempp, *supra*]

(6) **Academic study of religion or the Bible:** [§1063] Academic study of religion or the Bible in the public schools does ***not*** violate the Establishment Clause—since the purpose and effect is secular (*i.e.*, to educate children about their importance, not to indoctrinate in religious tenets). [Abington School District v. Schempp, *supra*]

(7) **History and patriotism:** [§1064] Recitation in public schools of religious references in historic documents (*e.g.*, Declaration of Independence), the flag salute, or the national anthem probably does ***not*** violate the Establishment Clause—the purpose and effect being secular (patriotic) rather than religious. [Engel v. Vitale, *supra*]

(8) **Equal access to facilities:** [§1065] Permitting student religious groups in secondary schools, as well as other noncurriculum-related student groups, to meet for religious purposes (including prayer) on school premises during noninstructional time does ***not*** violate the Establishment Clause. In granting equal access to ***both*** secular and religious speech, the school does not endorse religion nor will secondary school students understand it to do so. [Board of Education v. Mergens, 496 U.S. 226 (1990)]

h. **Policies of public schools to "accommodate" religion:** [§1066] Policies of public schools to accommodate religion need not violate the Establishment

Clause—even though their purpose and effect may seem to favor religion—if: (i) they do not involve religious programs in the public schools, and (ii) they further, rather than threaten, the "free exercise" of religion.

(1) **Released time—off premises:** [§1067] Programs in which participating children go to religious classes conducted at religious centers ***away from*** the public school do not violate the Establishment Clause. This is regarded as merely an "accommodation" to religious needs, the question of "aid to religion" being "one of degree." [Zorach v. Clauson, 343 U.S. 306 (1952)]

(2) **Dismissed time:** [§1068] "Dismissed time" is distinguished from released time in that ***all*** students are dismissed early one day a week to encourage attendance at religious classes held off public school premises. It follows from *Zorach* that this type of program is valid, despite its religious purpose.

(3) **Absence for holidays:** [§1069] Excusing children from public school to attend religious services (*e.g.*, on Ash Wednesday or Yom Kippur) does not violate the Establishment Clause, despite its religious purpose. This also follows from *Zorach.*

i. **General government regulation benefiting religion:** [§1070] Government action that benefits religion violates the Establishment Clause only if its purpose and effect is to sponsor or advance religion. If it has a secular purpose and effect, it is valid. (*Note:* It is also valid even though it has a "religious" purpose if its effect is merely to "accommodate" religion (*see supra*, §1066) or if it is helpful or necessary to religious liberty; *see* discussion of the Free Exercise Clause, below.)

(1) **Religious oath requirement for public office:** [§1071] Requiring a religious oath for public office is invalid—its purpose and effect being to sponsor religion and burden religious liberty. [Torcaso v. Watkins, 367 U.S. 488 (1961)]

(2) **Sunday closing laws:** [§1072] Laws requiring businesses or government offices to close on Sundays are valid; such laws have a secular purpose and effect (even though originally to aid religion), are advocated by labor and business, and are designed to create a day of rest and relaxation. [McGowan v. Maryland, 366 U.S. 420 (1961)]

(3) **Murder, theft, and adultery laws:** [§1073] Laws prohibiting and/or punishing murder, theft, or adultery are also valid; even though their effect coincides with religious tenets, the purpose and effect is secular (although religion obtains incidental benefits).

(4) **Insulating churches from liquor outlets:** [§1074] Zoning laws that bar liquor outlets within a prescribed distance of designated institutions (including churches) are probably valid because of their secular "environmental" purpose. But a law that gives churches the power to veto applications for liquor licenses near them violates the Establishment Clause. It delegates discretionary government power to churches, thus

giving them the ability to advance religion. It also entangles churches in the processes of government. [Larkin v. Grendel's Den, Inc., 459 U.S. 116 (1982)]

j. **Public acknowledgments of religion:** [§1075] American history is replete with government recognition of our religious heritage and with official expressions of religious beliefs. This does ***not*** violate the Establishment Clause unless, "in reality, it establishes a religion or religious faith, or tends to do so." [Lynch v. Donnelly, 465 U.S. 668 (1984)]

(1) **Prayers at opening sessions of public bodies:** [§1076] A state legislature's practice of opening each legislative day with a prayer by a state-paid chaplain does ***not*** violate the Establishment Clause. Such practice was actually authorized by the Congress that proposed the Establishment Clause and is "deeply embedded" in our history and tradition. Since adults are not readily susceptible to religious indoctrination, the practice is "a tolerable acknowledgment" of widely held beliefs. [Marsh v. Chambers, 463 U.S. 783 (1983)]

(a) **Compare—prayer at graduations:** [§1077] The practice of public school officials having members of the clergy give invocation and benediction prayers at graduation ceremonies ***does violate*** the Establishment Clause. The setting is analogous to the classroom because of subtle coercive pressures on students to participate in the religious exercise at a most significant occasion in the student's life. The atmosphere at the opening session of a legislature is different because adults are free to enter and leave with little constraint. [Lee v. Weisman, 112 S. Ct. 2649 (1992)]

(2) **Christmas Nativity scene:** [§1078] A city's inclusion of a Nativity scene in the context of a larger annual Christmas display does ***not*** violate the Establishment Clause. The purpose is not "motivated wholly by religious considerations," but is rather to take account of the "historical origins" of Christmas, and the beneficial effect for religion is only "indirect, remote, and incidental." [Lynch v. Donnelly, *supra*]

(a) **Compare:** However, a Nativity scene in the county courthouse, with the message "Glory to God in the Highest" (in Latin), and with ***no*** surrounding secular objects (such as Santa Claus, reindeer and sleigh, candy-striped poles, etc.) ***does*** violate the Establishment Clause because it denotes government endorsement and support of religion. [County of Allegheny v. American Civil Liberties Union Greater Pittsburgh Chapter, 492 U.S. 573 (1989)]

1) **Contrast:** On the other hand, a display containing a Christmas tree, Chanuka menorah, and a sign declaring the city's "salute to liberty" does ***not*** have the effect of endorsing or supporting religion, and does ***not*** violate the Establishment Clause. [County of Allegheny v. American Civil Liberties Union Greater Pittsburgh Chapter, *supra*]

(3) **Other examples:** [§1079] On similar analysis, it would appear that the following are also valid: official proclamation of a National Day of

Prayer; making Thanksgiving and Christmas national holidays; public compensation of chaplains in Congress and the military; making "In God We Trust" the national motto; inclusion of "One nation under God" in the pledge of allegiance to the flag; hanging religious paintings in publicly supported galleries; and providing chapels in the Capitol for worship and meditation. [Lynch v. Donnelly, *supra*]

4. **Scope of Free Exercise Clause**

a. **Purpose:** [§1080] If the purpose of a statute or other governmental action is to single out religion for adverse treatment, or to hinder (or discriminate against) a particular religion, it violates the Free Exercise Clause unless it is narrowly tailored to advance a compelling state interest. Such laws will survive strict scrutiny only in rare cases. [Church of the Lukumi Babalu Aye, Inc. v. City of Hialeah, 113 S. Ct. 2217 (1993)]

(1) **Example—clergy disqualification:** [§1081] Forbidding members of the clergy from holding public office has been held to violate the Free Exercise Clause. The state justification for the law—that clergy in public office would create religious divisiveness—was not supported by American experience. [McDaniel v. Paty, 435 U.S. 618 (1978)]

(2) **Example—animal sacrifice:** [§1082] City ordinances that barred ritual animal sacrifice with the object of suppressing a religion that employed this as a principal form of devotion violate the Free Exercise Clause. The justifications for the laws (protecting public health and preventing cruelty to animals) could be served by methods short of flatly prohibiting all religious sacrifices. [Church of the Lukumi Babalu Aye, Inc. v. City of Hialeah, *supra*]

b. **"Beliefs" vs. "action" or "conduct":** [§1083] A distinction must be made between a statute that "interferes" with religious beliefs and a statute that "interferes" with conduct that a person wishes to engage in (or to refrain from engaging in) because of her religion.

(1) **Beliefs:** [§1084] The freedom to hold religious beliefs is absolute. The government may not compel anyone to accept a particular creed. [Cantwell v. Connecticut, 310 U.S. 296 (1940)]

(a) **Example—flag salute:** [§1085] Requiring all public school pupils to salute the flag and recite the pledge of allegiance is invalid as applied to children whose religious scruples forbid it—government cannot require affirmation of a belief. [West Virginia State Board of Education v. Barnette, 319 U.S. 624 (1943)—freedom of speech and religion provisions of First Amendment forbid requiring flag salute by any person who has ideological objection]

(2) **Conduct:** [§1086] Action (or inaction) undertaken because of religious beliefs is ***not absolutely*** protected by the Free Exercise Clause.

(a) **Prior approach—balancing test:** [§1087] Under the prior approach, when a government regulation, enacted for a secular purpose, either burdened conduct required by some religious belief or required conduct forbidden by some religious belief, the Court balanced the following three factors:

1) **Severity of the burden:** Serious burdens can arise when government regulation makes action or inaction demanded by one's religion illegal; *i.e.*, the individual must choose between criminal prosecution or forsaking a religious duty (illustrated below). But the Court also invalidated some regulations that do not make the religious duty illegal, but make pursuit of religious obligations more difficult—usually financially burdensome (illustrated below).

2) **Strength of state interest:** The Court determined whether the state interest is "of the highest order"—using such terms as "compelling" and "important."

3) **Alternative means:** The Court also inquired whether the state could satisfy its interest by means that impose a lesser burden on religion.

(b) **Current rule:** [§1088] The Court has now ruled that the Free Exercise Clause affords ***no right to a religious exemption*** from a ***neutral*** law that happens to impose a substantial burden on religious practice—as long as the law is otherwise constitutionally applied to persons who engage in the action for nonreligious reasons. [Employment Division, Department of Human Resources of Oregon v. Smith, 494 U.S. 872 (1990)—no exemption from drug laws for Native American Church's sacramental use of peyote]

1) **Polygamy:** [§1089] A statute making polygamy illegal was upheld as applied to Mormons whose religion demanded polygamy. [Reynolds v. United States, 98 U.S. 145 (1878)]

2) **Sunday closing law:** [§1090] A Sunday closing law was upheld as applied to a Sabbatarian (Orthodox Jew) who must now refrain from working two days each week. [Braunfeld v. Brown, 366 U. S. 599 (1961)]

3) **Draft laws:** [§1091] The Court has stated that the Free Exercise Clause does not require draft exemption for any religious objectors to military service. And it has upheld a Selective Service Act exemption that was limited to those who are religiously opposed to "war in ***any*** form" as applied to religious conscientious objectors to a ***particular*** war. [Gillette v. United States, 401 U.S. 437 (1971)]

4) **Veterans' educational benefits:** [§1092] The Court upheld the denial of veterans' educational benefits to conscientious objectors who performed alternative civilian service. [Johnson v. Robison, 415 U.S. 361 (1974)]

5) **Taxes:** [§1093] Some early decisions invalidated a vendor's license tax (flat fee) when applied to those whose religion required them to sell religious literature, because it operated as a prior restraint on the dissemination of religious ***ideas***. [Murdock v. Pennsylvania, 319 U.S. 105 (1943)] More recently, the Court has upheld application of general taxes to religiously motivated activity. *Examples:*

   a) ***Social Security tax*** applied to an Amish employer whose beliefs forbade payment and receipt of Social Security benefits. [United States v. Lee, 455 U.S. 252 (1982)]

   b) ***Sales and use tax*** applied to sale of religious material (books and tapes) by a religious organization. [Jimmy Swaggart Ministries v. Board of Equalization of California, 493 U.S. 378 (1990)]

   c) ***Charitable deduction from federal income tax*** was denied for fixed price payments that members made to the Church of Scientology in exchange for sessions to increase spiritual awareness and teach the tenets of the faith. [Hernandez v. Commissioner of Internal Revenue, 490 U.S. 680 (1989)]

6) **Racial discrimination:** [§1094] The IRS denied tax exempt status to private schools whose religious beliefs required them to practice racial discrimination in admissions, etc. [Bob Jones University v. United States, 461 U.S. 574 (1983)]

7) **Compulsory military training:** [§1095] A state regulation requiring all students wishing to attend the state university to take a course in military training was upheld as applied to those whose religious beliefs forbade such training. [Hamilton v. Regents of University of California, 293 U.S. 245 (1934)]

8) **Military dress:** [§1096] Air Force refusal to exempt from its uniform dress requirements an Orthodox Jewish psychologist who wanted to wear a yarmulke while on duty at a military hospital was upheld. [Goldman v. Weinberger, 475 U.S. 503 (1986)]

9) **Prisoners' rights:** [§1097] The standard of review is different for claims by prisoners: Courts must afford deference to prison officials; and prison regulations that impinge on free exercise rights of prisoners are valid if "reasonably related to legitimate penological objectives." [O'Lone v. Estate of Shabazz, 482 U.S. 342 (1987)]

10) **Incidental effects of government programs:** [§1098] The Free Exercise Clause does not require government to justify otherwise lawful programs whose incidental effect happens to interfere with the practice of certain religions. [Lyng v. Northwest Indian Cemetery Protective Association, 485 U.S. 439

(1988)—government's building a road on public land that is sacred to Indians' religion does not require Free Exercise Clause justification even though it would virtually destroy Indians' ability to practice their religion]

(c) **Decisions upholding "free exercise" claims:** [§1099] In a few cases, the Court ***has required an exemption*** from a neutral, generally applicable law for religiously motivated action, most frequently when the Free Exercise Clause appears in conjunction with other constitutional protections.

1) **Right of parents to educate their children:** [§1100] A law compelling school attendance to age 16 was applied to Amish parents who sincerely believed, as a fundamental tenet of their faith (rather than from personal or philosophical conviction), that high school would endanger salvation. *Held:* The state's strong interest in universal education was outweighed by the Free Exercise Clause and the constitutional rights recognized in *Pierce v. Society of Sisters* (*supra*, §461), since the Amish prepared their children for life as adults in the Amish community, which has been productive and law-abiding. [Wisconsin v. Yoder, 406 U.S. 205 (1972)]

2) **Distribution of literature, solicitation of funds, use of public streets and parks, etc.:** [§1101] The doctrines that have resulted in violations of "free speech" have also led to violations of the Free Exercise Clause when the case involves religious groups. [*See, e.g.*, Cantwell v. Connecticut, *supra*, §1084]

3) **Unemployment compensation:** [§1102] A law requiring applicant to accept "suitable work" (including work on Saturday) or lose benefits was applied to a Sabbatarian (Seventh Day Adventist). *Held:* Where the state system ***provides for individual exemptions*** depending on the particular circumstances of an applicant's unemployment, it may not refuse to extend that system to cases of "religious hardship" without compelling reasons. [Sherbert v. Verner, 374 U.S. 398 (1963); *and see* Thomas v. Review Board of Indiana Employment Security Division, 450 U.S. 707 (1981); Hobbie v. Unemployment Appeals Commission, 480 U.S. 136 (1987)]

a) **Establishment Clause issues:** [§1103] Even though the exemptions for religion in the above cases may be said to have a "religious purpose," they do ***not*** violate the Establishment Clause—because "accommodating" these religious beliefs, as required by the Free Exercise Clause, is not government sponsorship of religion and neither does it result in excessive government involvement with religion.

1/ **Permissible accommodation:** [§1104] Similarly, the government may accommodate religion by alleviating burdens on religious exercise even though it would not be required to do so by the Free Exercise Clause. [Church of Jesus Christ of Latter-Day Saints v. Amos, 483 U.S. 327 (1987)—exemption of religious organizations from ban on religious discrimination in employment]

2/ **Compare—"absolute" religious exemption:** [§1105] However, a law that gives Sabbath observers an ***unqualifed*** right not to work on whatever day they designate as their Sabbath—regardless of the burden this may impose on the employer or fellow workers—goes beyond "accommodation." It violates the Establishment Clause because it has a "***primary effect*** that impermissibly advances a ***particular religious*** practice." [Estate of Thornton v. Caldor, Inc., 472 U.S. 703 (1985)]

c. **"Accommodations" that benefit only some religions:** [§1106] Accommodations for religion may not discriminate on the basis of religious affiliation or belief. But an accommodation that happens to produce "a de facto discrimination among religions"—*i.e.*, results in benefiting some religions but not others—does ***not*** violate either the Establishment Clause or Free Exercise Clause if there is a "neutral, secular basis for the lines government has drawn." [Gillette v. United States, *supra,* §1091—draft exemption only for those religious objectors to ***all*** wars has neutral and secular purpose of effectively raising armies in a fair and evenhanded way]

5. **What Are Protectible "Religious Beliefs"?**

a. **"Truth" of beliefs:** [§1107] The First Amendment forbids courts (or juries) from finding that any person's asserted religious beliefs are untrue—since many of the most traditional and accepted religious beliefs could not be proved today. [United States v. Ballard, 322 U.S. 78 (1944)]

(1) **Note:** Courts must respect sincerely held religious beliefs even though they may not appear to be logical, consistent, or comprehensible to others. [Thomas v. Review Board of Indiana Employment Security Division, *supra*, §1102]

b. **Good faith:** [§1108] However, courts ***can*** determine whether a person ***sincerely believes*** the asserted religious tenets. [United States v. Ballard, *supra*—person prosecuted for mail fraud for soliciting funds for his religious movement asserted that he was divine messenger, had divine healing powers, had talked to Jesus, etc.]

c. **Definition of "religion":** [§1109] Religious beliefs need not be theistic to qualify for constitutional protection. [Torcaso v. Watkins, *supra*, §1071—listing Buddhism, Taoism, Ethical Culture, and Secular Humanism as religions that do not teach belief in the existence of God] But the Court has said that religious beliefs must constitute more than merely a philosophic rejection of contemporary secular values. [Wisconsin v. Yoder, *supra*, §1100] Although the Court has not stated an authoritative constitutional definition of "religion," neither has it ever held any asserted religious beliefs not to be "religious" for First Amendment purposes.

(1) **Statutory interpretation:** [§1110] In construing "religious belief" in the Selective Service Act, the Court has perhaps suggested a constitutional definition: The belief must occupy a place in the believer's life parallel to that occupied by orthodox religious beliefs. Such a belief may be internally derived, but it must be something beyond a merely political or philosophical view. [United States v. Seeger, 380 U.S. 163 (1965)]

6. **Judicial Resolution of Disputes Involving Church Doctrine:** [§1111] In disputes between a local congregation and a general church hierarchy involving the right to church property (or the right to be a church official), the First and Fourteenth Amendment guarantees of religious liberty forbid courts from determining ecclesiastical questions (*i.e.*, questions of religious doctrine and practice) to resolve the case. [Presbyterian Church v. Hull Church, 393 U.S. 440 (1969); Serbian Eastern Orthodox Diocese v. Milivojevich, 426 U.S. 696 (1976)] At least absent fraud or collusion when the church tribunal allegedly acts in bad faith for secular purposes, the ***decision of the church tribunal is conclusive***—despite the claim that it has not complied with its own rules.

a. **Rationale:** Judicial inquiry into such matters would constitute "excessive government entanglement" with religion; also, church members ***impliedly consent*** to be bound by hierarchical church decisions on ecclesiastical questions.

(1) **Congregational churches:** This rationale may extend to church members impliedly consenting to be bound by decisions of a majority of the congregation in a local church that has no general affiliation. [Watson v. Jones, 80 U.S. 679 (1871)]

(2) **Personal rights:** And the rationale may extend to disputes where personal, rather than property, rights are involved.

b. **Alternative approach:** [§1112] Civil courts may also use "neutral principles" of property law—not involving questions of religious doctrine or practice—to resolve church property disputes. For example, the courts may examine the deeds to the property, state statutes on implied trusts, and the church rules; or the court may adopt a presumptive rule of majority representation—and in the absence of a church rule implying a trust to the general church, the court may award the property to the entity that has legal title. [Jones v. Wolf, 443 U.S. 595 (1979)]

7. **Standing**

a. **Free Exercise Clause:** [§1113] In accordance with the general doctrine of standing (*see supra*, §§43-46), a person asserting violation of the Free Exercise Clause must: (i) show a ***direct personal injury*** due to the challenged action, and (ii) ordinarily, claim an ***interference with her own religious beliefs***. [McGowan v. Maryland, *supra*, §1072—store employees, convicted of violating Sunday closing laws, had no standing to attack law as violating Free Exercise Clause since they did not allege infringement of their own religious freedom]

b. **Establishment Clause:** [§1114] But persons asserting violation of the Establishment Clause need not allege infringement of particular religious freedoms to have standing. It is enough that they are ***directly affected*** by the action complained of.

(1) **Example:** Department store employees prosecuted for Sunday closing law violation could claim that the law violates the Establishment Clause. [McGowan v. Maryland, *supra*]

(2) **Example:** Parents of public school children have standing to challenge public school practices (Bible reading) as violating the Establishment Clause. [Abington School District v. Schempp, *supra*, §1063]

H. OTHER LIMITATIONS ON GOVERNMENTAL POWER

1. Restrictions on Power of Eminent Domain

a. **Fifth Amendment:** [§1115] The Fifth Amendment provides in part: ". . . nor shall private property be taken for public use without just compensation."

(1) **Federal government:** [§1116] This is ***not*** an implied grant to the federal government of a general power to take, provided it pays. Rather, it is a restriction that applies only if, through some ***other*** constitutional provision, the substantive power to take is independently granted.

(2) **State government:** [§1117] The Fifth Amendment restraint on the power of eminent domain applies to the states through the Fourteenth Amendment Due Process Clause. [Chicago, Burlington & Quincy Railroad v. Chicago, 166 U.S. 226 (1897)]

b. **Substantive requirements**

(1) **Property:** [§1118] "Property" interests are not created by the Constitution, but are derived from independent sources such as state or federal law. They may include intangible (as well as tangible) interests, such as trade secrets. [Ruckelshaus v. Monsanto Co., 467 U.S. 986 (1984)]

(2) **Public use:** [§1119] Note that the "taking" must be for a "public use." If not taken for this purpose, the private property may not be appropriated by government ***at all***, even if "just compensation" is paid.

(a) **Broadly defined:** [§1120] The Court's role in determining whether the taking is for a "public use" is ***extremely narrow***. A use is held to be "public" if it is ***rationally related*** to a ***conceivable*** public purpose—***e.g.***, if it furthers health, welfare, safety, moral, social, economic, political, or even aesthetic ends. The Court will ***not*** consider the desirability of a particular taking, or the extent to which the property must be taken in order to satisfy the public purposes. [Berman v. Parker, 348 U.S. 26 (1954)]

1) **And note:** Uses may be "public" if there is public advantage or benefit, even though the property is not ***used*** by the general

public. Thus, the state may authorize takings and use by private persons or companies if thought to be in the public interest. [Hawaii Housing Authority v. Midkiff, 467 U.S. 229 (1984)—transfer of property from owners to lessees to reduce concentration of land ownership]

(3) **"Taking" vs. "regulation":** [§1121] The crucial issue is whether the government action is a ***taking***, requiring just compensation, or merely a ***regulation*** under the police power (not requiring compensation).

(a) **No clear formula:** [§1122] The Court has been unable to develop any "set formula" for determining when a "taking" occurs. Rather, the Court asks whether ***"justice and fairness" require*** that economic loss caused by public action must be ***compensated by the government*** and thus borne by the public as a whole, or whether the loss should remain concentrated on those few persons subject to the public action. [Penn Central Transportation Co. v. New York City, 438 U.S. 104 (1978)]

(b) **Appropriation or permanent invasion:** [§1123] A "taking" will almost always be found if there is an ***actual appropriation*** or a ***permanent physical invasion*** of private property by the government or by authorization of state law. This is true regardless of the state's interest or the economic impact on the owner. [Loretto v. Teleprompter Manhattan CATV Corp., 455 U.S. 904 (1982)—statute required landlords to allow television cables on their buildings] Illustrations of such government action held to constitute a "taking" include:

1) ***Formal condemnation*** of property for some public use.

a) ***Passing property to heirs***—although the government has broad authority to ***regulate*** the descent and devise of property, ***abolishing*** these rights is a taking. [Hodel v. Irving, 481 U.S. 704 (1987)]

2) ***Requirement that a right-of-way easement*** be granted by the property owner to permit others to traverse the property. [Nollan v. California Coastal Commission, 483 U.S. 825 (1987)]

a) *But note:* A city may require owners to dedicate an interest in their property as a condition for developing it, but only if the ***city makes*** some sort of ***individualized determination*** that the required dedication is related both in nature and extent (*i.e.*, there is some "rough proportionality") to the impact of the proposed development. [Dolan v. City of Tigard, 114 S. Ct. _____ (1994)]

3) ***Direct flights*** over private property adjacent to federal or municipal airports that are ***so low and frequent*** as to destroy the property's present use. [United States v. Causby, 328 U.S. 256 (1946); Griggs v. Allegheny County, 369 U.S. 84 (1962)]

4) ***Federal dam construction*** resulting in repeated flooding of private property. [United States v. Cress, 243 U.S. 316 (1917)]

5) ***Government requirement that public be given free access*** to privately developed waterway, thus unreasonably impairing the value of the property and its owners' reasonable expectations. [Kaiser Aetna v. United States, 444 U.S. 164 (1979)]

a) *Compare:* Requiring the owner of a shopping center to provide access to persons desiring to distribute handbills is not a taking since it does not unreasonably impair the value or use of the property as a shopping center. [Pruneyard Shopping Center v. Robins, *supra*, §896]

6) ***Statute, which in addition to charging a fee for court clerk's services*** in keeping private funds deposited in an ***interpleader action***, also provided that the ***interest*** on the deposited funds goes to the state, and was therefore "not reasonably related to the costs of using the courts." [Webb's Fabulous Pharmacies, Inc. v. Beckwith, 445 U.S. 925 (1980)]

(c) **Exceptions:** [§1124] Examples of government action held ***not*** to be a "taking" include:

1) ***Military destruction of strategic private property*** simply to avoid its falling into enemy hands, and the destruction of private property to stop the spread of a fire have been held ***not*** to be "takings"—public need outweighing private injury. [United States v. Caltex, Inc., 344 U.S. 149 (1952)]

2) ***Forfeiture of property used in connection with crime*** was not a "taking," despite innocence of the property owner (*e.g.*, lessor)—at least where owner voluntarily entrusted the property to wrongdoers and did not show that he did "all that he reasonably could to avoid having the property put to an unlawful use." [Calero-Toledo v. Pearson Yacht Leasing Co., 416 U.S. 663 (1974)]

3) ***A temporary, unplanned occupation of private property by the military during a riot*** was not a "taking" when done primarily to defend the property rather than the general public interest. [National Board of Y.M.C.A. v. United States, 395 U.S. 85 (1969)]

(d) **Severe economic impact:** [§1125] Government action that amounts to only a ***temporary*** physical invasion of property, that adversely affects property value, or that prohibits the most beneficial use of the property does not ***necessarily*** result in a "taking," since reduction in economic value is an inevitable effect of much government regulation. The Court has stated that it is a ***matter of degree***. [Pennsylvania Coal Co. v. Mahon, 260 U.S. 393 (1922)]

1) **No economically valuable use:** [§1126] A regulation that denies ***all*** economically beneficial or productive use of land is, from the owner's point of view, equivalent to a physical appropriation. It thus is a "taking" unless principles of nuisance or property law that existed when the owner acquired the land make the use prohibitable. [Lucas v. South Carolina Coastal Council, 112 S. Ct. 2886 (1992)]

2) **Other significant factors:** [§1127] A restriction on use of property may constitute a "taking" if not "***reasonably necessary*** to the effectuation of a ***substantial*** public purpose," or if it has an "***unduly harsh*** impact" on the "distinct ***investment-backed expectations***" of the owner. But the Court balances the ***public need*** against the ***private cost***, and no compensation is required for burdens imposed on ***"all similarly situated property"*** in order to produce "***widespread*** public benefit." [Penn Central Transportation Co. v. New York City, *supra*, §1122]

3) **Examples:** [§1128] The following were held ***not*** to be a "taking."

   a) ***State-ordered destruction*** of cedar trees that were spreading disease to apple orchards was ***not*** a "taking," despite great reduction of value—since cedar trees were causing harm to an important state industry. [Miller v. Schoene, 276 U.S. 272 (1928)]

   b) ***Zoning ordinance*** restricting use of property and causing reduction in value was ***not*** a "taking," if it substantially advanced legitimate state interests and did not extinguish a fundamental attribute of ownership. [Agins v. City of Tiburon, 447 U.S. 255 (1980)—ordinance permitted as many as five houses on five-acre tract]

   c) ***State restriction*** on use of property designated as "landmark" was ***not*** a "taking"—at least when owner could continue to obtain a "reasonable return" on investment—since restriction was reasonably related to public policy of historic preservation and owner's proposed use was inconsistent with that policy. [Penn Central Transportation Co. v. New York City, *supra*]

4) **Taxes:** [§1129] A tax is not deemed a "taking"—even when it is so excessive as to render continuation of a business unprofitable, so that the owner is forced to shut down. [City of Pittsburgh v. Alco Parking Corp., 417 U.S. 369 (1974)]

(4) **"Just" compensation:** [§1130] If a "taking" is found, the property owner normally must be paid the ***"fair market value"*** of the property. Absent special circumstances, ***neither*** the value of the private owner's unique need for the property nor the value of the gain to the taker are compensable. [United States v. 564.54 Acres of Land, 441 U.S. 506 (1979)]

(a) **Note:** If, after the taking, the owner has some property left whose value has been ***enhanced*** as a result thereof, the gain in value may be considered as an offset against the value of the property taken. [Blanchette v. Connecticut General Insurance, 419 U.S. 102 (1974)]

c. **Remedy:** [§1131] If a "taking" occurs, just compensation must be paid for damages suffered during the ***entire*** time that the property was "taken." The government ***cannot*** disallow damages for the period of time between enactment of the challenged regulation and its ultimate invalidation. [First English Evangelical Lutheran Church v. County of Los Angeles, 482 U.S. 304 (1987)]

d. **Procedural requirements:** [§1132] When the federal or state government exercises its power of eminent domain, due process requires that it give the property owner reasonable notice and a reasonable opportunity to be heard and offer evidence regarding the amount of compensation due her. [Bragg v. Weaver, 251 U.S. 57 (1919)]

(1) **But note:** Due process does ***not*** require that the condemnation of land occur in advance of its occupation by the condemning authority [Bailey v. Anderson, 326 U.S. 203 (1945)]; nor does it require a hearing on the necessity and expediency of the taking [Bragg v. Weaver, *supra*].

2. **Prohibition Against Involuntary Servitude**

a. **Thirteenth Amendment:** [§1133] The Thirteenth Amendment provides: "Neither slavery nor involuntary servitude, except as a punishment for crime whereof the party shall have been duly convicted, shall exist within the United States, or any place subject to their jurisdiction." Thus, the Thirteenth Amendment prevents slavery or involuntary servitude from being practiced anywhere in the United States, whether by a state, the federal government, or a private individual. It is a complete prohibition.

b. **What is involuntary servitude?**

(1) **Peonage:** [§1134] This amendment prohibits peonage—*i.e.*, impressing one into the personal service of the creditor in order to liquidate a debt. Although the amendment excepts punishment of crime, the state may not make the nonpayment of the debt, or the refusal to perform personal services to liquidate the debt, the crime itself.

(a) **Example:** The Court held void a state criminal statute making failure to render services, for which an advance was received and for which no repayment had been made, prima facie evidence of an intent to defraud. [Pollock v. Williams, 322 U.S. 4 (1944)]

(b) **Example:** The Court also invalidated a federal statute that permitted release of convicts to employers who, pursuant to agreement with the convicts, paid their fine in exchange for agreed services, where the statute made breach of the agreement by the convict a crime. [United States v. Reynolds, 235 U.S. 133 (1914)]

(2) **Exceptional circumstances:** [§1135] There are exceptional situations where performance of a personal obligation has always been enforced.

(a) **Example:** In *Robertson v. Baldwin*, 165 U.S. 275 (1897), the Court upheld a statute that provided that seamen who desert their vessel in violation of their contracts may be arrested and forcibly returned to the vessel for service and may be criminally prosecuted for desertion.

(b) **And note:** Similarly, military conscription was upheld in the *Selective Draft Law Cases*, 245 U.S. 366 (1918).

3. **Impairment of Contractual Obligations**

a. **State government**

(1) **Constitutional provision:** [§1136] Article I, Section 10 (Contract Clause) provides: "No State shall . . . pass any . . . Law impairing the Obligation of Contracts. . . ."

(a) **Applicable to state legislation:** [§1137] Since only the legislature can ***"pass"*** any law, the Contract Clause applies only to state legislation, not decisions by state courts. Thus, the overruling of a prior decision by a state court is not prohibited by this clause, even though the reversal may affect contracts. [Tidal Oil Co. v. Flanagan, 263 U.S. 444 (1924)]

(b) **"Impairs":** [§1138] A law that ***"impairs"*** is one that ***substantially*** invalidates, releases, or extinguishes the obligations of a contract, or that derogates substantial contractual rights. [Home Building & Loan Association v. Blaisdell, 290 U.S. 398 (1923)] The more substantial the impairment, the greater the justification that must be shown by the state.

(c) **"Obligation":** [§1139] This connotes not only the terms of the contract but also the ***legal rules in force when the contract is made*** and which enter into and comprise a part of the agreement; ***i.e.***, it is presumed that the contracting parties adopt the terms of their bargain in reliance on the law in effect at the time the agreement is reached. However, the law is not required to remain static, since only the legitimate expectations of the parties regarding the law are deemed obligations to the government. [United States Trust Co. v. New Jersey, 431 U.S. 1 (1977)]

(d) **"Contracts":** [§1140] This includes both public agreements (*i.e.*, those entered into by a state either as a sovereign or in its proprietary capacity) and private bargains (*i.e.*, those entered into between persons). It includes both executed agreements and executory agreements. [Fletcher v. Peck, 10 U.S. (6 Cranch) 87 (1810)—land grant case; Dartmouth College v. Woodward, 17 U.S. (4 Wheat.) 518 (1819)—college charter case]

(2) **Limitations on protection afforded to private contracts**

(a) **Modification reasonable and necessary for public purpose:** [§1141] Not all substantial "impairments" of contracts are deemed unconstitutional. Thus, although the Contract Clause prevents state destruction of ***all*** rights or ***all*** enforcement of existing contracts, rights and responsibilities in a private contract can be ***modified*** by legislation that: (i) serves an ***important and legitimate*** public interest, and (ii) is a ***reasonable and narrowly tailored means*** of promoting that interest.

1) **Factors considered:** [§1142] In determining these issues, the Court will consider, among other things, the ***severity*** of the impairment, the ***reasonable reliance*** and expectations of the contracting parties, the ***strength and breadth*** of the social-economic problem involved, whether the law serves the ***general*** public welfare or benefits only ***special interests***, whether the law operates in an ***area already regulated*** by the state, and whether the impact of the law is ***permanent*** (rather than temporary) or ***immediate*** (as opposed to gradual). [Allied Structural Steel Co. v. Spannaus, 438 U.S. 234 (1978); Energy Reserves Group Inc. v. Kansas Power & Light Co., 459 U.S. 400 (1983)]

   a) **General applicability:** [§1143] The Court will more likely uphold a law that imposes a general rule of conduct on all persons within the purpose of the regulation than a law that is limited to altering the contractual duties of persons who are parties to existing contracts. Otherwise, people could obtain immunity from state regulation by private contractual arrangements. [Exxon Corp. v. Eagerton, 462 U.S. 176 (1983)]

2) **Modification of contract remedy:** [§1144] Without "impairing the obligation" of a contract, the ***remedy*** provided by the legislature to enforce that obligation may be modified, as long as the modification is reasonable and does not impair substantial contractual rights. [Von Hoffman v. City of Quincy, 71 U.S. (4 Wall.) 535 (1867)]

   a) **Example:** A state could not retroactively impair the obligation of a debtor to pay interest after the maturity of the debt, where the contract is silent, but it could shorten the statute of limitations applicable to suit on the contract, as long as a reasonable time is given in which the contract can be enforced.

(b) **Deference to legislative judgment:** [§1145] Courts generally give substantial deference to a legislature's judgment regarding the reasonableness of, and necessity for, laws that impair the obligations of private contracts. [East New York Savings Bank v. Hahn, 326 U.S. 230 (1945)] Ultimately, however, the Court makes its own judgment regarding these requirements.

(3) **Limitations on protection afforded to public contracts**

(a) **Subsequent impairments:** [§1146] Subsequent impairments of public contracts are subject to basically similar limitations as private contracts: an important public interest and a reasonable and narrowly tailored means of promoting that interest (*see supra*, §1141).

(b) **Less deference to legislative judgment:** [§1147] However, where a public contract is involved, the legislature's own self-interest is at stake (*i.e.*, the legislature is modifying its own obligation). Therefore, its judgment as to whether the modification is both (i) ***reasonable*** under the circumstances, ***and*** (ii) ***narrowly tailored*** to an ***important*** state purpose is given less deference. [United States Trust Co. v. New Jersey, *supra*, §1139—state repeal of financial covenant in state bonds held invalid because not essential to meet public need for mass transit and not reasonable in that importance of public mass transit was foreseeable at time state sold bonds with covenant]

1) **But note:** The protection of the Contract Clause is limited by a rule of construction that requires that public contracts be construed narrowly against the grantee. [Charles River Bridge v. Warren Bridge, 36 U.S. (11 Pet.) 420 (1837)]

a) **Example:** Although a state may contract irrevocably to exempt property from taxation, whenever in doubt, such contracts are usually construed as revocable and as providing only an exemption from some, but not all, types of taxation. [*See, e.g.*, Hale v. Iowa State Board of Assessment and Review, 302 U.S. 95 (1937)—income from state and municipal bonds, which by statute was "exempt from taxation," held subject to state income tax, since the exemption was construed as only providing a property tax exemption]

(c) **Ab initio impairments of reserved powers:** [§1148] The Contract Clause does not require a state to adhere to a contract by which the state surrenders, ab initio, an essential attribute of its sovereignty. Thus, a state cannot bargain away its power of eminent domain or its police powers, or enter into a contract prohibiting the exercise of such powers.

1) **Example:** A state's grant of an exclusive privilege to maintain a toll bridge does not prevent the state from later taking and paying for the bridge under its power of eminent domain. [West River Bridge Co. v. Dix, 47 U.S. 507 (1848)]

2) **Example:** Similarly, a lottery company chartered by the state for 25 years could be put out of business three years later by legislation adopted under the exercise of the state's police powers. [Stone v. Mississippi, 101 U.S. 814 (1879)]

3) **Compare—financial contracts:** [§1149] However, a state can enter into contracts that are binding as to the exercise of its ***taxing and spending powers***. [New Jersey v. Wilson, 11 U.S. (7 Cranch) 164 (1812)—Contract Clause prohibits impairment of permanent tax exemption granted by state]

b. **Federal government:** [§1150] The Contract Clause does ***not apply*** to the national government. Federal legislation adjusting economic interests may be applied retroactively as long as Congress has a "rational" purpose. [Usery v. Turner Elkhorn Mining Co., 428 U.S. 1 (1976)]

4. **Prohibition Against Ex Post Facto Laws**

a. **Constitutional provisions:** [§1151] Article I, Section 9, Clause 3 provides: "No . . . ex post facto law shall be passed"; and Article I, Section 10, Clause 1 provides: "No state shall . . . pass any ex post facto law." These clauses prohibit ***both federal and state legislatures*** from passing ex post facto laws.

b. **Definition:** [§1152] An ex post facto law is one that retroactively alters the law in a ***substantially prejudicial*** manner, so as to deprive a person of any right (civil, criminal, or political) previously enjoyed, for the purpose of ***punishing*** the person ***for some past activity***. [Cummings v. Missouri, 71 U.S. (4 Wall.) 277 (1867)]

(1) **Compare:** Thus, a statute is ***not*** ex post facto if its principal purpose is regulation of some present status or activity, as opposed to punishment for past acts. [Hawker v. New York, 170 U.S. 189 (1898)—upholding statute prohibiting future practice of medicine by any person previously convicted of felony, because principal purpose deemed to be protection of health and safety of citizens, rather than additional punishment for convicted doctors]

c. **Retroactive effects:** [§1153] A statute retroactively ***alters*** the law in a substantially prejudicial manner if it: (i) ***makes criminal an act innocent when done***, and punishes such act, or (ii) ***prescribes greater punishment for an act than the law provided when it was committed***.

(1) **Example:** A statute enacted after the Civil War required all officeholders, teachers, and preachers to execute an oath, swearing they had not participated in the rebellion. This requirement was held ***invalid*** as an attempt to punish for past acts, since the oath had no relationship to fitness to practice. [Cummings v. Missouri, *supra*]

(2) **Compare:** But since deportation of aliens is not deemed to be "punishment," a statute authorizing deportation for conduct that took place prior to enactment of the statute (and which was not grounds for deportation at that time) is ***not*** an ex post facto law. [Harisiades v. Shaughnessy, *supra*, §152]

I. SAFEGUARDS IN THE ADMINISTRATION OF CRIMINAL JUSTICE

The following discussion covers the few aspects of "constitutional criminal procedure" presently contained in Constitutional Law courses. A thorough discussion of these topics, and many other topics not touched upon herein, is contained in the Criminal Procedure Summary.

1. **Right to Counsel**

   a. **In federal courts**

      (1) **Constitutional provision—Sixth Amendment:** [§1154] "In all criminal prosecutions, the accused shall enjoy the right . . . to have the Assistance of Counsel for his defense."

      (2) **Effect:** [§1155] The Sixth Amendment entitles an accused in federal courts to the assistance of counsel unless this right has been knowingly and intelligently waived. If an accused desires counsel but cannot afford to hire his own, defense counsel must be appointed by the trial court. [Johnson v. Zerbst, 304 U.S. 458 (1938); Walker v. Johnston, 312 U.S. 275 (1941)]

   b. **In state courts:** [§1156] The Sixth Amendment is incorporated by the Due Process Clause of the Fourteenth Amendment, and thus the same right to counsel must be afforded in state courts. [Gideon v. Wainwright, *supra*, §398]

   c. **Scope of right**

      (1) **Nature of charge—felony vs. misdemeanor:** [§1157] The right to counsel is constitutionally required in all prosecutions that ***result*** in actual ***imprisonment***—whether the offense be classified as felony or misdemeanor. [Argersinger v. Hamlin, 407 U.S. 25 (1972)]

         (a) **Effect:** [§1158] If the trial judge concludes that the offense is punishable by imprisonment, she must afford counsel to the accused; ***otherwise***, ***no jail sentence*** may be imposed.

         (b) **Indigents:** [§1159] Counsel need not be appointed for indigent defendants where the crime is punishable by imprisonment, but upon conviction no imprisonment occurs. [Scott v. Illinois, 440 U.S. 367 (1979)]

2. **Use of Involuntary Confessions**

   a. **In federal courts**

      (1) **Constitutional provision:** [§1160] The Fifth Amendment provides: "No person . . . shall be compelled in any criminal case to be a witness against himself. . . ."

      (2) **Effect:** [§1161] An involuntary or coerced confession is deemed ***inadmissible*** in federal courts. [Bram v. United States, 168 U.S. 532 (1897)]

   b. **In state courts:** [§1162] The Fifth Amendment provision prohibiting the use of involuntary or coerced confessions is incorporated into the Due Process Clause of the Fourteenth Amendment, and thus is binding in state, as well as federal, criminal prosecutions. [Brown v. Mississippi, 297 U.S. 278 (1936)]

   c. **Certain confessions inadmissible even though voluntary:** [§1163] Under certain circumstances, even a ***voluntary*** confession may be inadmissible.

(1) ***Miranda***: [§1164] In *Miranda v. Arizona*, 384 U.S. 436 (1966), the Court held that a confession obtained from an accused during custodial interrogation—before or after formal charges are filed, and regardless of voluntariness—would not be admissible unless it first appeared that the police had clearly informed the accused (i) of his right to ***remain silent***; (ii) that ***anything he said might be used against him***; and (iii) that he had the ***right to consult with counsel*** (and, if indigent, that he had the right to appointed counsel) at the time of the interrogation.

(a) **Rationale:** "In custody" interrogations are ***inherently compulsive***, and hence there is a greater need to protect an accused's constitutional rights. This greater need justifies the requirement that the prosecution make an affirmative showing that these rights were protected where it seeks to use ***any*** statements (inculpatory or exculpatory) obtained from the accused during such interrogations.

3. Privilege Against Self-Incrimination

a. In federal courts

(1) **Constitutional provision:** [§1165] The privilege against self-incrimination springs from the same Fifth Amendment provision barring the use of involuntary confessions: "No person . . . shall be compelled in any criminal case to be a witness against himself. . . ."

(2) **Effect:** [§1166] In any federal proceeding, ***civil or criminal***, a witness (whether or not a party to the action) cannot be compelled to give evidence of a ***testimonial*** or communicative nature that might subject him to any criminal prosecution.

b. **In state courts:** [§1167] The Fourteenth Amendment Due Process Clause incorporates the Fifth Amendment privilege against self-incrimination, so that an accused cannot be forced to give such evidence himself in state courts either. [Malloy v. Hogan, *supra*, §398]

c. **No comment on failure to testify in own defense:** [§1168] In both federal and state courts, a defendant's failure to take the witness stand in his own defense is treated as tantamount to a claim of the privilege. Hence, no adverse inference of guilt can be drawn therefrom, and neither the judge nor the prosecutor is permitted to make any adverse comment to the jury about the defendant's failure to testify. [Griffin v. California, 380 U.S. 609 (1965)]

4. Exclusion of Evidence Obtained by Illegal Searches and Seizures

a. In federal courts

(1) **Fourth Amendment:** [§1169] "The right of the people to be secure in their persons, houses, papers, and effects, against unreasonable searches and seizures, shall not be violated, and no Warrants shall issue, but upon probable cause, supported by Oath or affirmation, and particularly describing the place to be searched, and the persons or things to be seized."

(2) **Effect:** [§1170] Evidence obtained in violation of this provision is ***inadmissible*** in the prosecution's case-in-chief in federal courts. [Elkins v. United States, 364 U.S. 206 (1960)]

(a) **"Good faith exception":** [§1171] But this exclusionary rule does not bar the admission of evidence obtained within the scope of a search warrant, even though the warrant is invalid (*e.g.*, ***not*** supported by probable cause), if: (i) the warrant was issued by a ***detached and neutral magistrate***, and (ii) the officer was ***neither dishonest nor reckless*** in preparing the affidavit and had an ***objectively reasonable belief*** that the warrant was valid. [United States v. Leon, 468 U.S. 897 (1984); Massachusetts v. Sheppard, 468 U.S. 981 (1984)]

b. **In state courts:** [§1172] The Due Process Clause of the Fourteenth Amendment incorporates the protection afforded by the Fourth Amendment, and has the same effect upon state criminal prosecutions that the Fourth Amendment has upon federal prosecutions; *i.e.*, illegally seized evidence or the fruits thereof must usually be excluded. [Mapp v. Ohio, 367 U.S. 643 (1961)]

c. **What constitutes unreasonable search or seizure:** [§1173] The Fourth Amendment protection extends to the unauthorized obtaining of physical evidence (documents, guns, drugs, etc.), to the interception of verbal communications (eavesdropping, wiretapping), and even to the observation of matters through an unauthorized invasion of privacy. (*See* detailed discussion in Criminal Procedure Summary.)

(1) **Fourth Amendment protects people, not places:** [§1174] The Fourth Amendment has been held to protect people, not places. Hence, the constitutional guarantee applies whether or not the evidence is obtained by any physical intrusion or trespass. [Katz v. United States, 389 U.S. 347 (1967)—excluding evidence obtained by electronic eavesdropping accomplished without any wiretap or physical trespass]

d. **Enforcement of constitutional prohibitions—exclusion of evidence:** [§1175] The Fourth Amendment, implemented by the Self-Incrimination Clause of the Fifth Amendment, forbids the federal government from convicting a person of a crime by using testimony or papers obtained by unreasonable searches and seizures as defined in the Fourth Amendment. [Boyd v. United States, 116 U.S. 616 (1886)] Such evidence is therefore ***inadmissible*** in federal courts ***whether seized by state or federal officers***. [Weeks v. United States, 232 U.S. 383 (1914); Elkins v. United States, *supra*] The same rule applies in state courts. [Mapp v. Ohio, *supra*]

5. **Cruel and Unusual Punishment**

a. **Constitutional provision:** [§1176] The Eighth Amendment provides ". . . nor [may] cruel and unusual punishments [be] inflicted."

(1) **State courts:** [§1177] The Eighth Amendment is incorporated in the Due Process Clause of the Fourteenth Amendment and thus applies to the states, as well as the federal government.

b. **Scope:** [§1178] The scope of the constitutional prohibition is two-fold.

(1) **Punishment disproportionate to crime:** [§1179] One approach is to determine whether the punishment is ***"excessive"—i.e.***, whether it is grossly disproportionate to the severity of the crime, or whether it is the purposeless imposition of severe punishment. The Court itself ultimately makes this judgment, informed by history, precedent, legislative attitudes, and the responses of sentencing juries.

(a) **Example—"cadena temporal":** [§1180] Twelve years in irons at hard labor, together with accessory penalties (loss of parental and property rights and surveillance for life after release), for a relatively minor offense (falsifying public records) is "grossly disproportionate" and thus invalid. [Weems v. United States, 217 U.S. 349 (1910)]

(b) **Example—punishment for illness:** [§1181] Conviction under a state statute that made it a crime to be ***addicted to the use of narcotics*** is invalid. Imprisonment for having a certain status (addict) that the individual is powerless to overcome is analogous to criminally prosecuting a person for being mentally ill or afflicted with a cold or venereal disease. [Robinson v. California, 370 U.S. 660 (1962)]

(c) **Capital punishment:** [§1182] The death penalty is "grossly disproportionate" for the offenses of (i) rape of an adult woman [Coker v. Georgia, 433 U.S. 584 (1977)]; and (ii) murder committed during a felony when the defendant does not kill, attempt to kill, or intend that a killing occur, and does not play a major role in the felony which shows reckless indifference to human life. [Enmund v. Florida, 456 U.S. 904 (1982), *as clarified by* Tison v. Arizona, 481 U.S. 137 (1987)]

1) **Juvenile offenders:** [§1183] The Supreme Court has unanimously agreed that at ***some age*** a juvenile cannot be considered fully responsible for murder, and therefore the death penalty would be "grossly disproportionate." However, a majority has concluded that there is no such national consensus forbidding the death penalty for capital crimes committed at the ages of 16 and older. [Stanford v. Kentucky, 492 U.S. 361 (1989)]

2) **Mental retardation:** [§1184] Similarly, there is no national consensus against executing mentally retarded people (who are not "idiots" or "lunatics" and thus "insane"). [Penry v. Lynaugh, 492 U.S. 302 (1989)]

(d) **Length of sentence:** [§1185] The length of a prison sentence cannot be grossly disproportionate to the severity of the crime. [Solem v. Helm, 463 U.S. 277 (1983)—life sentence without possibility of parole for seventh nonviolent felony is "grossly disproportionate"] But substantial deference must be given to sentence decisions of legislatures and sentencing courts, and successful challenges to the length of a sentence alone are rare. [Rummell v. Estelle, 445 U.S. 263 (1980)—upholding life sentence, ***with*** parole possibility, for multiple nonviolent offender]

(2) **Punishment "barbaric" regardless of crime:** [§1186] A second approach is to determine whether the punishment itself is disapproved by a national consensus of our society, irrespective of the crime.

(a) **Example:** A state may not impose the death penalty on a prisoner who is insane at the ***time of the punishment***. [Ford v. Wainwright, 477 U.S. 399 (1986)]

(b) **Example:** Congress may not strip an army deserter of citizenship—because making an accused a "stateless person, deprived of the right to have rights" is considered too cruel a punishment for any crime. [Trop v. Dulles, 356 U.S. 86 (1958)]

c. **Capital punishment:** [§1187] The death penalty is not, under all circumstances, cruel and unusual punishment. If the sentencing body (judge or jury) is given adequate guidance as to both ***aggravating and mitigating*** factors about the crime and the defendant relevant to sentencing, ***and*** if there is a review procedure to ensure against imposition of the death sentence for discriminatory reasons, capital punishment is permissible. [Gregg v. Georgia, 428 U.S. 153 (1976)]

(1) **Undue discretion:** [§1188] However, death penalties imposed pursuant to statutory standards that permit ***unbridled*** discretion, and under which the penalty may be ***selectively and capriciously applied***, violate the Eighth and Fourteenth Amendments. [Furman v. Georgia, 408 U.S. 238 (1972)]

(a) **Limited discretion:** [§1189] It is enough, however, if the sentencer is required to find at least one ***adequately defined*** aggravating factor; the sentencer is ***not*** required to weigh the aggravating and mitigating factors pursuant to any specific standards. [Zant v. Stephens, 462 U.S. 862 (1983)]

(b) **Racially disproportionate statistics:** [§1190] Some degree of discretion in the criminal justice system is fundamental and provides substantial benefits to defendants. As long as the capital sentencer's discretion is properly confined, the fact that statistics show that the death sentence is most frequently imposed on black defendants who kill white victims does not present such an unacceptable risk of racial prejudice in the capital sentencing system as to violate the Eighth and Fourteenth Amendments. [McCleskey v. Kemp, 481 U.S. 279 (1987)]

(2) **Mandatory death penalty:** [§1191] Mandatory capital punishment for a broad category of homicides, with no meaningful opportunity for consideration of mitigating factors regarding the crime or defendant, is cruel and unusual. [Woodson v. North Carolina, 428 U.S. 280 (1976)—killing of a police officer; Sumner v. Shuman, 483 U.S. 66 (1987)—murder by inmate serving life sentence without possibility of parole]

(a) **Compare:** But the death sentencing procedure may have some "mandatory aspects"—*e.g.*, death penalty required if the sentencing jury finds an aggravating factor and ***no*** mitigating factors. [Blystone v. Pennsylvania, 494 U.S. 299 (1990)]

(3) **Mitigating factors:** [§1192] The capital sentencing procedures must ***not explicitly*** or ***implicitly restrict*** the sentencer from considering such mitigating factors as any aspect of a defendant's background (*e.g.*, mental retardation or an abused childhood), character, or record and any of the circumstances of the offense that the defendant proffers as relating to his "personal moral culpability" for a sentence less than death. [Lockett v. Ohio, 438 U.S. 586 (1978); Penry v. Lynaugh, *supra*, §1184]

(a) **Unanimity:** [§1193] Nor may the capital sentencing procedures require the jury to unanimously find a mitigating factor before considering it. Such a requirement could lead to a death sentence even though almost all of the jurors thought it to be inappropriate. [McKoy v. North Carolina, 494 U.S. 433 (1990)]

(b) **Burden of proof:** [§1194] However, as long as the state has the burden of proving aggravating factors, the burden of proving mitigating factors may be placed on the defendant. [Walton v. Arizona, 497 U.S. 639 (1990)]

(4) **Permissible factors:** [§1195] The sentencing jury ***may*** consider evidence of defendant's probable future dangerousness (including psychiatric testimony which need not be based on personal examination). [Barefoot v. Estelle, 463 U.S. 880 (1983)] To this end, the jury ***may*** be told that the governor has power to commute a sentence of "life imprisonment without possibility of parole." Such instruction may be given even if state law forbids the jury to be told that the governor also has power to commute a death sentence—because the omission will not tend to skew the jury to favor the death sentence. [California v. Ramos, 463 U.S. 992 (1983)]

(a) **Victim impact statement:** [§1196] The sentencing jury may also consider evidence (and argument by the prosecutor) that describes the personal characteristics of the victim and the effect of the crime on the victim's family. States may legitimately permit the jury to assess the harm caused as a result of the crime as well as the defendant's moral culpability. [Payne v. Tennessee, 501 U.S. 808 (1991)—*overruling* Booth v. Maryland, 482 U.S. 496 (1987)]

6. Right to Trial by Jury

a. Petit jury

(1) **Constitutional provision:** [§1197] The Sixth Amendment provides: "In all criminal prosecutions, the accused shall enjoy the right to speedy and public trial, by an impartial jury of the State and district wherein the crime shall have been committed. . . ."

(2) **Effective in state and federal courts:** [§1198] Under the above provision, a defendant in a federal court charged with any ***serious offense***

(as distinguished from a petty offense) is entitled to trial by a jury. [Patton v. United States, 281 U.S. 276 (1930)] And the right is deemed so "fundamental" that it is fully incorporated by due process in state proceedings as well. [Duncan v. Louisiana, *supra*, §398]

(3) **What constitutes "trial by jury"**

(a) **Number of jurors:** [§1199] The number of jurors in federal criminal trials is 12, but this is pursuant to statute [Fed. R. Crim. P. 23] and is ***not constitutionally required*** [Williams v. Florida, 399 U.S. 78 (1970)]. The Constitution requires a sufficient number of jurors to provide ***adequate group deliberation*** and a ***fair cross section*** of the community. [Ballew v. Georgia, 435 U.S. 223 (1978)]

1) **Less than twelve jurors:** [§1200] Thus, state rules have been upheld allowing the use of six jurors [Williams v. Florida, *supra*]; but five jurors have been deemed too few to meet constitutional requirements [Ballew v. Georgia, *supra*].

(b) **Unanimous verdict**

1) **Federal courts:** [§1201] The Sixth Amendment right to jury trial is deemed to give a defendant in ***federal*** court the right to a unanimous jury verdict. [*See* Apodaca v. Oregon, *supra*, §397]

2) **State courts:** [§1202] However, the Court has upheld ***state*** convictions based on a verdict by only a "substantial majority" of the jurors—as low as 75% (nine to three verdict). [Johnson v. Louisiana, 406 U.S. 356 (1972)]

a) **Comment:** This is one of the unusual situations in which ***not all aspects*** of one of the Bill of Rights is incorporated by the Fourteenth Amendment—so that the right receives greater protection in federal than in state courts. (*See supra*, §397.)

b) **Note:** The Court has ***rejected*** the argument that allowing less than unanimity in the verdict undermines the ***reasonable doubt*** standard required by due process (*see infra*, §1227); the fact that three jurors disagree does ***not*** in itself establish a reasonable doubt.

c) **But note:** When a jury is as small as six persons, the verdict must be ***unanimous***. [Burch v. Louisiana, 441 U.S. 130 (1979)]

(4) **"Serious" vs. "petty" offenses:** [§1203] Since a jury trial is guaranteed only where a "serious" offense is charged, it becomes necessary to distinguish between "serious" and "petty" (nonserious) offenses. The Court looks to the maximum potential sentence. [Duncan v. Louisiana, *supra*]

(a) **Potential sentence:** [§1204] Any offense that carries a potential sentence of ***more than six months*** is a "serious" offense, so that a jury trial ***must*** be afforded on demand, and this is true even in cases where the actual sentence imposed is less than six months. [Baldwin v. New York, 399 U.S. 66 (1970)]

b. **Selection of jurors**

(1) **Constitutional source:** [§1205] The Sixth Amendment guarantees an accused the right to ***trial*** before "an ***impartial*** jury ***of the state and district*** wherein the crime shall have been committed." This guarantee is incorporated in the Fourteenth Amendment Due Process Clause and is therefore binding on the states. [Duncan v. Louisiana, *supra*]

(a) **Note:** The guarantee is construed to require that ***trial and grand juries*** in both federal and state courts be both ***"impartial" and*** drawn from a ***fair cross section*** of the community. [Taylor v. Louisiana, 419 U.S. 522 (1975)]

(2) **Requirement that jurors be drawn from "fair cross section of community":** [§1206] The right to a "jury trial" presupposes that the jury venire will be drawn from a pool ***broadly representative*** of the community at large. If there is systematic disproportion from a fair community cross section either mandated by statute or resulting from consistent practice, the only remaining issue is whether there is significant justification of this infringement, irrespective of whether there was discriminatory purpose.

(a) **Application**

1) **Systematic exclusions invalidated:** [§1207] A defendant is deprived of the constitutional right to a jury trial if any identifiable segment playing a major role in the community is systematically excluded or underrepresented by a particular selection process for the grand or petit jury panel. However, the requirement of a fair cross section may be overcome by a significant governmental interest that is incompatible with that process. [Duren v. Missouri, 439 U.S. 357 (1979)] *Examples:*

a) ***Systematic exclusion of blacks*** from petit jury panels has been held to be a denial of equal protection of law. [Patton v. Mississippi, 332 U.S. 463 (1947)]

b) ***Systematic exclusion of Mexican-born*** citizens from petit jury panels has been held to be a denial of equal protection. [Hernandez v. Texas, 347 U.S. 475 (1954)]

c) ***Exclusion of women*** from petit jury panels unless they volunteered for jury service has been held to be a denial of Sixth and Fourteenth Amendment rights to a "representative" jury. [Taylor v. Louisiana, *supra*]

1/ So is the ***underrepresentation*** of women resulting from the automatic exemption from jury service for any woman requesting not to serve. [Duren v. Missouri, *supra*]

d) ***Substantial underrepresentation of Mexican-Americans from grand jury selection*** has been held to be a prima facie denial of equal protection. [Castaneda v. Partida, 430 U.S. 482 (1977)—prima facie case not rebutted by showing that Mexican-Americans constituted "governing majority" in county]

2) **Compare—"considerable leeway" granted where no systematic exclusion shown:** [§1208] Where there is no claim that the jury panel was chosen in a manner that systematically excluded or discriminated against any identifiable segment of the community, "considerable leeway" is granted in selection of trial jurors. States are free to prescribe "relevant qualifications" and to provide "reasonable exemptions" from jury service. [Taylor v. Louisiana, *supra*]

a) **Proportionate representation not required:** [§1209] The right to a "jury trial" does ***not*** require proportionate representation of all the component groups in the community. [Akins v. Texas, 325 U.S. 398 (1945)]

1/ Indeed, state rules ***requiring*** proportional ***racial*** representation on jury panels have been held to ***violate*** equal protection—*i.e.*, race may not be considered as a factor either in inclusion or exclusion from jury service. [Cassell v. Texas, 339 U.S. 282 (1950)]

b) **"Blue ribbon" panels permitted:** [§1210] The Court has upheld a state's system of choosing "blue ribbon" jury panels (requiring special experience, etc.) to try certain kinds of cases. [Fay v. New York, 332 U.S. 261 (1947)]

3) **Peremptory challenges of jurors from particular groups permitted:** [§1211] The fair cross section required at the venire stage may be disrupted during the jury selection process to serve a legitimate state interest. Thus, peremptory challenges to eliminate prospective jurors from groups that might unduly favor one side are permitted to assure "an ***impartial*** jury." [Holland v. Illinois, 493 U.S. 474 (1990)]

(b) **Standing to challenge:** [§1212] A defendant convicted by a jury panel that is not fairly chosen may challenge the verdict on this ground alone. The defendant ***need not*** prove that the verdict was ***affected*** by the exclusion, or that any different outcome was likely had the jury been properly chosen. The verdict will be reversed simply because an improperly selected jury ***deprives*** the accused of the constitutional right to a "jury trial"; no other prejudice need be shown. [Taylor v. Louisiana, *supra*]

1) **Defendant need not be member of excluded group:** [§1213] Thus, a defendant may raise the constitutional challenge even where he is ***not*** a member of the group allegedly excluded. [Taylor v. Louisiana, *supra*—male rape defendant had standing to challenge systematic exclusion of women from jury panel that convicted him]

2) **Excluded persons may file civil suit:** [§1214] The persons ***excluded*** from juries solely because of their race, etc., ***also*** have standing to challenge the jury selection process. Of course, their attack will not be on the conviction. Rather, they are entitled to file a civil suit for injunctive or declaratory relief to establish their right to serve on such juries. [Carter v. Jury Commission, 396 U.S. 320 (1970)]

(3) **Impartial jury:** [§1215] Both the accused and the accuser have a constitutional right to an impartial jury. Although a juror may have a preconceived notion as to the guilt or innocence of the accused, she must be able to lay aside her impression or opinion and render a verdict based on the evidence presented to her. [Irvin v. Dowd, 366 U.S. 717 (1961)]

(a) **Effect of pretrial publicity:** [§1216] Where a community has been repeatedly exposed to inflammatory publicity regarding an accused, due process may require a change of venue to obtain an impartial jury. [Rideau v. Louisiana, 373 U.S. 723 (1963)—reversing conviction where state court refused change of venue notwithstanding fact that an interview between accused and sheriff, containing admissions of capital crimes charged, was telecast three times in the community]

(b) **Protection against prejudice during trial:** [§1217] A jury cannot be subjected to possible influence or prejudicial associations during a criminal trial. [Turner v. Louisiana, 379 U.S. 466 (1965)—reversing conviction where jury deliberated in custody of two deputy sheriffs who had given key testimony against defendant during trial]

(c) **Death penalty cases:** [§1218] A state may not automatically exclude for cause all prospective jurors who express a doubt or scruple about the death penalty. [Witherspoon v. Illinois, 391 U.S. 510 (1968)] The standard for determining when a prospective juror should be excluded for cause is whether the juror's views would prevent or substantially impair the performance of his duties in accordance with his instructions and oath. [Wainwright v. Witt, 469 U.S. 412 (1985)] Thus, if a juror's doubts or scruples about the death penalty prevent or substantially impair the performance of his duties, he may be excluded from the jury, and the fact that this may result in a "death qualified" jury does not infringe a defendant's constitutional rights. [Lockhart v. McCree, 476 U.S. 162 (1986)]

7. **Right to Public Trial**

a. **In federal courts:** [§1219] In federal courts, a public trial is expressly guaranteed by the Sixth Amendment.

b. **In state courts:** [§1220] This right is also guaranteed in state courts. A secret trial violates the Due Process Clause of the Fourteenth Amendment. [*In re* Oliver, 333 U.S. 257 (1948)]

c. **Suppression hearing:** [§1221] The right extends to a hearing to suppress wrongfully seized evidence that is conducted prior to the presentation of evidence of guilt. It may be outweighed only by a compelling and narrowly tailored interest articulated in findings by the trial judge. [Waller v. Georgia, 467 U.S. 39 (1984)]

d. **Scope of the right:** [§1222] The right to a public trial belongs only to the ***accused***, so that members of the public (*e.g.*, the press) do not have standing under the Sixth Amendment to complain of any exclusion. [Gannett Co. v. DePasquale, 443 U.S. 368 (1979)—holding that the press can be excluded under the Sixth Amendment from hearings on pretrial motions; *but see supra*, §1005]

8. **Right to Fair Trial:** [§1223] In addition to the foregoing rights specifically mentioned in the Constitution, the Court has deemed certain types of conduct so unfair in either state or federal court as to violate due process under the Fifth and Fourteenth Amendments. Such unfairness is usually coupled with a showing that the conduct complained of resulted in identifiable prejudice to the accused. On occasion, however, the Court has held that the conduct involves such a probability of prejudice that it is inherently lacking in due process—*i.e.*, actual prejudice need ***not*** be shown. *Examples:*

a. **Trial publicity:** [§1224] The Court has held in several cases that inflammatory publicity given to a crime or to the trial thereon may have so prejudiced the minds of potential jurors as to prevent the accused from receiving a fair trial (*see supra*, §1216).

(1) **Media coverage of trial:** [§1225] Radio, television, or photographic coverage of a criminal trial for public broadcast does not—when properly controlled—violate due process unless the defendant shows prejudicial effect on trial participants or jury inability to fairly adjudicate the case. [Chandler v. Florida, 449 U.S. 560 (1981)]

(2) **Protection of jury impartiality:** [§1226] A conviction must be reversed where the trial court fails to take such steps as are reasonably necessary to protect the impartiality of the jury. [Sheppard v. Maxwell, 384 U.S. 333 (1966)—trial judge failed to control coverage by news media so that "bedlam reigned" and inflammatory stories were held to have so aroused public opinion as to deny accused a fair trial]

9. **Burden of Proof:** [§1227] The Due Process Clause requires proof ***beyond a reasonable doubt*** of every fact necessary to constitute the crime with which the defendant is charged. [*In re* Winship, *supra*, §400]

a. **Proceedings to which applicable:** [§1228] This requirement applies in every proceeding in which violation of a criminal law is charged, or as to which criminal sanctions may be imposed.

(1) **Juvenile proceedings:** [§1229] It applies in juvenile proceedings, at least where the juvenile is charged with violation of a criminal law. [*In re* Winship, *supra*—whether juvenile is "delinquent" must be proved beyond reasonable doubt]

(2) **Appellate review:** [§1230] Since defendant's guilt must be proved beyond a reasonable doubt, the question of whether, after viewing the evidence in the light most favorable to the prosecution, any rational trier of fact could have found the essential elements of the crime beyond a reasonable doubt is a question of law cognizable in an appeal or a habeas corpus proceeding. [Jackson v. Virginia, 443 U.S. 307 (1979)]

10. **Requirement of Certainty in Criminal Statutes:** [§1231] Although all statutes must be definite and certain to be enforceable, this is a fundamental requirement regarding criminal statutes. The statute must give "fair warning" of the conduct that it makes a crime; *i.e.*, it must be sufficiently explicit to inform those who are subject to it exactly what conduct on their part will render them liable to its penalties. Moreover, the requirement of certainty ***prevents arbitrary and discriminatory enforcement*** of criminal statutes (*i.e.*, it assures explicit standards to guide the police as well as the public). [Grayned v. City of Rockford, 408 U.S. 104 (1972)]

a. **Application**

(1) **Vagueness:** [§1232] Statutes may be held invalid because of vagueness in defining ***what conduct constitutes*** the crime. *Examples:*

(a) ***To be a member of a "gang."*** [Lanzetta v. New Jersey, 306 U.S. 451 (1939)]

(b) ***To engage in conduct*** on city sidewalks in a manner ***"annoying" to passersby***. [Coates v . Cincinnati, 402 U.S. 611 (1971)]

(c) ***To wander city streets late at night*** "without lawful business and . . . [without giving a] satisfactory account of himself." [Palmer v. City of Euclid, 402 U.S. 544 (1971)]

b. **Effect of mens rea requirement:** [§1233] Vagueness in language may sometimes be cured by a requirement that the defendant have a specific intent to do that which is forbidden in vague language. [*See* Screws v. United States, *supra*, §713—statute made it a crime to ***willfully*** violate the "constitutional rights" of others]

11. **Rights on Appeal**

a. **Appeal of state conviction**

(1) **In state courts:** [§1234] A state is ***not required*** by the Federal Constitution ***to provide appellate review*** of alleged errors in the trial. [National Union of Marine Cooks v. Arnold, 348 U.S. 37 (1954)] However, if it does provide such review, it cannot do so in a way that unfairly discriminates against some convicted defendants on account of their poverty. Such discrimination violates the Due Process and Equal Protection Clauses of the Fourteenth Amendment. *Examples:*

(a) **Right to transcript:** [§1235] This requires that the state furnish an indigent defendant with a free transcript of the trial court proceedings, to the extent necessary to enable him to perfect his right to appeal. [Griffin v. Illinois, *supra*, §568]

1) ***Whether the entire transcript must be provided*** depends on the nature of the arguments that the defendant wishes to raise on appeal and the availability of alternative devices that could serve the same function. [Britt v. North Carolina, 404 U.S. 226 (1971)— same rule applies where defendant seeks transcript of prior mistrial in preparation for retrial]

2) ***If the defendant makes out a "colorable" need for a complete transcript***, the burden is ***on the prosecution*** to show that only a portion thereof is required for an effective appeal, or that some "alternative device" would serve the same function—*e.g.*, a statement of facts agreed to by both sides, or a full narrative statement based on the trial judge's notes or the court reporter's untranscribed notes. [Mayer v. City of Chicago, 404 U.S. 189 (1971)]

(b) **Right to counsel:** [§1236] A state's failure to appoint counsel to represent an indigent defendant on a direct appeal from a criminal conviction constitutes a denial of the Fourteenth Amendment, where nonindigents can have the benefit of counsel on their appeals. [Douglas v. California, *supra*, §568—state appellate court's procedure of going through appellate record to ascertain if any good would be served by appointment of counsel held not sufficient protection, so that failure to appoint counsel violated the Fourteenth Amendment]

1) **Right extends to appeal of right:** [§1237] The right to counsel extends only to proceedings in which the accused has a ***right*** to appellate review—normally, to an intermediary appellate court. If the indigent's conviction has been affirmed by such appellate court, the state is ***not*** required to furnish him with counsel to assist in seeking a ***discretionary*** review by the state supreme court, or to seek certiorari from the United States Supreme Court. [Ross v. Moffitt, *supra*, §569]

a) **Rationale:** The fact that an indigent defendant at this stage has had a trial transcript, a brief by appointed counsel on the first appeal as a matter of right, and often a judicial opinion on that appeal is deemed to assure him an "adequate opportunity to present his claims" when seeking discretionary review.

12. **Post-Conviction Procedures**

a. **In federal courts:** [§1238] By special statutory provision [28 U.S.C. §2254], a federal court may review a state conviction by means of a petition for a writ of habeas corpus.

(1) **Exhaustion of state remedies:** [§1239] The requirement of 28 U.S.C. section 2254 that the petitioner for habeas corpus have "exhausted the

remedies available in the courts of the State" is interpreted by the Court to mean that petitioner need only have exhausted those state remedies ***still available*** at the time she files in federal court for habeas corpus.

(2) **Right to be heard in federal court:** [§1240] If the applicant for federal habeas corpus has exhausted state remedies and claims a violation of the federal Constitution, a federal statute, or a treaty directly bearing upon her conviction, the federal court may reexamine the state criminal conviction. [Fay v. Noia, 372 U.S. 391 (1963)]

(a) **Effect:** The result is that most constitutional claims that were developed in the state courts may be heard in the federal habeas corpus proceeding. [Fay v. Noia, *supra*]

(b) **Compare:** However, if the constitutional claim was not developed in the state court because petitioner failed to comply with a state procedural rule requiring such claims to be made, the claim may be heard for the first time in the federal court only if: (i) there is a showing of ***cause*** for noncompliance with the state rule, and (ii) there is some showing of ***actual prejudice***, ***or*** (iii) failure to consider the claim will result in a ***fundamental miscarriage of justice*** (*e.g.*, petitioner shows actual innocence). [Keeney v. Tamayo-Reyes, 112 S. Ct. 1715 (1992)]

1) **"Cause":** Ignorance or inadvertent error by petitioner's lawyer does ***not*** constitute "cause." Petitioner must bear the risk of attorney error. [Coleman v. Thompson, 501 U.S. 722 (1991)]

(c) **And note:** Where the prisoner had a full and fair opportunity in the state court to litigate certain claims not directly related to the issue of guilt (*e.g.*, a search and seizure claim), such claims are not a proper basis for a grant of federal habeas corpus relief. [Stone v. Powell, 428 U.S. 465 (1976)]

13. **Retroactive Application of Determinations Regarding Constitutional Rights of Accused:** [§1241] In recent years, the Court has had to consider repeatedly whether its decisions, recognizing some right of an accused in the criminal process, are to be applied retroactively—*i.e.*, whether the decision is merely a guidepost for future criminal prosecutions, or can be invoked by persons previously convicted (without benefit of the constitutional protection involved) to gain their freedom or, at the very least, a new trial. (For general discussion of retroactivity concept, *see supra*, §§112-113.)

a. **Factors governing:** [§1242] The Court usually determines whether its opinion is to be given retroactive effect on the basis of the following factors:

(1) **Purpose to be served:** If the major purpose of the new constitutional doctrine is to overcome some aspect of criminal trial procedure that substantially impedes its ***truth-finding function***, and therefore raises serious questions about the accuracy of guilty verdicts in the past, the new doctrine will be given retroactive effect. However, if the integrity of the truth-finding function is not challenged by the new doctrine, the Court will go on to consider these other factors:

(2) **Reliance by police:** The extent of reliance by law enforcement officials on the old standards is considered.

(3) **Effect:** Also, the effect on the administration of justice of a retroactive application of the new standard is considered by the Court.

b. **Rules applied retroactively:** [§1243] Under this approach, the Court has given retroactive effect to those decisions that affect "the ***very integrity of the fact-finding process***"—so that the previous standard posed a "clear danger of convicting the innocent." [Johnson v. New Jersey, 384 U.S. 719 (1966)]

(1) **Example:** The decisions establishing a criminal defendant's ***right to counsel*** at trial [Gideon v. Wainwright, *supra*, §1156] and on appeal [Douglas v. California, *supra*, §1236] were given retroactive effect because the assistance of counsel is fundamental to the truth-determining process at each of these stages.

(2) **Example:** Likewise, the decision in *Griffin v. Illinois* (*supra*, §1235), establishing an indigent defendant's right to a free transcript on appeal of his conviction has a retroactive effect. [Eskridge v. Washington Prison Board, 357 U.S. 214 (1958)]

c. **Rules not applied retroactively:** [§1244] However, where the Court concludes that ***other safeguards*** were available to protect the integrity of the truth-determining process at trial, and the interests of justice would be ***adversely affected*** by reversing convictions obtained in reliance on the previous standards, the new rule will ***not*** be applied retroactively. [Johnson v. New Jersey, *supra*]

(1) **Example:** The decision in *Mapp v. Ohio* (*supra*, §1172) barring use in state courts of evidence obtained by illegal search or seizure does not apply retroactively. *Rationale:* The rule's purpose is to ***deter unlawful searches***; and this has no bearing on the guilt or innocence of the accused. Hence, the ends of justice do not require retroactive application. [Linkletter v. Walker, 381 U.S. 618 (1965)]

(a) **Note:** A similar result and reasoning applies to the decision in *Katz v. United States* (*supra*, §1174) prohibiting use of evidence obtained by electronic eavesdropping. [Desist v. United States, 394 U.S. 244 (1969)]

(2) **Example:** The decision in *Miranda v. Arizona* (*supra*, §1164) limiting police right to interrogate criminal suspects has no retroactive effect. *Rationale:* Deprivation of counsel during the investigative stage does not necessarily impair the integrity of the ***truth-determining*** process at ***trial***. [Johnson v. New Jersey, *supra*]

(a) **Note:** The same result (and rationale) applies to the decision in *United States v. Wade*, 388 U.S. 218 (1967), dealing with an accused's right to counsel at a police lineup. But if the accused can show that the lineup was so unfairly constructed that ***due process*** was violated through admission of eyewitness identification, retroactive relief may be available. [Stovall v. Denno, 388 U.S. 293 (1967)]

(3) **Example:** The decision in *Griffin v. California* (*supra*, §1168), prohibiting adverse comment on an accused's failure to testify in his own defense, also has no retroactive application. *Rationale:* The purpose of the rule (to preserve the accusatorial system) would not be advanced by retroactive application. [Tehan v. United States *ex rel.* Shott, 382 U.S. 406 (1966)]

(4) **Example:** And the decision in *Duncan v. Louisiana* (*supra*, §1203), requiring states to afford jury trials in all cases involving serious criminal offenses, does not apply retroactively. *Rationale:* A nonjury trial is not necessarily unfair. [DeStefano v. Woods, 392 U.S. 631 (1968)]

d. **Cases on appeal:** [§1245] Even if the new rule is not given retroactive effect to all persons previously convicted, it will still be applied to cases ***pending*** on direct appeal at the time the new rule is announced—even if the new rule constitutes a "clear break with the past." [Griffith v. Kentucky, 479 U.S. 314 (1987)—*overruling* United States v. Johnson, 457 U.S. 1139 (1982)]

REVIEW QUESTIONS

FILL IN
ANSWER

1. Congress enacts a statute providing that the Supreme Court may no longer hear appeals in cases arising under the National Labor Relations Act. Is the statute valid? ________

2. Jones, a resident of Arizona, sues the State of Arizona in federal court for breach of contract. The State moves to dismiss on the ground that federal jurisdiction is barred by the Eleventh Amendment. What ruling? ________

3. Jones, a resident of Arizona, sues the City of New Orleans in a federal court for breach of contract. The City moves to dismiss on the ground that federal courts have no jurisdiction because of the Eleventh Amendment. How should the court rule? ________

4. Jones, a resident of Arizona, files suit in federal court to enjoin the governor of Arizona from enforcing a state law that allegedly violates Jones's constitutional rights. The governor moves to dismiss on the ground that federal jurisdiction is barred by the Eleventh Amendment. What ruling? ________

5. Does the Supreme Court have mandatory appellate jurisdiction where a state court has held a federal statute invalid? ________

6. Bob Brown files a class action in federal court on behalf of himself and all other state citizens under age 21 challenging the validity of a state law restricting the sale of liquor to those over age 21. By the time the case reaches the Supreme Court, Bob Brown is 23 years of age. Should the action be dismissed as "moot"? ________

7. Which, if any, of the following have standing to sue in federal court? ________

   (A) Charlene Cook files suit to challenge exclusionary zoning practices by City, alleging that the challenged zoning made it too expensive for her to purchase a home in City.

   (B) Society files suit challenging a state law requiring disclosure of Society's membership, alleging that the law infringes its members' freedom of association.

   (C) Environmental protection group files suit to block further oil drilling on the ground that it is contrary to the public interest.

   (D) State files suit on behalf of its citizens (as "parens patriae") to contest federal spending measures.

8. Donald Douglas files suit as a federal taxpayer challenging money appropriations made by Congress to the F.B.I. because of allegedly improper activities by the F.B.I. The Government moves to dismiss on the ground that Douglas lacks standing. How should the court rule? ________

9. The Supreme Court of State X has affirmed a judgment in a case involving a substantial federal question. However, state common law issues were also involved in the case. Is the state court judgment reviewable in the United States Supreme Court? ________

10. A statute has recently been enacted making certain business practices criminal. Sheila Jones is in fear of being prosecuted by the state under this new law because she regularly engages in the practices now prohibited. Jones claims that the statute violates her constitutional rights. Is any relief available to Jones in federal court? ________

11. Mary Adams files suit challenging a state election law that provides that an incumbent (person presently holding state office) shall be listed first on the ballot. Adams claims that this gives the incumbents a big advantage in any election. Should the action be dismissed as involving a "political question"? ________

12. Assume that the Supreme Court has just held a state statute unconstitutional. Will this decision ever be given ***retroactive*** effect? ________

13. Congress enacts legislation imposing an excise tax of $50,000 per annum on all firearms dealers. The monies thus collected fund a government project to reimburse victims of violent crimes. The tax is invalid since its principal effect is to discourage the sale of firearms. True or false? ________

14. Congress passes a statute authorizing exclusion of all alien terrorists. John Kendrick has arranged with Sien Rourke to give a series of lectures on the Irish dilemma. The Attorney General has confidential information concerning Rourke's membership in a terrorist organization. Can Kendrick successfully challenge Rourke's exclusion because it interferes with Kendrick's right of association and therefore violates his First Amendment rights? ________

15. A Mexican citizen enters the United States illegally, but obtains a job and establishes permanent residence here. Twenty years later, his illegal entry is discovered and he is seized for deportation. Is he entitled to a hearing before being expelled? ________

16. State X enacts a law prohibiting naturalized citizens from holding state office during the first five years following their naturalization. Is the law valid? ________

17. Congress enacts a law that provides that a naturalized citizen will lose her citizenship by enlisting in the armed services of a hostile foreign government. Is the law constitutional? ________

18. Is it permissible for either House of Congress to issue subpoenas to witnesses and to take their testimony on matters not currently the subject of pending legislation? ________

19. The President appoints Rudolph Rich to the Federal Resources Board, and obtains the "advice and consent" of the Senate, which is required for the appointment. Can the President later remove Rich from the Federal Resources Board ***without*** the approval of the Senate? ________

20. Due to an extreme shortage of natural gas, and without waiting for Congress to act, the President declares an emergency and orders federal officers to take possession of all available gas storage tanks and to supervise a program of allocations drawn up by the President. The owners of the gas challenge the seizure on the ground that the President has no such power. In whose favor should the Court rule? ________

21. A congressional committee investigating foreign policy asks the Secretary of State for certain information. The Secretary refuses on the ground that the information relates to high-level secret talks, and the President has directed him to assert executive privilege. Will the Secretary's claim of privilege be upheld? ________

22. State X enacts a law that provides that resident aliens may receive welfare benefits only if they are citizens of countries that provide similar benefits for United States citizens. Is the law valid? ________

23. If a state statute conflicts with a treaty obligation, which prevails? ________

24. If an act of Congress conflicts with a treaty obligation of the United States, which prevails? ________

25. The city of Old York is on the verge of bankruptcy. To save it from bankruptcy, the state legislature passes emergency legislation authorizing the city to issue "scrip," which shall be legal tender for payment of all obligations owing by the city, and that persons receiving such scrip from the city may use it as legal tender for paying their private obligations within the state. Is the statute valid? ________

26. Is freedom of association and expression a "privilege and immunity" of national citizenship within the meaning of the Fourteenth Amendment? ________

27. Is the right of interstate travel a "privilege and immunity" of national citizenship within the meaning of the Fourteenth Amendment? ________

28. State Z enacts a law providing that foreign corporations must pay a fee of $50,000 for a permit to sell certain types of securities within the state, whereas domestic corporations have to pay only $500 for the same permit. Acme, Inc., a foreign corporation, attacks this as violating Article IV, Section 2 (Interstate Privileges and Immunities Clause). Is Acme correct? ________

29. Congress enacts a law imposing a permit fee of $10 per annum for vehicles entering national parks. Is this law valid as applied to cars and trucks owned by State X that are required to enter the park lands for state purposes? ________

30. State X requires "all motor vehicles operated on state highways" to have a license plate issued by state authorities upon payment of a specified fee. Can this statute be applied constitutionally to federal cars and trucks using state roads? ________

31. Is a state income tax on the salaries of federal employees valid? ________

32. State X enacts a sales tax that requires a seller to collect from a purchaser 5% of the amount of the sale, and to remit it to the state. Is this tax valid as applied to sales made

by a seller to a private contractor who is working for the United States Government on a "cost plus" basis (so that the ***cost*** of the tax is ultimately passed on to the federal government)? ________

33. Is the regulation of interstate commerce an "exclusive" power of Congress? ________

34. Does Congress have the power to regulate interstate commerce solely for the purpose of furthering ***state*** laws or policies? ________

35. Can Congress, under its commerce power, regulate an activity that is purely intrastate? ________

36. Congress enacts a law expressly authorizing the states to require out-of-state milk producers to conform to local testing and inspection standards as a condition for selling their milk within the state. The effect is that each state sets its own standards, and this makes it very difficult and expensive for out-of-state producers to compete with local producers. Is the law valid? ________

37. Congress enacts a law requiring that all hospitals maintain certain minimum emergency room facilities. State X, however, has a law requiring hospitals in its state to contain much more complete emergency room facilities. Is the State X law valid? ________

38. State X enacts a law requiring national airlines servicing local airports to comply with safety standards substantially the same as the safety standards established by the Federal Aviation Administration. Is the State X law valid? ________

39. The State of Maine enacts a law prohibiting the shipment outside the state of any lobsters taken from state waters. The purpose of the law is to protect the state's lobster beds from being depleted by the heavy demands of out-of-state consumers. Its effect is to cause consumers throughout the country to pay considerably higher prices because of the nonavailability of Maine lobsters. Is the law valid? ________

40. In the absence of federal regulation, state regulation of interstate commerce is permissible as long as it is nondiscriminatory and does not regulate a subject matter that requires uniform national regulation. True or false? ________

41. The State of Kansas enacts a law that requires any vehicle using Kansas highways to be equipped with special mufflers and emission control devices not required in most other states. The purpose is to limit the noise and smoke emissions along Kansas highways. Is the law valid as applied to out-of-state vehicles using Kansas roads? ________

42. The State of Kentucky enacts a law providing that all bourbon whisky sold in the state be sold at the lowest price available anywhere in the nation. Is the law valid? ________

43. The Missouri Tax Commissioner seeks to impose a property tax on trucks belonging to Ace Cattle Co. Ace resists on the ground that it is a Texas corporation and none of its trucks were actually in Missouri on tax assessment day (although Ace admits that it regularly sends its trucks in and out of Missouri as part of its cattle-raising operations). Who wins? ________

a. Should the amount of tax be apportioned on the basis of the average physical presence of the trucks within the taxing state? ________

44. The Kansas Tax Commissioner seeks to impose a property tax on cattle that were located on a feed lot in Kansas on tax assessment day. The owner of the cattle resists on the ground that the cattle had been raised in Texas and were being trucked to a slaughterhouse in Illinois, and were merely being fattened up for a few days in Kansas while en route. Who wins? ________

a. Should the amount of tax be apportioned based on the number of days the cattle were in Kansas? ________

45. Interstate Railway has its headquarters in Alabama, with scheduled trips to and from Texas. May Texas validly levy a privilege tax on Railway's gross revenues derived from Texas, if properly apportioned? ________

46. General Encyclopedia Co. has a sales office in Illinois. Salespeople from this office solicit orders from customers in Illinois and Iowa. All orders are forwarded to the company's home office in Nebraska, where they are formally "accepted," and from which the books are shipped directly to the customer.

a. May Illinois impose a sales tax on sales made to Illinois customers? ________

b. May Iowa impose a sales tax on the sales made in Iowa? ________

47. Iowa law requires that all sales solicitors pay a $100 annual fee for a license to solicit sales in Iowa. Can this law be constitutionally applied to the salespeople working out of General Encyclopedia's Illinois office? ________

48. Iowa law requires that any foreign corporation seeking to do business in Iowa must pay $10,000 annually for the right to do business in the state, whereas local corporations pay no more than $100 annually for the same permission. Is the law valid? ________

49. The State of Maine imposes a tax of $1 per pound on all lobsters exported from Maine to foreign nations. The tax is designed to conserve Maine lobsters from excessive foreign demand. Is the tax valid? ________

50. "Any right enumerated in the Bill of Rights will receive the same protection against state action as against federal." True or false? ________

51. State X welfare authorities adopt a regulation that provides for the immediate cutoff of welfare payments to any welfare recipient who fails to report for work on county work projects when told to do so. Pursuant to this regulation, and without any sort of hearing, Paul's welfare benefits are cut off because he failed to report for work on a county road project to which he had been assigned. Is the termination of Paul's benefits proper? ________

52. State X enacts a law prohibiting drugstores from selling contraceptives to any person under age 16. The law is challenged on the ground that the age 16 classification

serves "no compelling state interest." The State seeks to uphold the law on the ground that it is valid as long as it serves a "rational purpose" (deterring younger persons from sexual relations). Which test should the court apply? ________

53. Allen, a former agent of the Central Intelligence Agency, makes a speaking tour of several Latin American countries during which he denounces the actions of the United States government. Allen also reveals the identities of several undercover CIA agents. As a result, the State Department revokes Allen's passport. Is this action valid? ________

54. A state law that grants widows, but not widowers, a property tax exemption necessarily violates equal protection. True or false? ________

55. Poverty is considered a suspect classification for purposes of equal protection analysis. True or false? ________

56. State X enacts a law requiring new political parties to submit nominating petitions bearing the signatures of at least 5% of all registered voters. Is this law valid? ________

57. State X enacts a law that denies persons convicted of a felony the right to vote in state elections. Does this violate the Equal Protection Clause? ________

58. The right to vote cannot be restricted on grounds other than residence, age, or citizenship in any election, unless some compelling state interest is served by the restriction. True or false? ________

59. "Local boundary lines are entitled to ***no*** consideration in apportioning congressional voting districts." True or false? ________

60. "Equal protection requires the same standard of proportionate representation in both federal and state elections. No deviation from the one person-one vote formula is permitted without substantial justification—regardless of whether the election is to Congress or to the city council." True or false? ________

61. The "one person-one vote" principle does not apply in the election of an official who performs only administrative functions—*e.g.*, the state treasurer. True or false? ________

62. In an effort to conserve available funds, School Board adopts a program limiting the number of classes in which students may enroll. Student challenges this program on the ground that it impairs the "constitutional right to a quality education," and that the limit on the number of classes serves no "compelling state interest" and is not the "least burdensome alternative" available. Who wins? ________

63. Is a filing fee required for bankruptcy proceedings violative of equal protection to indigents? ________

64. State Y grants to Meadowbrook Race Track, Inc. (a private company) the exclusive right to operate horse races in the state. Meadowbrook enforces a policy whereby persons under age 21 are excluded from the track. Bobby, a minor, challenges this policy as discriminatory "state action" by State Y. Is he correct? ________

65. Do any of the constitutional amendments ***expressly*** prohibit private (as opposed to governmental) actions affecting the rights of other citizens? ________

66. The Fourteenth Amendment is a limitation on state action, and is not a source of power to the federal government. True or false? ________

67. All federal civil rights legislation is based on the Thirteenth, Fourteenth, or Fifteenth Amendment. True or false? ________

68. State X has a statute that bans exhibition of films containing any form of nudity. In reviewing the constitutionality of this statute, the court will presume it is constitutional until its invalidity is shown beyond a reasonable doubt. True or false? ________

69. State X enacts a law making it a crime "to advocate or join with others to advocate the practice of peaceful civil disobedience." Is the statute valid? ________

70. In determining whether a law that restricts freedom of speech is constitutional, it must be shown that the expression was directed to inciting, and likely to incite, ***imminent*** lawless action. True or false? ________

71. The *Daily Bugle* publishes an article by a sportswriter accusing Coach of "throwing" a football game. Coach sues *Daily Bugle* for defamation. The evidence shows that the reporter who wrote the story had no reasonable ground for believing the story was true when she wrote it. The *Daily Bugle* cannot claim any constitutional privilege for this publication because Coach is not a public official or candidate for public office. True or false? ________

72. "Gay Way" is a magazine published by homosexuals and designed to reach the homosexual community. Its pages often contain pictures of nude males and females embracing members of their own sex.

    a. In determining whether the magazine is "obscene," it must be shown to appeal to the prurient interest of homosexuals. The fact that it would ***not*** appeal to the prurient interest of the rest of the community is to be disregarded. True or false? ________

    b. In determining whether this magazine is "obscene," the fact that it is being published for a profit is to be disregarded. True or false? ________

    c. The determination of whether this magazine is "obscene" must be made in light of the contemporary moral standards of the "community" nationwide and not just statewide standards. True or false? ________

    d. If the magazine is found to be "obscene," then any magazine dealer or distributor who sells "Gay Way" can be punished along with the publisher of the magazine. True or false? ________

73. To protect minors, City adopts an ordinance providing that billboards may not carry advertisements that display bare female breasts or buttocks. Is the ordinance valid? ________

74. City enacts an ordinance making it a crime for persons to use designated four-letter words in public speeches or debates. Is the ordinance valid? ________

75. To preserve neighborhood stability, City passes an ordinance prohibiting the posting of "for sale" signs on real estate. Is this ordinance valid? ________

76. Congress enacts a law banning the importation of any "obscene" materials into this country and authorizing customs officials to seize and destroy such materials without any hearing or other proceedings. Is the law valid? ________

77. Is symbolic conduct (conduct such as display of objects or mode of dress) always protected to the same extent as "pure" speech? ________

78. Municipality accepts advertisements for commercial products in its buses. However, it refuses to permit its buses to carry political advertisements. Candidate Jones claims this impairs her freedom of expression in public places. Is she right? ________

79. City adopts an ordinance that requires all persons seeking to hold a parade or demonstration on City streets to obtain a license or permit at least three days in advance from the police commissioner. Is this ordinance valid? ________

80. State enacts an ordinance that homeowners are entitled to a special exemption from the property tax provided they file a sworn oath "that they have never been a member of any group dedicated to the violent overthrow of the state or federal government." Is the oath requirement valid? ________

81. State School Board requires all employees to take an oath "to support the federal and state constitutions and to oppose the overthrow of the federal and state governments by illegal means." Employees who refuse are subject to summary discharge (without a hearing). Is the Board's requirement constitutional? ________

82. State School Board requires all prospective employees to take an oath "that they have never been a member of any group dedicated to the violent overthrow of the state or federal government." Persons who once belonged to such groups are barred from employment by the Board. Is the Board's requirement constitutional? ________

83. State University adopts a rule that all personnel abstain from participation in political campaigns or controversies involving the administration of the University. Professor Wallbanger writes a letter to the editor of the *Daily Bugle* highly critical of the manner in which the president of the University is allocating research funds. Wallbanger is fired for violating the University rule. Is he entitled to reinstatement? ________

84. State requires all persons seeking to be licensed as teachers to list all organizations in which they have been members for the past 10 years. Is this requirement valid? ________

85. Does a news reporter have a constitutional right to withhold the sources of her news stories when disclosure is sought in a ***civil*** action? ________

86. State X enacts a state law designed to further vocational guidance for high school students. All high school students are to receive aptitude tests and individual

counseling based on the test results. Public school personnel are assigned to perform these functions at all schools, public and private. Maude challenges this law as constituting financial aid to parochial schools in violation of the Establishment Clause. Is Maude's challenge valid? ________

87. State X exempts from local property taxation any real estate used exclusively for purposes of charitable, educational, and religious worship. Angela attacks this law as violating the Establishment Clause. Is Angela's challenge valid? ________

88. State X enacts a law providing that all students attending public schools shall be let out early on the Jewish High Holy Days to enable Jewish students to attend religious services. Mark attacks this law as violating the Establishment Clause. Will Mark's challenge be successful? ________

89. State X enacts a law that requires that all children within the state attend public or private schools through the eighth grade. Jeremiah attacks this law as infringing his right to educate his children at home, which he claims is a basic tenet of a new religious group he leads. Will Jeremiah's challenge be successful? ________

90. Because of limitations in staff and facilities, public school students in State X are required to attend classes four hours a day, six days a week. Paul, a Seventh-Day Adventist, challenges the requirement that his children attend school on Saturdays as interfering with the "free exercise" of their religion (which prohibits such activities on Saturday). Is Paul's challenge valid? ________

91. State X enacts a law requiring all students at State University to take basic military training. Marsha, a student at State University, claims this law infringes her freedom of conscience and belief because she is a pacifist. Will Marsha's challenge be successful? ________

92. State X enacts a law requiring employers to allow employees time off with pay to attend religious services on Good Friday. Harry Jones, an avowed atheist, challenges the law on the ground that it violates both the Establishment and Free Exercise Clauses of the Constitution. State X moves to dismiss Jones's suit on the ground that he has no standing to challenge the law because, being an atheist, it cannot be said to interfere with his personal rights or beliefs. How should the Court rule on the state's motion to dismiss? ________

93. Requiring the owner of a shopping center to provide access to persons desiring to distribute handbills constitutes a taking. True or false? ________

94. Does the Constitution expressly limit the federal government's power to impair contractual obligations? ________

95. Congress enacts a law providing that resident aliens are subject to deportation if they have "ever" been convicted of a narcotics offense. A resident alien challenges this law on the ground that it would operate to impose additional punishment for conduct that took place prior to enactment of the statute. Is the law valid? ________

96. Mary Smith has been subpoenaed to give testimony before a grand jury investigating organized crime. Mary is indigent and demands that the court appoint an attorney to advise her and appear with her before the grand jury. Is Mary entitled to such assistance? ________

97. Is a person entitled to counsel in a state criminal trial even where the crime charged carries no prison sentence? ________

98. Is a ***unanimous*** verdict constitutionally required in both federal and state prosecutions? ________

99. D is charged with speeding; the maximum sentence for this offense is a $50 fine. Does D have a constitutional right to trial by jury? ________

100. D is a black man. He is tried and convicted by a jury consisting of both whites and blacks. He appeals his conviction solely on the ground that Asian-Americans had been systematically excluded from the jury and therefore the jury is not representative of the community. Does D (not being Asian himself) have standing to raise the exclusion of Asian-Americans? ________

101. D is on trial for murder. State law requires that if D claims the killing was accidental or justified, she must bear the burden of proof on this issue; failing this, the killing will be deemed to have been with malice aforethought. Is this law valid? ________

102. D, an indigent, is convicted of murder. After affirmance of his conviction by the state supreme court, D seeks appointment of counsel to assist him in seeking certiorari from the United States Supreme Court. Is D constitutionally entitled to such assistance? ________

103. Which of the following factors is entitled to the greatest weight in determining whether a new decision by the Supreme Court affecting the administration of criminal justice will be given retroactive effect? ________

(A) Police officers have acted in reasonable reliance on former decisions of the Court.

(B) The primary purpose and effect of the new standard is to deter police misconduct and disregard for constitutional rights of defendants.

(C) The new decision was formulated for the purpose of ending some aspect of criminal procedure that raised questions as to the accuracy of guilty verdicts in the past.

ANSWERS TO REVIEW QUESTIONS

1. **YES** — Article III, Section 2 expressly gives Congress the power to regulate the ***appellate*** (but not original) jurisdiction of the Supreme Court. [§§3, 16-26]

2. **MOTION GRANTED** — The Eleventh Amendment bars suits by a private citizen against any state (including the state in which the citizen resides). [§6]

3. **MOTION DENIED** — The Eleventh Amendment prohibits suits by a private citizen against a ***state***, but this does not apply to subdivisions of a state. [§10]

4. **MOTION DENIED** — The "stripping doctrine" of *Ex parte Young* is applicable. [§11]

5. **NO** — Nearly all the Supreme Court's appellate jurisdiction is by certiorari. [§§22-23]

6. **NO** — Although the class representative's individual controversy may have become moot, he may continue to pursue a class action as long as the claims of other class members survive. [§41]

7. **ONLY (B)** — (A) No standing because general financial ability is not sufficient "direct and immediate injury" as result of challenged practice. [§§44, 46]

   (B) Standing because disclosure of membership would also affect the ability of the group to obtain members; thus, the infringement of members' constitutional rights also causes injury to the group itself. [§57]

   (C) No standing because standing cannot be predicated upon claim of injury to the public at large. [§§44, 47]

   (D) No standing because the state may not assert the claims of its citizens against the federal government with respect to a federal spending program. [§61]

8. **MOTION GRANTED** — There is not sufficient "nexus" between his status as taxpayer and the allegedly illegal activities of the F.B.I. [§50]

9. **DEPENDS** — If the state court judgment can be supported entirely by a state ground and clearly indicates that it is based on state law, the Supreme Court will not review. [§§73-76]

10. **YES** — As long as no criminal prosecution is yet pending, federal declaratory relief is available. (Declaratory relief is deemed to produce much less tension with state interests than enjoining a pending state prosecution.) [§§84-88]

11. **NO** — The mere fact that the suit seeks protection of a political ***right*** does not mean it presents a political question. [§109]

12. **YES** — The Court's declaration of unconstitutionality has full retroactive effect in all cases still open on appeal and as to all events regardless of when they occur. [§112]

13. **FALSE** A tax that also has the effect of regulating will be upheld if Congress has the power to regulate the subject of the taxed activity or if the dominant intent of the tax is to raise revenue (which can be shown by the fact that the tax in fact raises revenue). Congress can regulate sales of firearms involving interstate commerce (which could include every sale of firearms under the affectation doctrine) and the tax here will apparently raise revenue. [§§133-137]

14. **NO** If Congress has a bona fide reason for excluding an alien, citizens may not complain that such exclusion interferes with their First Amendment rights. [§151]

15. **YES** Due process protections are available to an alien resident in the United States (whether here legally or ***illegally***). [§152]

16. **NO** The rights of native-born and naturalized citizens are equal; hence, this limitation would be a violation of the Fourteenth Amendment Equal Protection Clause. [§156]

17. **MAYBE** Congress can take away citizenship where the citizen, through words or conduct, manifests an intent to relinquish citizenship. Enlisting in the armed services of a hostile foreign government may manifest such intent. [§157]

18. **YES** It is the ***power*** to legislate, which implies the power to investigate; pendency of legislation is not essential. [§§160-161]

19. **MAYBE** It depends on the status of the Federal Resources Board. If it is strictly an arm of the executive branch, appointees are removable by the President at will. However, if this is an administrative agency created by Congress, removal may be limited to the causes specified in the statute creating the agency. [§§176, 178]

20. **OWNERS** The President has no inherent law-making power in internal affairs. [Youngstown Sheet & Tube v. Sawyer] (Note, however, that parts of *Youngstown* indicate that the President has inherent power to act in cases of great national emergency as long as Congress has not expressly denied such power.) [§§182, 189-190]

21. **MAYBE** This is an open question. [§§194, 197]

22. **NO** No state regulation (direct or indirect) is permitted in the field of external affairs. The statute here would be viewed as an attempt to influence welfare policies of other countries. [§204]

23. **TREATY** A state statute that conflicts with a treaty provision is invalid. [§208]

24. **LAST IN TIME** Acts of Congress are of equal weight with treaties and thus, the last expression of the sovereign will control where there is a conflict. [§209]

25. **NO** "Coinage of money" is an exclusive ***federal*** power, and the issuance of scrip as legal tender for private debts would probably be so regarded. [§223]

26. **NO** The Bill of Rights is ***not*** included in the Privileges and Immunities Clause. [Slaughterhouse Cases] [§231]

27. **MAYBE** Source of this right is unclear, but ***it is*** constitutionally protected. [§§230, 465-467]

28. **NO** The Interstate Privileges and Immunities Clause protects only "citizens" of each state, and a corporation is not a "citizen." [§236] (*Note:* Acme may be able to attack this statute on Commerce Clause or equal protection grounds. [§§291, 381])

29. **YES** Generally, the federal government may tax state government property or activities, as long as the federal tax does not discriminate by taxing them and not other property or activities similarly situated. Furthermore, operation of these vehicles is not an activity that is unique to state sovereignty. In addition, the tax may be upheld as a user fee. [§245]

30. **NO** State laws may not tax or burden federal activities. [§§247-248]

31. **YES** No unreasonable burden on the federal government is deemed imposed thereby. [§250]

32. **YES** *See Alabama v. King & Boozer.* [§§251-252]

33. **NO** Although the Commerce Clause grants to Congress the power to regulate interstate commerce, it is deemed ***concurrent*** with state power over transactions occurring within the state. [§261]

34. **YES** This is deemed a valid exercise of congressional power; there need be no national goal served thereby. [§266]

35. **YES** As long as it has a ***national economic effect***, *i.e.*, ***affects*** more than one state. [§§271-272]

36. **YES** Congress's broad power over interstate commerce includes the power to ***authorize the states*** to regulate where they otherwise would not have power to do so—even where the effect is to ***discriminate*** against interstate commerce. [§280]

37. **YES** There is no apparent intent to supersede state regulation of hospitals, and the field is not one that apparently requires uniform national regulation. There is no direct conflict with the federal law because compliance with the state law would also constitute compliance with the federal. (Result would be contra, of course, if the state law made ***compliance*** with federal law more difficult or expensive.) [§§283-289]

38. **NO** Where Congress has provided complete regulation of a particular field (interstate airlines), ***any*** state regulation is preempted; it need not conflict. [§§283-289]

39. **NO** Regulations for protection of local natural resources are usually not upheld. [§§295-296]

40. **FALSE** The nature and extent of the burden on interstate commerce must also be ***outweighed*** by the interests served by the state regulation. [§§309-319]

41. **NO** The burden on interstate carriers in complying with the stricter Kansas standards would outweigh whatever interests Kansas has. [§315]

42. **NO** This may force sellers to lower prices elsewhere. The Twenty-First Amendment does not allow state regulation on the local sale of liquor if the practical effect is to regulate liquor prices in other states. [§326]

43. **TAX COMMISSIONER** Property tax may properly be imposed if there is a "nexus" between the taxing state and instrumentalities used to convey commodities interstate. [§§338-339]

a. **YES** This is required where instrumentalities have more than one taxable situs. [§§340-346]

44. **OWNER** Commodities in the course of interstate shipment are exempt from local tax. Here, the "break" in transit was ***not*** intended to end the interstate movement, and hence the goods remained exempt. (Result would be different if they were on feed lot pending owner's disposition.) [§§347-349]

a. **NO** Either the goods are taxable or they are not; there is no apportionment where goods are in the course of interstate shipment. [§347]

45. **YES** Privilege taxes may be imposed if the activity taxed has a substantial nexus to the taxing state, the tax is fairly apportioned, the tax does not discriminate against interstate commerce, and the tax fairly relates to services provided by the taxing state. [§§350-351]

46.a. **YES** Maintenance of a local sales office is a sufficient taxable incident even though the sale was technically made in Nebraska (order "accepted" there). [§374]

b. **NO** Sales solicitors ("drummers") representing an out-of-state manufacturer are not a sufficient taxable incident where the sale was consummated outside the state (order accepted in Nebraska). [§375]

47. **NO** Flat license fees may not be levied upon interstate sales solicitors even if local sales people are subject to the same tax. [§359]

48. **PROBABLY NOT** Under the Equal Protection Clause, a state may not impose more onerous taxes or other burdens on foreign corporations than on domestic corporations unless the discrimination is rationally related to a legitimate state purpose. Here, there is no showing of a legitimate state purpose. [§381]

49. **NO** The Import-Export Clause prohibits states from taxing exports after they have begun their physical entry into the stream of exportation. Thus, assuming the lobsters have entered this "stream," they are not subject to the tax. [§387]

50. **FALSE** Not all rights have been incorporated by the Fourteenth Amendment, and ***certain*** aspects of an incorporated right may be treated differently in state courts. [Apodaca v. Oregon] [§§393-399]

51. **NO** A welfare recipient has a protectible interest in continued receipt of welfare payments, and due process requires some sort of hearing prior to termination. [§416]

52.	**COMPELLING STATE INTEREST**	State regulation of contraceptives invades the constitutional right of privacy, and is subject to the strict standard of scrutiny. [§§441, 446]
53.	**YES**	It is reasonable to revoke the passport of a person whose conduct in foreign countries presents a serious danger to national security and foreign policy. [§§470-471]
54.	**FALSE**	It has been found substantially related to the achievement of an important governmental objective. [§561]
55.	**FALSE**	The Supreme Court has said that poverty standing alone is not a suspect classification. [§565]
56.	**PROBABLY**	State requirements that new political parties demonstrate public support to get on the ballot have been upheld where the requirements were not unduly burdensome because they further a "compelling" state interest. [§§585-586]
57.	**NO**	Disenfranchising felons is expressly authorized in the Fourteenth Amendment. [§616]
58.	**FALSE**	In "special interest" elections, different standards apply. [§§617-618]
59.	**TRUE**	Avoiding fragmentation of political subdivisions does not justify deviations from population for congressional districts. [§§626-627]
60.	**FALSE**	Slightly greater percentage deviations are allowed for local government apportionment than for state and congressional, as long as justifying factors exist. [§634]
61.	**FALSE**	Equal protection is applicable to the election of all officials who perform normal ***governmental*** functions. [§641]
62.	**SCHOOL BOARD**	A student's right to a particular quality of education is ***not*** a right guaranteed by the Constitution. Consequently, statutes regulating education are reviewable under the traditional rational basis test. [§657]
63.	**NO**	There is no constitutional right to discharge one's debts through bankruptcy proceedings. The filing fee helps make bankruptcy proceedings self-supporting. [§659]
64.	**NO**	State action will not be found merely because the state has granted a monopoly to a private business. To constitute "state action," there must be ***significant*** state involvement with the ***challenged action*** of the private party. (No showing that state authorized or encouraged Meadowbrook to exclude Bobby.) [Jackson v. Metropolitan Edison Co.] [§§679, 682]
65.	**YES**	The Thirteenth Amendment ban on slavery. [§§702-703]
66.	**FALSE**	The Enabling Clause of the Fourteenth Amendment authorizes Congress to enforce the amendment by "appropriate legislation," and this is a major source of power in the civil rights area. [§§704-715]

67. **FALSE** Provisions of the Civil Rights Act of 1964 have been upheld as a valid exercise of Congress's power under the Commerce Clause. [§719]

68. **FALSE** When government restricts freedom of expression, the Court weighs the importance of First Amendment rights with the nature and scope of the restraint, the type and strength of the government interest, and whether the restriction is narrowly tailored to achieve that interest. [§737]

69. **NO** Mere advocacy is not enough. [§754]

70. **TRUE** At least, this is the most recent formulation of the "clear and present danger" test. [Brandenburg v. Ohio] [§754]

71. **FALSE** Coach would apparently fall in the category of a "public figure," which is covered by the constitutional privilege. [§§768-770]

72.a. **TRUE** *Mishkin v. New York.* [§787]

b. **TRUE** Commercial activity does not narrow the protections of the First Amendment. (*Compare:* "Pandering" in advertising may be considered.) [§§791-792]

c. **FALSE** The Court has rejected the contention that community standards be determined on a "national" basis. [§789]

d. **FALSE** Dealers must be shown to have ***knowledge of contents***. [§§795-796]

73. **NO** Not all nudity is obscene, even as to minors. [§§782, 784, 862]

74. **NO** Offensiveness alone is not enough (no direct tendency to cause immediate acts of violence). [§807]

75. **NO** *Linmark Associates, Inc. v. Township of Willingboro.* [§822]

76. **NO** Although the government has the power to exclude "obscene" materials from import into this country, adequate procedural safeguards must be afforded. [§859]

77. **NO** If there is an important state interest independent of the speech aspects of the conduct, it may be regulated despite the incidental limitation on speech. [§861]

78. **NO** A city transit system is not a "public forum." [§§893-895]

79. **DEPENDS** On whether the ordinance sets forth clearly defined standards to govern the issuance of the permits. [§§898-905]

80. **NO** Due process requires that the burden be on the state to prove that a person is not qualified for the exemption. Placing upon the taxpayer the affirmative burden of proving by loyalty oath that she was not engaged in the forbidden activity is unconstitutional. [§§975-976]

81. **YES** *Connell v. Higginbotham; Cole v. Richardson.* [§§980-981]

82. **NO** "Mere membership" is not enough (must have been "knowing" and with "specific intent to further unlawful aims"). [§983]

83. **YES** Wallbanger's exercise of First Amendment rights cannot serve as a basis for dismissal from public employment. [§989]

84. **NO** This law is too broad. It would force prospective teachers to reveal their association with many organizations that have no bearing on their loyalty or professional competence. [§§996-997]

85. **MAYBE** The Court has not ruled on this. *Branzburg v. Hayes* applies to ***criminal*** proceedings. [§1003]

86. **YES** *Meek v. Pittenger.* [§1036]

87. **NO** Neither the purpose nor the effect of the exemption is the advancement or inhibition of religion. [Walz v. Tax Commissioner] [§1051]

88. **NO** *Zorach v. Clauson.* [§§1067-1069]

89. **PROBABLY NOT** There is no right to a religious exemption from a neutral law that happens to impose a substantial burden on religious practice, notwithstanding *Wisconsin v. Yoder,* which struck down compulsory attendance in ***high school*** for Amish based on ***long history*** of preparing children for life. [§§1088, 1100]

90. **PROBABLY NOT** There is no right to a religious exemption from a neutral law that happens to impose a substantial burden on religious practice. [§1088]

91. **NO** *Hamilton v. Regents of University of California.* [§1095]

92. **MOTION DENIED** A person claiming violation of the Free Exercise Clause must show some infringement of his personal beliefs, but ***all persons who are directly affected by the action complained of have standing*** to attack state action in violation of the Establishment Clause. [§§1113-1114]

93. **FALSE** This does not unreasonably impair the value or use of the property as a shopping center. [§1123]

94. **NO** Article I, Section 10 imposes such a limitation on the power of the ***states***. Federal legislation adjusting economic interests retroactively is permissible if done for a rational purpose. [§§1136, 1150]

95. **YES** Deportation is not considered "punishment" for ex post facto purposes. [Harisiades v. Shaughnessy] [§1153]

96. **NO** The right to counsel is limited to criminal ***prosecutions***. [§1154-1159]

97. **NO** The right to counsel is constitutionally required only in prosecutions that result in actual imprisonment. [§1157-1159]

98. **NO** Unanimity is required in federal, but not state, prosecutions. [§§1201-1202]

99. **NO** A jury trial is guaranteed only where a "serious" offense is charged. An offense is "serious" if it carries a potential sentence of more than six months. Thus, this is not a "serious" offense. [§§1203-1204]

100. **YES** A defendant may raise this challenge even when he is not a member of the group allegedly excluded. [§1213]

101. **NO** Prosecution must prove ***every element*** of the crime charged beyond a reasonable doubt. Malice aforethought is an essential element of murder and must be ***proved by the prosecution***. [§1227]

102. **NO** The right of counsel on appeal extends only to proceedings in which the accused has the ***right*** of appellate review. [§1237]

103. **(C)** New standards will always be given retroactive effect so as to protect the integrity of the truth-finding process. [§§1242-1243]

SAMPLE EXAM QUESTION I

A State X statute makes it a misdemeanor to "distribute any leaflet within 20 feet of an election booth while such booth is open for election purposes." Jones knowingly violates this statute by distributing handbills supporting his candidacy for mayor. He does so on the advice of his counsel, who tells him that the statute was unconstitutional. A criminal prosecution for violation of the statute is subsequently commenced against Jones.

Another state statute makes it a misdemeanor to "distribute in a public place any leaflet which does not have printed thereon the name of a person responsible for printing said leaflet, except that this requirement shall not apply to the distribution of political leaflets." Smith desires to print and distribute an anonymous leaflet urging citizens to keep their children in integrated public schools. He consults the prosecuting attorney, who tells him that he is not certain whether such a leaflet would fall within the "political leaflet" exception. Smith distributes the leaflet. The day prior to such distribution, the State X Supreme Court rules in another case that the "political leaflet" exception applies only to leaflets concerning candidates for public office or issues on the ballot. When the prosecutor learns of this ruling, he initiates criminal proceedings against Smith.

What defenses should Jones and Smith raise against their respective prosecutions, and what rulings should result? Discuss.

SAMPLE EXAM QUESTION II

Assume that the United States has recently adopted the following statute:

> Whoever travels in interstate or foreign commerce or uses any facility in interstate or foreign commerce, including the mail, with intent to: (a) Incite a riot, or to organize, promote, encourage, or carry on a riot, or to commit any act of violence in furtherance of a riot, or to aid and abet any person in inciting a riot or committing any act of violence in furtherance of a riot, and (b) thereafter performs or attempts to perform any overt act specified in paragraph (a), shall be fined not more than $10,000 or imprisoned not more than five years, or both.
>
> For purposes of this chapter: A riot is a public disturbance, involving acts of violence by assemblages of three or more persons, which poses an immediate danger of damage or injury to property or persons.

A, a militant racist, comes to your office. He tells you that immediately after he made an impassioned speech in another state, members of his audience engaged in rioting, burning, looting, and killing. Nevertheless, he wishes to continue advocating his philosophy through speeches and correspondence of similar content in other states.

Can A immediately challenge the constitutionality of the Act by a suit in a federal court? Assuming suit is possible, what constitutional grounds might A urge and with what likely result? Discuss.

SAMPLE EXAM QUESTION III

D, a State X corporation, maintains a vessel which transports cargo among several states on the Great Lakes. The vessel, equipped with hand-fired coal boilers, emits smoke of a density and duration that exceeds the limits imposed by the Smoke Abatement Code of Lakeport, a city in State X. Violations are punishable by a $100 fine, 30 days imprisonment, or both. No such code exists in other ports visited by the vessel. Pursuant to a comprehensive federal statute governing seagoing safety, the Coast Guard has inspected, approved, and licensed D's vessels (including boilers and fuel).

D's vessel puts into State X's ports for occasional refueling and repairs. Loading and unloading is done at main terminals located in other states. State X has levied its personal property tax on the full value of D's vessel, and no such tax is imposed by the other states visited.

After trials in State X courts, D is convicted of violating Lakeport's Smoke Abatement Code ***and*** is found liable for the State X property tax. State X's highest court has affirmed both decisions, and the United States Supreme Court has granted review. What should be the decision of the Supreme Court, and for what reason? Discuss.

SAMPLE EXAM QUESTION IV

A state statute provides scholarship grants of $2,000 per year for any military veteran enrolled in college. This statute is, in turn, limited by the state's so-called Jones Act, which prohibits distribution of monetary grants to "any person who presently supports, is a member of, or in the past year has been a member or supporter of, any organization known by him to advocate the violent overthrow of the state government."

The Jones Act requires that each applicant for a grant submit a sworn statement declaring that he meets the conditions imposed by that Act. The State Welfare Department is then directed to investigate each application, and in case of any doubt, to hold a hearing at which the applicant has the burden of showing that he is not barred by the Act from receiving the scholarship grant.

Z brings suit in state court to have the Jones Act declared invalid insofar as it limits scholarship grants. He alleges that he is a veteran; that, although not presently attending college, he has been accepted for enrollment at the start of the next term; and that he would be deprived of a state scholarship because, as a matter of conscience, he cannot submit the sworn statement required by the Jones Act.

Accepting his allegations as true, the state courts decide against Z on the ground that the state may condition scholarship grants on whatever grounds it chooses, since such grants are strictly a matter of legislative grace.

On review by the United States Supreme Court, what federal constitutional issues are presented and how should they be resolved? Discuss.

SAMPLE EXAM QUESTION V

A State X statute provides that "an employee entitled to vote in a general election may absent himself from his employment for four hours between the opening and closing of the polls without penalty and any employer who deducts wages for that absence is guilty of a misdemeanor." D, a railroad corporation doing business in State X and engaged in interstate commerce, has company regulations providing that "employees may absent themselves for the purpose of voting on election day for any number of hours, provided that advance notice is given designating the particular hours of absence, and provided further that wages shall not be paid for any absences in excess of two hours." Federal legislation regulates the work hours of railroad employees, but does not deal with the voting situation. After trial in a State X court, D is convicted of violating the State X statute upon proof that wages for two hours were deducted for many of its employees who absented themselves, after giving notice, for four hours on election day.

(1) On appeal to the highest court of State X, what federal constitutional questions may be raised by D, and how should they be resolved? Discuss.

(2) Assume that on appeal the highest court of State X holds the statute invalid on the sole ground that it infringes a particular provision of the State X Constitution. What federal remedy, if any, would be available to the State X prosecutor? Discuss.

SAMPLE EXAM QUESTION VI

A statute of State X concerning adoption states that only agencies licensed by the State may place children for adoption, and that the primary duty of such agencies shall be to promote the best interests of the child, including his or her moral and spiritual well-being.

Another section of the statute provides: "The race and religious affiliation of the adoptive parents shall be the same as that of the natural parents, or in the case of illegitimate children, that of the mother."

Husband (H) and Wife (W) apply to Agency, a duly licensed nonprofit corporation, to adopt the next available illegitimate black child. H is black; W is white; and both are professed agnostics. Their application is rejected after an Agency investigation. In a letter to H and W, Agency states, "Although our investigator found you highly qualified to be adoptive parents in other respects, we must reject your application because the social problems created by the difference in your ethnic backgrounds and your lack of religious affiliation combine to indicate that the requested adoption would not be in the best interests of the child."

H and W file suit in the appropriate State X court seeking a declaratory judgment that the quoted requirements of the statute are unconstitutional, and an order compelling Agency to process and approve their application. The trial court denies relief, and the State Supreme Court affirms.

Assuming all questions are properly preserved, discuss the issues that are likely to arise on review by the United States Supreme Court and how they should be resolved.

SAMPLE EXAM QUESTION VII

Dave contracts with the General Housing Administration, a federal agency, to carry bulk building materials to be used in the construction of a postal building between highway points within State X. After entering into the contract, he performs services only for the government.

State X's laws require any commercial carrier to obtain a permit from the state's Public Utility Commission, which is granted upon proof of financial responsibility and the safety of the carrier's equipment. Dave never obtains a permit.

On several occasions while engaged in the performance of his government contract, Dave is arrested by state highway patrolmen, in each case for violating a state statute which prohibits any speed "greater than is reasonable or prudent having due regard for the traffic on, and the surface and width, of the highway." On the last such occasion, after Dave had ignored the prior citations, his driver's license is suspended by State X's Director of Motor Vehicles pursuant to statute, pending an administrative hearing which Dave has the right to request. Concurrently therewith, Dave is ordered by the State X Public Utility Commission to cease transportation of all goods until he obtains a permit therefor.

Dave continues to perform his contract without regard to suspension of his driver's license or the required carrier's permit. He is subsequently arrested and charged with violating State X statutes making it a crime for any person to drive on state highways while his driver's license is suspended, or to carry goods for hire on the highways without a permit therefor.

What constitutional defenses may be raised by Dave to the charges of (1) transporting goods for hire without a permit, (2) driving while his license was suspended, and (3) speeding? Discuss.

SAMPLE EXAM QUESTION VIII

A statute of State A requires submission of all motion picture films, books, magazines, and newspapers to the State Obscenity Commission for examination prior to issuance by the Commission of a permit allowing their public exhibition, sale, or distribution. The Commission is directed to refuse a permit if the item submitted contains obscene matter, which is defined as "matter dealing with sex in a manner appealing to prurient interest, that is, matter having a tendency to excite lustful thoughts."

D distributes films for public exhibition and magazines for sale to the public throughout State A. He applies to the Commission for a permit to distribute a film entitled *The Decameron*, and a picture magazine called *Love*, but refuses to submit either the film or the magazine for examination.

(1) Is the Commission constitutionally authorized, by reason of D's refusal, to deny him a permit to distribute: (a) The film? (b) The magazine? Discuss.

(2) Assume that D is constitutionally required to submit the film, so that the Commission may examine it for obscenity. Does the statutory test for "obscene matter" satisfy constitutional requirements? Discuss.

ANSWER TO SAMPLE EXAM QUESTION I

As to Jones

Freedom of Speech: Jones might argue that the State X statute violates his First Amendment rights (made applicable to the states by the Fourteenth Amendment). In *Mills v. Alabama*, 384 U.S. 214 (1966), the Supreme Court held that a state statute prohibiting any campaigning on election day was invalid as applied to a newspaper editorial encouraging voters to vote in a certain way. However, the present case is distinguishable from *Mills*, since the statute prohibits only campaigning within 20 feet of election booths and forbids only one type of activity (leafletting). Thus, *Mills* is of little help to Jones.

It has been held that ***certain types of public property may be shut off entirely*** to the exercise of First Amendment activities. [Adderly v. Florida, 385 U.S. 39 (1966); Cox v. Louisiana, 377 U.S. 288 (1965)] To come within this rule, the property must be either not open to the general public or such that exercise of First Amendment activities would interfere with its normal use. In the present case, some, but not all, election booths may meet this requirement. An election booth may be set up in a city hall, firehouse, courthouse, college dormitory, fraternal lodge or private home. Some such locations are either not open to the general public, or are property on which leafletting would interfere with the property's normal use (*e.g.*, courthouse while trial is being held). Other locations (*e.g.*, city hall) ***are*** generally open to the public; and the legislature could not prohibit all First Amendment activities thereon.

Even if a location cannot be absolutely closed to First Amendment activities, many such activities are subject to reasonable regulation as to time, place, and manner. In deciding whether a regulation is constitutional, the Court ***weighs the substantiality of the state interest against the First Amendment interest***. Specifically with regard to election laws, the Court has stated that the greater the restriction the regulation imposes on the right to vote, the more substantial the state interest must be. [*See* Burdick v. Takushi, 112 S. Ct. 2059 (1992)] Here, the regulation imposes little on voting rights. Requiring a leafletter to stand 20 feet away from an election booth does little to prevent the leafletter from disseminating his message; he is still well within the visual and aural range of voters. Moreover, the regulation probably serves a compelling interest—the smooth operation of elections. Leafletting within 20 feet of an election booth might confuse those waiting in line to use the booth and might make it more difficult to process voters. It also could intimidate voters. For these reasons, the Court has upheld a regulation forbidding campaigning activity within 100 feet of a polling place. [Burson v. Freeman, 112 S. Ct. 1846 (1992)] Thus, the regulation here likely will be upheld.

Scienter: Jones cannot successfully argue that he inadvertently violated the law. It has been held that a statute making it unlawful to possess an obscene writing or book was invalid because it did not require knowledge of the contents of the book. [Smith v. California, 361 U.S. 147 (1959)] But that case was based on the chilling effect the statute would have if book sellers could be prosecuted for possessing obscene books without knowledge of their contents—*i.e.,* sellers would probably stock only books that, after a cursory examination, appeared totally "pure." In the present case, the statute has no such chilling effects: Leafletters know when they are within 20 feet of an election booth, and thereby violating the law. Moreover, Jones knowingly violated the statute and even consulted an attorney for advice. Hence, any contention that he had no such knowledge or that the statute chilled his First Amendment rights would not be accepted.

As to Smith

Freedom of Speech; Vagueness: Smith's obvious defense is that the statute is void for vagueness. Whenever a statute touches First Amendment freedoms, it must be drawn with special precision. Otherwise the statute will have a chilling effect—*i.e.,* a person who fears violating the statute will restrict his speech to avoid even constitutionally protected expression.

In the present case the statute prohibits distribution of leaflets without the sponsor's name printed thereon, unless the leaflet is a "political leaflet." The term "political leaflet" is vague, as attested by the fact that the prosecuting attorney did not know whether Smith's leaflet was "political." Because of this uncertainty, all leafletters (except perhaps those leafletting for candidates for public office) would identify the person responsible for printing the leaflets. But in so identifying the sponsor, the leafletters may be forgoing their First Amendment rights. Hence the statute's vagueness and concomitant chilling effect render it unconstitutional.

Overbreadth: The prosecutor might argue that any statutory vagueness was cured by the State Supreme Court's ruling before Smith distributed the leaflet. But since the court interpreted "political leaflet" to mean only a leaflet concerning candidates for public office or issues on the ballot, the interpretation itself probably violates the First Amendment. Any state interest in knowing the sponsors of leaflets does not justify demanding disclosure of the sponsors of ***all*** nonelection leaflets. The statute, as construed by the court, would require disclosure of many leaflets that carry messages of great public interest and are clearly within the First Amendment. The state has no pressing interest in disclosure of sponsors; and anonymity may be important. Even as construed, therefore, the statute has a "chilling effect"—*i.e.,* sponsors, if identified, might alter the content of their leaflets so as to avoid any public, private, or governmental reprisals. This in turn renders the statute as interpreted unconstitutional.

Discrimination: The court's interpretation is likewise unconstitutional for the related reason that it discriminates between types of leaflets on the basis of their contents. Rather than regulating the time, place, or manner of leafletting (as in the Jones problem above), the statute regulates only leaflets which are not of a special type. The Supreme Court has held that, absent substantial justification, a state statute permitting only some kinds of speech on certain property violates equal protection. [Chicago Police Department v. Mosely, 408 U.S. 92 (1972)] Similarly, permitting distribution of only certain types of leaflets without disclosure of sponsors probably violates equal protection, since the state apparently could not offer a substantial justification for such discrimination.

ANSWER TO SAMPLE EXAM QUESTION II

Enjoining the Federal Statute ("Ripeness"): For A to immediately challenge the constitutionality of the statute, the issue must be "ripe" for decision. Article III limits the jurisdiction of the federal courts to "cases" or "controversies." Furthermore, the Federal Declaratory Judgment Act permits a final judgment declaring rights and liabilities of parties only in cases of "actual controversy." To satisfy these requirements, A must show that he wants to engage in specific activities and that there is a real likelihood that the statute will be enforced against him. The facts do not indicate that prosecution against A has been threatened or that the statute has been enforced against anyone in the past (although this may be relatively unimportant due to the statute's recent enactment).

The greatest ripeness problem is that A has apparently not expressed a desire to engage in specific activities proscribed by the statute. Rather, he wishes to continue advocating his philosophy through speech and correspondence with content "similar" to the earlier speech.

Since the composition of his audience is likewise not specific, it is possible that none of the speeches would "incite, organize, promote, or encourage a riot" (and therefore fall within the statute's proscription). Unless A can show that his speechmaking and correspondence, given their content and audience, regularly or inevitably incite or promote riots, the issue may not be "ripe"; and A may have to await criminal prosecution before challenging the constitutionality of the statute.

Congressional Power: ***Assuming*** A can maintain his action for declaratory relief, he might argue that the statute is unconstitutional because Congress had no power to enact it. However, the statute is clearly supported by the ***Commerce Clause***. Under that clause, Congress has plenary power over the channels and facilities of interstate commerce and can properly prohibit certain persons or pieces of correspondence from entering into interstate commerce. The fact that the proscribed overt act takes place in only one state is irrelevant, since the act is only necessary to prove that the defendant had a certain intent when he traveled in interstate commerce or used interstate communication facilities. Furthermore, Congress has power to regulate all commerce activity, whether or not interstate, if it affects more than one state. Under this basis, almost any activity can be regulated. The present statute apparently satisfies this standard, since riots, as defined, could rationally be found to have effects beyond the state in which they occur.

Right to Travel: A might also argue that the statute violates his constitutional right to travel. The right to travel freely between states is a privilege of national citizenship which is almost absolute as against state interference. However, the right is not absolute, and can be overriden by a substantial or compelling governmental interest. And, the government's interest is afforded substantially greater weight where federal rather than state interests are involved.

In the present case, the federal government's interest is in preventing persons from causing riots. If militants are permitted to travel from state to state, inciting riots in each, local authorities would be hindered in taking effective action; and the federal government might be forced to combat this serious evil. Against this strong federal interest, the statute in question impinges upon the right to travel in only a minor way. Militants are not barred from interstate travel, and can avoid the terms of the statute simply by refraining from inciting or encouraging riots in the destination states. Since the impingement on A's right to travel is minor and the federal government's interest in preventing interstate travel of riot-provokers is substantial, there is probably no constitutional violation on this ground.

Freedom of Speech: A could also attack the statute on the ground it violates his First Amendment right to freedom of speech. Again, however, this right is not absolute, even though it occupies a preferred position among all constitutional rights. The test for determining when government may punish advocacy of illegal action is not clear. In *Dennis v. United States* and *Yates v. United States*, the Court said the test involved the imminence of the evil occurring ***and*** the gravity or seriousness of the evil advocated. The more serious the evil, the less imminent it need be. The *Brandenburg v. Ohio* test, however, makes imminence an ***independent*** requirement and says nothing about the seriousness of the evil. Furthermore, *Brandenburg* appears to require an evil intent by the speaker. To complicate matters even more, the Court in *Brandenburg* approvingly cited the *Dennis* and *Yates* decisions. Possibly *Brandenburg* meant that imminence is only an independent factor when the evil being advocated is not extremely serious, in which case *Brandenburg* would be consistent with *Dennis* except insofar as it also seems to require an evil intent by the advocate.

The statute in question appears to punish only advocacy that will produce an imminent evil. It expressly prohibits speech that incites or promotes a riot, and "riot" is defined to mean a public disturbance that poses an immediate danger of damage or injury. But since a riot exists whenever violence is perpetrated against people or property by three or more persons, the statute does ***not*** require the danger to be serious. For example, a person would violate the act if he incited three persons to violently kick out the window of an abandoned warehouse. Similarly, the statute only requires that the advocate intend to incite others to commit an immediate evil: It does not require that the evil intended be serious.

Applying the *Brandenburg* test, the statute may be constitutional, since it requires the evil advocated to be imminent. However, *Brandenburg* also appears to require an evil intent. The statute in question requires only an intent to incite or promote an immediate evil, no matter how minor the evil may be; and this may not satisfy the evil intent test. The statute, however, apparently would be constitutional under the *Dennis-Yates* test, since it requires no showing of evil intent. Hence, the validity of the statute on this basis may depend upon which test is applied.

Overbreadth and Vagueness: Even if the statute is valid under the *Dennis-Yates* or *Brandenburg* tests for advocacy, it is still probably unconstitutional on its face under the First Amendment. The statute—which is clearly addressed to speech as such—not only proscribes advocacy of criminal acts, but also penalizes encouragement and the aiding and abetting of such acts. This may include speech that would, by itself, be quite harmless; and since speech falling short of advocacy is proscribed, the statute is overbroad. Moreover, the statute is unconstitutionally vague: An individual who wishes to make a speech could not determine beforehand whether his proposed speech could be considered as "encouraging" a riot, and thus might severely censor his speech or not make the speech at all. Such "chilling effects" are not permitted under the First Amendment.

The statute in question is also overbroad for a second reason. It penalizes not only advocacy of criminal conduct, but also ***attempts*** to advocate illegal conduct. Since an attempt violation could be based upon nonadvocating speech, expression could be punished even though it did not satisfy the *Dennis-Yates* or *Brandenburg* standards—clearly an unconstitutional proscription.

In sum, since the statute is vague, punishes speech short of advocacy, and may punish advocacy that does not satisfy the *Dennis-Yates* or *Brandenburg* standards, it is unconstitutional.

ANSWER TO SAMPLE EXAM QUESTION III

Decision on Smoke Abatement

Preemption: D might argue that the Lakeport Smoke Abatement Code is preempted by the federal statute and hence is invalid under the Supremacy Clause. Although there may be no direct conflict between the two statutes, the Lakeport act cannot be upheld if Congress intended the federal statute to constitute complete and exclusive regulation of the area.

The federal statute is a comprehensive act governing safety of seagoing vessels. If Lakeport's act required additional safety features on vessels, it would probably be found preempted by the federal act. But the Lakeport act is an air pollution measure which presumably does not deal with safety requirements at all. It is unlikely that Congress, when passing the safety act, intended to prevent states or their subdivisions from regulating smoke output or other nonsafety aspects of shipping vessels.

If the legislative history were examined, however, one might find statements indicating that the federal bill was passed to alleviate problems created by varying state specifications for vessels. Any such indication would support D's argument that states or their subdivisions, unable to demand different boiler specifications under a safety act, should not be able to destroy the uniformity of the federal act under the guise of pollution, health, or other nonsafety measures. A comparison of the federal statute and the Lakeport act might also reveal that boilers meeting the pollution standards set by the Lakeport act could not satisfy the federal safety requirements—in which case the Lakeport act would clearly be invalid. Assuming this is not the case, however, and assuming the legislative history does not indicate that Congress intended to displace local pollution measures, the Lakeport act would not be preempted by the federal safety statute.

Commerce Clause: D might also contend that the Lakeport act violates the Commerce Clause. However, absent conflicting federal legislation and subject to certain limitations, states may regulate local activities even though the regulation affects interstate commerce. One limitation is that states may never discriminate against interstate commerce; but this does not invalidate the Lakeport act, since local smoke emitters are also apparently subject to the act.

Whether nondiscriminatory state legislation violates the Commerce Clause must be determined by the "balancing" test. Under this test, the Court weighs the detriment to the national interest imposed by the legislation against the strength and merit of the state's interest in the regulation. Here, the Lakeport act seems to impose only a minor burden on interstate commerce. Because no other ports visited by D's vessel have a similar act, there is no indication that compliance with the act would prevent the vessel from docking at other ports. However, the cost of bringing vessels up to the Lakeport standards ***would*** be relevant to the Court's determination, as would information on how many ships would satisfy Lakeport's act without alteration of boilers. This information is of course not provided.

On the other hand, Lakeport's interest in clean air, since it is one involving health, safety, or social welfare, is afforded greater deference than an act designed merely to protect economic interests. Lakeport's interest in safeguarding the health of its residents could well be defeated if vessels docking there were allowed to pollute the air with dense clouds of smoke. Since the burden on interstate commerce is probably minor and the benefit of the act substantial, and since there is no indication that Lakeport's interest could be effectively served by less burdensome legislation, the act would similarly be valid under the Commerce Clause.

Decision on Property Tax

Situs: As a general proposition, a state may levy an ad valorem property tax on instrumentalities of interstate commerce if the instrumentality has acquired a "taxable situs" within the state, thereby satisfying the ***Due Process Clause***. A taxable situs always exists in the state of domicile, although if the instrumentality receives benefits or protection from other states, it may be taxable by them as well. In the present case, the vessel is owned by a State X corporation, so State X is the ***domiciliary state*** and may levy an ad valorem tax on the vessel.

Apportionment: The domiciliary state need ***not*** apportion the value of interstate instrumentalities unless the taxpayer can prove that a certain part of the instrumentalities have acquired a taxable situs elsewhere. To do this, the taxpayer must show either that the instrumentalities are permanently located elsewhere, or that they were habitually employed in interstate commerce in other states and thereby acquired a taxable situs there. D's vessel probably meets the second criterion. Although not located permanently in some other state, it does all of its cargo hauling between other states, and docks in State X only for occasional refueling and repairs. The vessel probably acquired a taxable situs in one or more of the other states in which it docks and, whether or not other states are in fact taxing the vessel, State X must apportion its tax to satisfy objections under the ***Commerce Clause***.

A method of apportionment will be upheld if it roughly reflects the instrumentality's average physical presence within the state. For example, if D's vessel spends 5% of its dock time in State X ports, State X should be allowed to levy its tax on 5% of the vessel's value. But the State X tax was levied on the full value of D's vessel. If D can show the vessel has acquired a taxable situs in some other state or states (*see* discussion above), the Court should find that this lack of apportionment is an unconstitutional burden on interstate commerce—in the absence of authorizing federal legislation.

ANSWER TO SAMPLE EXAM QUESTION IV

Freedom of Association: The state court decision failed to consider whether the Jones Act benefits are unconstitutionally conditioned, in that they violate the First Amendment prohibition of abridgments on freedom of association. This prohibition applies to the states through the Due Process Clause of the Fourteenth Amendment.

Vagueness: The Jones Act prohibits distribution of scholarship aid to any person who is a member of or supports a group known to him to advocate the violent overthrow of the state government. This standard is vague because of the term "supports," which could encompass not only membership and active participation, but also attendance at meetings and even mere sympathy for the organization. An individual who considered applying for Jones Act benefits in the future might well be chilled by this vague standard: *e.g.*, he might avoid any conduct or speech that could possibly be construed as support for a group advocating overthrow of the state government (even though constitutionally protected). Hence, the standard violates the First Amendment.

Overbreadth: The Jones Act standard is also overbroad. The state may deny governmental benefits for associating with certain groups only when the group engages in activities not constitutionally protected ***and*** the individual is an active member of the group, has knowledge of the group's illegal advocacy, and has the specific intent that the group's aims be accomplished. Under the Jones Act, benefits would be denied even where the applicant is only a passive member or supporter. Moreover, the prohibition against distribution of benefits applies even though the applicant has no specific intent to further the group's unlawful aims. A denial based on such conduct is likewise unconstitutional under the First Amendment.

Burden of Proof: Even if the substantive standard found in the Jones Act was not vague and overbroad (*see* discussion above), the Act would be unconstitutional on the ground that the applicant has the burden of proof at the hearing provided under the Act. Where the state imposes a civil "penalty" by conditioning benefits upon the applicant's speech or associations (in contrast to imposing a civil disability in order to serve a legitimate state regulatory end), the First Amendment requires that the ***state*** bear the burden of showing that the applicant engaged in unprotected speech or association.

Right to a Hearing: Placing the burden of proof on the wrong party seems particularly objectionable in the present case, since due process usually requires some form of notice and hearing before an individual may be deprived of liberty or property interests by the state. The interest in obtaining scholarship aid under the Jones Act may be such a "property interest" that requires a hearing before deprivation. An applicant who appears to satisfy all of the legitimate conditions to aid under the Act seemingly has a legitimate claim to the grant; and before the state withholds benefits, the applicant should be given a hearing at which the state has the burden of proving the applicant engaged in speech or association that is not constitutionally protected.

Standing and Ripeness: Although the Jones Act is constitutionally deficient in a number of respects, Z may not challenge the Act unless he has standing—which requires a direct and immediate personal injury due to the Act's unconstitutional requirements. Z has alleged that he is a veteran, that he has been accepted for enrollment at the start of the next term, and that, as a matter of conscience, he could not submit the sworn statement required by the Jones Act. These allegations establish standing, since Z's unwillingness to satisfy the allegedly unconstitutional requirement will have the immediate injurious effect of depriving him of scholarship aid.

The constitutionality of the sworn statement requirement is also "ripe," since Z has been accepted for college and it appears clear that the allegedly unconstitutional requirement will be enforced against him.

However, Z may not have standing to attack the constitutionality of the burden of proof requirement at the hearing. Since he has refused to submit a sworn statement and will not receive a hearing, he may not be injured by the requirement that he carry the burden of proof. Furthermore, the burden of proof issue may not be ripe, since the burden of proof requirement may never be applied to him. However, if the Court believes Z has a substantial chance of succeeding in his contention, there is little reason to prohibit him from challenging the second stage of the proceedings. The "real likelihood of harm" requirement would be satisfied, and a comprehensive attack on the statutory scheme is consistent with notions of judicial economy.

Conclusion: Z will clearly prevail in his challenge. The requirement of a sworn statement is both unconstitutionally vague and overbroad, and placing the burden of proof on the applicants at the hearing violates the First Amendment and due process. Z has standing to challenge the sworn statement requirement and the issue is ripe. He should also have standing to attack the burden of proof requirement, and this issue should also be found ripe—since Z's challenge to the statement requirement is so substantial that he will likely be faced in the near future with the burden of proving he is not barred from receiving scholarship aid. Even if Z does not yet have standing to attack this requirement and the issue is not yet ripe, he will certainly be able to do so once he prevails in his attack against the statement requirement.

ANSWER TO SAMPLE EXAM QUESTION V

(1) **Preemption:** The first constitutional issue is whether the federal legislation preempts the state statute, making the latter invalid under the Supremacy Clause. Although there is no direct conflict between the state and federal legislation, there may be a conflict in policy or a congressional intent to occupy the field. For example, the federal act may have been enacted to achieve national uniformity in working hours of railroad employees. Such an objective would be frustrated by the State X act since railroad service in State X on election day might be inferior to service in other states. Also, D, a railroad doing interstate business, would be required by the state act to make special arrangements on election day for employees in only one state. Any congressional interest in uniformity should be given considerable weight in resolving the preemption question, because operation of the railroads is of substantial national interest.

Of course, a review of the legislative history may instead reveal that Congress wished to leave this problem to the states. Even so, however, such legislative history must be considered in light of the countervailing factors discussed above. The national interest in railroad operations, the desirability of uniformity in such operations, and the fact that railroad operations are extensively regulated by Congress would probably outweigh anything less than overwhelming evidence that state rules on election leaves of absence are permissible. If the State X Supreme Court agrees that the state act is in conflict with the policy of the federal legislation, the state act is invalid.

Commerce Clause: A second possible constitutional objection to the State X statute is that it constitutes improper regulation of interstate commerce and is therefore invalid under the Commerce Clause. The act is clearly not invalid on the ground that it discriminates against interstate commerce since it applies to all employers in the state. Hence the State X court should apply the "balancing test" used to determine if nondiscriminatory legislation is an unreasonable burden on interstate commerce—*i.e.,* weighing the extent of the burden on interstate commerce against the strength and merit of the state interest in regulation. Although few facts are given, it is probable that a required four-hour leave of absence will severely hamper the operations of a number of interstate enterprises. For example, goods traveling from State Y to State Z may be delayed a full day because of the railroad's decreased work force in State X and passenger service could become unsafe. In the present case, D already gives a leave of absence, but only with advance notice. Presumably the advance notice requirement exists so that the employer can, despite leaves of absence, schedule the day's operations in the way that will have the least effect on its passenger and cargo service. By not requiring advance notice from employees, the State X statute makes it exceedingly difficult for the employer to do this.

Balanced against this burden on interstate commerce is the state's interest in having its residents take an active role in the democratic process. Statutes furthering such an interest involving the social welfare are generally accorded more weight than statutes protecting local economic interests. However, the state's interest could probably be achieved in a manner that would be less burdensome on interstate commerce; *e.g.,* leaves of absence only for the first or last hours of the shift. Such a provision would enable all workers to vote en route to work or returning home, and would not disrupt the middle of companies' shifts. Furthermore, the act could have provided for advance notice of absence so that the employer could make necessary arrangements for adequate service. Since the act does place a substantial burden on interstate commerce, and since the state's interest could be protected by less burdensome legislation, the act could be found invalid under the Commerce Clause.

Due Process and Equal Protection: The state act is not vulnerable on either due process or equal protection grounds, since it falls within the category of economic and social legislation. Such legislation is upheld under the Due Process Clause unless no reasonable state of facts can be conceived to support it, or unless it bears no rational relationship to the end sought. State X could reasonably have concluded that the statute in question would lead to a larger voter turnout. As for equal protection, any rational classification or discrimination is valid. Thus the statute could not be invalidated on the ground that only employees entitled to vote are eligible for the paid leave of absence.

Contracts Clause: Similarly, the state act does not impair the obligation of contracts (as prohibited by Article I, Section 10). The proscription of the Contracts Clause is not absolute: The reasonableness of the state legislation is the test when the law regulates only private contracts; and legislative judgment is usually afforded substantial deference. In the present case, the state has a strong interest in increasing voter turnout while the employment contracts allegedly impaired will only be affected one day each year. Balanced against the state's interest, this impairment is not substantial enough to constitute a Contracts Clause violation.

Just Compensation Clause: Finally, the State X statute is not an unconstitutional taking of property without just compensation. Such takings are prohibited by the Fifth Amendment, and this prohibition applies to the states under the Fourteenth Amendment Due Process Clause. But any legislation involving the state's police power places some burden on the use of the property, so that the line between permissible regulation and a taking is a matter of degree. In deciding whether an act constitutes a taking, the court generally balances the public need against the private cost. As discussed above, there is a substantial state interest here in increasing participation in the electoral process; and the cost to the employers is minimal because of the infrequency of general elections. Thus, the act should be held a valid exercise of the state's police power rather than an unconstitutional taking.

(2) **Adequate State Ground:** If the highest court of State X holds the statute invalid on the sole ground that it infringes a provision of the State X constitution, the State X prosecutor would be confronted by the doctrine of adequate state grounds. Despite the presence of a federal question in the case, the Supreme Court will not review state court judgments if the state court judgment can be supported entirely on a state ground. The doctrine does not apply where the state ground is not "adequate" (*e.g.,* where it does not dispose of the entire issue). The facts do not disclose what the state constitutional provision is, so it cannot be determined whether the state ground is really adequate. However, if the state court relied on a due process clause or impairment of contracts provision in the state constitution, the prosecutor may be foreclosed from further action.

ANSWER TO SAMPLE EXAM QUESTION VI

State Action: As will be discussed below, the adoption agency's decision probably violates the First Amendment freedoms of religion as applicable to the states through the Fourteenth Amendment, the Fourteenth Amendment Equal Protection Clause, and right to marry, which is part of the constitutional right of privacy. Since these constitutional provisions apply only to state action and the adoption agency here is a private corporation, a preliminary issue arises as to whether the adoption agency's action constitutes state action.

State action includes not only action by the state, but also certain actions undertaken by ostensibly private individuals where the individuals are performing exclusive government functions or there is significant government involvement. Here, it is uncertain whether adoption services will be considered to be an exclusive government function since, historically, the government has not been the only entity running adoption agencies. Moreover, the mere fact that the adoption agency has been licensed by the state or indeed that it has been given a monopoly will not be enough to make the agency's action state action. [Jackson v. Metropolitan Edison Co., 419 U.S. 345 (1974)] However, where a private individual's action is compelled by state law, there is sufficient government involvement for the individual's action to constitute state action. [Peterson v. City of Greenville, 373 U.S. 244 (1963)] Since the adoption agency here was compelled by the state statute to discriminate on the basis of race and religion, the agency's action constitutes state action.

Race and Equal Protection: The State X statute contains an explicit racial classification. Such classifications are "suspect" and will not be upheld unless they are necessary to accomplish some substantial or compelling state objective. In the present case, the state's interest is in promoting the best interests of the child. Under certain circumstances, a racially mixed family may affect the child's well-being, and this interest may satisfy the substantial state interest test. But the statute would not permit adoption even where a thorough investigation indicated that, because of the community's racial mix or other factors, an interracial adoption would have no adverse effect on the child. Since a statute that takes account of such special cases would protect the state's interest just as well as the existing statute, the statute could be held to violate equal protection.

Right to Marry: The statute may also be an impermissible burden on the constitutional right to marry. As exemplified by the present case, the statute effectively prohibits racially mixed couples from adopting children of any race, thereby imposing a direct and substantial disability upon anyone who marries a person of a different race. Unless the Court concludes the state has a substantial compelling interest in so acting (*see* discussion above), imposition of this disability could be unconstitutional.

Freedom of Religion: The letter from the adoption agency states a second ground for rejection, namely, the parents' lack of religious affiliation. The State X statute provides that adoptive parents shall have the same religious affiliation as the child's natural parents. This requirement may be unconstitutional, under both the Establishment and Free Exercise Clauses of the First Amendment (applicable to the states by the Fourteenth Amendment).

Free Exercise: The "same religion" requirement imposes an indirect burden on the exercise of religion since a couple not affiliated with a major religious group may have to wait years before an agency can provide a child. Likewise, members of very small religious denominations may never be able to adopt a child. This statutory burden could be unconstitutional unless the state cannot protect its important interest in the child's well-being by alternative means. Since a statute requiring consideration of the effect of religious differences on a case-by-case basis would probably serve the state's interest equally well, the indirect burden is probably impermissible.

Definition of "Religion": The Free Exercise Clause only prohibits the imposition of burdens on religious beliefs or conduct. H and W are professed agnostics, and it is questionable whether agnosticism is a religious belief. However, the Supreme Court has never held any asserted religious beliefs not to be religious for First Amendment purposes; and if H and W possess beliefs that occupy a place in their lives parallel to that occupied by orthodox religious beliefs, the Free Exercise Clause should prevent the imposition of burdens on their beliefs not necessary to achieve a compelling state interest.

Establishment: The "same religion" requirement may also violate the Establishment of Religion Clause of the First Amendment. The statute has a purpose to aid religion—*i.e.,* it is specifically designed to promote the child's spiritual well-being. The statute also aids religion generally, and certain religious denominations in particular. Where either the purpose or effect of a statute is to aid religion, the statute will usually violate the Establishment Clause. Since both tests are satisfied here, the Court would likely hold the statute unconstitutional on this basis.

ANSWER TO SAMPLE EXAM QUESTION VII

Federal Immunity from State Regulation

Transporting goods for hire without a permit: The Supremacy Clause has been held impliedly to require that activities of the federal government be free from burdensome state regulation. This means that the states may neither ***unduly interfere*** with the functioning of federal agencies, nor directly control work that a contractor is performing for the United States. The states may, however, regulate government contractors as long as the regulation does not prescribe the manner in which they are to perform their contracts.

In the present case, Dave is a contractor performing services ***only*** for the federal government. If he must comply with the State X requirement that commercial carriers obtain permits from the Public Utility Commission, granted only to financially responsible carriers which use safe equipment, the federal government's operations could be severely hindered: Not only might the processing procedure delay construction, but the state standards restrict the federal government's initial choice of carriers. Thus, since Dave is probably immune from the permit requirement, he cannot constitutionally be prosecuted for failure to satisfy the requirement.

Driving while license suspended: Since Dave is a carrier, a state requirement that all persons driving motor vehicles have a valid operator's license would clearly interfere with his work for the federal government. As noted earlier, such a requirement could unduly limit the government's choice of contractors and interfere with operations after the contract is entered into. In a case involving a federal employee, rather than a contractor, it was held the state could not require the employee to obtain a driver's license to operate a mail truck. [Johnson v. Maryland, 254 U.S. 51 (1920)] This same immunity would presumably extend to federal contractors while they are operating vehicles pursuant to their contract.

In the present case, however, Dave did not simply refuse to obtain a driver's license: He had a license when he began performing his contract, and lost it only after ignoring a number of speeding citations. Whether Dave should be immune from prosecution under these circumstances is not clear.

The state could take the position that if Dave is not immune from the speeding charges (*see* discussion below), he cannot be immune from charges arising from his failure to honor the license suspension—which is the penalty for ignoring the citations. This argument is not persuasive, however, and is inconsistent with the principle of governmental immunity. If the speeding charges are valid, the state does have an interest in punishing Dave; but where there is a conflict, this interest must yield to the federal interest in carrying on its operations free from undue state interference.

Moreover, the state's interest in punishing Dave was probably achieved for the most part by suspending his license, since he may not legally operate a motor vehicle except in the course of his work for the federal government. If the state does not think this limitation is an adequate punishment, it can take legal action to enforce the traffic fines, something the state has apparently not yet done. In any event, the fact that the state may lawfully cite Dave for speeding should not permit it to interfere with federal operations. Thus, since Dave was engaged in the performance of his contract at the time he was arrested for driving while his license was suspended, he cannot be prosecuted constitutionally for this offense.

Speeding: Dave's immunity should not extend to speeding violations, since the federal interest is not unduly interfered with or impaired by enforcing the speed law against Dave. When the federal government entered into its contract with Dave, it presumably did not contemplate that Dave would exceed the speed limit when delivering supplies. The facts do not indicate any interest of the federal government that would be served by allowing Dave to freely violate the speed law, and since governmental immunity should arise only when a conflict exists between the state interest (in protecting against the harms of speeding) and federal interests, immunity should not shield Dave from the speeding charges.

Vagueness: However, Dave may avoid conviction on the speeding charges on the ground the state speeding law is vague. The statute will not be held void "on its face," since neither the statute nor Dave's conduct concerns freedom of speech or any other constitutional right. If it is void for vagueness at all, it must therefore be because it is vague as applied. A less strict standard is employed as to this type of statute than as to statutes that concern a constitutional right and are allegedly void on their face because of a potential chilling effect on the exercise of constitutional rights.

The speeding statute requires that drivers not drive at speeds "greater than what is reasonable under the circumstances." Persons of common intelligence would probably differ as to application of the statute, so that there could be significant disparities in enforcement; *i.e.,* on any given stretch of highway at any given time, one law enforcement officer might believe 40 m.p.h. to be a reasonable speed, while a second officer might consider 70 m.p.h. reasonable. A motorist in turn might feel 50 m.p.h. is reasonable. Whether the motorist is cited, therefore, depends on which officer observes him.

Because of this vagueness and probable discrepancies in application, Dave should be able to avoid prosecution under the statute unless, perhaps, he was driving at a speed that no person of common intelligence would believe reasonable (*e.g.,* 80 m.p.h. in a school zone). Unless Dave is such a "hardcore" violator, however, the state should not be allowed to prosecute him on the speeding charges.

ANSWER TO SAMPLE EXAM QUESTION VIII

(1) **Censorship Systems**

(a) **Movies:** Although governments generally may not censor speech before it is uttered or published, some forms of prior restraint and censorship are permitted. But to be upheld, censorship plans must contain adequate procedural and judicial safeguards. In the area of movie censorship, such a system must contain at least the following procedural safeguards:

(i) The standards for imposing censorship (or denying a license) must be narrowly drawn, reasonable, and definite. That is, only "obscene" films or films otherwise not protected under the Constitution may be covered by the censorship program.

(ii) The censor must promptly seek a judicial injunction if a permit is not issued.

(iii) In the judicial proceeding, the censor must bear the burden of proving that the film is not protected.

(iv) The judicial determination must be rendered promptly.

[Freedman v. Maryland, 380 U.S. 51 (1965)]

Censorship programs that satisfy these procedural safeguards are permitted on the ground that movies differ from other forms of expression, and that the time delays inherent in the programs are relatively less burdensome.

The statute in question fails to satisfy these safeguards. First, the statute allows denial of a permit even in cases where the film is not "obscene" according to constitutional standards (*see* discussion in (2), below). Second, the statute says absolutely nothing about judicial proceedings; and as indicated, for the statute to be valid it must require the censorship board promptly to seek a judicial injunction, the censor must have the burden of proving the film is unprotected, and there must be a prompt judicial determination. The State A statute allows the State Obscenity Commission to refuse permits without any judicial determination on whether the film is unprotected.

If the State A statute were not invalidated, there would be an undue burden on First Amendment freedoms. After the Commission refused to issue a permit, the applicant would be forced to seek judicial relief before his film could be exhibited (or run the risk of criminal prosecution by exhibiting it). Without a statutory provision for expedited judicial determination, the applicant might face lengthy delays before a decision was reached. Absent a statutory allocation of the burden of proof, the judge might give the Commission's ruling a presumption of validity. Because of these failings, the State A statute is invalid; and the Commission may not constitutionally deny D a permit even though he refused to submit his film.

(b) **Magazines:** Although some licensing systems are permissible for films, government may not establish any form of licensing board to which publications must be submitted for advance approval of content. The rationale for this distinction is that the time delays inherent in censorship systems impose an undue burden on publications, while such delays do not overly burden the distribution of films.

Thus, a state wishing to control the content of publications may proceed against distribution of an item only after it has had some distribution. If a court then determines that the item is obscene, it may enjoin further distribution. The State A statute requires neither prior distribution nor a judicial hearing, but permits the state to censor books, magazines, and newspapers whenever the Commission determines they are obscene. The statute is therefore void on its face; and the Commission may not deny D's application for a permit to distribute his magazine.

(2) **Obscenity:** Not every depiction of sex is obscene. The Supreme Court has held that several separate elements must be present before an item can be deemed obscene. [Miller v. California, 413 U.S. 15 (1973)] First, the dominant theme of the material when considered as a whole must appeal to a prurient interest in sex. In determining this, the Court considers whether the material appeals to an average person's prurient interest in sex. Second, the material must affront contemporary community standards relating to sexual matters in such a way as to be patently offensive. The "standards" examined need not be "national"; a statewide standard has been upheld. Third, as a whole the material must lack political, literary, scientific, or artistic value. There must be separate proof of each of these three elements before material can be deemed obscene.

The State A statute defines obscene matter as "matter dealing with sex in a manner appealing to prurient interest, that is, matter having a tendency to excite lustful thoughts." This definition clearly fails to satisfy the standard set forth above. For example, although the statute speaks of "appealing to prurient interest," it is not at all clear ***whose*** prurient interest must be appealed to before material can be determined obscene. Under the State A standard, a children's magazine presumably could be labeled obscene (and therefore banned from display or distribution) if it had a tendency to excite lustful thoughts in child molesters. But, as noted above, material may generally not constitutionally be considered obscene unless it appeals to the average person's prurient interest in sex. Thus, the State A statute is unconstitutional.

Moreover, even if the statutory language satisfied the "prurient interest" requirement, the statute fails to require that material affront contemporary community standards before it can be deemed obscene. Under the statute, a book that has a tendency to excite lustful thoughts in some readers could be determined obscene by the Commission even though the great majority of the public might consider the book unobjectionable. Since a state may not treat material as obscene unless it is patently offensive, this is another basis for holding the State A provision invalid. The statute is likewise unconstitutional in that it would permit a finding of obscenity even as to material that has serious political, artistic, scientific or literary value; *e.g.,* medical books containing pictures of naked persons could be banned despite the obvious value of such books to the scientific community.

Although states are free to adopt obscenity standards more stringent than that announced in *Miller*, and states have occasionally been permitted to define obscenity in terms varying somewhat from the *Miller* standard, the State A statute is so broad and general that it almost certainly is invalid. In effect, the act gives the Commission power to declare obscene anything which might appeal to any person's prurient interest, regardless whether the material has any redeeming virtues. Any definition permitting such results clearly fails to satisfy constitutional standards.

TABLE OF CASES

Abate v. Mundt - §634
Abington School District v. Schempp - §§1055, 1062, 1063, 1114
Abood v. Detroit Board of Education - §§726, 985
Adams Manufacturing Co. v. Storen - §372
Adamson v. California - §394
Adderley v. Florida - §895
Addington v. Texas - §§405, 428
Aetna Life Insurance Co. v. Haworth - §27
Afroyim v. Rusk - §157
Agins v. City of Tiburon - §1128
Aguilar v. Felton - §1036
Akins v. Texas - §1209
Alabama v. King & Boozer - §251
Alaska v. Arctic Maid - §332
Albertini, United States v. - §895
Albertson v. Subversive Activities Control Board - §968
Alexander v. United States - §846
Alexander v. Virginia - §846
Allegheny Pittsburgh Coal Co. v. County Commission - §487
Allen v. Wright - §46
Allgeyer v. Louisiana - §434
Allied Structural Steel Co. v. Spannaus - §1142
Amalgamated Food Employees Union v. Logan Valley Plaza, Inc. - §678
Ambach v. Norwick - §551
American Party of Texas v. White - §§584, 585
American Textile Manufacturers Institute v. Donovan - §128
Anastaplo, *In re* - §§998, 999
Anderson v. Celebrezze - §588
Anderson v. Dunn - §162
Anderson v. Liberty Lobby, Inc. - §763
Anderson v. Martin - §511
Apodaca v. Oregon - §§397, 1201
Aptheker v. Secretary of State - §472
Arcara v. Cloud Books, Inc. - §867
Argersinger v. Hamlin - §1157
Arkansas Writers' Project v. Ragland - §1018
Arnett v. Kennedy - §§409, 419
Asarco, Inc. v. Idaho State Tax Commission - §357
Asarco, Inc. v. Kadish - §53
Ashwander v. Tennessee Valley Authority - §78
Associated Industries of Missouri v. Lohman - §367
Associated Press v. Walker - §770
Association of Data Processing Service Organizations, Inc. v. Camp - §45
Attorney General v. Soto-Lopez - §599
Austin v. Michigan Chamber of Commerce - §§933, 934
Austin v. New Hampshire - §330
Austin v. United States - §440
Bacchus Imports, Ltd. v. Dias - §325
Baggett v. Bullitt - §981
Bailey v. Anderson - §1132
Bailey v. Drexel Furniture Co. - §138
Baird v. State Bar - §999
Baker v. Carr - §§44, 101, 109, 625
Baldwin v. Fish & Game Commission - §238
Baldwin v. New York - §1204
Ball v. James - §618
Ballard, United States v. - §§1107, 1108
Ballew v. Georgia - §§1199, 1200
Bank of Augusta v. Earle - §236
Bantam Books, Inc. v. Sullivan - §833
Barefoot v. Estelle - §1195
Barenblatt v. United States - §§973, 974
Barnes v. Glen Theatre, Inc. - §865
Barron v. Baltimore - §390
Barrows v. Jackson - §§56, 686
Barry v. Barchi - §424
Bates v. State Bar of Arizona - §828
Batson v. Kentucky - §497
Bazemore v. Friday - §529
Bearden v. Georgia - §571
Beauharnais v. Illinois - §§755, 756
Bell v. Burson - §408
Bell v. Maryland - §687
Bellotti v. Baird - §454
Belmont, United States v. - §217
Benton v. Maryland - §398
Berman v. Parker - §1120
Bernal v. Fainter - §547
Bethel School District v. Fraser - §941
Bibb v. Navajo Freight Lines, Inc. - §315
Bigelow v. Virginia - §§810, 813
Bishop v. Wood - §§406, 409
Bivens v. Six Unknown Named Agents - §714
Blake v. McClung - §237
Blanchette v. Connecticut General Insurance - §130
Blount v. Rizzi - §§853, 858
Blum v. Yaretzsky - §§680, 689
Blystone v. Pennsylvania - §1191
Board of Curators v. Horowitz - §423
Board of Directors of Rotary International v. Rotary Club of Duarte - §736
Board of Education v. Allen - §1030
Board of Education v. Mergens - §1065
Board of Education v. Pico - §943
Board of Education of Kiryas Joel Village School District v. Grumet - §1025
Board of Regents v. Roth - §§405, 406, 408
Board of Trustees of State University of New York v. Fox - §821
Bob Jones University v. United States - §1094
Boddie v. Connecticut - §§572, 574, 576

Bolger v. Youngs Drug Products Corp. - §§811, 813, 822
Bolling v. Sharpe - §§401, 512
Bond v. Floyd - §982
Boos v. Barry - §874
Booth v. Maryland - §1196
Bose Corp. v. Consumers Union - §764
Boston Stock Exchange v. State Tax Commission - §329
Bowen v. Kendrick - §1043
Bowers v. Hardwick - §463
Bowsher v. Synar - §177
Boyd v. United States - §1175
Boyle v. Landry - §33
Bradfield v. Roberts - §1041
Bradley v. Public Utilities Commission - §321
Bragg v. Weaver - §1132
Bram v. United States - §1161
Brandenburg v. Ohio - §754
Braniff Airways v. Nebraska Board of Equalization - §339
Branti v. Finkel - §988
Branzburg v. Hayes - §1003
Braunfeld v. Brown - §1090
Breard v. City of Alexandria - §312
Brewster, United States v. - §§167, 169
Bridges v. California - §908
Britt v. North Carolina - §1235
Broadrick v. Oklahoma - §§739, 741, 991
Brockett v. Spokane Arcades, Inc. - §§743, 785
Brotherhood of Locomotive Firemen v. Chicago, Rock Island & Pacific Railroad - §314
Brotherhood of Railroad Trainmen v. Virginia - §953
Brown v. Board of Education - §§512, 524
Brown v. Glines - §951
Brown v. Hartladge - §921
Brown v. Maryland - §384
Brown v. Mississippi - §1162
Brown v. Socialist Workers '74 Campaign Committee - §936
Brown v. Thomson - §633
Browning Ferris Industries of Vermont, Inc. v. Kelso Disposal, Inc. - §440
Buck v. Kuykendall - §320
Buckley v. Valeo - §§172, 589, 926, 929, 935, 967
Bullock v. Carter - §§577, 650
Burch v. Louisiana - §1202
Burdick v. Takushi - §§918, 922
Burns v. Richardson - §640
Burson v. Freeman - §920
Burton v. Wilmington Parking Authority - §682, 691
Butler v. Michigan - §786
Butler, United States v. - §51
Butterworth v. Smith - §917
CBS v. FCC - §1012
CBS, Inc. v. Democratic National Committee - §§689, 1014
Caban v. Mohammed - §559
Cabell v. Chavez-Salido - §551
Calero-Toledo v. Pearson Yacht Leasing Co. - §§415, 1124
Califano v. Aznavorian - §471
Califano v. Jobst - §603
Califano v. Torres - §600
Califano v. Webster - §561
California v. Ramos - §1195
California v. Stewart - §68
California v. Zook - §289
California Medical Association v. Federal Election Commission - §927
California Retail Liquor Dealers Association v. Medical Aluminum, Inc. - §324
Caltex, Inc., United States v. - §1124
Campbell v. Hussey - §283
Canton Railroad v. Rogan - §351
Cantwell v. Connecticut - §§1022, 1084, 1101
Capital Cities Cable, Inc. v. Crisp - §324
Capitol Greyhound Lines v. Brice - §§362, 363
Carey v. Brown - §606
Carey v. Population Services International - §§57, 446
Carolene Products Co., United States v. - §436
Carrington v. Rash - §609
Carroll v. Princess Anne County - §843
Carter v. Carter Coal Co. - §115
Carter v. Jury Commission - §1214
Cassell v. Texas - §1209
Castaneda v. Partida - §§496, 1207
Causby, United States v. - §1123
Central Hudson Gas & Electric Corp. v. Public Service Commission - §820
Central Railroad v. Pennsylvania - §346
Chae Chan Ping v. United States - §209
Chandler v. Florida - §1225
Chaplinsky v. New Hampshire - §§781, 806
Chapman v. Meier - §624
Charles River Bridge v. Warren Bridge - §1147
Chicago & Grand Trunk Railway v. Wellman - §42
Chicago, Burlington & Quincy Railroad v. Chicago - §1117
Chicago Police Department v. Mosley - §§606, 872
Chicago Teachers Union v. Hudson - §986
Church of Jesus Christ of Latter-Day Saints v. Amos - §104
Church of the Lukumi Babalu Aye, Inc. v. City of Hialeah - §§1080, 1082
Cincinnati, City of v. Discovery Network Inc. - §826
Citizens Against Rent Control v. Berkeley - §928
City of - *see* name of city
Civil Rights Cases - §670

Clark v. Allen - §209
Clark v. Community for Creative Non-Violence - §862
Clark v. Jeter - §562
Clark Distilling Co. v. Western Maryland Railroad - §282
Classic, United States v. - §700
Cleburne v. Cleburne Living Center, Inc. - §§580, 581
Clements v. Fashing - §651
Cleveland Board of Education v. LaFleur - §666
Cleveland Board of Education v. Loudermill - §420
Coates v. Cincinnati - §§745, 1232
Coe v. Errol - §348
Cohen v. California - §§784, 807
Cohen v. Cowles Media Co. - §1009
Coker v. Georgia - §1182
Colautti v. Franklin - §458
Cole v. Richardson - §981
Colegrove v. Green - §625
Coleman v. Miller - §105
Coleman v. Thompson - §1240
Colorado Anti-Discrimination Commission v. Continental Air Lines, Inc. - §289
Columbus Board of Education v. Penick - §§514, 524
Commercial Pictures Corp. v. Regents - §851
Committee for Public Education v. Nyquist - §§1037, 1045, 1046
Committee for Public Education v. Regan - §§1048, 1049
Commonwealth Edison Co. v. Montana - §358
Communist Party v. Subversive Activities Control Board - §967
Communist Party of Indiana v. Whitcomb - §§753, 993
Complete Auto Transit, Inc. v. Brady - §§320, 351, 358, 372
Connecticut v. Doehr - §427
Connell v. Higginbotham - §980
Connick v. Myers - §990
Connor v. Finch - §648
Consolidated Edison Co. v. Public Service Commission - §932
Constantine, United States v. - §138
Container Corp. of America v. Franchise Tax Board - §357
Cooley v. Board of Wardens of Philadelphia - §306
Cooper v. Mitchell Brothers' Santa Ana Theater - §847
Cornelius v. NAACP Legal Defense & Education Fund - §894
County of Allegheny v. American Civil Liberties Union Greater Pittsburgh Chapter - §1078
Cox v. Louisiana - §§808, 895
Cox v. New Hampshire - §897
Cox Broadcasting Corp. v. Cohn - §§65, 69, 1007
Craig v. Boren - §§57, 555, 559
Craig v. Harney - §914
Cramp v. Board of Public Instruction - §745
Crawford v. Los Angeles Board of Education - §544
Cress, United States v. - §1123
Crist v. Bretz - §397
Cruikshank, United States v. - §701
Cruzan v. Director, Missouri Department of Health - §§479, 480
Cummings v. Missouri - §§1152, 1153
Curtis Publishing Co. v. Butts - §770
Curtiss-Wright Export Corp., United States v. - §§125, 201, 203, 205

Dallas, City of, v. Stanglin - §727
Dalton v. Specter - §184
Dames & Moore v. Regan - §218
Damico v. California - §94
Dandridge v. Williams - §653
Daniels v. Williams - §412
Darby Lumber, United States v. - §§265, 272
Dartmouth College v. Woodward - §1140
Davis v. Bandemer - §639
Davis v. Passman - §693
Dawson v. Delaware - §722
Dayton Board of Education v. Brinkman (1979) - §507
Dayton Board of Education v. Brinkman (1977) - §§507, 521, 524
Dean Milk Co. v. City of Madison - §298
DeJonge v. Oregon - §965
Dennis v. United States - §§753, 754
Department of Revenue v. James B. Beam Distilling Co. - §327
DeShaney v. Winnebago County Department of Social Services- §413
Desist v. United States - §1244
DeStefano v. Woods - §1244
Detroit v. Murray Corp. - §253
Detroit, United States v. - §§254, 256
Doe v. Bolton - §§237, 457
Doe v. McMillan - §168
Dolan v. City of Tigard - §1123
Dombrowski v. Pfister - §§87, 92, 97
Doran v. Salem Inn, Inc. - §86
Doremus v. Board of Education - §49
Doremus, United States v. - §137
Douglas v. California - §§568, 1236, 1243
Douglas v. City of Jeannette - §84
Duke Power Co. v. Carolina Environmental Study Group, Inc. - §436
Dun & Bradstreet, Inc. v. Greenmoss Builders, Inc. - §§774, 775, 776
Dunbar Stanley Studios, Inc. v. Alabama - §360

Duncan v. Louisiana - §§396, 398, 1198, 1203, 1205, 1244
Dunn v. Blumstein - §§593, 607
Duren v. Missouri - §1207
Dusch v. Davis - §638

East New York Savings Bank v. Hahn - §1145
Eastland v. United States Servicemen's Fund - §165
Edelman v. Jordan - §§7, 12
Edenfield v. Fane - §831
Edge Broadcasting Co., United States v. - §825
Edmonson v. Leesville Concrete Co. - §688
Edwards v. Aguillard - §1059
Edwards v. California - §292
Edwards v. South Carolina - §869
Eichman, United States v. - §864
Eisenstadt v. Baird - §446
Elfbrandt v. Russell - §§965, 982
Eli Lilly & Co. v. Sav-On-Drugs, Inc. - §320
Elkins v. United States - §§1170, 1175
Ellis v. Brotherhood of Railway, Airline & Steamship Clerks - §985
Elrod v. Burns - §988
Employment Division, Department of Human Resources of Oregon v. Smith - §1088
Energy Reserves Group Inc. v. Kansas Power & Light Co. - §1142
Engel v. Vitale - §§1055, 1056, 1064
England v. Louisiana State Board of Medical Examiners - §99
Enmund v. Florida - §1182
Epperson v. Arkansas - §1058
Erznoznik v. Jacksonville - §873
Eskridge v. Washington Prison Board - §1235
Estate of - *see* name of party
Eu v. San Francisco County Democratic Central Committee - §§923, 924
Evans v. Abney - §684
Evans v. Cornman - §612
Evans v. Newton - §684
Evansville-Vanderburgh Airport Authority District v. Delta Airlines, Inc. - §364
Everson v. Board of Education - §§49, 1022, 1028, 1050
Ex parte - *see* party name
Examining Board of Engineers v. de Otero - §547
Exxon Corp. v. Eagerton - §1143
Exxon Corp. v. Wisconsin Department of Revenue - §357

FCC v. League of Women Voters - §1015
FCC v. National Citizens Committee - §1016
FCC v. Pacifica Foundation - §1017
Fay v. New York - §1210
Fay v. Noia - §1240
Federal Deposit Insurance Corp. v. Mallen - §425
Federal Election Commission v. Massachusetts Citizens for Life, Inc. - §933
Federal Election Commission v. National Conservative Political Action Committee - §930
Federal Election Commission v. National Right to Work Committee - §927
Feiner v. New York - §808
Ferguson v. Skrupa - §434
Fiallo v. Bell - §564
First English Evangelical Lutheran Church v. County of Los Angeles - §1131
First National Bank v. Bellotti - §932
Fitzpatrick v. Bitzer - §14
564.54 Acres of Land, United States v. - §1130
Flagg Bros., Inc. v. Brooks - §681
Flast v. Cohen - §§43, 52
Fletcher v. Peck - §§21, 1140
Florida Lime & Avocado Growers, Inc. v. Paul - §289
Florida Star v. B.J.F. - §1007
Foley v. Connelie - §551
Ford v. Wainright - §1186
Fordice, United States v. - §530
Fort Gratiot Sanitary Landfill, Inc. v. Michigan Department of Natural Resources - §304
Forsyth County, Georgia v. Nationalist Movement - §§898, 902
Fortson v. Morris - §645
Fousha v. Louisiana - §476
Freedman v. Maryland - §§849, 853, 854, 858, 859
Freeman v. Maryland - §855
Freeman v. Pitts - §528
Fresno County, United States v. - §249
Friedman v. Rogers - §815
Frisby v. Schultz - §880
Frontiero v. Richardson - §557
Frothingham v. Mellon - §§50, 52
Fuentes v. Shevin - §426
Fullilove v. Klutznick - §§541, 707, 720
Furman v. Georgia - §1188
FW/PBS Inc. v. City of Dallas - §853

Gaffney v. Cummings - §§632, 636
Gannett Co. v. DePasquale - §§1005, 1222
Garcia v. San Antonio Metropolitan Transit Authority - §243
Garner v. Los Angeles Board of Public Works - §996
Garnett, *Ex parte* - §124
Garrison v. Louisiana- §§759, 767
Geduldig v. Aiello - §558
General Motors Corp. v. Washington - §352
General Trading Co. v. Iowa Tax Commission - §377
Gentile v. State Bar of Nevada - §911
Geofroy v. Riggs - §214
Georgia v. McCollum - §688
Gerlach Live Stock Co., United States v. - §142

Gertz v. Robert Welch, Inc. - §§768, 769, 771, 772, 776, 780
Gibbons v. Ogden - §275
Giboney v. Empire Storage & Ice Co. - §957
Gibson v. Florida Legislative Investigation Committee - §§973, 974
Gideon v. Wainwright - §§398, 1156, 1243
Gillette v. United States - §§1091, 1106
Gilligan v. Morgan - §104
Gillock, United States v. - §166
Gilmore v. City of Montgomery - §531
Ginsberg v. New York - §797
Ginzburg v. United States - §§791, 792
Gitlow v. New York - §§721, 751
Globe Newspaper Co. v. Superior Court - §1004
Goldberg v. Kelly - §408, 416
Goldman v. Weinberger - §1096
Goldwater v. Carter - §103
Gomez v. Perez - §563
Gomillion v. Lightfoot - §§109, 502
Gooch v. United States - §265
Good Real Property, United States v. - §415
Gooding v. Wilson - §809
Gordon v. Lance - §646
Goss v. Lopez - §§406, 408, 421
Grace, United States v. - §869
Graham v. Richardson - §§545, 546
Grand Rapids School District v. Ball - §1036
Gravel v. United States - §166
Graves v. New York *ex rel.* O'Keefe - §250
Grayned v. City of Rockford - §§895, 1231
Great Atlantic & Pacific Tea Co. v. Cottrell - §319
Green v. New Kent County School Board - §520
Greer v. Spock - §895
Gregg v. Georgia - §1187
Griffin v. Breckenridge - §§697, 702
Griffin v. California - §§1168, 1244
Griffin v. County School Board - §§98, 532
Griffin v. Illinois - §§568, 1235, 1243
Griffith v. Kentucky - §1245
Griffiths, *In re* - §547
Griggs v. Allegheny County - §1123
Griswold v. Connecticut - §§442, 446
Grossman, *Ex parte* - §181
Guest, United States v. - §§464, 696, 715

H. P. Hood & Sons v. DuMond - §§295, 310
Hadley v. Junior College District - §641
Hague v. CIO - §869
Haig v. Agee - §§471, 736
Hale v. Iowa State Board of Assessment and Review - §1147
Hamilton v. Regents of University of California - §1095
Hamling v. United States - §§789, 794, 796
Hampton v. Mow Sun Wong - §401
Hancock v. Train - §258
Hans v. Louisiana - §6
Harisiades v. Shaughnessy - §§152, 1153
Harlow v. Fitzgerald - §199
Harper v. Virginia Board of Elections - §§577, 610
Harper v. Virginia Department of Taxation - §112
Harper & Row v. Nation Enterprises - §962
Harris v. McRae - §§460, 565, 576, 605
Harris County Commissioners' Court v. Moore - §96
Hauenstein v. Lynham - §208
Hawaii Housing Authority v. Midkiff - §1120
Hawker v. New York - §1120
Hazelwood School District v. Kuhlmeier - §942
Head Money Cases - §209
Healy v. James - §901
Healy v. The Beer Institute, Inc. - §326
Heart of Atlanta Motel, Inc. v. United States - §§272, 276, 719
Heffron v. International Society for Krishna Consciousness - §§871, 879
Heller v. New York - §845
Helvering v. Davis - §142
Henneford v. Silas Mason Co. - §§366, 377
Henry v. Mississippi - §75
Herb v. Pitcairn - §73
Herbert v. Lando - §762
Hernandez v. Commissioner of Internal Revenue - §1093
Hernandez v. New York - §499
Hernandez v. Texas - §§491, 1207
Hicklin v. Orbeck - §§234, 237. 239, 240
Hicks v. Miranda - §91
Hill v. Stone - §613
Hills v. Gautreaux - §523
Hines v. Davidowitz - §286
Hirabayashi v. United States - §492
Hobbie v. Unemployment Appeals Commission - §102
Hodel v. Indiana - §§272, 276
Hodel v. Irving - §1123
Hodel v. Virginia Surface Mining & Reclamation Association - §§272, 273
Hodgson v. Minnesota - §456
Holland v. Illinois - §1211
Holmgren v. United States - §155
Holt Civic Club v. City of Tuscaloosa - §619
Home Building & Loan Association v. Blaisdell - §1138
Honda Motor Co. v. Oberg - §438
Hooper v. Bernalillo County Assessor - §599
Hostetter v. Idlewild Bon Voyage Liquor Corp. - §§322, 323
Houchins v. KQED - §1004
Hudgens v. NLRB - §§678, 896
Huffman v. Pursue, Ltd. - §89
Hughes v. Alexandria Scrap Corp. - §299

Hughes v. Oklahoma - §296
Hughes v. Superior Court - §957
Hughes Bros. Timber Co. v. Minnesota - §349
Humphrey's Executor v. United States - §178
Hunt v. Washington State Apple Advertising Commission - §§58, 303
Hunter v. Erickson - §544
Hunter v. Underwood - §504
Hurtado v. California - §399
Hustler Magazine v. Falwell - §779
Hutchinson v. Proxmire - §§168, 771
Hutto v. Finney - §13
Hynes v. Mayor of Oradell - §881

Ibanez v. Florida Department of Business & Professional Regulation - §820
Immigration & Naturalization Service v. Chadha - §186
In re - see name of party
Ingraham v. Wright - §422
International Brotherhood of Teamsters v. Vogt, Inc. - §956
International Harvester Co. v. Department of Treasury - §371
International Society for Krishna Consciousness, Inc. v. Lee - §894
Irvin v. Dowd - §1215
Itel Containers International Corp. v. Huddleston - §389

J.E.B. v. Alabama *ex rel.* T.B. - §559
Jackson v. Metropolitan Edison Co. - §§679, 689
Jackson v. Virginia - §1230
James v. Valtierra - §565
Japan Line, Ltd. v. County of Los Angeles - §389
Jenkins v. Georgia - §§789, 793
Jenness v. Fortson - §586
Jimenez v. Weinberger - §668
Jimmy Swaggart Ministries v. Board of Equalization of California - §1093
Johnson v. Louisiana - §1202
Johnson v. Maryland - §258
Johnson v. New Jersey - §§1243, 1244
Johnson v. Robison - §§488, 578, 1092
Johnson v. Zerbst - §1155
Johnson Oil Refining Co. v. Oklahoma - §342
Johnson, United States v. (1982) - §1245
Johnson, United States v. (1966) - §164
Jones v. Alfred H. Mayer Co. - §702
Jones v. Helms - §468
Jones v. North Carolina Prisoners' Labor Union - §947
Jones v. Wolf - §1112
Joseph v. Carter & Weekes Stevedoring Co. - §351
Joseph Burstyn, Inc. v. Wilson - §851
Joseph E. Seagram & Sons, Inc. v. Hostetter - §326
Juidice v. Vail - §90

Kadrmas v. Dickinson Public Schools - §658
Kahn v. Shevin - §561
Kahriger, United States v. - §§137, 138
Kaiser Aetna v. United States - §1123
Kansas v. Colorado - §119
Karcher v. Daggett - §627
Kassel v. Consolidated Freightways Corp. - §§305, 315
Katz v. United States - §§1174, 1244
Katzenbach v. McClung - §272
Katzenbach v. Morgan - §§704, 706, 710
Keeney v. Thompson - §1240
Keller v. State Bar of California - §987
Kelley v. Johnson - §463
Kendall v. United States *ex rel.* Stokes - §191
Kent v. Dulles - §469
Kentucky Whip & Collar Co. v. Illinois Central Railroad - §266
Ker v. California - §398
Kern-Limerick, Inc. v. Scurlock - §252
Keyes v. School District No. 1 - §§515, 516, 519
Keyishian v. Board of Regents - §§981, 983
Kilbourn v. Thompson - §161
Kingsley Books, Inc. v. Brown - §844
Kingsley International Pictures Corp. v. Regents - §852
Kleindienst v. Mandel - §150
Kleppe v. New Mexico - §159
Klopfer v. North Carolina - §398
Kokinda, United States v. - §895
Konigsberg v. State Bar - §§998, 999
Korematsu v. United States - §492
Kosydar v. National Cash Register Co. - §387
Kovacs v. Cooper - §§882, 890
Kramer v. Union Free School District - §611
Kras, United States v. - §§574, 659
Kunz v. New York - §900
Kusper v. Pontikes - §622
Kwong Hai Chew v. Colding - §152

Ladue, City of, v. Gilleo - §892
Laird v. Tatum - §36
Lakewood v. Plain Dealer Publishing Co. - §904
Lalli v. Lalli - §564
Lamb's Chapel v. Center Moriches Union Free School District - §894
Lamont v. Postmaster General - §728
Landmark Communications, Inc. v. Virginia - §§916, 1007
Lanzetta v. New Jersey - §1232
Larkin v. Grendel's Den, Inc. - §1074
Larson v. Domestic & Foreign Commerce Corp. - §5
Larson v. Valente - §1025
Lassiter v. Department of Social Services - §431
Law Students Civil Rights Research Council v. Wadmond - §§980, 1000

Leathers v. Medlock - §1019
Lee v. International Society for Krishna Consciousness - §894
Lee, United States v. - §1093
Lee v. Weisman - §1077
Lehman v. City of Shaker Heights - §895
Lehr v. Robertson - §407
Leis v. Flynt - §408
Leisy v. Hardin - §282
Lemon v. Kurtzman - §§1026, 1032, 1045
Leon, United States v. - §1171
Leslie Miller, Inc. v. Arkansas - §258
Levitt v. Committee for Public Education - §1048
Levy v. Louisiana - §563
Lewis v. City of New Orleans - §809
Lincoln County v. Luning - §10
Lincoln Federal Labor Union v. Northwestern Iron & Metal Co. - §437
Lindsey v. Normet- §§655, 661
Lindsley v. Natural Carbonic Gas Co. - §485
Liner v. Jafco, Inc. - §37
Linkletter v. Walker - §1244
Linmark Associates, Inc. v. Township of Willingboro - §822
Little v. Streater - §573
Lochner v. New York - §435
Lockett v. Ohio - §1192
Lockhart v. McCree - §1218
Logan v. Zimmerman Brush Co. - §410
Lombard v. Louisiana - §683
Loretto v. Teleprompter Manhattan CATV Corp. - §891
Los Angeles v. Preferred Communications, Inc. - §1011
Los Angeles City Council v. Taxpayers for Vincent - §891
Los Angeles, City of, v. Lyons - §35
Lottery Case - §265
Louisiana v. United States - §500
Lovell v. City of Griffin - §898
Loving v. Virginia - §§444, 510, 511
Lubin v. Panish - §650
Lucas v. 44th General Assembly - §631
Lucas v. South Carolina Coastal Council - §1126
Lugar v. Edmondson Oil Co. - §685
Lynch v. Donnelly - §§1075, 1078, 1079
Lyng v. International Union - §938
Lyng v. Northwest Indian Cemetery Protective Association - §1098

McCardle, *Ex parte* - §26
McCarthy v. Philadelphia Civil Service Commission - §600
McClesky v. Kemp - §§498, 1190
McCollum v. Board of Education - §1060
McCray v. United States - §137
McCulloch v. Maryland - §§120, 122, 227, 248
McDaniel v. Paty - §1081
McDermott v. Wisconsin - §267
McDonald v. Board of Elections - §623
McDonald v. Santa Fe Trail Transportation Co. - §703
McGoldrick v. Berwind-White Coal Mining Co. - §374
McGowan v. Maryland - §§485, 1072, 1113, 1114
McGrain v. Daugherty - §160
McKesson Corp. v. Florida Division of Alcoholic Beverages & Tobacco - §9
McKoy v. North Carolina - §1193
McLaughlin v. Florida - §§510, 511
McLemore, United States v. - §4
McLeod v. J. E. Dilworth Co. - §§375, 377
Mackey v. Montrym - §424
Madden v. Women's Health Center, Inc. - §905
Mahan v. Howell - §633
Maher v. Roe - §§576, 605
Maine v. Taylor - §298
Malloy v. Hogan - §§398, 1167
Malone v. Bowdoin - §5
Mapp v. Ohio - §§1172, 1175, 1244
Marbury v. Madison - §§17, 21
Marchetti v. United States - §138
Marcus v. Search Warrant - §845
Marsh v. Alabama - §§676, 896
Marsh v. Chambers - §1076
Marston v. Lewis - §594
Martin v. Hunter's Lessee - §21
Martin v. Mott - §103
Martin v. Struthers - §888
Martinez v. Bynum - §§579, 600
Maryland v. Baltimore Radio Show, Inc. - §25
Maryland v. Louisiana - §61
Maryland v. Wirtz - §272
Massachusetts v. Mellon - §§60, 61
Massachusetts v. Oakes - §749
Massachusetts v. Sheppard - §1171
Massachusetts Board of Retirement v. Murgia - §578
Masson v. New Yorker Magazine, Inc. - §760
Mathews v. Diaz - §545
Mathews v. Eldridge - §§414, 417
Mathews v. Lucas - §§562, 564
Maurer v. Hamilton - §287
Mayer v. City of Chicago - §1235
Mayor of Philadelphia v. Educational Equality League - §496
Meek v. Pittenger - §§1036, 1047
Meese v. Keene - §834
Memorial Hospital v. Maricopa County - §592
Memphis v. Greene - §508
Memphis Light, Gas & Water Division v. Craft - §408

Metro Broadcasting, Inc. v. Federal Communications Commission - §541
Metromedia, Inc. v. City of San Diego - §§827, 875, 889
Metropolitan Life Insurance Co. v. Ward - §§281, 382
Meyer v. Grant - §931
Meyer v. Nebraska - §461
Miami Herald Publishing Co. v. Tornillo - §1013
Michael M. v. Sonoma County Superior Court - §560
Michelin Tire Corp. v. Wages - §§260, 385
Michigan v. Long - §76
Middlesex County Ethics Committee v. Garden State Bar Association - §90
Milk Control Board v. Eisenberg Farm Products - §317
Milk Wagon Drivers' Union v. Meadowmoor Dairies, Inc. - §955
Milkovich v. Lorain Journal Co. - §778
Miller v. California - §§781, 782, 783, 789, 790, 793, 802
Miller v. Schoene - §1128
Miller Bros. v. Maryland - §380
Milliken v. Bradley (1977) - §525
Milliken v. Bradley (1974) - §522
Mills v. Alabama - §§66, 919
Minneapolis Star & Tribune Co. v. Commissioner of Revenue - §1018
Minnesota v. Barber - §§297, 313
Minnesota v. Blasius - §349
Minnesota v. Clover Leaf Creamery Co. - §311
Minnesota State Board for Community Colleges v. Knight - §730
Mintz v. Baldwin - §313
Miranda v. Arizona - §§1164, 1244
Mishkin v. New York - §787
Mississippi Tax Commission, United States v. (1975) - §252
Mississippi Tax Commission, United States v. (1973) - §323
Mississippi University for Women v. Hogan - §559
Missouri v. Holland - §§59, 212, 214
Mistretta v. United States - §129
Mitchell v. Forsyth - §199
Mitchell v. W. T. Grant Co. - §426
Mitchum v. Foster - §83
Mobil Oil Corp. v. Vermont Commissioner of Taxes - §357
Mobile, City of, v. Bolden - §509
Monitor Patriot Co. v. Roy - §765
Moore v. City of East Cleveland - §462
Moore v. Ogilvie - §§39, 643
Moore v. Sims - §89
Moorman Manufacturing Co. v. Bair - §356
Moose Lodge v. Irvis - §§687, 689
Morrison v. Olson - §§173, 176
Morton v. Mancari - §542
Mt. Healthy Board of Education v. Doyle - §994
Mueller v. Allen - §1038
Murdock v. City of Memphis - §74
Murdock v. Pennsylvania - §1093
Myers v. United States - §176

NAACP v. Alabama - §§56, 72, 726, 966, 967
NAACP v. Button - §§747, 953
NAACP v. Claiborne Hardware Co. - §§959, 960, 978
NLRB v. Fainblatt - §274
NLRB v. Jones & Laughlin Steel Corp. - §§271, 275
National Bellas Hess, Inc. v. Illinois Department of Revenue - §380
National Board of Y.M.C.A. v. United States - §1124
National Cable Television Association v. United States - §183
National Geographic Society v. California Board of Equalization - §379
National League of Cities v. Usery - §243
National Society of Professional Engineers v. United States - §816
National Union of Marine Cooks v. Arnold - §1234
Near v. Minnesota - §§832, 836
Nebbia v. New York - §437
Nebraska Press Association v. Stuart - §§837, 909
Nevada v. Hall - §15
New Jersey v. Wilson - §1149
New Orleans v. Dukes - §486
New York v. Ferber - §798
New York v. United States - §244, 245
New York City Transit Authority v. Beazer - §487
New York State Club Association v. New York City - §736
New York Times v. Sullivan - §§758, 759, 761, 765, 767, 768, 772, 776, 778, 779, 780, 812
New York Times Co. v. United States - §832
Nippert v. City of Richmond - §§332, 359
Nixon v. Administrator of General Services - §§196, 463
Nixon v. Fitzgerald - §198
Nixon, United States v. - §§101, 106, 193, 194, 195
Nollan v. California Coastal Commission - §1123
Nordlinger v. Hahn - §487
Norfolk & Western Railway v. Missouri Tax Commission - §§343, 344
North American Co. v. SEC - §276
North Dakota Board of Pharmacy v. Snyder's Drug Stores - §437
North Georgia Finishing, Inc. v. Di-Chem, Inc. - §426
Northeast Bancorp, Inc. v. Board of Governors - §281

Northwestern States Portland Cement Co. v. Minnesota - §§353, 354, 355
Norwood v. Harrison - §531
Nyquist v. Mauclet - §555

O'Bannon v. Town Court Nursing Center - §411
O Brien v. Brown - §108
O'Brien v. Skinner - §623
O'Brien, United States v. - §§861, 862
O'Connor v. Donaldson - §§474, 475
Ohio v. Akron Center for Reproductive Health - §456
Ohio Civil Rights Commission v. Dayton Christian Schools, Inc. - §90
Ohralik v. Ohio State Bar Association - §§817, 830
Oklahoma Publishing Co. v. District Court - §838
Oliver, *In re* - §§398, 1220
O'Lone v. Estate of Shabazz - §1097
Oregon v. Mitchell - §§698, 699, 704, 709
Organization For a Better Austin v. Keefe - §884
Orito, United States v. - §801
Orr v. Orr - §559
Ortwein v. Schwab - §575
Osborne v. Ohio - §§748, 799
O'Shea v. Littleton - §§35, 93
Ott v. Mississippi Valley Barge Line Co. - §342
Owen v. City of Independence - §713

Pacific Gas & Electric Co. v. Public Utilities Commission - §1014
Pacific Mutual Life Insurance Co. v. Haslip - §438
Pacific States Telegraph & Telephone Co. v. Oregon - §107
Palko v. Connecticut - §396
Palmer v. City of Euclid - §1232
Palmer v. Thompson - §532
Palmore v. Sidoti - §511
Panama Refining Co. v. Ryan - §126
Papish v. Board of Curators - §992
Paradise, United States v. - §537
Parham v. Hughes - §560
Parham v. J. R. - §429
Paris Adult Theatre I v. Slaton - §§781, 800
Parker v. Brown - §318
Parker v. Levy - §951
Pasadas de Puerto Rico Associates v. Tourism Company of Puerto Rico - §824
Pasadena Board of Education v. Spangler - §527
Passenger Cases - §466
Patsone v. Pennsylvania - §549
Patton v. Mississippi - §1207
Patton v. United States - §1198
Paul v. Davis - §§406, 463
Paul v. Virginia - §466
Payne v. Tennessee - §1196
Peel v. Illinois Attorney Registration & Disciplinary Commission - §828
Pell v. Procunier - §§946, 979
Penn Central Transportation Co. v. New York City - §§1122, 1127, 1128
Pennekamp v. Florida - §909
Pennhurst State School & Hospital v. Halderman - §11
Pennsylvania v. Board of Trusts - §684
Pennsylvania v. Nelson - §§284, 288
Pennsylvania v. Union Gas Co. - §14
Pennsylvania Coal Co. v. Mahon - §1125
Pennzoil Co. v. Texaco, Inc. - §90
Penry v. Lynaugh - §§1184, 1192
Perez v. Campbell - §227
Perez v. United States - §§273, 274
Perry Education Association v. Perry Local Educators' Association - §§870, 872, 894
Personnel Administrator of Massachusetts v. Feeney - §556
Peterson v. City of Greenville - §683
Philadelphia v. New Jersey - §293
Philadelphia Newspapers, Inc. v. Hepps - §777
Phoenix, City of, v. Kolodziejski - §613
Pickering v. Board of Education - §§989, 990
Pierce v. Society of Sisters - §§461, 1100
Pike v. Bruce Church, Inc. - §§297, 316
Pink, United States v. - §219
Pinkus v. United States - §786
Pittsburgh, City of, v. Alco Parking Co. - §1129
Pittsburgh Press Co. v. Pittsburgh Human Relations Committee - §816
Planned Parenthood v. Ashcroft - §§445, 448
Planned Parenthood v. Danforth - §§450, 452, 453, 454
Planned Parenthood of Southeastern Pennsylvania v. Casey - §§448, 449, 450, 451, 457
Plyler v. Doe - §552
Poe v. Ullman - §34
Poelker v. Roe - §605
Pointer v. Texas - §398
Pollock v. Farmers' Loan & Trust Co. - §116
Pollock v. Williams - §1134
Pope v. Illinois - §789
Poulos v. New Hampshire - §905
Powell v. McCormack - §110
Presbyterian Church v. Hull Church - §1111
Press Co. v. Pittsburg Human Relations Committee - §819
Press-Enterprise Co. v. Superior Court (1986) - §1005
Press-Enterprise Co. v. Superior Court (1984) - §1006
Price, United States v. - §715
Primus, *In re* - §953
Prize Cases - §188
Procunier v. Martinez - §950
Prudential Insurance Co. v. Benjamin - §§280, 328

Pruneyard Shopping Center v. Robins - §§724, 896, 1123
Public Utilities Commission v. Pollak - §689

Quill Corp. v. North Dakota - §§376, 380
Quilloin v. Walcott - §463

R.A.V. v. City of St. Paul - §807
R.M.J., Matter of - §828
Radio Station WOW, Inc. v. Johnson - §67
Rahrer, *In re* - §282
Railroad Commission v. Pullman Co. - §95
Raymond Motor Transportation, Inc. v. Rice - §315
Red Lion Broadcasting Co. v. FCC - §§1011, 1012
Redrup v. New York - §804
Reed v. Reed - §557
Reeves, Inc. v. Stake - §299
Regan v. Taxation with Representation of Washington - §937
Regan v. Wald - §471
Regents of University of California v. Bakke - §539
Reid v. Covert - §213
Reidel, United States v. - §800
Reitman v. Mulkey - §690
Rendell-Baker v. Kohn - §§680, 689
Renton, City of, v. Playtime Theatres, Inc. - §§802, 885
Rescue Army v. Municipal Court - §§32, 77
Reynolds v. Sims - §§631, 636
Reynolds v. United States - §1089
Reynolds, United States v. - §1134
Rice v. Santa Fe Elevator Corp. - §287
Richardson v. Belcher - §654
Richardson v. Ramirez - §616
Richardson, United States v. - §52
Richmond, City of, v. J. A. Croson Co. - §§533, 534
Richmond Newspapers, Inc. v. Virginia - §1005
Rideau v. Louisiana - §1216
Riley v. National Federation of the Blind of North Carolina - §§725, 855, 888
Rivera v. Minnich - §433
Rizzo v. Goode - §93
Robel, United States v. - §990
Roberts v. United States Jaycees - §§463, 727, 736
Robertson v. Baldwin - §1135
Robinson v. California - §1181
Rodriguez v. Popular Democratic Party - §645
Roe v. Wade - §§442, 447, 458
Roemer v. Board of Public Works - §1042
Rogers v. Bellei - §157
Rogers v. Lodge - §505
Rome, City of, v. United States - §717
Rosario v. Rockefeller - §621
Rosenblatt v. Baer - §§761, 766
Ross v. Moffitt - §§569, 1237
Rostker v. Goldberg - §560
Roth v. United States - §§781, 782, 783
Roudebush v. Hartke - §110
Rowan v. United States Post Office - §883
Royster Guano Co. v. Virginia - §488
Ruckelshaus v. Monsanto Co. - §1118
Rummel v. Estelle - §1185
Runyon v. McCrary - §§463, 702
Rust v. Sullivan - §938
Rutan v. Republican Party of Illinois - §988

Sable Communications of California, Inc. v. FCC - §786
Saia v. New York - §882
Sailors v. Board of Education - §§644, 645
Salyer Land Co. v. Tulare Water Storage District - §§618, 642
Samuels v. Mackell - §88
San Antonio Independent School District v. Rodriguez - §§582, 652, 657
San Francisco Arts & Athletics, Inc. v. United States Olympic Committee - §961
Santosky v. Kramer - §432
Scales v. United States - §965
Schacht v. United States - §750
Schad v. Borough of Mount Ephraim - §803
Schechter Poultry Co. v. United States - §126
Scheuer v. Rhodes - §11
Schick v. Reed - §180
Schilb v. Kuebel - §398
Schlesinger v. Ballard - §561
Schlesinger v. Reservists Committee - §48
Schneider v. Rusk - §156
Schneider v. State - §887
Schneiderman v. United States - §157
Scott v. Germano - §647
Scott v. Illinois - §1159
SCRAP, United States v. - §45
Screws v. United States - §§671, 713, 1233
Scripto v. Carson - §378
Seattle Times Co. v. Rhinehart - §839
Seeger, United States v. - §1110
Selective Draft Law Cases - §1135
Serbian Eastern Orthodox Diocese v. Milivojevich - §1111
Shapero v. Kentucky Bar Association - §828
Shapiro v. Thompson - §§467, 591
Sharpnack, United States v. - §259
Shaughnessy v. United States *ex rel.* Mezei - §151
Shaw v. Reno - §543
Sheet Metals Workers' International Association v. Equal Employment Opportunity Commission - §536
Sheldon v. Sill - §2
Shelley v. Kraemer - §686
Shelton v. Tucker - §997

Sheppard v. Maxwell - §§913, 1226
Sherbert v. Verner - §1102
Shreveport Rate Case - §272
Shuttlesworth v. City of Birmingham - §§903, 904
Sibron v. New York - §38
Sierra Club v. Morton - §§44, 47
Simon v. Eastern Kentucky Welfare Rights Organization - §46
Simon & Schuster, Inc. v. Members of the New York Crime Victims Board - §738
Sinclair v. United States - §160
Skinner v. Oklahoma- §§445, 604
Slaughterhouse Cases - §§231, 392
Smith v. Allwright - §674
Smith v. California - §§795, 796
Smith v. Daily Mail Publishing Co. - §1007
Snepp v. United States - §836
Sniadach v. Family Finance Corp. - §426
Snowden v. Hughes - §496
Socialist Labor Party v. Gilligan - §79
Solem v. Helm - §1185
Sonzinsky, United States v. - §137
Sosna v. Iowa - §597
South Carolina v. Baker - §245
South Carolina v. Katzenbach - §§65, 716
South Carolina State Highway Department v. Barnwell Bros. - §§305, 307
South-Central Timber Development, Inc. v. Wunnicke - §301
South Dakota v. Dole - §141, 244
Southeastern Promotions, Ltd. v. Conrad - §853
Southern Pacific Co. v. Arizona - §309
Southern Pacific Co. v. Gallagher - §367
Spector Motor Service, Inc. v. O'Connor - §351
Speiser v. Randall - §976
Spence v. Washington - §864
Spevack v. Klein - §1001
Sporhase v. Nebraska - §§239, 296
Standard Oil Co. v. Peck - §347
Stanford v. Kentucky - §1183
Stanley v. Georgia - §§799, 800
Stanley v. Illinois - §664
Starns v. Malkerson - §596
Staub v. Baxley - §903
Steffel v. Thompson - §85
Steward Machine Co. v. Davis - §141
Stolar, *In re* - §999
Stone v. Graham - §1061
Stone v. Mississippi - §1149
Stone v. Powell - §1240
Storer v. Brown - §587
Stovall v. Denno - §1244
Strauder v. West Virginia - §491
Street v. New York - §§750, 866
Sturges v. Crowninshield - §228
Sugarman v. Dougall - §548
Sullivan, United States v. - §267
Sumner v. Shuman - §1191
Supreme Court of New Hampshire v. Piper - §§234, 237
Supreme Court of Virginia v. Friedman - §237
Swann v. Adams - §632
Swann v. Charlotte-Mecklenburg Board of Education - §§525, 538

Takahashi v. Fish and Game Commission - §549
Talley v. California - §877
Tancil v. Woolls - §511
Tashjian v. Republican Party of Connecticut - §925
Tate v. Short - §570
Taylor v. Louisiana - §§1205, 1207, 1208, 1212, 1213
Tehan v. United States *ex rel.* Shott - §1244
Terrace v. Thompson - §549
Terry v. Adams - §675
Texas, United States v. - §8
Texas v. Johnson - §864
Texas Monthly, Inc. v. Bullock - §1052
Thirty-Seven Photographs, United States v. - §859
Thomas v. Review Board of Indiana Employment Security Division - §§1102, 1107
Thornburgh v. Abbott - §949
Thornhill v. Alabama - §954
Thornton, Estate of, v. Caldor, Inc. - §1104
Tidal Oil Co. v. Flanagan - §1137
Tileston v. Ullman - §54
Tilton v. Richardson - §1042
Time, Inc. v. Firestone - §771
Time, Inc. v. Hill - §780
Times Film Corp. v. City of Chicago - §849
Tinker v. Des Moines Independent School District - §§863, 940
Tison v. Arizona - §1182
Toll v. Moreno - §553
Toomer v. Witsell - §237
Torcaso v. Watkins - §§1071, 1109
Town of Lockport v. Citizens for Community Action - §646
Trafficante v. Metropolitan Life Insurance Co. - §47
Train v. New York - §191
Trainor v. Hernandez - §90
Trinova Corp. v. Michigan Department of Treasury - §351
Trop v. Dulles - §1186
Turner v. Fouche - §566
Turner v. Louisiana - §217
Turner v. Safley - §945
Turner Broadcasting System v. FCC - §§738, 1018, 1019, 1020
12-200 Ft. Reels, United States v. - §801

Twining v. New Jersey - §§230, 466
TXO Production Corp. v. Alliance Resources Corp. - §438

Union Tank Line Co. v. Wright - §341
United Building & Construction Trades Council v. Mayor & Council of Camden - §§235, 302
United Jewish Organizations v. Carey - §543
United Mine Workers v. Illinois Bar Association - §953
United Public Workers v. Mitchell - §31
United States v. - *see* name of defendant
United States Civil Service Commission v. National Association of Letter Carriers - §742
United States Department of Agriculture v. Moreno - §§487, 662
United States Department of Agriculture v. Murry - §667
United States Department of Commerce v. Montana - §630
United States *ex rel.* Knauff v. Shaughnessy - §151
United States *ex rel.* Mezei - §151
United States Parole Commission v. Geraghty - §41
United States Postal Service v. Council of Greenburgh Civic Associations - §895
United States Railroad Retirement Board v. Fritz - §485
United States Trust Co. v. New Jersey - §§1139, 1147
University of Pennsylvania v. Equal Employment Opportunity Commission - §944
Usery v. Turner Elkhorn Mining Co. - §1150

Valley Forge Christian College v. Americans United - §52
Vance v. Bradley - §486
Vance v. Terrazas - §157
Veazie Bank v. Fenno - §134
Village of Arlington Heights v. Metropolitan Housing Development Corp. - §§503, 504
Village of Belle Terre v. Boraas - §656
Village of Hoffman Estates v. Flipside, Hoffman Estates, Inc. - §741
Village of Schaumburg v. Citizens for a Better Environment - §729
Virginia, *Ex parte* - §671
Virginia State Board v. Virginia Citizens Consumer Council - §818
Vitek v. Jones - §405
Vlandis v. Kline - §665
Von Hoffman v. City of Quincy - §1144

WHYY, Inc. v. Borough of Glassboro - §331
W. T. Grant Co., United States v. - §40
Wade, United States v. - §1244
Wainwright v. Witt - §1218
Walker v. City of Birmingham - §860
Walker v. Johnston - §1155
Walker v. Sauvinet - §399
Wallace v. Jaffree - §1057
Waller v. Georgia - §1221
Walters v. National Association of Radiation Survivors - §418
Walton v. Arizona - §1194
Walz v. Tax Commission - §§1023, 1024, 1026, 1051
Ward v. Rock Against Racism - §886
Warth v. Seldin - §46
Washington v. Davis - §§493, 501, 506
Washington v. Harper - §§430, 477
Washington v. Seattle School District - §544
Washington v. Texas - §398
Washington v. United States - §257
Washington Revenue Department v. Association of Washington Stevedoring Companies - §§351, 386
Waters v. Churchill - §990
Watkins v. United States - §971
Watson v. Jones - §1111
Watts v. United States - §750
Webb's Fabulous Pharmacies, Inc. v. Beckwith - §1123
Weber v. Aetna Casualty & Surety Co. - §563
Webster v. Reproductive Health Services - §§459, 460
Weeks v. United States - §1175
Weems v. United States - §1180
Weinberger v. Salfi - §669
Weiner v. United States - §178
Welton v. Missouri - §294
Wesberry v. Sanders - §626
West Coast Hotel Co. v. Parrish - §437
West River Bridge Co. v. Dix - §1148
West Virginia State Board of Education v. Barnette - §1085
Western & Southern Life Insurance Co. v. California Board of Equalization - §§281, 381
Whalen v. Roe - §463
Whitcomb v. Chavis - §637
White v. Massachusetts Council of Construction Employers - §§300, 302
White v. Regester - §§632, 637
White v. Weiser - §§628, 629
Wickard v. Filburn - §272
Widmar v. Vincent - §§876, 1053
Wieman v. Updegraff - §983
Williams v. Florida - §§1199, 1200
Williams v. Rhodes - §583
Williams v . Standard Oil - §117
Williams, United States v. - §695
Williams v. Vermont - §368
Williamson v. Lee Optical Co. - §§437, 486
Winship, *In re* - §§400, 1227, 1229

Wisconsin v. Constantineau - §406
Wisconsin v. Mitchell - §734
Wisconsin v. Yoder - §§1100, 1109
Witherspoon v. Illinois - §1218
Witters v. Washington Department of Services for the Blind - §1039
Wolff v. McDonnell - §948
Wolman v. Walker - §§1029, 1031, 1033, 1035
Wolston v. Reader's Digest Association - §771
Wood v. Georgia - §915
Woods v. Cloyd Miller Co. - §146
Woodson v. North Carolina - §1191
Wooley v. Maynard - §§84, 723
Wright v. Council of Emporia - §526
Wygant v. Jackson Board of Education - §535

Yakus v. United States - §127
Yates v. United States - §§753, 754
Yick Wo v. Hopkins - §§491, 495
Young v. American Mini Theatres, Inc. - §§802, 885
Young, *Ex parte* - §§11, 80
Youngberg v. Romeo - §478
Younger v. Harris - §§88, 92
Youngstown Sheet & Tube Co. v. Sawyer - §§189, 190

Zablocki v. Redhail - §602
Zacchini v. Scripps-Howard Broadcasting Co. - §1008
Zant v. Stephens - §1189
Zauderer v. Office of Disciplinary Council - §§828, 829
Zemel v. Rusk - §§471, 733
Zobel v. Williams - §598
Zobrest v. Catalina Foothills School District - §1034
Zorach v. Clauson - §§1067, 1068, 1069
Zschernig v. Miller - §204
Zurcher v. Stanford Daily - §1010
Zwickler v. Koota - §95

INDEX

A

ABORTION
equal protection, §605
funding, §576
substantive due process, §§447-460
ABSTENTION, §§95-99
AD VALOREM TAX, §§337-349
"ADEQUATE STATE GROUND," §§73-76
ADMIRALTY AND MARITIME POWER, §124
ADVISORY OPINIONS, §§28-36
AGE DISCRIMINATION, §559
ALIENS
See also Equal protection
congressional authority over, §§149-152
APPEAL
See Judicial review; Supreme Court
APPELLATE REVIEW
See also Judicial review
Eleventh Amendment, §9
obscenity, §793
rights on appeal, §§1234-1240, 1245
federal procedures, §§1238-1240
retroactivity, §1245
state courts, §§1234-1237
right to counsel, §§1236-1237
transcript, §1235
APPORTIONMENT, LEGISLATIVE, §§606-607
APPORTIONMENT OF TAXES
See State taxation of interstate commerce
"ARISING UNDER," §3
ASSOCIATION, FREEDOM OF, §§963-1001
See also Fundamental rights; Speech
disclosure of association, §§966-974
compulsory disclosure, §§966-968
legislative investigations, §§969-974
limitations, §§970-974
nexus requirement, §974
overriding legislative interest, §973
loyalty oaths, §§980-983
ballot qualifications, §§991, 993-994
bar admissions, §§995-1001
government employment, §983
membership disclosure, §983
past membership, §§996-1000
memberships, §996
"knowledge" requirement, §§999-1000
unprotected advocacy or
activities, §§963-965, 975-978
civil penalties, §§975-978
culpability of group, §964
culpability of individual, §965
ATTACHMENT, §§427, 685

B

"BALANCE OF INTERESTS" TEST, §§309-319
BALLOT QUALIFICATIONS
equal protection, §624
loyalty oaths, §993
BANKRUPTCY
nonfundamental right, §659
BAR ADMISSION, §§995-1001
BENIGN DISCRIMINATION
See Equal Protection
BILL OF RIGHTS
See also Individual rights as limitations
constitutional guarantee, §§390-397
national citizenship, §§231, 392
selective incorporation, §§395-400
BOND ELECTIONS
See Fundamental Rights, right to vote
BROADCASTING
See Speech
BURDEN OF PROOF, §§1227-1230

C

CAMPAIGN FUNDING, §§926-936
CAPITAL PUNISHMENT, §§1182-1184, 1187-1196
CASE AND CONTROVERSY LIMITATIONS, §§27-42
CENSORSHIP
See Speech
CERTAINTY REQUIREMENT
criminal statutes, §§1231-1233
CERTIORARI, §§22-25
"CITIZEN" STANDING, §48
CITIZENSHIP
rights of, §§233-238, 695-701
CLASSIFICATIONS
See Equal protection
"CLEAR AND PRESENT DANGER" TEST, §752
COERCED CONFESSIONS
See Self-incrimination
COLLUSIVE SUITS, §42
COMMERCE CLAUSE, §§261-389
"channels" of interstate commerce, §§263-270
after interestate commerce "ends," §§267-270
intrastate commerce, §270
limitations, §268
regulation of persons, §269
federal police power, §264
furthering state law, §266
motive irrelevant, §265
concurrent power, §261
constitutional provision, §262
Due Process Clause and, §336
equal protection and, §281
foreign commerce, §§260, 327, 383-389
individual rights limitation, §277
interstate commerce, §261
Interstate Privileges and Immunities Clause, §302
national economic effect, §§271-277
commercial and noncommercial activities covered, §272
congressional findings, §273
congressional intent, §276

individual rights limitation, §277
limitless power, §275
substantial relationship, §276
racial discrimination, §272
scope of, §§262-277
state regulation of interestate commerce, §§278-327
Congressional power in general, §279
expressed authorization or prohibition, §§280-282
equal protection limitation, §281
reversal of Court, §282
supersession/preemption doctrine, §§283-289
applicable beyond interstate commerce, §284
completeness of federal scheme, §288
federal and state similarity, §289
federal or local matter, §287
general statutory intent, §283
uniform national regulation, §286
where Congress has not acted, §§290-327
discrimination against interstate commerce, §§291-304
absence of alternatives exception, §298
conservation of natural resources, §296
discriminatory impact prohibited, §303
environmental protection, §293
excluding incoming trade, §292
higher prices for incoming trade, §294
requiring business operations locally, §297
restricting outgoing trade, §295
state as market participant exception, §§299-302
liquor regulations, §§322-327
local transactions, §290
nondiscriminatory regulation, §§305-391
balancing test, §§309-319
economic regulations, §§317-318
judicial role, §311
reciprocity agreements, §319
social welfare, health, and safety, §§312-316
subject matter test, §§306-308
permit or license requirements, §§320-321
taxation. *See* Foreign commerce; State taxation of interstate commerce
two theories for broad scope, §262
COMMERCE POWER
See Commerce Clause
COMMERCIAL SPEECH
See Speech
COMPANY TOWNS, §676
CONCURRENT POWERS, §§226-228
CONFESSIONS
See Self-incrimination
CONGRESSIONAL HEARINGS, §§969-974
CONGRESSIONAL IMMUNITY, §§164-169
CONGRESSIONAL INVESTIGATIONS, §§160-163, 969-974
CONGRESSIONAL MEMBERSHIP
jurisdiction, §110
CONGRESSIONAL POWER
See Enforcement of constitutional rights; Legislative power
CONSCIENTIOUS OBJECTORS, §§1091-1092
CONSCRIPTION
equal protection, §560
religious freedom, §§1091-1092, 1095-1096
war power, §144
CONSERVATION OF NATURAL RESOURCES, §296
See also Commerce Clause
CONTEMPT POWER
investigatory power, §§162, 969, 971
CONTRACEPTIVES, §446
CONTRACT CLAUSE, §§1136-1150
CORPORATIONS
campaign financing, §§932-933
COUNSEL, RIGHT TO, §§1154-1159
constitutional provisions, §§1154-1155
federal courts, §§1154-1159
state courts, §1156
criminal proceedings only, §§1157-1159
appeals, §§1236-1237
felony vs. misdemeanor, §§1157-1159
CREDITORS' REMEDIES
due process, §§426-427
state action, §§681, 685
CRIMINAL APPEALS, §§568-569, 1234-1240
CRIMINAL PROSECUTIONS
enjoining. *See* Enjoining state action
mootness, §38
CRUEL AND UNUSUAL PUNISHMENT, §§1176-1196

D

DEATH PENALTY
See Capital punishment
DECLARATORY RELIEF
advisory opinions and, §§30-36
civil, §§89-92
criminal, §§84-88
DEFAMATION, §§755-780
criminal libel, §767
damages, §§774-777
group libel, §756
intentional infliction of emotional distress, §779
invasion of privacy, §780
malice, §§759-764
not protected, §755
opinions, §778
political candidates, §766
private individuals, §§772-777
public figures, §§768-771
public issues, §757
public officials, §§758-767
DELAY EXCEPTION TO ABSTENTION, §98
DELEGATION OF POWER
external affairs, §205
legislative powers, §§126-129
standards requirement, §§127-128
to judicial branch, §129
DESEGREGATION
See Equal protection
DILUTION OF RIGHTS, §§710-711

DISABILITY BENEFITS
due process, §411
illegitimate children, §668
DIVORCE
See Due process; Fundamental rights
"DOING BUSINESS" TAXES, §§350-360
DRAFT CARD BURNING, §862
DRIVER'S LICENSE, §424
DRUMMERS, §§375, 377
DUE PROCESS, §§402-480, 663-669
causes of action, §410
Commerce Clause and, §336
defamation by government, §406
interests not enumerated, §441
"liberty," §§405-407
defamation by government, §406
loss of employment, §406
persons protected, §402
procedural due process, §§403-433
attachment, §427
civil forfeiture, §415
creditors' remedies, §426
"deprivation," §§412-413
disability benefits, §§417-418
driver's license, §424
government employment, §§409-410, 419-420
hearing, §414
institutionalization, §§428-429
irrebuttable presumptions, §§663-669
disability benefits, §668
employment fitness, §666
"needy" status, §667
parental fitness, §664
residency, §§428-429
mentally ill, §§428-429, 462-464
paternity, §433
suspension from school, §§421-423
academic dismissal, §423
corporal punishment, §422
temporary suspension, §421
test, §§411, 436
unbiased tribunal, §403
utility services, §408
welfare, §416
property, §§408-410
public employment, §§409, 419-420
state taxation of commerce, §§334, 336
substantive due process, §§434-480
economic interests, §§434-440
business regulation, §436
public health, §436
public safety, §436
punitive damages, §§438-440
rational relationship, §436
personal liberties, §441
divorce, §597
familial rights, §462
marital rights, §444
privacy, §§442-462
abortion, §§447-460
contraceptives, §446
interests not protected, §463
procreation, §445
source, §401
travel, §§464-472
voting, §473
DURATIONAL REQUIREMENTS, §§595-597

E

EDUCATION
See also Equal protection; Religious freedom
due process, §§421-423, 461
nonfundamental right, §657
religious schools. *See* Religious freedom
ELEVENTH AMENDMENT, §§6-15
appellate review, §9
subdivision of states, §10
EMINENT DOMAIN POWER, §§1115-1132
constitutional provision, §§1115-1117
just compensation, §§1130-1131
procedure, §1132
public use, §§1119-1120
"taking," §§1121-1129
government regulation, §§1123-1129
noncompensable, §§1124-1129
ENABLING CLAUSES
See also Enforcement of constitutional rights
privileges and immunities, §232
ENFORCEMENT OF CONSTITUTIONAL RIGHTS, §§692-720
Congressional power, §§692-694
against government action, §693
against private action, §694
Enabling Clauses, §§692, 702-717
Fifteenth Amendment, §§716-717
"rational" finding, §§716-717
Fourteenth Amendment, §§704-715
"basis" for determination, §704
definitive power, §704
government vs. private action, §§712-715
federal officials, §714
private individuals, §715
state officials, §713
limitations, §§708-711
constitutional conflict, §709
enforcement vs. dilution, §710
expansion vs. dilution, §711
literacy tests, §§704, 706
remedial power, §§705-707
future violations, §706
prior violations, §707
prohibiting constitutional conduct, §705
Thirteenth Amendment, §§702-703
"rational" determination, §702
scope, §703
Necessary and Proper Clause, §§695-701
interstate travel, §§696-698
right to petition government, §701
right to vote, §§699-700
rights of national citizenship, §695
other sources of power, §§718-720

commerce power, §719
taxing and spending powers, §720
ENJOINING STATE ACTION, §§84-99
abstention, §95
comity, §§84, 88
pending civil proceedings, §§89-92
pending criminal prosecutions, §88
criminal prosecutions
not pending, §§84-87
declaratory relief, §§85-86
irreparable injury, §§84-85
pending, §§83, 88, 91
declaratory relief, §§85-86
defined, §91
extraordinary circumstances, §84
free speech, §§87-88
inconvenience, §88
ENUMERATED POWERS, §119
EQUAL PROTECTION, §§481-669
aliens, discrimination against, §§545-553
congressional plenary power, §545
federal—traditional test, §545
illegal aliens, §552
participation in government, §551
states—strict scrutiny test, §§545-553
bar admission, §547
civil service, §548
land ownership, §549
welfare, §546
Supremacy Clause, §553
benign discrimination, §§533-543
remedying past discrimination, §§534-543
business, §§541-542
education, §§538-540
legislative apportionment, §543
strict scrutiny, §533
classifications, need for, §483
constitutional provisions, §§401, 481-482
elderly, discrimination against, §578
fundamental rights. *See* Fundamental rights
gender discrimination, §§554-561
against men, §§559-560
against women, §§557-558
remedies for past discrimination, §561
de facto discrimination, §556
"quasi-suspect" test, §§555-556
generally, §483
illegitimate children, discrimination against, §§562-564
"quasi-suspect" test, §562
valid discrimination, §564
irrebuttable presumptions. *See* Irrebuttable presumptions
mentally retarded, discrimination against, §§580-581
poor, discrimination against, §§565-577
de facto discrimination, §§567-577
criminal appeals, §§568-569
divorce, §572
fine or imprisonment, §§570-571
paternity actions, §573
voting, §577
no discrimination, §§574-576
abortion, §576
bankruptcy, §574
welfare appeals, §575
not "suspect," §565
race and ethnic discrimination, §§489-544
benign discrimination, §§533-543
"de facto" discrimination, §§506-509
Fifteenth Amendment, §509
Thirteenth Amendment, §508
traditional test, §506
intentional discrimination ("de jure") requirement §§493-505, 507
impermissible motive, §§501-505
effect of, §504
judicial inquiry, §503
standard of review, §505
"on its face," §494
unequal administration, §§495-500
burden of proof, §§496-499
race and national origin, §§489-492
exception, §492
racial segregation—"suspect" classification, §§510-532
closing of facilities, §532
education, §§512-532
aid to segregated schools, §531
de facto segregation, §507
dual systems, §517
proving segregation, §§514-519
remedies, §§520-532
guidelines, §525
termination of duty to integrate, §§529-530
uniracial schools, §518
scope of application, §513
strict scrutiny test, §511
repeal of remedies, §544
strict scrutiny test, §§490-491
traditional test, §§484-487
EX POST FACTO LAWS, §§1151-1153
EXCLUSIVE AND UNIQUE POWERS
See Intergovernmental relations
EXECUTIVE AGREEMENTS, §§215-219
EXECUTIVE POWER, §§170-199
executive privilege, §§193-199
immunity from civil damages, §198
scope, §§194-197
generally, §170
scope of powers, §§171-192
appointments, §171
legislation, §§182-190
emergency situations, §§189-190
removals, §§174-178
veto power, §§185-186
military powers, §§187-188
pardons, §§179-181
EXECUTIVE PRIVILEGE, §§193-199
EXPORTS
See State taxation of interstate commerce

F

FACIAL CHALLENGES, §§747-749
FAIR TRIAL, §§1223-1226
trial publicity, §§1224-1226
FEDERAL COURTS
See Judicial power; Supreme Court
FEDERAL LANDS, §259
FEDERAL QUESTION JURISDICTION, §§70-76
FEDERAL SYSTEM
See Intergovernmental relations
FIELD TRIPS, §1029
FIFTEENTH AMENDMENT
See Enforcement of constitutional rights; Fundamental rights, right to vote
FIGHTING WORDS, §§805-807
FLAG DESECRATION, §864
FLAG SALUTE CASES, §1064
FOREIGN AFFAIRS, §§200-219
constitutional provisions, §200
delegation, §205
domestic powers compared, §§201-204
executive agreements, §§215-219
federal exclusivity, §§203-204
treaty power, §§206-214
conflicts with, §§207-209
Congressional acts, §209
state laws, §208
generally, §206
independent source of power, §§211-214
limitations, §§212-214
"supreme law of the land," §207
FOREIGN COMMERCE, §§260, 327, 383-389
regulation, §260
taxation by states, §§383-389
Commerce Clause, §§388-389
Import-Export Clause, §§327, 383
of exports, §387
of imports, §§384-386
Twenty-First Amendment and, §327
FOREIGN RELATIONS JURISDICTION, §103
FOURTEENTH AMENDMENT
See Enforcement of constitutional rights; Individual rights as limitations
FREEDOM OF EXPRESSION
See also Speech
facial challenges, §§747-749
FRIENDLY SUITS, §42
FUNDAMENTAL RIGHTS, §§441-480, 582-662
See also Due process; Equal protection
freedom of association, §§583-589. *See also* Association, freedom of
funding presidential campaigns, §589
political candidates, §§584-588
political parties, §§583-584
freedom of speech, §606. *See also* Speech
international travel, §§469-472
interstate travel, §§464-468, 590-600
impermissible durational requirements, §§590-600
medical care, §592
voting, §§593-594
welfare, §591
state benefits, §§598-599
valid residence requirements, §§595-600
divorce, §597
tuition, §596
nonfundamental rights, §§652-667
See also Irrebuttable presumptions
bankruptcy, §659
bus transportation, §658
disability benefits, §654
education, §657
housing, §§655-656, 661
"important" rights, §§660-662
traditional, "rational basis" test, §652
welfare, §653
right of privacy, §§442-463. *See also* Privacy
abortion, §§447-460, 605
marriage, §§444, 602-603
procreation, §§445, 604
right to be a candidate, §§649-651
right to vote, §§473, 607-648
apportionment, congressional distress, §§626-630
among states, §630
"equal population" requirement, §626
equal protection and, §625
preserving boundaries, §627
preserving incumbent seats, §629
apportionment, state legislative districts, §§631-648
appointment vs. election, §645
multi-member districts, §§637-638
"one person-one vote" rule, §641
permissible deviations, §§632-636
preserving boundaries, §633
preserving incumbent seats, §636
relevant officials, §§641-645
remedies, §§647-648
armed forces, §609
basis, §§473, 607
bond elections, §613
denial of right, §§608-619
valid restrictions, §§615-619
felons, §616
limiting vote "effectiveness," §§620-624
absentee ballots, §623
ballot qualifications, §624
primary elections, §§621-622
poll tax, §610
remedies for malapportionment, §§647-648
special purpose elections, §§617-619
supermajority requirements, §646
rights of mentally ill, §§474-478
strict scrutiny test, §§441, 582

G

GENDER DISCRIMINATION, §§554-561
See also Equal protection
GENERAL WELFARE CLAUSE, §§131-132, 142

GOVERNMENT BENEFITS
aliens, §545
loyalty oaths, §§980-982
GOVERNMENT EMPLOYMENT
See Aliens; Association, freedom of; Equal protection
GROUP LIBEL, §756

H

HABEAS CORPUS
See Post-conviction procedures
HOUSING, §§655-656, 661

I

ILLEGITIMATES, DISCRIMINATION AGAINST, §§562-564
IMMUNITY
See Self-incrimination
IMPEACHMENT, Senate jurisdictions, §106
IMPLIED POWERS, §§120-124
IMPORT-EXPORT CLAUSE, §§260, 327, 383-387
See also State taxation of interstate commerce
IMPORTS, CENSORSHIP OF
See Speech, prior restraint
IMPOSTS
See Foreign commerce
INDIVIDUAL RIGHTS AS LIMITATIONS
See also Due process; Equal protection; Fundamental rights; Irrebuttable presumptions; Speech; "State action" requirement
Bill of Rights, §§390, 398
Fourteenth Amendment, §§391-401
Due Process Clause, §§393-400
other incorporated rights, §400
provisions incorporated, §398
provisions not incorporated, §399
selective incorporation, §§394-399
Equal Protection Clause, §401
INHERENT SOVEREIGN POWERS, §§125, 189, 203
INSTRUMENTALITIES OF COMMERCE, §§338-346
INTERGOVERNMENTAL IMMUNITY, §§241-259
INTERGOVERNMENTAL RELATIONS, §§220-259
concurrent powers, §§226-228
exclusive powers, §§221-225
generally, §220
intergovernmental immunity, §§241-259
federal regulation of states, §244
federal taxation of states, §245
general rule, §241
intergovernmental differences, §242
state regulation of federal government, §§258-259
state taxation of federal government, §§246-257
congressional power, §246
congressional silence, §§247-257
income tax, §250
on federal property, §248
parties dealing with United States, §249
property tax, §§253-256
sales tax, §§251-252
intergovernmental privileges and immunities, §§229-240
national citizenship, §§229-232
Bill of Rights, §231
constitutional provision, §229
defined, §230
Enabling Clause, §232
right to travel, §§464-472, 590-594, 614. *See also* Fundamental rights; Enforcement of constitutional rights
uncertain source, §§465-467
state citizenship, §§233-240
Commerce Clause, §240
constitutional provision, §233
general rule, §234
protected persons, §§237-239
INTERSTATE CARRIERS, §§361-363
INTERSTATE COMMERCE
See Commerce Clause
INTERSTATE PRIVILEGES AND IMMUNITIES CLAUSE, §§229-230, 302
INTERSTATE TRAVEL
See Fundamental rights; Enforcement of constitutional rights
INVASION OF PRIVACY
See Defamation; Privacy
INVESTIGATORY POWER, §§160-163
enforcement, §162
implied, §160
limitations, §163
scope, §161
INVOLUNTARY CONFESSIONS
See Self-incrimination
INVOLUNTARY SERVITUDE, §§1133-1135
IRREBUTTABLE PRESUMPTIONS, §§663-669
decline of doctrine, §669
disability benefits; illegitimate children, §668
food stamps, §667
parental custody, §664
pregnancy and employee fitness, §666
residency status, §665
right to hearing, §663

JK

JUDICIAL POWER, §§1-117
effect of unconstitutionality, §§111-117
partial invalidity, §§114-117
retroactivity, §§112-113, 1241-1245
federal court jurisdiction, §§3-5
limitations, §§27-110
abstention, §§95-99
advisory opinions, §§28-36
case or controversy, §§27-42
enjoining state action, §§84-94
declaratory relief, §§30-36, 85-92
injunctions, §§80-94
mootness, §§37-41
political questions, §§100-110
ripeness, §32
standing, §§43-62

associations, §58
citizens, §48
state, §§59-61
taxpayers, §§49-53
third-party rights, §§54-58
strict necessity, §§77-79
scope, §§3-15
"arising under," §3
Eleventh Amendment, §§6-15
limitations, §§8-15
sovereign immunity, §4
source, §§1-2
Supreme Court jurisdiction, §§16-26
appellate, §§20-26
appeal, §§22-24
certiorari, §§22-25
congressional limitations, §26
judicial review, §21. *See also* Judicial review
original, §§16-19
JUDICIAL REVIEW
federal questions, §§70-72
international travel restrictions, §471
lower federal court judgments, §§24-25
prior restraints, §§844-848
state court judgments, §§23, 63-76. *See also* State court judgments
state criminal judgments. *See* Post-conviction procedures
substantive due process, §§434-436
JURY SELECTION, §§1205-1218
constitutional provisions, §1205
death penalty cases, §1218
impartial jury, §§1215-1218
pretrial publicity, §1216
"representative cross section," §§1206-1214
blue ribbon jurors, §1210
systematic exclusion, §1207
standing to challenge, §§1212-1214
JURY TRIAL, §§1197-1218
constitutional provisions, §§1197-1198
selection of jurors. *See* Jury selection
serious vs. petty offenses, §§1203-1204
what constitutes, §§1199-1202
number of jurors, §§1199-1200
unanimous verdict, §§1201-1202

L

"LEGAL INCIDENCE" OF TAX, §252
LEGISLATIVE POWER, §§118-169
See also Enforcement of constitutional rights
commerce power, §130. *See also* Commerce Clause
congressional immunity, §§164-169
constitutional basis, §164
persons covered, §166
rationale, §165
scope, §§167-169
legislative acts, §168
political acts, §169
delegation of powers, §§126-129
standards, §127
to judicial branch, §129
external affairs, §148
generally, §118
investigatory power, §§160-163. *See also* Investigatory power
naturalization and citzenship, §§149-157
aliens, §§150-153. *See also* Equal protection
congressional authority over, §§150-152
deportation, §152
exclusion, §151
constitutional provision, §149
loss of citizenship, §157
naturalization, §§154-156
Necessary and Proper Clause, §121
over D.C., §225
property power, §§158-159
scope of federal powers, §§119-125
enumerated powers, §119
implied powers, §§120-125
any appropriate means, §122
inherent powers, §125
spending power, §§139-143
constitutional provision, §131
limitations, §§142-143
general welfare, §142
individual rights, §143
scope, §§139-141
taxing power, §§131-138
constitutional provision, §131
independent power, §132
regulatory purpose or effect, §§133-138
congressional power to regulate, §134
no power to regulate, §§135-138
war power, §§144-147
broad scope, §§145-147
post-war powers, §§146-147
constitutional provision, §144
LIQUOR REGULATIONS
Commerce Clause, §§322-327
LITERACY TESTS, §§704, 706
LOCAL BUSINESS, §§290-304
LOYALTY OATHS, §§980-983
See also Association, freedom of

M

MAILS
censorship, §§856-859
prisons, §§948-950
MARITAL RIGHTS
See Due process; Fundamental rights
MARITIME POWER
See Admiralty and maritime power
MEDICAL CARE, §§479-480, 592
MEMBERSHIP DISCLOSURE
See Association, freedom of
MENTALLY ILL PERSONS, §§428-429, 474-478
MILITARY AND WAR POWERS, §§144-147, 187-190
MILITARY STATUTES, §104
MILK PRICE CASES, §§295, 298, 316
MOOT CASES, §§37-41
criminal convictions, §38
recurring issues, §39

MOTION PICTURES
See Obscenity; Speech

N

NATIONAL ORIGIN, §§489-492
NATIONAL SECURITY
See also Loyalty oaths; War power
travel, §470
NATURALIZATION AND CITIZENSHIP
See also Legislative power
national citizen, §§229-232, 695
NECESSARY AND PROPER CLAUSE, §§695-701
NEWS REPORTER'S PRIVILEGE, §1003
See also Speech
NEXUS TEST
See Association, freedom of; State taxation of interstate commerce; Taxpayers' actions
NONFUNDAMENTAL RIGHTS, §§652-669

O

OATH OF OFFICE, §1071
OATHS, LOYALTY
See Loyalty oaths
OBSCENITY, §§781-804, 845-859
See also Speech
appellate review, §793
as question of law, §§793-796
book dealers, §845
broadcasting, §1018
business licenses, §854
community standards, §§782, 786, 789
defined, §§782-792
elements, §§783-792
patently offensive, §788
prurient interest, §§784-787
deviant audience, §787
"pandering," §791
without social value, §790
importation, §§801, 859
minors, §§797-799
not protected, §781
obscene mail, §§857-858
prior restraints, §§832-859
foreign governments, §834
informal government action, §833
procedural safeguards, §§842-859
importation, §§801, 859
mail, §§856-858
movie censorship, §§849-852
municipal theaters, §853
private possession, §§800-801
public exhibition, §853
transportation, §801
zoning, §§802-804
ONE PERSON-ONE VOTE RULE, §641

P

PARADES, MEETINGS, AND DEMONSTRATIONS
See Speech
PAROCHIAL SCHOOLS
See Religious freedom
PARTIAL INVALIDITY, §§114-117
PATRONAGE, §988
PENDING PROCEEDINGS
civil, §§89-92
criminal, §88
PENUMBRA DOCTRINE, §442
PEONAGE, §1134
PICKETING
See Speech
POLITICAL QUESTIONS, §§100-110
apportionment. *See* Apportionment, legislative
congressional membership, §110
defined, §101
examples, §§103-110
political rights distinguished, §109
POLITICAL RIGHTS
jurisdiction, §109
political questions distinguished, §109
POLL TAX, §610
POLYGAMY, §1089
POOR, DISCRIMINATION AGAINST, §§565-577
See also Equal protection
POST-CONVICTION PROCEDURES, §§1238-1240
POWERS RETAINED BY STATES
federal legislative power, §119
intergovernmental relations, §221
taxation, §§328, 334
PRESIDENTIAL POWER
See Executive power
PRESS, FREEDOM OF
See Speech
PRETRIAL PUBLICITY
See Jury trial
PRIMARIES, §§621-622, 925
PRIOR RESTRAINT
See Speech
PRIVACY
equal protection, §§601-605
abortion, §605
marriage, §§602-603
invasion of privacy, §780
substantive due process, §§442-462
abortion, §§447-460, 605
contraceptives, §446
familial rights, §462
interests not protected, §463
marriage, §444
procreation, §§445, 604
PRIVATE OBSCENITY
See Obscenity; Privacy
PRIVILEGES AND IMMUNITIES
See also Enforcement of constitutional rights
Bill of Rights and, §231
defined, §230
discrimination, §§238-239
Enabling Clause, §232
Fourteenth Amendment, §231
individual liberties, §392
intergovernmental tax immunity. *See* Intergovernmental relations

Interstate Privileges and Immunities Clause, §§233-239
Commerce Clause and, §240
persons protected, §§234-236
right to travel, §§467-472, 590-594. *See also* Travel, right to
PROCREATION, §445
PROPERTY POWER, §§158-159
PUBLIC FIGURES, §§768-771
See also Defamation; Speech
PUBLIC HEALTH AND WELFARE, §§312-316
See also Commerce Clause
PUBLIC INTEREST
standing, §§47-53
taxpayers' suits, §§49-53
PUBLIC TRIAL, §§1219-1222
PUBLICITY
publication of private performance, §1008
trial, §§1224-1226

Q

"QUASI-SUSPECT" TEST, §§555, 562

R

RACE DISCRIMINATION
See Commerce Clause; Equal protection; Fundamental rights
RATIONAL BASIS TEST, §§484-488
See also Traditional test
RECIPROCITY AGREEMENTS, §319
REGULATION
See also Commerce Clause
eminent domain, §§1115-1132
taxing and spending powers, §§133-141
RELIGIOUS FREEDOM, §§1021-1114
"accommodations" benefiting religion, §1106
animal sacrifice, §1082
beliefs, §§1083-1085
conduct, §§1086-1105
conscientious objectors, §§1091-1092, 1064-1065
constitutional provisions, §§1021-1022
counseling agencies, §1043
draft, §1091
education, §§1024-1069, 1092, 1100
beneficial regulations, §§1070-1074
Bible reading, §§1055-1056
compulsory education, §1100
equal access, §1065
evolution, §§1058-1059
financial aid to religious schools, §§1027-1039, 1042-1050
"auxiliary" services, §§1035-1036
direct aid, §§1040-1050
field trips, §1029
guidance services, §§1035-1036
health services, §§1032-1034
maintenance and repair, §1046
racial discrimination, §1094
secular purpose, §1026
silent prayer, §1057
testing, §1048
textbooks, §§1030-1031
transportation, §1028
tuition credits, §§1037-1039
universities, §1042
flag-salute cases, §1085
prayers, §§1055-1056
released time, §§1060, 1067
subjects taught, §§1058-1059, 1063
employment discrimination, §§1072, 1079
Establishment Clause, §§1023-1079
Free Exercise Clause, §§1080-1106
hospitals, §1041
incidental effects, §1098
judicial resolution of church disputes, §§1111-1112
military dress, §1096
polygamy, §1089
prisoners' rights, §1097
protectible beliefs, §§1107-1110
public acknowledgments, §§1075-1079
racial discrimination, §1094
religion defined, §§1109-1110
standing, §§1113-1114
Establishment Clause, §1114
Free Exercise Clause, §1113
state regulations
oath of office, §1071
public solicitation and canvassing, §1101
qualification for office, §1071
Sunday closing laws, §§1072, 1090
tax exemptions, §§1051-1052
three-pronged test, §1026
unemployment compensation, §1102
use of public facilities, §§1053, 1065
RIPENESS, §32

S

SALES TAXES
See State taxation of interstate commerce
SEARCHES AND SEIZURES, §§1169-1175
constitutional provisions, §§1169-1172
federal courts, §§1169-1171
state courts, §1172
defined, §§1173-1174
exclusionary rule, §1170
"good faith exception," §1171
newspaper office, §1010
SEGREGATION
See Equal protection
SELECTIVE INCORPORATION, §§395-400
SELF-INCRIMINATION
constitutional provisions, §§1165-1168
federal courts, §§1165-1166
state courts, §1167
disclosures, §§968, 1001
effect of claiming privilege, §1168
involuntary confessions, §§1160-1164
constitutional provisions, §§1160-1162
federal courts, §§1160-1161
state courts, §1162
inadmissible voluntary confessions, §§1163-1164
Miranda rule, §1164
SEPARATION OF POWERS, §§1-3

checks and balances, §§2-3
delegation, §§1-3
executive power, §§170-199. *See also* Executive power
judicial power, §§1-117. *See also* Judicial power
legislative power, §§118-169. *See also* Legislative power
"SEVERABILITY CLAUSE," §117
SEX DISCRIMINATION, §§554-561
SHOPPING CENTERS, §678
SIGNIFICANT STATE INVOLVEMENT
See Individual rights as limitations
SMITH ACT, §753
SOUND TRUCKS, §882
SOVEREIGN IMMUNITY, §4
SPECIAL PURPOSE ELECTIONS, §§617-619
SPEECH, §§721-1020
See also Association, freedom of; Defamation; Obscenity
boycotts, §§959-960
Brandenburg test, §754
broadcasting, §§1012-1017
cable television, §§1019-1020
editorializing, §1015
"fairness doctrine," §§1012-1013
indecent speech, §1017
ownership limitations, §1016
political advertising, §1014
censorship. *See* Speech, prior restraint
"clear and present danger" test, §752
commercial speech, §§810-831
content regulation, §§810, 814-817
definition, §§811-813
illegal matters, §816
overbreadth doctrine inapplicable, §817
prior restraint, §818
scope of protection, §§819-831
billboards, §827
burden, §820
casino advertising, §824
contraceptives, §823
"for sale" signs, §822
legal services, §§828-831
lottery, §825
required disclosures, §829
Communist Party membership, §967
constitutional provisions, §§721-735
association, freedom of, §§726-727
belief, freedom of, §722
conduct protected, §§731-735
freedom not to speak, §§723-725
receiving information, §728
solicitation of funds, §729
copyright, §962
defamation. *See* Defamation
Dennis-Yates test, §753
disclosure of associations, §§966-974
compulsory disclosure, §§966-968
general standard, §967
legislative investigations, §§969-974
privilege against self-incrimination, §§968, 1001
disclosure of beliefs, §§995-1001
bar membership, §§998-1000
"chilling" effect, §997
knowledge requirement, §§999-1000
obstructing investigations, §§998-1000
elections, §§918-936
campaign activities, §§918-936
campaign expenditures, §§929-934
corporations, §§932-934
political action committees, §930
campaign promises, §921
closed primaries, §925
contribution limitations, §§926-928
ballot measures, §928
financial disclosures, §§935-936
political party restrictions, §§923-925
write-in voting, §922
fighting words, §§805-806
hostile audience, §§808-809
in general, §750
justice, administration of, §§906-917
in court, §907
out of court, §§908-917
pending proceedings, §§910-911
press, §909
type of proceeding, §§931-917
labor picketing, §§954-958
limitations
clear and present danger, §752
conduct, §861
facial invalidity, §§740, 747-749
in general, §§736-737
licensing, §§898-903
overbreadth doctrine, §§741-745
time, place, and manner restrictions, §§871-889
vagueness, §§745-746
military discipline, §951
NAACP membership, §967
obscenity. *See* Obscenity
practice of law, §§952-953
press, freedom of, §§1002-1010, 1013
criminal trials, access to, §§1005-1006
government information, access to, §1004
office searches, §1010
reporter's privilege, §1003
taxation of, §§1019-1020
prior restraint, §§832-860
broadcasting, §1011
challenging invalid injunctions, §860
commercial speech, §820
defined, §832
exceptions, §§835-841
fair trials, §§837-838
national security, §836
obscenity, §840
pretrial discovery, §839
public property, §841
government action, §§833-834
judicial review, §859
policy against, §832
procedural safeguards, §§842-859
business licenses, potentially obscene materials, §854
charitable solicitors, licenses, §855
importation, obscene materials, §859
injunctions, §844
mails, use of, §§856-858

movie censorship, §§849-852
municipal theaters, §853
notice and hearing requirement, §843
seizure of books and films, §§845-848
where allowed, §§945-951
prisoners' rights, §§945-950
mail, §§948-950
news interviews, §946
prison regulations, §945
prison unions, §947
public employment, restrictions on, §§979-1001
disclosure of associations, §§966-974, 995-1001
loyalty oaths and conduct standards, §§980-994
ballot position, §993
compulsory unionism, §§984-986
expression of views, §989
government employees, §§983-991
group membership, §983
patronage, §988
political activities, §991
support of Constitution, §980
vagueness, §981
when proper, §§981-986, 990-991
public places, §§868-905
in general, §868
injunctions, §905
licensing, §§897-904
challenging, methods of, §904
defined standards, §899
no censorship, §898
speeches, meetings, and parades, §897
when permit is necessary, §904
no public forum, §§893-897
private property, §896
public property, §895
public forums, §§869-870
public schools, §940
classrooms, §941
libraries, §943
publications, §942
soliciting and canvassing, §§881, 888
time, place, and manner regulations, §§871-889
content neutral, §§872-876
billboards, §875
drive-in theaters, §873
foreign embassies, §874
state university facilities, §876
homes, §880
narrowly tailored, §§886-888
purpose and means test, §§877-885
sound trucks, §882
unwanted mail, §883
zoning, §885
total ban, §§889-892
symbolic conduct, §§861-867
armbands, §863
automatic reversals, §866
draft card burning, §862
flag desecration, §864
nonexpressive conduct, §867
nudity, §865
school protests, §861
subject to regulation, §861
taxation of press, §1018
trademarks, §961
unlawful action, advocacy of, §§750-754
criminal penalties, §§751-754
background, §751
Brandenburg test, §728
"clear and imminent danger," §752
Dennis-Yates test, §753
substantial government interest, §753
imminence vs. gravity, §753
Smith Act, §753
utility bill inserts, §990
SPENDING POWER, §§139-143
See also Legislative power
STANDING
See generally, §§43-62
associations, §58
citizens, §48
collusive suits, §42
freedom of expression, §§87-88
individual injury requirement, §44
jury selection, §§1215-1218
nature of injury, §45
parens patriae, §61
religious freedom, §§1212-1214
taxpayers' actions, §§49-53
third-party rights, §§54-58
"STATE ACTION" REQUIREMENT, §§670-691
acts of government "agents," §671
in general, §670
no public function, §§677-681
creditors' remedies, §681
monopoly businesses, §679
regulated businesses, §680
shopping centers, §678
public or government functions, §§672-676
company towns, §676
elections, §§673-675
significant state involvement, §§682-691
attachment procedures, §685
government approval, §689
judicial enforcement, §§686-687
peremptory challenges, §688
private discrimination, §§683-684
restrictive covenants, §§686-687
state policy, §690
symbiotic relationship, §691
STATE COURT JUDGMENTS
"adequate state grounds," §§73-76
criminal. *See* Post-conviction procedures
federal and nonfederal grounds, §§69-72
federal question, §§70-72
finality, §§65-69
habeas corpus. *See* Post-conviction procedures
judicial review. *See* Judicial review
rights on appeal, §§1234-1237
state procedural rules, §72
unclear grounds, §76
STATE PROCEDURAL RULES, §72
STATE PROCEEDINGS, ENJOINING
See Enjoining state action

STATE STATUTES
declaratory relief, §§85-86
judicial review. *See* Judicial review
STATE TAXATION OF FOREIGN COMMERCE
See Foreign commerce
STATE TAXATION OF INTERSTATE COMMERCE, §§328-382
ad valorem property taxes, §§337-349
apportionment, §§341-345
cargo in transit, §§347-349
"break" in transit, §349
"nexus," §§338-340
airport use tax, §364
apportionment, §§341-345, 355-357, 372
Commerce Clause, §§335, 338
congressional supremacy, §328
discriminatory taxes, §§329-333
Equal Protection Clause, §331
Interstate Privileges and Immunities Clause, §330
"doing business" taxes, §§350-357
adequate contacts, §354
four-part test, §351
net income taxes, §§353-357
"single-factor" formula, §356
drummers, §§359, 375, 377
due process, §336
foreign corporations, §§381-382
franchise tax, §§350-357
in general, §328
"instrumentalities" of commerce, §§338-346
interstate carriers, §§361-363
license taxes, §§350-357, 360
net income taxes, §§353-357
nondiscriminatory taxes, §§334-336
occupation tax, §§350-357
peddlers, §360
privilege tax, §§350-357
sales tax, §§365-375
by "consumer" state, §§373-375
by "seller" state, §§368, 370-372
sufficient contacts, §374
severance tax, §358
taxable situs, §§338-340, 367-369
use taxes, §§365-380
by "consumer" state, §§366-368
by "seller" state, §369
collection by "seller" state, §§376-380
drummers, §377
mail solicitation, §380
office in state, §379
STRICT NECESSITY DOCTRINE, §§77-79
STRICT SCRUTINY TEST, §§441, 489-492, 511
See also Equal protection; Fundamental rights
SUNDAY CLOSING LAWS, §§1072, 1090
SUPERSESSION DOCTRINE, §§283-289
See also Commerce Clause
SUPREMACY CLAUSE, §§226-228, 247
SUPREME COURT
See also Judicial review
appeal, §§22, 24
appellate jurisdiction, §§20-25
congressional regulation, §§17, 22, 26
certiorari, §§22-25
power of judicial review, §21. *See also* Judicial power; Judicial review
trial jurisdiction, §§16-19
SUSPECT CRITERIA
See Equal protection
SUSPENSION FROM SCHOOL, §421
See also Due process
SYMBOLIC SPEECH, §§861-866
See also Speech
SYNDICALISM STATUTES, §§750-754

T

TAX EXEMPTIONS
religious freedom, §§1051-1052
"TAXES," §§132- 133
TAXING POWER, §§131-138
See also Intergovernmental relations; Legislative power; State taxation of interstate commerce
TAXPAYERS' ACTIONS, §§49-53
TENTH AMENDMENT
See also Powers retained by states
standing, §60
TEXTBOOKS, §§1030-1031
THIRTEENTH AMENDMENT
See Enforcement of constitutional rights; Equal protection; Individual rights as limitations
TRADITIONAL TEST, §§484-487
See also Equal protection; Fundamental rights
TRANSCRIPTS, RIGHT TO, §1235
TRAVEL RIGHT TO
fundamental right, §§464-472, 590-594
national security, §§469-472
area restrictions, §470
passports, §470
privileges and immunities, §§229-230, 590-594
substantive due process, §§464-468
TREATY POWER, §§206-214
TRIAL BY JURY
See Jury trial
TRIAL PUBLICITY, §§1224-1226
TUITION CREDITS, §1037
TWENTY-FIRST AMENDMENT, §§322-327

U

UNBIASED TRIBUNAL, RIGHT TO, §403
UNCONSTITUTIONALITY, EFFECT OF, §§111-117
criminal cases, §113
partial invalidity, §§114-117
retroactive effect, §§112-113
"Severability Clause," §117
USE TAXES, §§365-380

V

VEHICLE SEARCHES
See Searches and seizures
VERDICT
See Jury trial
VETO POWER, §§185-186

VOTING RIGHTS
See Fundamental rights

W X Y

WAR POWER, §§144-147
See also Legislative power
presidential power, §§187-188
WARRANTS
See Searches and seizures

WELFARE BENEFITS
aliens, §546
appeals of, §575
as nonfundamental right, §653
procedural due process, §414

Z

ZONING
First Amendment, §885
nonobscene entertainment, §803

CONSTITUTIONAL LAW

Jesse H. Choper

1996 Supreme Court Supplement

HARCOURT BRACE LEGAL AND PROFESSIONAL PUBLICATIONS, INC.
EDITORIAL OFFICES: 176 W. Adams, Suite 2100, Chicago, IL 60603

REGIONAL OFFICES: New York, Chicago, Los Angeles, Washington, D.C.
Distributed by: **Harcourt Brace & Company** 6277 Sea Harbor Drive, Orlando, FL 32887 (800)787-8717

PROJECT EDITOR
Steven J. Levin, B.A., J.D.
Attorney At Law

SERIES EDITOR
Elizabeth L. Snyder, B.A., J.D.
Attorney At Law

QUALITY CONTROL EDITOR
Blythe C. Smith, B.A.

SUPPLEMENT TO GILBERT
"CONSTITUTIONAL LAW" SUMMARY
(Twenty-Seventh Edition)

August 1996

Page	Revision

3 **Delete** para. 4) [§11]; substitute the following:

4) **Suits against state officials:** [§11] Subject to the situation described *supra*, §7, the Eleventh Amendment does not bar suits against state officials acting pursuant to state law but allegedly in violation of the complainant's rights under the ***Constitution*** or ***federal law***.

4 **Delete** para. 5) [§14]; substitute the following:

5) **Congressional enforcement of Fourteenth Amendment:** [§14] The broadest exception to state immunity from private suits in federal court concerns statutory causes of action passed by Congress pursuant to section 5 of the Fourteenth Amendment (giving Congress power to enforce provisions of the amendment). *Rationale:* The Fourteenth Amendment embodies significant limitations on state authority, thus allowing Congress (in enforcing its provisions) to provide for private suits against the states that are otherwise impermissible under the Eleventh Amendment. [Fitzpatrick v. Bizter, 427 U.S. 445 (1976)]

a) **No exception for Commerce Clause:** However, Congress has no power ***under the Commerce Clause***—either to regulate commerce "among the several States" or "with the Indian Tribes"—to abrogate state immunity under the Eleventh Amendment. [Seminole Tribe of Florida v. Florida, 116 S. Ct. 1114 (1996), *overruling* Pennsylvania v. Union Gas Co., 491 U.S. 1 (1989)]

12 **Insert** the following after para. (b) [§58]:

1) **Congressional conferral of standing:** The third prong of the *Hunt* "test" (above) is ***not*** part of the "case or controversy" requirement of Article III. The "direct and immediate injury" required by Article III is satisfied by the *Hunt* test's first prong—*i.e.*, that one of the association's members himself have standing. Thus, Congress may grant standing to an association to sue for damages on behalf of its members even though *Hunt's* third prong would appear otherwise to preclude such standing. [United Food & Commercial Workers Union Local 751 v. Brown Group, Inc., 116 S. Ct. 1529 (1996)]

24 **Insert** the following after para. (a) [§128]:

(b) **Independent constitutional authority:** Whatever the required specificity of standards may be for congressional delegations of power, they are more flexible when the entity exercising the delegated authority has independent power over the subject matter. [Loving v. United States, 116 S. Ct. 1737 (1996)—congressional delegation to President in respect to military court martials]

41 **Insert** the following after para. (2)(a) of §228:

d. **Absence of federal and state power—Qualifications Clauses:** The provisions of Article I, Section 2, Clause 2 and Article I, Section 3, Clause 3—enumerating the age, citizenship, and residence requirements for members of Congress—are exclusive. Neither Congress nor the states may alter or add to these qualifications, because this would be contrary to the Framers' intent of a uniform national legislature elected by the people voting for whom they wish. [United States Term Limits, Inc. v. Thornton, 115 S. Ct. 1846 (1995)—invalidating state preclusion from election ballot of candidates who have served more than a certain number of terms, because preclusion's sole purpose is to impose additional qualification of term limits]

51 **Delete** para. (a) [§276]; substitute the following:

(a) **"Substantial" effect required?** [§276] The modern opinions have stated that the intrastate activity regulated by Congress must have a "***substantial relationship*** to interstate commerce" [North American Co. v. SEC, 327 U.S. 686 (1946)], or a "***substantial effect***" on interstate commerce [Heart of Atlanta Motel, Inc. v. United States, *supra*, §272].

52 **Insert** the following after para. (b) [§277]:

(c) **Not limitless power:** The Court has recently made clear that the power of Congress to regulate commerce, although very broad, does have limits. To be within Congress's power under the Commerce Clause, a federal law must either regulate economic or commercial activity that can ***substantially affect*** interstate commerce or require that the regulated activity be ***connected to interstate commerce***. [United States v. Lopez, 115 S. Ct. 1624 (1995)] In *Lopez*, the Court held that a federal statute barring possession of a gun in a school zone does not "substantially affect" interstate commerce, noting that there were no congressional findings to help the Court to evaluate whether the regulated activity had such a substantial effect.

62 **Delete** paras. (c) and 1) [§§332, 333]; substitute the following:

(c) **Finding discrimination:** [§332] If a state tax singles out interstate commerce for taxation, the Court ordinarily will not "save" the tax by finding other state taxes imposed only on local commerce (which might arguably eliminate the "apparent" discrimination against interstate commerce). [Nippert v. City of Richmond, 327 U.S. 416 (1946)]

1) **"Compensatory" tax exception:** [§333] However, a facially discriminatory tax ***may*** be upheld if the state shows that the tax was designed simply to make interstate commerce bear a burden ***no greater*** than that already imposed on intrastate commerce by an ***identified tax***. [Associated Industries of Missouri v. Lohman, 511 U.S. 641 (1994)]

a) **Equivalent events:** The "compensatory" (or "complementary") taxes must tax persons who are in essentially the same class, ***i.e.***, engaged in essentially the same transaction. (*See*, ***e.g.***, sales and use taxes, discussed below.)

69 **Insert** the following before para. d. [§374]:

(b) **Sales tax on services performed outside state:** If the ***sale*** of the service is consummated within the state (*e.g.*, the sale of a bus ticket), the seller state may impose a sales tax on the full amount of the sale—even though this covers some service (*e.g.*, bus transportation) that takes place outside the state. No other state can claim to be the site of the sale. [Oklahoma Tax Commission v. Jefferson Lines, Inc., 115 S. Ct. 1331 (1995)]

77 **Insert** the following after para. (b) [§407]:

(c) **Prison discipline:** Disciplinary action by prison officials to punish a prisoner's misconduct does ***not*** encroach upon a "liberty" interest unless it results in a restraint that imposes "atypical and significant hardship in relation to the ordinary incidents of prison life." [Sandin v. Conner, 115 S. Ct. 2293 (1995)—30-day segregated confinement was ***not*** outside range of hardship normally expected by prisoner serving 30 years to life]

83 **Delete** para. 1) [§439]; substitute the following:

1) **Amount:** [§439] "Grossly excessive" damages—*i.e.*, those that are unreasonably high to vindicate the state's interests in punishment and deterrence—are invalid. [TXO Production Corp. v. Alliance Resources Corps., 509 U.S. 443 (1993)] Although there is no "bright line" marking the constitutional limits for punitive damages, a person must receive fair notice of their possible magnitude. The Court has indicated it will look to the following factors in determining whether the defendant had adequate notice that a severe penalty might be imposed: (i) the degree of reprehensibility of the defendant's conduct, (ii) the disparity between the actual or potential harm suffered by the plaintiff and the amount of punitive damages awarded, and (iii) the difference between the punitive damages awarded and the criminal and civil penalties authorized for comparable misconduct. [BMW of North America, Inc. v. Gore, 116 S. Ct. 1589 (1996)]

92 **Insert** the following after para. (a) of §487; reletter subsequent paras. accordingly:

(b) **Example:** Several municipalities passed ordinances banning discrimination in housing, employment, etc., based on sexual orientation. In response, the state voters adopted a constitutional amendment prohibiting any state or local action protecting the status of persons based on their homosexual, lesbian, or bisexual orientation. *Held:* A state constitutional provision that identifies persons by a single trait and then denies them the right to seek ***any*** specific protections from the law—no matter how local or widespread the injury—is so unprecedented as to imply animosity toward such persons and is thus not related to any legitimate state interest. [Romer v. Evans, 116 S. Ct. 1620 (1996)]

99 **Insert** the following before para. a/ [§523]; reletter subsequent para. accordingly:

a/ **Example:** It is impermissible for a court to impose a remedy whose purpose is to attract nonminority students from outside the school district. This remedy seeks indirectly to accomplish the interdistrict transfer of students that cannot be accomplished directly. [Missouri v. Jenkins, 115 S. Ct. 2038 (1995)]

103 **Delete** para. 3) [§541]; substitute the following:

3) **Congressional power:** [§541] The standard for judging all racial classifications drawn by the federal government is the same as for state and local action: strict scrutiny. These classifications violate the equal protection component of the Fifth

Amendment Due Process Clause unless they are ***narrowly tailored*** measures that further ***compelling*** government interests. [Adarand Constructors, Inc. v. Pena, 115 S. Ct. 2097 (1995), *overruling* Metro Broadcasting, Inc. v. Federal Communications Commission, 497 U.S. 547 (1990)]

a) **Comment:** In applying strict scrutiny, the Court ***may*** give deference to congressional judgment in light of Congress's special power under Section 5 of the Fourteenth Amendment to enforce equal protection (*see infra*, §§704-715) [Fullilove v. Klutznick, 448 U.S. 448 (1980)—upholding set aside for minority businesses of 10% federal grants for public works projects], but this is unclear.

103 **Delete** para. 4) [§543]; substitute the following:

4) **Legislative apportionment:** [§543] Race may be considered in drawing up new voting districts—without subjecting the districting scheme to strict scrutiny—as long as (i) no racial group has its overall voting strength minimized [United Jewish Organizations v. Carey, 430 U.S. 144 (1977)] and (ii) the district's shape and demographics (as well as more direct evidence of legislative purpose) show that race was ***not*** the dominant and controlling factor, *i.e.*, that other districting principles (such as respecting municipal borders) were not ***subordinated*** to race [Miller v. Johnson, 115 S. Ct. 2475 (1995)].

a) **Burden of proof:** The challenger bears the burden of proving the race-based motive. [Shaw v. Hunt, 116 S. Ct. 1894 (1996)]

106 **Insert** the following after para. (a) [§558]:

(b) **Nature of heightened scrutiny:** The "important government objective" advanced to justify categorization on the basis of gender must be ***genuine***—not hypothesized for the purpose of litigation defense. Neither may the government's justification rely on ***overbroad generalizations*** about males and females that will create or perpetuate the legal, social, and economic inferiority of women. [United States v. Virginia, 116 S. Ct. 2264 (1996)]

1) **Example:** When a state military school's policy of admitting only men was challenged, the state justified the policy by claiming that: (i) offering a diversity of educational approaches within the state (*e.g.,* some schools having men only, some schools having women only, and some schools having both) yields important educational benefits, and (ii) females ***generally*** would not be able to meet the school's physical requirements and would not do well under the school's adversative approach to education. The Supreme Court found these arguments unavailing. There was no evidence that the single-sex school in question was established or had been maintained with a view toward fostering a diversity of educational opportunities, and there was some evidence that ***some*** women could meet the school's physical requirements and thrive under the school's adversative approach. [United States v. Virginia, *supra*]

107 **Insert** the following after para. (c) of §561:

(4) **Single-sex education:** The Court has not resolved the validity of a system of single-sex education. But if such diverse educational opportunities are not even-handed—*i.e.,* are not "separate but equal"—they violate equal protection. [United States v. Virginia, *supra*—separate college for women who were excluded from

Virginia Military Institute was a "pale shadow" in terms of curricular choice, faculty status, funding, prestige, and alumni]

118 **Insert** the following after para. 4) [§630]:

a) **Census:** Nor does a strict mathematical standard apply to the federal government's choice of methods when it conducts the decennial census. [Wisconsin v. City of New York, 116 S. Ct. 1091 (1996)—decision by Secretary of Commerce, to whom Congress delegated its authority over the census, not to statistically adjust census figures need have only a reasonable relation to accomplishing "actual Enumeration" of the population as required by Article I, Section 2, Clause 3]

125 **Insert** the following after para. 2.b. of §671:

c. **Definition of government "agency":** A corporation created by a special federal statute "for the furtherance of governmental objectives," with the President having permanent authority to appoint a majority of the directors, is "part of the government for purposes of the First Amendment," even though the authorizing statute disclaims this fact. [Lebron v. National Railroad Passenger Corp., 115 S. Ct. 961 (1995)—Amtrak]

150 **Insert** the following after para. (2) [§821]; renumber subsequent paras. accordingly:

(3) **Regulating consumer choice:** If the government's reason for banning truthful commercial speech is not to protect consumers from deception or overreaching, but rather is because the government believes that the public will respond irrationally to the advertising, the regulation will ***almost never*** be upheld. [44 Liquormart, Inc. v. Rhode Island, 116 S. Ct. 1495 (1996)—view of five Justices in separate opinions]

151 **Insert** the following after para. (4) [§823]; renumber subsequent paras. accordingly:

(5) **Disclosing alcoholic strength of beer:** A law prohibiting beer bottle labels from displaying alcohol content has been held invalid. Although the government's interest in preventing "strength wars" is ***substantial***, the government did not carry its burden of showing that the law advanced this interest in a ***direct and material way***. [Rubin v. Coors Brewing Co., 115 S. Ct. 1585 (1995)]

(6) **Liquor price advertising:** A law prohibiting advertising of retail prices of alcoholic beverages has been held invalid. It was ***more extensive than necessary*** to serve the state's interest in keeping prices high so as to keep consumption low. The state could directly accomplish its goal (for example, by establishing minimum prices) without any restriction on speech. [44 Liquormart, Inc. v. Rhode Island, *supra*]

(a) **Twenty-First Amendment:** Although the Twenty-First Amendment affects state power to regulate interstate commerce (*supra*, §§322-327), it does ***not*** qualify First Amendment rights. [44 Liquormart, Inc. v. Rhode Island, *supra*]

152 **Insert** the following after para. 1) [§831]:

(c) **Mail solicitation of personal injury victims:** A state may prohibit personal injury lawyers from sending mail solicitations to victims and their relatives for 30 days following an accident. Studies demonstrated that such advertising intrudes on the privacy of victims (a "substantial" interest) and reflects poorly on lawyers. [Florida Bar v. Went For It, Inc., 115 S. Ct. 2371 (1995)]

169 **Insert** the following after para. (a) [§930]; renumber subsequent paras. accordingly:

(b) **Political parties:** A law that limits political parties from making expenditures that are independent of—(*i.e.*, not actually coordinated with) the candidate is also invalid. [Colorado Republican Federal Campaign Committee v. Federal Election Commission, 116 S. Ct. 2309 (1996)]

170 **Insert** the following after para. (a) [§936]:

(b) **Campaign literature:** Speech intended to influence the electoral process occupies the core of protection afforded by the First Amendment. Therefore, laws that require disclosure of the identity of those who author such documents are subject to "exacting scrutiny." [McIntyre v. Ohio Elections Commission, 115 S. Ct. 1511 (1995)—state interests in providing information or in preventing fraud and libel are insufficient to justify ban on ***all*** anonymous campaign literature]

180 **Delete** paras. d) [§989] and e) [§990]; substitute the following; renumber subsequent para. accordingly:

d) **Expression of views:** [§989] A government employer may restrict speech of public employees on a "matter of public concern" only when, ***on balance***, the public employee's right ***as a citizen*** to comment on issues of public interest are outweighed by the government's significant interest as an employer in efficient performance of public service. [Pickering v. Board of Education, 391 U.S. 563 (1968)]

1/ **Job related speech:** [§990] In contrast, a government employer has no special burden of justification in restricting speech of public employees that concerns nothing more than their employment conditions, their personal status in the workplace, or other "internal office affairs." [Connick v. Myers, 461 U.S. 138 (1983)]

2/ **Independent contractors:** The principles in *Pickering v. Board of Education, supra*, §989, with respect to speech on matters of public concern, and *Elrod v. Burns* and *Branti v. Finkel, supra*, §988, with respect to political party affiliation—adjusted to weigh the government's interest as a contractor rather than as an employer—apply to retaliatory ***termination*** or ***nonrenewal*** of existing commercial relationships with independent government contractors. [Board of County Commissioners v. Umbehr, 116 S. Ct. 2342 (1996); O'Hare Truck Service Inc. v. City of Northlake, 116 S. Ct. 2353 (1996)]

181 **Insert** the following after para. f) [§991]:

g) **Ban on honoraria:** Government may not forbid ***all*** government employees (specifically, lower echelon executive branch employees) from receiving compensation for speeches, appearances, or articles—even when these expressive actions have no nexus to their employment and thus could not pose the danger (or appearance) of (i) improper influence by the payor or (ii) improper use by the employee of knowledge or resources acquired in the course of the government employment. [United States v. National Treasury Employees Union, 115 S. Ct. 1003 (1995)] This ban on honoraria was especially vulnerable under the First Amendment because it burdened only speech and not other off-duty activities that may pose the same dangers of misuse of public employment, and because it applied to a broad category of expression by a massive number of potential speakers.

186 **Insert** the following after para. (b) of §1013:

(c) **Compare—parades:** Nor may the state require private citizens who organize a parade to express their collective views to include among the marchers a group imparting a message that the organizers oppose. The First Amendment gives the organizers the right to choose the content of what may be expressed or not expressed through the parade. [Hurley v. Irish-American Gay, Lesbian & Bisexual Group of Boston, 115 S. Ct. 2338 (1995)]

187 **Insert** the following after para. (5) [§1017]:

(a) **Cable channels:** For similar reasons, the First Amendment is not violated by a law that ***permits*** cable operators to forbid "patently offensive" sex-related materials on channels that the law requires them to lease to third parties. [Denver Area Educational Telecommunications Consortium Inc. v. FCC, 116 S. Ct. 2374 (1996)—law is "sufficiently tailored" response to "compelling" interest in protecting children]

1) **Compare:** But a law that permits cable operators to forbid such materials on "public access" channels is invalid. Since the cable operators agree with municipalities to reserve these public, governmental, and educational channels in exchange for the award of cable franchises, the cable operator's First Amendment interest in control is very weak. Furthermore, locally accountable bodies that normally supervise these channels make it likely that children will be protected. [Denver Area Educational Telecommunications Consortium Inc. v. FCC, *supra*]

2) **Compare:** Similarly a law that requires cable operators to segregate all sex-related materials on a blocked and separate channel, which may be unblocked only on written request of subscribers, is not narrowly or reasonably tailored and thus is invalid. [Denver Area Educational Telecommunications Consortium Inc. v. FCC, *supra*—less restrictive alternatives include honoring subscriber's request to block ***by phone***, or a "lock-box" controlled by parents]

193 **Insert** the following after para. f. [§1053]; reletter subsequent paras. accordingly:

g. **Public funds:** Nor does a state university's giving funds for printing a student newspaper that promotes a distinctly Christian viewpoint violate the Establishment Clause as long as the program is neutral toward religion in extending benefits to recipients whose ideologies are broad and diverse. [Rosenberger v. Rector and Visitors of the University of Virginia, 115 S. Ct. 2510 (1995)] The Court distinguished programs making money payments directly to sectarian institutions by noting that here the university made payments directly to the printing companies. One member of the majority also noted that the source of funds for this program was not taxation but fees from students, any of whom might possibly opt out if they objected to funding religious activities.

196 **Insert** the following after para. 1) of §1078:

(3) **Religious displays in public forums:** Permitting the Ku Klux Klan to display a Latin cross in the plaza surrounding the statehouse does ***not*** violate the Establishment Clause because the plaza was a traditional public forum open to expression of all private groups on equal terms—at least when the display is accompanied by a

sign disclaiming government endorsement. [Capitol Square Review & Advisory Board v. Pinette, 115 S. Ct. 2440 (1995)—no majority opinion]

205 **Delete** para 2) of §1124; substitute the following:

2) ***Forfeiture of property used in connection with crimes*** was not a "taking" even though property owner (*e.g.*, lessor or co-owner) did not know that property was to be put to such use—at least where (i) "innocent" owner ***voluntarily entrusted*** the property to wrongdoer and (ii) forfeiture law affords judge ***some discretion*** to prevent inequitable application. [Calero-Toledo v. Pearson Yacht Leasing Co., 416 U.S. 663 (1974); Bennis v. Michigan, 116 S. Ct. 994 (1996)]

Notes

Notes

Notes

Notes

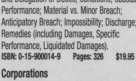

LAW SCHOOL LEGENDS SERIES

America's Greatest Law Professors on Audio Cassette

Wouldn't it be great if all of your law professors were law school legends? You know — the kind of professors whose classes everyone fights to get into. The professors whose classes you'd take, no matter what subject they're teaching. The kind of professors who make a subject sing. You may never get an opportunity to take a class with a truly brilliant professor, but with the Law School Legends Series, you can now get all the benefits of the country's greatest law professors…on audio cassette!

Administrative Law

Professor To Be Announced
Call For Release Date

TOPICS COVERED (Subject to Change): Classification Of Agencies; Adjudicative And Investigative Action; Rule Making Power; Delegation Doctrine; Control By Executive; Appointment And Removal; Freedom Of Information Act; Rule Making Procedure; Adjudicative Procedure; Trial Type Hearings; Administrative Law Judge; Power To Stay Proceedings; Subpoena Power; Physical Inspection; Self Incrimination; Judicial Review Issues; Declaratory Judgment; Sovereign Immunity; Eleventh Amendment; Statutory Limitations; Standing; Exhaustion Of Administrative Remedies; Scope Of Judicial Review.

3 Audio Cassettes
ISBN 0-15-900189-7 $39.95

Agency & Partnership

Professor Richard J. Conviser
Chicago Kent College of Law

TOPICS COVERED: Agency: Creation; Rights And Duties Of Principal And Agent; Sub-Agents; Contract Liability–Actual Authority: Express And Implied; Apparent Authority; Ratification; Liabilities Of Parties; Tort Liability–Respondeat Superior; Frolic And Detour; Intentional Torts. *Partnership:* Nature Of Partnership; Formation; Partnership By Estoppel; In Partnership Property; Relations Between Partners To Third Parties; Authority of Partners; Dissolution And Termination; Limited Partnerships.

3 Audio Cassettes
ISBN: 0-15-900351-2 $39.95

Antitrust Law

Professor To Be Announced
Call For Release Date

TOPICS COVERED (Subject to Change): How U.S. Antitrust Lawyers And Economists Think And Solve Problems: Antitrust Law's First Principle — Consumer Welfare Opposes Market Power; Methods Of Analysis — Rule Of Reason, Per Se, Quick Look; Sherman Act Section 1 — Civil And Criminal Conspiracies In Unreasonable Restraint Of Trade; Sherman Act Section 2 — Illegal Monopolization And Attempts To Monopolize; Robinson Patman Act Price Discrimination And Related Distribution Problems; Clayton Act Section Section 7 — Mergers And Joint Ventures; Antitrust And Intellectual Property; U.S. Antitrust And International Competitive Relationships — Extraterritoriality, Comity, And Convergence; Exemptions And Regulated Industries; Enforcement By The Department Of Justice, Federal Trade Commission, National Association Of State Attorneys General, And By Private Litigation; Price And Non-Price Restraints.

2 Audio Cassettes
ISBN: 0-15-900341-5 $39.95

Bankruptcy

Professor Elizabeth Warren
Harvard Law School

TOPICS COVERED: The Debtor/Creditor Relationship; The Commencement, Conversion, Dismissal and Reopening Of Bankruptcy Proceedings; Property Included In The Bankruptcy Estate; Secured, Priority And Unsecured Claims; The Automatic Stay; Powers Of Avoidance; The Assumption And Rejection Of Executory Contracts; The Protection Of Exempt Property; The Bankruptcy Discharge; Chapter 13 Proceedings; Chapter 11 Proceedings; Bankruptcy Jurisdiction And Procedure.

4 Audio Cassettes
ISBN: 0-15-900273-7 $45.95

Civil Procedure

By Professor Richard D. Freer
Emory University Law School

TOPICS COVERED: Subject Matter Jurisdiction; Personal Jurisdiction; Long-Arm Statutes; Constitutional Limitations; In Rem And Quasi In Rem Jurisdiction; Service Of Process; Venue; Transfer; Forum Non Conveniens; Removal; Waiver; Governing Law; Pleadings; Joinder Of Claims; Permissive And Compulsory Joinder Of Parties; Counter-Claims And Cross-Claims; Ancillary Jurisdiction; Impleader; Class Actions; Discovery; Pretrial Adjudication; Summary Judgment; Trial; Post Trial Motions; Appeals; Res Judicata; Collateral Estoppel.

5 Audio Cassettes
ISBN: 0-15-900322-9 $59.95

Commercial Paper

By Professor Michael I. Spak
Chicago Kent College Of Law

TOPICS COVERED: Introduction; Types Of Negotiable Instruments; Elements Of Negotiability; Statute Of Limitations; Payment-In-Full Checks; Negotiations Of The Instrument; Becoming A Holder-In-Due Course; Rights Of A Holder In Due Course; Real And Personal Defenses; Jus Teril; Effect Of Instrument On Underlying Obligations; Contracts Of Maker And Indorser; Suretyship; Liability Of Drawer And Drawee; Check Certification; Warranty Liability; Conversion Of Liability; Banks And Their Customers; Properly Payable Rule; Wrongful Dishonor; Stopping Payment; Death Of Customer; Bank Statement; Check Collection; Expedited Funds Availability; Forgery Of Drawer's Name; Alterations; Imposter Rule; Wire Transfers; Electronic Fund Transfers Act .

3 Audio Cassettes
ISBN: 0-15-900275-3 $39.95

Conflict Of Laws

Professor Richard J. Conviser
Chicago Kent College of Law

TOPICS COVERED: Domicile; Jurisdiction; In Personam, In Rem, Quasi In Rem; Court Competence; Forum Non Conveniens; Choice Of Law; Foreign Causes Of Action; Territorial Approach To Choice/Tort And Contract; "Escape Devices"; Most Significant Relationship; Governmental Interest Analysis; Recognition Of Judgments; Foreign Country Judgments; Domestic Judgments/Full Faith And Credit; Review Of Judgments; Modifiable Judgments; Defenses To Recognition And Enforcement; Federal/State (Erie) Problems; Constitutional Limits On Choice Of Law.

3 Audio Cassettes
ISBN: 0-15-900352-0 $39.95

Constitutional Law

By Professor John C. Jeffries, Jr.
University of Virginia School of Law

TOPICS COVERED: Introduction; Exam Tactics; Legislative Power; Supremacy; Commerce; State Regulation; Privileges And Immunities; Federal Court Jurisdiction; Separation Of Powers; Civil Liberties; Due Process; Equal Protection; Privacy; Race; Alienage; Gender; Speech And Association; Prior Restraints; Religion—Free Exercise; Establishment Clause.

5 Audio Cassettes
ISBN: 0-15-900319-9 $45.95

Contracts

By Professor Michael I. Spak
Chicago Kent College Of Law

TOPICS COVERED: Offer; Revocation; Acceptance; Consideration; Defenses To Formation; Third Party Beneficiaries; Assignment; Delegation; Conditions; Excuses; Anticipatory Repudiation; Discharge Of Duty; Modifications; Rescission; Accord & Satisfaction; Novation; Breach; Damages; Remedies; UCC Remedies; Parol Evidence Rule.

4 Audio Cassettes
ISBN: 0-15-900318-0 $45.95

Copyright Law

Professor Roger E. Schechter
George Washington University Law School

TOPICS COVERED: Constitution; Patents And Property Ownership Distinguished; Subject Matter Copyright; Duration And Renewal; Ownership And Transfer; Formalities; Introduction; Notice, Registration And Deposit; Infringement; Overview; Reproduction And Derivative Works; Public Distribution; Public Performance And Display; Exemptions; Fair Use; Photocopying; Remedies; Preemption Of State Law.

3 Audio Cassettes
ISBN: 0-15-900295-8 $39.95

Corporations

By Professor Therese H. Maynard
Loyola Marymount School of Law

TOPICS COVERED: Ultra Vires Act; Corporate Formation; Piercing The Corporate Veil; Corporate Financial Structure; Stocks; Bonds; Subscription Agreements; Watered Stock; Stock Transactions; Insider Trading; 16(b) & 10b-5 Violations; Promoters; Fiduciary Duties; Shareholder Rights; Meetings; Cumulative Voting; Voting Trusts; Close Corporations; Dividends; Preemptive Rights; Shareholder Derivative Suits; Directors; Duty Of Loyalty; Corporate Opportunity Doctrine; Officers; Amendments; Mergers; Dissolution.

4 Audio Cassettes
ISBN: 0-15-900320-2 $45.95

Criminal Law

By Professor Charles H. Whitebread
USC School of Law

TOPICS COVERED: Exam Tactics; Volitional Acts; Mental States; Specific Intent; Malice; General Intent; Strict Liability; Accomplice Liability; Inchoate Crimes; Impossibility; Defenses;

For more information visit our World Wide Web site at http://www.gilbertlaw.com or write for a free 32 page catalog: Harcourt Brace Legal and Professional Publications, 176 West Adams, Ste. 2100, Chicago, Illinois 60603

Insanity; Voluntary And Involuntary Intoxication; Infancy; Self-Defense; Defense Of A Dwelling; Duress; Necessity; Mistake Of Fact Or Law; Entrapment; Battery; Assault; Homicide; Common Law Murder; Voluntary And Involuntary Manslaughter; First Degree Murder; Felony Murder; Rape; Larceny; Embezzlement; False Pretenses; Robbery; Extortion; Burglary; Arson.
4 Audio Cassettes
ISBN: 0-15-900279-6 $39.95

Criminal Procedure
By Professor Charles H. Whitebread
USC School of Law
TOPICS COVERED: Incorporation Of The Bill Of Rights; Exclusionary Rule; Fruit Of The Poisonous Tree; Arrest; Search & Seizure; Exceptions To Warrant Requirement; Wire Tapping & Eavesdropping; Confessions (Miranda); Pretrial Identification; Bail; Preliminary Hearings; Grand Juries; Speedy Trial; Fair Trial; Jury Trials; Right To Counsel; Guilty Pleas; Sentencing; Death Penalty; Habeas Corpus; Double Jeopardy; Privilege Against Compelled Testimony.
3 Audio Cassettes
ISBN: 0-15-900281-8 $39.95

Evidence
By Professor Faust F. Rossi
Cornell Law School
TOPICS COVERED: Relevance; Insurance; Remedial Measures; Settlement Offers; Causation; State Of Mind; Rebuttal; Habit; Character Evidence; "MIMIC" Rule; Documentary Evidence; Authentication; Best Evidence Rule; Parol Evidence; Competency; Dead Man Statutes; Examination Of Witnesses; Present Recollection Revived; Past Recollection Recorded; Opinion Testimony; Lay And Expert Witness; Learned Treatises; Impeachment; Collateral Matters; Bias, Interest Or Motive; Rehabilitation; Privileges; Hearsay And Exceptions.
5 Audio Cassettes
ISBN: 0-15-900282-6 $45.95

Family Law
Professor To Be Announced
TOPICS COVERED (Subject to change): National Scope Of Family Law; Marital Relationship; Consequences Of Marriage; Formalities And Solemnization; Common Law Marriage; Impediments; Marriage And Conflict Of Laws; Non-Marital Relationship; Law Of Names; Void And Voidable Marriages; Marital Breakdown; Annulment And Defenses; Divorce — Fault And No-Fault; Separation; Jurisdiction For Divorce; Migratory Divorce; Full Faith And Credit; Temporary Orders; Economic Aspects Of Marital Breakdown; Property Division; Community Property Principles; Equitable Distribution; Marital And Separate Property; Types Of Property Interests; Equitable Reimbursement; Alimony; Modification And Termination Of Alimony; Child Support; Health Insurance; Enforcement Of Orders; Antenuptial And Postnuptial Agreements; Separation And Settlement Agreements; Custody Jurisdiction And Awards; Modification Of Custody; Visitation Rights; Termination Of Parental Rights; Adoption; Illegitimacy; Paternity Actions.
3 Audio Cassettes
ISBN: 0-15-900283-4 $39.95

Federal Courts
Professor To Be Announced
TOPICS COVERED (Subject to change): History Of The Federal Court System; "Court Or Controversy" And Justiciability; Congressional Power Over Federal Court Jurisdiction; Supreme Court Jurisdiction; District Court Subject Matter Jurisdiction—Federal Question Jurisdiction, Diversity Jurisdiction And Admiralty Jurisdiction; Pendent And Ancillary Jurisdiction; Removal Jurisdiction; Venue; Forum Non Conveniens; Law Applied In The Federal Courts; Federal Law In The State Courts; Collateral Relations Between Federal And State Courts; The Eleventh Amendment And State Sovereign Immunity.
3 Audio Cassettes
ISBN: 0-15-900296-6 $39.95

Federal Income Tax
By Professor Cheryl D. Block
George Washington University Law School
TOPICS COVERED: Administrative Reviews; Tax Formula; Gross Income; Exclusions For Gifts; Inheritances; Personal Injuries; Tax Basis Rules; Divorce Tax Rules; Assignment Of Income; Business Deductions; Investment Deductions; Passive Loss And Interest Limitation Rules; Capital Gains & Losses; Section 1031, 1034, and 121 Deferred/Non Taxable Transactions.
4 Audio Cassettes
ISBN: 0-15-900284-2 $45.95

Future Interests
By Dean Catherine L. Carpenter
Southwestern University Law School
TOPICS COVERED: Rule Against Perpetuities; Class Gifts; Estates In Land; Rule In Shelley's Case; Future Interests In Transferor and Transferee; Life Estates; Defeasible Fees; Doctrine Of Worthier Title; Doctrine Of Merger; Fee Simple Estates; Restraints On Alienation; Power Of Appointment; Rules Of Construction.
2 Audio Cassettes
ISBN: 0-15-900285-0 $24.95

Law School ABC's
By Professor Jennifer S. Kamita
Loyola Marymount Law School, and
Professor Rodney O. Fong
Golden Gate University School of Law
TOPICS COVERED: Introduction; Casebooks; Hornbooks; Selecting Commercial Materials; Briefing; Review; ABC's Of A Lecture; Taking Notes; Lectures & Notes Examples; Study Groups; ABC's Of Outlining; Rules; Outlining Hypothetical; Outlining Assignment And Review; Introduction To Essay Writing; "IRAC"; Call Of The Question Exercise; Issue Spotting Exercise; IRAC Defining & Writing Exercise; Form Tips; ABC's Of Exam Writing; Exam Writing Hypothetical; Practice Exam And Review; Preparation Hints; Exam Diagnostics & Writing Problems.
4 Audio Cassettes
ISBN: 0-15-900286-9 $45.95

Law School Exam Writing
By Professor Charles H. Whitebread
USC School of Law
TOPICS COVERED: With "Law School Exam Writing," you'll learn the secrets of law school test taking. In this fascinating lecture, Professor Whitebread leads you step-by-step through his innovative system, so that you know exactly how to tackle your essay exams without making point draining mistakes. You'll learn how to read questions so you don't miss important issues; how to organize your answer, how to use limited exam time to your maximum advantage; and even how to study for exams.
1 Audio Cassette
ISBN: 0-15-900287-7 $19.95

Professional Responsibility
By Professor Erwin Chemerinsky
USC School of Law
TOPICS COVERED: Regulation of Attorneys; Bar Admission; Unauthorized Practice; Competency; Discipline; Judgment; Lawyer-Client Relationship; Representation; Withdrawal; Conflicts; Disqualification; Clients; Client Interests; Successive And Effective Representation; Integrity; Candor; Confidences; Secrets; Past And Future Crimes; Perjury; Communications; Witnesses; Jurors; The Court; The Press; Trial Tactics; Prosecutors; Market; Solicitation; Advertising; Law Firms; Fees; Client Property; Conduct; Political Activity.
3 Audio Cassettes
ISBN: 0-15-900288-5 $39.95

Real Property
By Professor Paula A. Franzese
Seton Hall Law School
TOPICS COVERED: Estates—Fee Simple; Fee Tail; Life Estate; Co-Tenancy—Joint Tenancy; Tenancy In Common; Tenancy By The Entirety; Landlord-Tenant Relationship; Liability For Condition Of Premises; Assignment & Sublease; Easements; Restrictive Covenants; Adverse Possession; Recording Acts; Conveyancing; Personal Property—Finders; Bailments; Gifts; Future Interests.
4 Audio Cassettes
ISBN: 0-15-900289-3 $45.95

Remedies
By Professor William A. Fletcher
University of California at Berkeley, Boalt Hall School of Law
TOPICS COVERED: Damages; Restitution; Equitable Remedies (including Constructive Trust, Equitable Lien, Injunction, and Specific Performance); Tracing; Rescission and Reformation; Specific topics include Injury and Destruction of Personal Property; Conversion; Injury to Real Property; Trespass; Ouster; Nuisance; Defamation; Trade Libel; Inducing Breach of Contract; Contracts to Purchase Personal Property; Contracts to Purchase Real Property (including Equitable Conversion); Construction Contracts; and Personal Service Contracts.
3 Audio Cassettes
ISBN: 0-15-900353-9 $45.95

Sales & Lease of Goods
By Professor Michael I. Spak
Chicago Kent College of Law
TOPICS COVERED: Goods; Contract Formation; Firm Offers; Statute Of Frauds; Modification; Parol Evidence; Code Methodology; Tender; Payment; Identification; Risk Of Loss; Warranties; Merchantability; Fitness; Disclaimers; Consumer Protection; Remedies; Anticipatory Repudiation; Third Party Rights.
3 Audio Cassettes
ISBN: 0-15-900291-5 $39.95

Secured Transactions
By Professor Michael I. Spak
Chicago Kent College of Law
TOPICS COVERED: Collateral; Inventory; Intangibles; Proceeds; Security Agreements; Attachment; After-Acquired Property; Perfection; Filing; Priorities; Purchase Money Security Interests; Fixtures; Rights Upon Default; Self-Help; Sale; Constitutional Issues.
3 Audio Cassettes
ISBN: 0-15-900292-3 $39.95

Torts
By Professor Richard J. Conviser
Chicago Kent College of Law
TOPICS COVERED: Essay Exam Techniques; Intentional Torts—Assault; Battery; False Imprisonment; Intentional Infliction Of Emotional Distress; Trespass To Land; Trespass To Chattels; Conversion; Defenses: Defamation—Libel; Slander; Defenses; First Amendment Concerns; Invasion Of Right Of Privacy; Misrepresentation; Negligence—Duty; Breach; Actual And Proximate Causation; Damages; Defenses; Strict Liability, Products Liability; Nuisance; General Tort Considerations.
4 Audio Cassettes
ISBN: 0-15-900185-4 $45.95

Wills & Trusts
By Professor Stanley M. Johanson
University of Texas School of Law
TOPICS COVERED: Attested Wills; Holographic Wills; Negligence; Revocation; Changes On Face Of Will; Lapsed Gifts; Negative Bequest Rule; Nonprobate Assets; Intestate Succession; Advancements; Elective Share; Will Contests; Capacity; Undue Influence; Creditors' Rights; Creation Of Trust; Revocable Trusts; Pourover Gifts; Charitable Trusts; Resulting Trusts; Constructive Trusts; Spendthrift Trusts; Self-Dealing; Prudent Investments; Trust Accounting; Termination; Powers Of Appointment.
4 Audio Cassettes
ISBN: 0-15-900294-X $45.95

Law School Legend Series FIRST YEAR PROGRAM

Includes Five Law School Legends Titles:

- **Civil Procedure**
  By Professor Richard D. Freer
  Emory University Law School
- **Contracts**
  By Professor Michael I. Spak
  Chicago Kent College Of Law
- **Criminal Law**
  By Professor Charles H. Whitebread
  USC School of Law
- **Real Property**
  By Professor Paula A. Franzese
  Seton Hall Law School
- **Torts**
  By Professor Richard J. Conviser
  Chicago Kent College of Law

Plus—

- **Law School Exam Writing**
  By Professor Charles H. Whitebread
  USC Law School

All titles are packaged in a convenient carry case. $250 if purchased separately. $195 if purchased as a set. Save $55.
ISBN: 0-15-900306-7 Set $195

All titles available at your law school bookstore or call to order: 1-800-787-8717

Wills, Trusts & Estates
Keyed to the Dukeminier Casebook
ISBN: 0-15-900127-7 192 pages $ 17.95

Also Available:

Accounting For Lawyers
ISBN: 0-15-900041-6 75 pages $ 12.95

Criminal Law Questions & Answers
ISBN: 0-15-900087-4 179 pages $ 12.95

Excelling on Exams/How to Study
ISBN: 0-15-900098-X 101 pages $ 12.95

Torts Questions & Answers
ISBN: 0-15-900126-9 174 pages $ 12.95

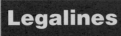

Legalines

Summary of Subjects Available

- Administrative Law
- Antitrust
- Civil Procedure
- Commercial Law
- Conflict of Laws
- Constitutional Law
- Contracts
- Corporations
- Criminal Law
- Criminal Procedure
- Decedents' Estates & Trusts
- Domestic Relations
- Enterprise Organization
- Estate & Gift Taxation
- Evidence
- Family Law
- Federal Courts
- Income Tax
- Labor Law
- Partnership & Corporate Taxation
- Property
- Real Property
- Remedies
- Sales & Secured Transactions
- Securities Regulation
- Torts
- Wills, Trusts & Estates

Current & Upcoming Software Titles

Gilbert Law Summaries
Interactive Software For Windows
Gilbert's Interactive Software features the full text of a Gilbert Law Summaries outline. Each title is easy to customize, print, and take to class. You can access the Lexis and Westlaw systems through an icon on the tool bar (with a valid student I.D.), as well as CaseBriefs Interactive Software, and Gilbert's On-Screen Dictionary Of Legal Terms (sold separately).

Administrative Law — Asimow
0-15-900205-2 — $27.95

Civil Procedure — Marcus, Rowe
0-15-900206-0 — $27.95

Constitutional Law — Choper
0-15-900207-9 — $27.95

Contracts — Eisenberg
0-15-900208-7 — $27.95

Corporations — Choper, Eisenberg
0-15-900209-5 — $27.95

Criminal Law — Dix
0-15-900210-9 — $27.95

Criminal Procedure — Marcus, Whitebread
0-15-900211-7 — $27.95

Evidence — Kaplan, Waltz
0-15-900212-5 — $27.95

Income Tax 1 — Asimow
0-15-900213-3 — $27.95

Property — Dukeminier
0-15-900214-1 — $27.95

Secured Transactions — Whaley
0-15-900215-X — $27.95

Torts — Franklin
0-15-900216-8 — $27.95

CaseBriefs
Interactive Software For Windows
Each title is adaptable to *all* casebooks in a subject area. For example, the Civil Procedure CaseBriefs title is adaptable to Civil Procedure by Cound, Hazard, Yeazell, etc... Simply select the casebook you're using when installing the software, and the program will do the rest! CaseBriefs is easy to customize, print, and take to class. You can access the Lexis and Westlaw systems through an icon on the tool bar (with a valid student I.D.), as well as Gilbert Law Summaries Interactive Software, and Gilbert's On-Screen Dictionary Of Legal Terms (sold separately).

Administrative Law — Adaptable To All Casebooks
0-15-900190-0 — $27.95

Civil Procedure — Adaptable To All Casebooks
0-15-900191-9 — $27.95

Conflict Of Laws — Adaptable To All Casebooks
0-15-900192-7 — $27.95

Constitutional Law — Adaptable To All Casebooks
0-15-900193-5 — $27.95

Contracts — Adaptable To All Casebooks
0-15-900194-3 — $27.95

Corporations — Adaptable To All Casebooks
0-15-900195-1 — $27.95

Criminal Law — Adaptable To All Casebooks
0-15-900196-X — $27.95

Criminal Procedure — Adaptable To All Casebooks
0-15-900197-8 — $27.95

Evidence — Adaptable To All Casebooks
0-15-900198-6 — $27.95

Family Law — Adaptable To All Casebooks
0-15-900199-4 — $27.95

Income Tax — Adaptable To All Casebooks
0-15-900200-1 — $27.95

Property — Adaptable To All Casebooks
0-15-900201-X — $27.95

Remedies — Adaptable To All Casebooks
0-15-900202-8 — $27.95

Torts — Adaptable To All Casebooks
0-15-900203-6 — $27.95

Wills, Trusts & Estates — Adaptable To All Casebooks
0-15-900204-4 — $27.95

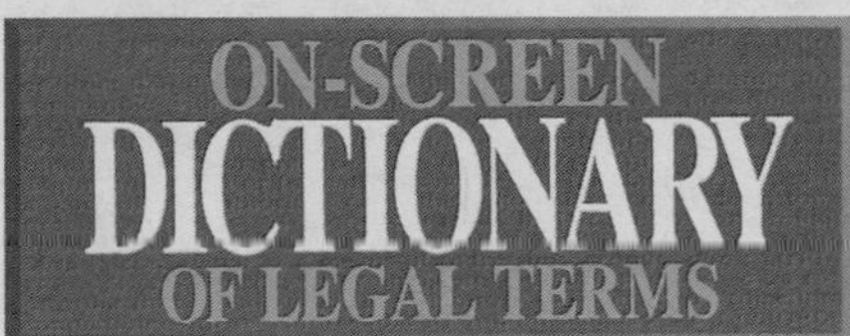

Gilbert's On Screen Dictionary Of Legal Terms:
Features over 3,500 legal terms and phrases, law school shorthand, common abbreviations, Latin and French legal terms, periodical abbreviations, and governmental abbreviations.

ISBN: 0-15-900-311-3 Macintosh $24.95
ISBN: 0-15-900-308-3 Windows $24.95

All titles available at your law school bookstore or call to order: 1-800-787-8717

Current & Upcoming Titles

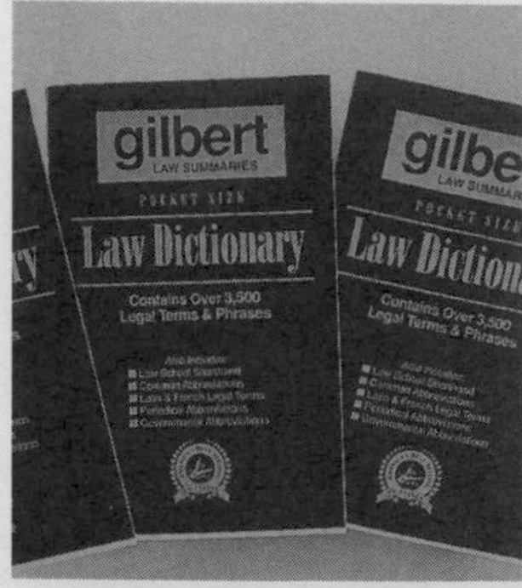

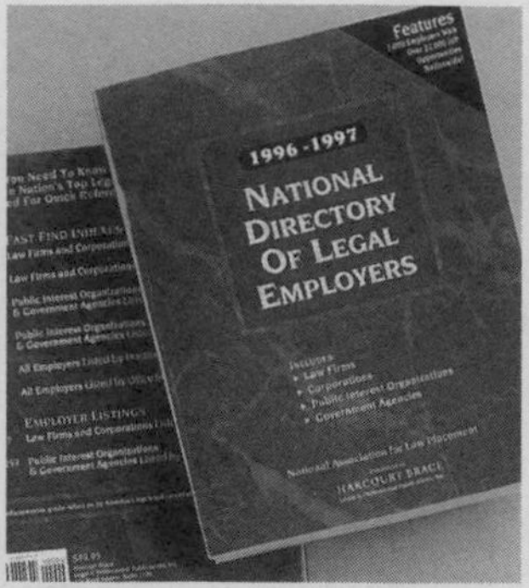

Gilbert's Pocket Size Law Dictionary
Gilbert

A dictionary is useless if you don't have it when you need it. If the only law dictionary you own is a thick, bulky one, you'll probably leave it at home most of the time — and if you need to know a definition while you're at school, you're out of luck!

With Gilbert's Pocket Size Law Dictionary, you'll have any definition you need, when you need it. Just pop Gilbert's dictionary into your pocket or purse, and you'll have over 3,500 legal terms and phrases at your fingertips. Gilbert's dictionary also includes a section on law school shorthand, common abbreviations, Latin and French legal terms, periodical abbreviations, and governmental abbreviations.

With Gilbert's Pocket Size Law Dictionary, you'll never be caught at a loss for words!

Available in your choice of 4 colors, $7.95 each:

- **Black** ISBN: 0-15-900255-9
- **Blue** ISBN: 0-15-900257-5
- **Burgundy** ISBN: 0-15-900256-7
- **Green** ISBN: 0-15-900258-3

Limited Edition: Simulated Alligator Skin Cover
- **Black** ISBN: 0-15-900316-4 $7.95

What Lawyers Earn: Getting Paid What You're Worth
NALP

"What Lawyers Earn" provides up-to-date salary information from lawyers in many different positions, all over the country. Whether you're negotiating your own salary — or you're just curious! — "What Lawyers Earn" tells you how much lawyers really make.

ISBN: 0-15-900183-8 $17.95

The 100 Best Law Firms To Work For In America
Kimm Alayne Walton, J.D.

An insider's guide to the 100 best places to practice law, with anecdotes and a wealth of useful hiring information. Also included are special sections on the top law firms for women and the best public interest legal employers.

ISBN: 0-15-900180-3 $19.95

The 1996-1997 National Directory Of Legal Employers
NALP

The National Association for Law Placement has joined forces with Harcourt Brace to bring you everything you need to know about 1,000 of the nation's top legal employers, fully indexed for quick reference.

It includes:

- Over 22,000 job openings.
- The names, addresses and phone numbers of hiring partners.
- Listings of firms by state, size, kind and practice area.
- What starting salaries are for full time, part time, and summer associates, plus a detailed description of firm benefits.
- The number of employees by gender and race, as well as the number of employees with disabilities.
- A detailed narrative of each firm, plus much more!

The National Directory Of Legal Employers has been published for the past twenty years, but until now has only been available to law school career services directors, and hiring partners at large law firms. Through a joint venture between NALP (The National Association For Law Placement) and Harcourt Brace, this highly regarded, exciting title is now available for students.

ISBN: 0-15-900179-X $49.95

Proceed With Caution: A Diary Of The First Year At One Of America's Largest, Most Prestigious Law Firms
William Formon

In "Proceed With Caution" the author chronicles the trials and tribulations of being a new associate in a widely coveted dream job. He offers insights that only someone who has lived through the experience can offer. The unique diary format makes Proceed With Caution a highly readable and enjoyable journey.

ISBN: 0-15-900181-1 $17.95

The Eight Secrets Of Top Exam Performance In Law School
Charles Whitebread

Wouldn't it be great to know exactly what your professor's looking for on your exam? To find out everything that's expected of you, so that you don't waste your time doing anything other than maximizing your grades?

In his easy-to-read, refreshing style, nationally-recognized exam expert Professor Charles Whitebread will teach you the eight secrets that will add precious points to every exam answer you write. You'll learn the three keys to handling any essay exam question, and how to add points to your score by making time work for you, not against you. You'll learn flawless issue spotting, and discover how to organize your answer for maximum possible points. You'll find out how the hidden traps in "IRAC" trip up most students... but not you! You'll learn the techniques for digging up the exam questions your professor will ask, before your exam. You'll put your newly-learned skills to the test with sample exam questions, and you can measure your performance against model answers. And there's even a special section that helps you master the skills necessary to crush any exam, not just a typical essay exam — unusual exams like open book, take home, multiple choice, short answer, and policy questions.

"The Eight Secrets of Top Exam Performance in Law School" gives you all the tools you need to maximize your grades — quickly and easily!

ISBN: 0-15-900323-7 $9.95

Guerrilla Tactics for Getting the Legal Job of Your Dreams
Kimm Alayne Walton, J.D.

Whether you're looking for a summer clerkship or your first permanent job after school, this revolutionary new book is the key to getting the job of your dreams!

"Guerrilla Tactics for Getting the Legal Job of Your Dreams" leads you step-by-step through everything you need to do to nail down that perfect job! You'll learn hundreds of simple-to-use strategies that will get you exactly where you want to go.

"Guerrilla Tactics" features the best strategies from the country's most innovative law school career advisors. The strategies in "Guerrilla Tactics" are so powerful that it even comes with a guarantee: Follow the advice in the book, and within one year of graduation you'll have the job of your dreams... or your money back!

Pick up a copy of "Guerrilla Tactics" today...and you'll be on your way to the job of your dreams!

ISBN: 0-15-900317-2 $24.95

Checkerboard Careers: How Surprisingly Successful Attorneys Got To The Top, And How You Can Too!
NALP

Fast paced and easy to read, "Checkerboard Careers" is an inspirational guide, packed with profiles and monologues of how successful attorneys got to the top and how you can, too.

ISBN: 0-15-900182-X $17.95

FREE! Gilbert Law Summaries 1st Year Survival Manual

Available from your BAR/BRI Bar Review Representative or write:

Gilbert Law Summaries
176 West Adams, Ste. 2100
Chicago, Illinois 60603

Also available on our World Wide Web site at http://www.gilbertlaw.com

To Order Any Of The Items In This Publications Catalog, Call Or Write:
Harcourt Brace Legal and Professional Publications, 176 West Adams, Ste. 2100, Chicago, Illinois 60603

1-800-787-8717